Mother and child

MANCHESTER
1824

Manchester University Press

To my mother,
Lesley (Earner) Byrne

Mother and child

Maternity and child welfare in Dublin 1922–60

Lindsey Earner-Byrne

Manchester University Press
Manchester and New York
distributed exclusively in the USA by Palgrave

Published by Manchester University Press
Oxford Road, Manchester M13 9NR, UK
and Room 400, 175 Fifth Avenue, New York, NY 10010, USA
www.manchesteruniversitypress.co.uk

Distributed exclusively in the USA by
Palgrave, 175 Fifth Avenue, New York,
NY 10010, USA

Distributed exclusively in Canada by
UBC Press, University of British Columbia, 2029 West Mall,
Vancouver, BC, Canada V6T 1Z2

British Library Cataloguing-in-Publication Data
A catalogue record for this book is available from the British Library

Library of Congress Cataloging-in-Publication Data applied for

ISBN 978 0 7190 7474 5 *hardback*

First published 2007

16 15 14 13 12 11 10 09 08 07   10 9 8 7 6 5 4 3 2 1

Edited and typeset by
Frances Hackeson Freelance Publishing Services, Brinscall, Lancs
Printed in Great Britain by
The Cromwell Press Ltd, Trowbridge

Contents

Abbreviations

AGF	Attorney General Files
CMO	County Medical Officer
CSSC	Catholic Social Service Conference
CSWB	Catholic Social Welfare Bureau
DDA	Dublin Diocesan Archives
ICPRS	Irish Catholic Protection and Rescue Society
IER	*Irish Ecclesiastical Record*
IESH	*Irish Economic and Social History*
IHA	*Irish Housewives Association*
IHS	*Irish Historical Studies*
IJMSc.	*Irish Journal of Medical Science*
IMA	Irish Medical Association
JCWSSW	Joint Committee of Women's Societies and Social Workers
JIFSMU	*Journal of the Irish Free State Medical Union*
JIMA	*Journal of the Irish Medical Association*
JMAÉ	*Journal of the Medical Association of Éire*
JSSISI	*Journal of the Statistical and Social Inquiry Society of Ireland*
JSSSI	*Journal of the Statistical and Social Society of Ireland*
MCS	Mother and child scheme
NAI	National Archives of Ireland
NLI	National Library of Ireland
RCSI, ML	Royal College of Surgeons Ireland, Mercer Library
Studies	*Studies: An Irish Quarterly Review of Letters, Philosophy and Science*
UCDA	University College Dublin Archives
WNHA	Women's National Health Association

Glossary of Irish words

An Bord Altranais	Nursing Board
Bean na hÉireann	The Women of Ireland *(journal)*
Bunreacht na hÉireann	Constitution of Ireland
Cumann na nGaedheal	Party of the Irish (political party)
Cumann na dTeachtaire	League of Women Delegates
Clann na Poblachta	Party of the Republic (political party)
Clann na Talmhan	Party of the Farmers (political party)
Dáil Éireann (Dáil)	Irish parliament
Fianna Fáil	Soldiers of Ireland (political party)
Ríocht na Midhe	*The Kingdom of Meath* (journal)
Saor an Leanbh	Save the Children
Saorstát Éireann	Irish Free State
Sinn Féin	Ourselves (political party)
Sláinte na nGaedheal	The Health of the Gaels
Taoiseach	Irish Prime Minister
Teach Ultáin	St Ultain's Hospital

Tables

Acknowledgements

I owe a debt of gratitude to more people than can be mentioned here, so I begin with a general expression of thanks to all those who have offered support and friendship during the writing of this book.

First and foremost I wish to thank my family, who have always believed in this project and have supported me in every way possible. To my parents and brother Adam, and to my brothers Graham and Patrick who did not live to see its publication, I am eternally grateful for your love. My thanks also to Daphne and Hilary Earner who supplied a roof, finance and good company when I was researching and writing this book. Also, my love and thanks to my grandmother, Moyra Earner, whose stories and life inspired my fascination with history. To my husband, Georg, and my daughter, Hannah Mae, for keeping me centred and laughing: thank you.

This book began its life as a Ph.D. thesis, so I wish to thank my academic supervisor, Professor Mary Daly, who was in reality much more than that. I also received encouragement and support from my colleagues in the School of History and Archives.

Maria Luddy and Margaret Ó hÓgartaigh read drafts of the manuscript and provided invaluable advice and suggestions. Both have gone out of their way to encourage me and their generosity was humbling.

In the course of this research I had the opportunity to meet many wonderful professionals in archives and libraries. I would like to thank all the staff of the National Archives of Ireland who foraged for Department of Health files on my behalf, especially Paddy who could find a needle in a haystack. I must also mention Catríona Crowe who was always ready to offer advice and assistance at a moment's notice. I also thank the staff of the National Library who were unfailingly helpful and cheerful. I am delighted that the course of research took me to the Dublin Diocesan Archives where I met David Sheehy. David not only led me to the most interesting material I worked on during my research; he also made many a Friday afternoon fly by with fascinating chat and insights.

The original thesis on which this book is based was prepared with financial assistance from the Open Postgraduate Scholarship, University College Dublin; the Lord Edward Fitzgerald Bursary; and a Government of Ireland Research Scholarship from the Irish Council for the Humanities and Social Sciences. Without this form of sponsorship I simply would not have been able to embark on this project.

Lastly, a special thanks to the team at Manchester University Press for their professionalism and patience.

Introduction

> The family is the core of human society and the mother, we are told, is the heart of the family. By virtue of her position, she has the responsibility of caring in a special way for the physical, mental, moral, and spiritual and social wellbeing of the family. What then can be more important than to assist in the work of guarding a mother's health, by helping her to solve the problems and anxieties which are preventing her from getting the maximum benefit from the medical services offered to her during pregnancy?[1]

Motherhood is a complex issue involving the mechanics of pregnancy and childbirth and the life experience of mothering and rearing children. Hence both the social realities and the cultural perceptions of motherhood are essential to the experience of mothering.[2] Motherhood, like childbirth, 'stands uncomfortably at the junction of two worlds of nature and culture',[3] and during the first half of the twentieth century the issue of maternal welfare raised many other social questions from family privacy to state responsibility. During the first few decades after Irish Independence in 1922, many mothers found it necessary to negotiate both the limited official relief services and the network of informal welfare services available in order to secure the welfare of the family. This book is concerned with the myriad of motives, conflicts and priorities behind the social and medical services offered to Dublin mothers by voluntary and religious organisations and by local and central governments. The envisaged role and reality of Irish motherhood not only exposed inherent contradictions in the societal response to tradition and modernity, but also called into question the appropriate role of charity and raised the thorny issue of responsibility. Tensions concerning religious territory, the domain of charity and the spectre of state control played a part in the move towards the development of a comprehensive maternity service in Ireland between the years 1922 and 1960.

This book draws from a wealth of literature on Irish culture, society and politics that had helped to elucidate aspects of life in Ireland during the first half of the twentieth century. In the last decade the scope of research on women in Irish history has expanded beyond feminism and nationalism to incorporate every aspect of women's lives from 'the ecclesiastical construction of the ideal Irish woman'[4] to the impact on women's domestic lives of running water.[5] The issue of maternity, however, has been conspicuously absent in the body of literature on Irish women.[6] Despite the centrality of the 'mothering experience' to women's lives, 'maternity' has not provided much allure for historians, primarily because it held little interest for contemporaries. Apart from the 'mother-and-child controversy' of 1951, the issue received little coverage. The controversy was ostensibly over the introduction of a free maternity scheme for all mothers, irrespective of income. In reality, however, it had more to do with political incompetence and disunity, religious and medical protectionism, and the dynamic of certain personalities. Although the controversy forms an essential part of the history of maternity policy, it also serves as a distraction in terms of maternity provision. Furthermore, despite the tendency of women's history to focus on the issue of female citizenship, there has been a reluctance to consider citizenship beyond political access to incorporate the notion of social citizenship. This study explores, through the issue of maternity welfare, the development of female 'social rights of citizenship' during the first forty years of Independence.[7]

Ireland is rarely considered in studies of welfare provision: welfare is commonly associated with industrialisation, modernisation and secularisation, and Ireland with agriculture, tradition and religion. In fact, it was the emphasis on tradition and the importance of religion that prompted initial welfare provision, and the history of Irish welfare policy is imbued with, and shaped by, the growing anxiety regarding the role of religion and tradition in modern Ireland. Work by Mel Cousins has opened the debate on the history of Irish welfare, but there has been nothing in the Irish context to rival the extensive study of women and welfare in other countries.[8]

While taking on board the warning against treating the development of welfare in any country as sui generis, this study analyses the particular cultural and social influences that impacted on the treatment of mothers in Ireland in general and Dublin in particular.[9] To this end, sources such as the papers of the two Roman Catholic Archbishops of Dublin, Dr Edward Byrne (1921–40) and Dr John Charles McQuaid (1940–72), have been invaluable in exposing the centrality of the Roman Catholic Church in the welfare and public health debates in relation to mothers during these years. The thousands of letters written by mothers to Dr Byrne have also afforded a rare insight into how mothers themselves viewed their position in society in terms of welfare provision. With the advantage of these sources, this work adds to a history that aims to provide not only a 'more complex picture of the totality of women's experiences',[10] but also an insight into the development of secular welfarism and social citizenship in modern Ireland.

In the 1920s and 1930s, the international preoccupation with state power and population development led to an increased emphasis on motherhood as a determining influence on national vitality and public health. In countries as different as France, Germany, Italy and Norway, feminists were declaring 'motherhood as a social function'.[11] In most Western European countries the main impetus behind the interest in maternal welfare was an international concern about the declining birth rate, which had reached a low point in many countries by 1933.[12] Ireland was a demographic anomaly in Western Europe. As a gathering of the Irish Statistical and Social Inquiry Society was informed in 1935, 'In no respect is this country more strikingly dissimilar from others than in the manner in which the population is recruited. With the lowest marriage rate in the world and one of the highest fertility rates (births per marriage) the Saorstát achieves a more or less average birth rate.'[13] The Irish demographic challenge came in the guise of a low marriage rate, and high emigration and infant mortality rates.

In 1939, as a result of an examination of the 1936 census, the Minister for Finance, Séan MacEntee, reassured the cabinet that every other country in Europe except Germany exceeded the percentage decline in Ireland's birth rate of 4.9 between 1926 and 1936.[14] Although he believed that the main problem was emigration, he conceded that the situation could be counteracted by an improvement in the survival rate of Irish children.[15] While the Irish state flirted with the rhetoric of population panic, ultimately both the demographic reality and social outlook of the state leaned more to the issue of public health as an objective in its own right. For many contemporaries working in the area of social services, the increased investment in maternity and child welfare services was regarded as 'one of the most convincing signs of an awakening of public interest in public health'.[16] Although it was hoped that improved public health might lead to an increase in national vitality and a comparable decrease in emigration, that wish should not detract from the fact that the desire to improve the physical health of Irish citizens was genuine. Consequently, from the late 1930s until the mid-1950s Ireland sought to confront its population problem with a strategy of counteraction against the tolls of infectious diseases and maternal and infant mortality. The Irish mother, therefore, was not targeted by pronatalist policies as in other European countries; instead she was the focus of debates and policies relating to the development of public health and the preservation of the social and the moral order.[17]

Prior to the Second World War, preventive maternity care was the preserve of the local authorities: they negotiated deals with charities and instigated a network of protection for mothers and their children. They were, however, not obliged to do so. For that reason the first identifiable feature of Ireland's maternity services was that they developed in a piecemeal fashion, varying hugely from county to county. The geography of the maternity and child welfare services that developed between 1922 and 1960 is crucial to the examination of the impact and tenor of those services. The maternity and child welfare services grew up around the county medical officer system, thereby rendering the service dependent on local initiative and regional variations. If a county did not appoint a county medical officer, and it was not obligatory to do so, then services for that county depended almost wholly on chance and charity. Often maternity hospitals proved crucial to the development of maternity and child welfare services in an area: the maternity hospital provided the core supervising antenatal clinics, referring patients to voluntary agencies for food and assistance, and arranging health visits.[18]

Dublin was exceptional in national terms, as it had the most comprehensive services for mothers and children, in both medical and welfare terms, and the most established network of charitable endeavour. Dublin was also well-endowed with three maternity hospitals, all of which were proactive in creating a canopy of integrated services for mothers, from medical attendance in hospital and at home to antenatal clinics and a referral system to maternity kitchens and other charitable facilities. Furthermore, despite its three voluntary maternity hospitals, Dublin had one of the worst infant mortality rates in the country for many years.[19] When central government was prompted into a more proactive response to maternity and child welfare in the early 1940s, it was primarily as a result of the soaring infant mortality rate in Dublin caused by the infectious disease gastro-enteritis and an awareness of the Beveridge Report (1942) in Britain.

From the beginning of the twentieth century, public health officials, medical experts and voluntary organisations drew attention to the connection between pregnancy and infant survival. Research into the impact of nutrition and antenatal care helped to broaden the contemporary understanding of pregnancy beyond childbirth. The more comprehensive view of pregnancy that emerged in the early twentieth century simultaneously expanded the social interpretation of maternity welfare. A mother's welfare began before the birth of her child and lasted well into the period of nursing. She was, therefore, entitled to medical care and nutritional and financial support. Nevertheless, the issue of assisting mothers to avail themselves of medical services and secure sufficient nutrition for themselves and their families was considerably more complicated than simple administration and organisation. The dilemma posed by the issue of maternity welfare drew in its train issues of religious and professional protectionism, money, morality and state power.

The first two chapters of this book chart the development of a maternity consciousness in public health terms and the social and moral complications that ensued. The nineteenth-century legacy of proselytism meant that the Roman Catholic Church was suspicious of, and hostile to, any Protestant or 'non-sectarian' organisations engaged in maternity and child welfare. Thus attention is also paid to the cultural association between morality and health, which did so much to complicate the development of a more comprehensive maternity and child welfare service in the succeeding years. Sectarian tensions undoubtedly limited the potential for co-operation between voluntary organisations and served as a distraction from the objective of infant protection. Nonetheless, the emphasis on moral supervision and religious-based charity, while restrictive and punitive, did also afford mothers room for negotiation. Chapter 3 explores the ways in which Catholic mothers negotiated the various relief options open to them. There is ample evidence that Catholic mothers were not merely passive recipients of assistance and advice, but were frequently active agents securing charity in exchange for allegiance. It was this fear of religious bargaining and the desire to limit secular or state intervention into social welfare that precipitated Roman Catholic involvement in maternity welfare. From this juncture the issue of maternity and child welfare became a virtually exclusive dialogue between the Roman Catholic Church and the Irish state, to the detriment of other religious and lay groups previously active in that arena.

Chapters 4 and 5 examine the impact of the Second World War, the emergence of a welfare state in Britain, an increasingly vociferous medical profession in alliance with a more proactive Roman Catholic diocese under McQuaid. McQuaid believed in the 'informal but effective concordat' established in the nineteenth century between the Catholic Church and nationalist leaders.[20] Consequently, he fought to maintain an established working relationship, one in which the state sought to 'supplement not supplant' Catholic voluntary effort in the field of social service.[21] In pursuit of that goal, McQuaid was involved in a positive sense in the government's drive to promote breastfeeding and reduce gastro-enteritis. However, the Archbishop was also assisted and encouraged in a policy of Catholic supremacy, whereby co-operation between different religious voluntary organisations was eschewed in favour of competition and exclusion. An analysis of the working relationship between the Archbishop of Dublin and the Department of Local Government and Public Health during the early 1940s provides the background of the difficulties that emerged in the late 1940s and early 1950s, when the state took a more 'secular' approach to maternity care.

By the 1940s the issues of infant mortality and infectious disease raised the profile of maternal health, allowing the state to take a more interventionist stance then previously justifiable: infectious diseases were accepted as a communal concern, enabling the state to encroach on the privacy of the family. Until the introduction of the ill-fated Public Health Act of 1947 the Irish state had no coherent policy in relation to maternal health and welfare. The attempts to introduce a free service for all mothers and children, irrespective of income, resulted in the infamous 'mother-and-child controversy' of 1950–51. While Chapter 5 offers a detailed analysis of this controversy in a political, cultural and medical sense, Chapter 6 explores the impact of the controversy on the progress of maternity care and analyses the meaning of the compromise scheme introduced in 1953 to Dublin mothers.

The final chapter examines the services provided for the unmarried mother and her child. The Irish state proscribed birth control, and while the rhetoric concerning motherhood was relatively non-prescriptive, a mother was only considered 'legitimate' if she was married. The unmarried mother was, therefore, in a particularly invidious position. Nonetheless, almost 100,000 illegitimate births were recorded between 1920 and 1970. The fate of both the mothers and the children was an indication of the social price that society was willing to pay for moral and cultural peace of mind. Frequently, these women faced detention in an institution, and their children died at between two and five times the rate of legitimate infants.[22] Many of the mothers fled to Britain rather than face the haphazard fate that awaited them and their children in Ireland. While the unmarried mother benefited from the mother-and-child scheme of 1953, she was virtually ignored by the Irish state, which operated a policy of stressing the moral aspect of the 'unmarried mother problem', thereby passing responsibility to the religious authorities. Neither Church nor State considered the single mother in terms of her citizenship; both institutions were concerned with the protection of her infant and the national disgrace caused by her propensity to emigrate, pregnant, to Britain. In the context of the wider debate on maternal welfare, the final section of this book completes an examination of maternity and child welfare with all its intricacies, including the role of religion, society, individuals and government.

Notes

1   M. Horne, 'An almoner's work in a maternity hospital', *Journal of the Irish Medical Association (JIMA)*, 34:202 (Apr. 1954), 105.
2   J. Lewis, *The Politics of Motherhood: Child and Maternal Welfare in England, 1900–1939* (London, 1980), p. 14.
3   A. Oakley, *Women Confined: Towards a Sociology of Childbirth* (Oxford, 1980), p. 7.
4   M. Valiulis 'Neither feminist nor flapper: the ecclesiastical construction of the ideal Irish woman', in M. O'Dowd and S. Wichert (eds), *Chattel, Servant or Citizen: Women's Status in Church, State and Society* (Belfast, 1995), pp. 168–78.
5   M. E. Daly, '"Turn on the tap": the state, Irish women and running water', in M. G. Valiulis and M. O'Dowd (eds), *Women and Irish History: Essays in Honour of Margaret MacCurtain* (Dublin, 1997), pp. 206–19.
6   There has been an attempt to deal with the issue of childbirth focusing on medical intervention and the development of different birthing practices. Caitríona Clear has looked at 'aspects of pregnancy and childbirth' and the issue of breastfeeding. See C. Clear, *Women of the House: Women's Household Work in Ireland 1922–1961: Discourses, Experiences, Memories* (Dublin, 2000); See also P. Kennedy (ed.), *Motherhood in Ireland: Creation and Context* (Cork, 2004), which, although not an historical study does contain certain chapters with historical dimensions.
7   H. Heclo, *Modern Social Policies in Britain and Sweden: From Relief to Income Maintenance* (London, 1974), p. 13.
8   M. Cousins, *The Birth of Social Welfare in Ireland, 1922–1952* (Dublin, 2003). See, for example, G. Bock and P. Thane (eds), *Maternity and Gender Policies: Women and the Rise of European Welfare States, 1880–1950* (London, 1991); Lewis, *The Politics of Motherhood*; J. Lewis (ed.), *Women's Welfare, Women's Rights* (London, 1983); S. Pedersen, *Family, Dependence, and the Origins of the Welfare State: Britain and France, 1914–1945* (New York, 1993); R. Fuchs, 'Morality and poverty: public welfare for mothers in Paris, 1870–1900', *French History*, 2:3 (Sept., 1988), 288–311; S. Michael, and S. Koven, 'Womanly duties: maternalist politics and the origins of the welfare

states in France, Germany, Great Britain and the United States, 1880–1920', *American History Review*, 4:95 (Oct. 1990), 1076–108.

9 Heclo, *Modern Social Policies in Britain and Sweden*, p. 14.

10 M. Ward, *The Missing Sex: Putting Women into Irish History* (Dublin, 1991), p. 18.

11 Bock and Thane, *Maternity and Gender Policies*, p. 8.

12 *Ibid.*, p. 10.

13 R. C. Geary, 'The future population of Saorstát Éireann and some observations on population statistics', *Journal of the Statistical and Social Inquiry Society of Ireland (JSSISI)* 89 (1935–36), 20.

14 S. MacEntee, 'Some observations on the population problem in this country', 1939; NAI, Dept. Taoiseach, S9684.

15 *Ibid.*

16 Anon., 'Maternity and child welfare,' *The Lancet*, 1 (19 June 1927), 407.

17 During the 1930s there was a wave of 'panic pronatalism' in Franco Spain, France and, to a lesser degree, in Britain and Scandinavia: Bock and Thane, *Maternity and Gender Policies*, p. 50.

18 This was the case in Dublin, Cork, Limerick and Drogheda.

19 In 1921 the national infant mortality rate was 77 per 1,000 registered births and for the Dublin registration area 134, for Belfast 115 and for Limerick 113. See *Annual Report of the Registrar-General, 1921* (Dublin, 1922), pp. xix–xx.

20 Larkin cited in D. Miller, *Church, State and Nation in Ireland 1898–1921* (Dublin, 1973), p. 493.

21 James Staunton to Taoiseach, J. A. Costello, 10 October 1950, DDA, McQuaid Papers, AB8/B/XVIII.

22 In 1923, the Registrar-General noted that the illegitimate death rate was six times the legitimate death rate. In 1940 the recorded illegitimate death rate was four times the legitimate death rate. See *Annual Report of the Registrar-General, 1923*, p. xviii; *Annual Report of the Registrar-General, 1940* (Dublin, 1941), p. viii.

1

Maternity and child welfare pre-Independence

So the babies' clubs were started
in a real viceregal way
With a feast of cakes from Scot-
land and a mighty flood o' tay,
An' Mrs Aberdeen was there in
her disinfected best,
An' swallowed with her tay as
Many microbes as the rest.[1]

The framework legislation passed in relation to public health, prior to Irish Independence, provided the backbone and logic for the haphazard system that persisted in Ireland until its overhaul in the early 1950s. However, the debates generated by certain pieces of legislation, and the tailoring and omission of others, provide interesting insights into the public health culture that emerged in pre-Independence Ireland. The theory of Ireland's sui generis needs was well established prior to 1922. This facilitated the centrality of debates regarding the role of religion, the state, voluntarism and the sanctity of the family. The resistance to adapting all British initiatives to the Irish context without question had its roots in a colonial past but this attitude, fuelled by national pride and financial realities, persisted throughout the twentieth century with regard to the creation of a welfare state. Maternity and child welfare often provided the pretext for debate on issues quite apart from mothers and children, which related to deep-seated fears regarding the power lines in Irish society. The boundaries between the spiritual and the temporal, state and voluntary body, central and local government, doctor and midwife, and husband and wife were challenged by the most unadventurous of measures in maternal and infant protection.

Irish public health: the nineteenth-century legacy

The tradition of preventive public health care in Ireland, however *ad hoc*, dated back to the first half of the nineteenth century.[2] The level of poverty and the fear of infectious diseases spurred the development of an impressive medical charities system based on the Dispensary Act of 1805[3] and the Fever Hospital Act of 1818.[4] Ronald Cassell noted that by 1841 'a year before the public health movement started in England, the theory that sickness caused poverty and that the state had to do something substantial about it was clearly formulated in Ireland'.[5] These developments were consolidated by the Medical Charities (Ireland) Act 1851,[6] which concentrated in the Irish Poor Law Commission 'medical relief and public health powers unprecedented in Ireland and unparalleled in the rest of the United Kingdom'.[7] Under the Act the Irish Poor Law Commission was empowered to regulate and define the role of the dispensary medical officers by insisting that they should be qualified in surgery, medicine and midwifery and should keep records. Between 1851 and 1872 the number of dispensary midwives employed in the country increased from 10 to 187.[8] Furthermore, the Medical Charities (Ireland) Act never mentioned the word 'destitute', and instead referred to the medical relief and care of 'poor persons', which facilitated a broader interpretation of entitlement.[9] Geary argues that the charities act removed the 'vestiges of paternalism and philanthropy' that clung to the dispensary system by making these institutions an 'integral part of the poor law system', and heralded the beginning of greater state involvement and increased centralisation.[10]

In 1925, the Department of Local Government and Public Health viewed the lack of definition of 'poor persons' in the 1851 act as an advantage because it allowed a 'liberal interpretation'.[11] Ruth Barrington also observed that the Irish poor law differed from the English version in the degree of emphasis on medical relief.[12] By 1862, the Poor Law (Ireland) Amendment Act legalised the admission into workhouse infirmaries of poor persons with non-contagious medical problems, facilitating, in effect, a conversion of the workhouse system into one of general hospitals. While this act legalised a growing trend, it ironically signalled the end of innovation in the public health care system in Ireland.[13] All other legislation affecting public health in the latter part of the nineteenth century, such as the Compulsory Vaccination (Ireland) Act (1885) and the Births and Deaths Registration (Ireland) Act (1864), originated in Britain.[14] Both were introduced despite opposition in Ireland from a section of the medical profession and the Catholic clergy respectively.[15] Even at this early stage in the development of a public health consciousness, the potential for a medico-religious alliance against state intervention was evident.

The vaccination and registration legislation reflected the trend towards prevention, regulation and control: the infectious nature of disease and the high rate of infant mortality encouraged contemporaries to approach public health from a communal as well as an individual perspective. Towards the end of the nineteenth century, public health policy continued to privilege the needs of the community over those of the individual. As a result, the language of legislation increasingly took on the 'syntax of compulsion'.[16] The Public Health (Ireland) Act of 1878 and the Local Government (Ireland)

Act of 1898 further established this approach, the former establishing new local authorities to administer preventive health services and certain curative services primarily for infectious disease. The 1898 Local Government Act established county councils and county borough councils which eventually became responsible for the administration of public health services, including tuberculosis services established under the tuberculosis acts, and the venereal disease scheme established under the Public Health (Prevention and Treatment of Disease) (Ireland) Act, 1917.[17]

Maternity and child welfare increasingly became the focus of public health legislation in the early twentieth century. Much of the legislation introduced was in keeping with the emerging regulation logic and was justified on the grounds of prevention: the prevention of maternal and infant mortality and morbidity. The Notification of Births Act, 1907, which enabled local authorities to require that all births be registered, and the compilation of statistics regarding mortality represented the first tentative steps in establishing maternity and child welfare services. This was only gradually extended to Ireland when Dublin embraced the legislation in 1910 after lobbying by public health campaigners and voluntary groups such as the Women's National Health Association (WNHA).[18] Dublin Corporation viewed the act's primary purpose as infant protection through the targeting of the poorer classes. It enabled health visitors, following the notification of a birth, to 'give advice … to mothers of the poorer classes on the feeding and rearing of infants'.[19] While it was acknowledged that the act was class-blind and that all births had to be notified, in practice the corporation's health visitors did not disturb the mothers of the middle and upper classes.[20] The Notification of Births Act, 1915, which was extended to Ireland, made the 1907 act compulsory and gave limited financial teeth to its good intentions.[21] It allowed for a 50 per cent recoupment of local authority spending on maternity and child welfare schemes to a maximum of £5,000 per annum.[22] These financial provisions only applied to urban districts in Ireland and did not oblige local authorities to set up maternity and child welfare schemes.[23] However, the powers afforded the Irish sanitary authorities were greater than those afforded their English counterparts, as the Irish legislation was not subject to amendments during the committee stage of the bill.[24]

Revealingly, the 1915 act allowed for the formation of urban committees on maternity and child welfare 'which shall include women'. This acknowledged the leading role played by women in public health and the widely held conviction that women were particularly suited to this form of work.[25] Irish women had already made inroads into maternal and child welfare. When reviewing the impact of the 1907 and 1915 acts, Lawson acknowledged the role of the Infant Aid Society in visiting Dublin mothers upon birth and the WNHA in establishing baby clubs for the propagation of mothercraft.[26] Margaret Ó hÓgartaigh argues that women physicians 'capitalised on the increasing interest in public welfare, and were active in the Babies' Clubs'.[27] What emerges from the work of Ó hÓgartaigh and Irene

Finn is a web of women active in the field of public health and welfare, mostly, though not exclusively, middle-class and Protestant, who populated committees, clubs, charities and hospitals and thus provided the network and precedence for later social feminists in Ireland.[28]

The Midwives (Ireland) Act, 1918, which was principally designed to regulate midwifery, also entitled any mother who did not qualify for free treatment under the medical charities system to the attention of skilled medical aid in the case of an emergency in connection with parturition.[29] Those working with necessitous mothers in Ireland were anxious that the midwives act should be extended to the country. The Lady Sanitary Officers in Dublin, who visited mothers under the Notification of Births Act, were active in the campaign to stamp out the practice of 'handy women'. The officers encouraged the centrality of maternity hospitals and promoted hospital births or births attended by hospital doctors and midwives. One Lady Sanitary Officer, Mrs E. Nally, feared that if the midwifery act were not extended to Ireland, the country would become 'the dumping ground for the inepts of Great Britain'.[30] The fear that legislation pertinent to mothers would not be translated appropriately to the Irish context was a constant theme in the pre-Independence years.

The early twentieth century witnessed an increase in social legislation that focused on welfare and health, thereby acknowledging the increasingly accepted link between these two aspects of life.[31] Between 1900 and 1921 Ireland benefited from the wave of liberal reforms in Britain, for example the Children's Act, 1908, the Old Age Pension Act, 1908 and the National Insurance Act, 1911.[32] The Old Age Pension Act was hugely popular in Ireland and caused official alarm owing to the enormous up-take: it appeared that a good many more Irish people lived to the age of seventy than the exchequer had calculated.[33] The National Insurance Act was also contentious: first, the medical benefit was not extended to Ireland and secondly, the maternity benefit, which was available to the wives of workers who qualified under the act, was altered to suit Irish conditions.[34] In theory, this act offered protection to working-class families against medical costs, the expense of childbirth and sanatorium treatment for tuberculosis.[35] However, the act was 'not designed for Irish conditions' as it was a health insurance system based on friendly societies, which hardly existed in Ireland.[36] Furthermore, the act was perceived in Ireland as a form of 'penal taxation'[37] and as a 'sudden and potentially catastrophic threat'[38] to the three voluntary maternity hospitals in Dublin city. The Rotunda,[39] the Coombe,[40] and the National Maternity Hospital[41] were powerful players in medical politics and public health policy. The hospitals objected to the fact that the thirty shillings maternity benefit would not be paid to mothers receiving hospital care. The logic for denying this payment to mothers receiving hospital care was based on the presumption that this care was generally provided free of charge. The hospitals feared that these women would opt for the money instead of hospital treatment, thus decimating the hospitals' client list.[42]

The hospitals also embellished their case by expressing a fear that such 'cash payments' would destroy the industry of private charity, thus establishing a formula for medical objections to state intervention in the arena of maternal welfare which was closely allied with religious (principally, though not exclusively, Roman Catholic) concerns.[43]

Henceforth, any threat to the medical profession's territory was married with a comparable risk to the benevolent instincts of charity. A compromise was found: mothers opting for hospital births would receive the maternity benefit subject to a deduction of five shillings which would be paid to the hospitals.[44] The issue of maternity benefit continued to be controversial even after its compromise introduction into Ireland. Irish women eagerly took advantage of this provision to such a degree that by the end of the first year there was considerable concern at the numbers availing themselves of the benefit. Barrington notes that by 1915 some 44,318 Irish mothers were in receipt of maternity benefit, which accounted for nearly half of all births.[45] However, those who entered the homes of the poor argued that the 'small maternity benefit of the insurance act scarcely ever reaches the mothers most in need of it. The wives of casual labourers – owing to the husband being in arrears with his contributions, due of course, in all cases to unemployment.'[46] There were also debates regarding the payment of the benefit which mirrored future debates regarding the payment of Children's Allowances (1944), with contemporaries arguing that the maternity benefit should be paid to the father in order to protect his domestic status as breadwinner and provider. This enraged Irish feminists, who commended the Women's Co-operative Guild[47] for fighting to have the benefit considered the 'property of mothers'.[48] Nonetheless, Irish feminists believed that the benefit was 'a first step in the right direction' and, crucially, they argued that it had 'drawn public attention to the grave needs of working-class mothers, and to a condition of affairs seriously affecting the future generations'.[49]

The Republican Maud Gonne drew attention to the near-starvation of many schoolgoing children and there was considerable disquiet that Ireland had not been included in the Provision of School Meals Act, 1906. However, when Gonne established the Ladies' School Dinner Committee she faced contemporary opposition on the grounds that children should be fed in the bosom of the family and that organised feeding of schoolchildren amounted to socialism.[50] A compromise, the Education (Provision of Meals) (Ireland) Act, 1914, allowed Irish Urban District Councils to make arrangements for the provision of meals for children attending national schools if children were unable to avail themselves of education as a result of hunger. The only public health legislation in relation to infant or child protection which was made mandatory in Ireland was the medical inspection of schoolchildren under the Public Health (Medical Treatment of Children) (Ireland) Act, 1919.[51] The fraught political climate in Ireland meant that the 1919 act was effectively shelved until after Independence. Indeed, in the wake of Independence the Minister for Local Government and Public Health, Séamus

A. Burke, appeared unsure of the act's relevance to Ireland:

> There was an English Act, and I assume it was drafted more with reference to the conditions in England than the conditions over here … The appointment of a medical inspector of schools would, I imagine, be an economic proposition for a big populous area like an English county, but might be altogether uneconomic for an area of the size of the average Irish county.[52]

When the issue of school medical inspections was tackled by an Irish administration in 1947, it brought with it the increasingly prominent anxiety regarding the sanctity of the family, the power of the state, and fears regarding socialism.

Infant protection: British wars and Irish babies

> [In 1912 there were] 156 tombstones for the Dublin babies who passed from the noise and crowding of the tenement house to the Kingdom of Heaven which is ever open to the little children. We ask, in all seriousness, is it not time our rulers took thought for this matter? What use to build Dreadnoughts and plan for regiments when children who, grown to full age, should man these are dying.[53]

The impact of war served to focus attention on infant mortality, which was considered an indicator both of national vitality and of the weaknesses in public health policy.[54] In Britain this awareness led to a series of investigative committees and reports, including the Inter-Departmental Committee on Physical Deterioration in 1904,[55] the National Conference of Infant Mortality in 1906 and 1908 and the Departmental Committee on Maternal Mortality in 1928.[56] These reports were heavily influenced by imperialist fears about the physical weakness of British subjects. The death tolls of the Crimean War (1853–54), the Boer Wars (1880–81, 1899–1902) and crucially, the Great War (1914–18) heightened contemporary awareness of the domestic battlefield against infant mortality. Public health, particularly the health of mothers and children, was increasingly regarded as a necessary form of national investment. The theory of counteraction and prevention emerged: in essence, the idea that began to infuse and enthuse public health activists was that infant lives could counteract the war losses and healthy citizens could prevent future military defeats. As Lawson argued, when extolling the virtues of the Notification of Births Act, 1915, 'The war is still with us, but the great loss of adult life caused thereby makes it the more incumbent on us to do what we can to protect the infant life we have.'[57] Dunwoody observes that the First World War brought the language, if not the reality, of social reform to Ireland. However, in providing the language it facilitated the debate, which ultimately led to significant pressure for change.[58] The war galvanised voluntary effort and witnessed a proliferation of local maternity and child welfare groups and initiatives.

In 1917 the Carnegie United Kingdom Trust sponsored investigations into maternity and infant welfare in the three Kingdoms.[59] The Irish report was compiled by Dr Edward Coey Bigger, the medical commissioner of the Local Government Board of Ireland and the Crown representative for Ireland on the General Medical Council.[60] Bigger's report was imbued with concern regarding population growth and 'imperialist preservation'.[61] He argued that infant protection was vital to national prosperity and national existence.[62]

Bigger proposed Dublin as the centre 'for the teaching of infant and child welfare work'.[63] He stressed the urgent need for mandatory legislation to provide for their welfare. Locating his argument in the realm of social investment, he wrote, 'No branch of public health work can affect so much at a moderate cost as that of maternity and infant welfare. Every mother, every infant and every child is of value to the country; we can no longer afford to waste their lives.'[64] Bigger isolated the tendency toward permissive legislation in Ireland, noting that it was insufficient to *permit* local authorities to provide for the care of mothers and children. He recommended 'repeated and systematic examination' of mothers during their pregnancy, thereby making the crucial connection between the supervision of pregnancy and the survival of the baby.[65]

Bigger's report was perspicacious in many respects, but most importantly for the future of maternity services, he identified a direct link between the mother's health, her surroundings and her child's survival. He prioritised ten factors which contributed to the death of infants, ranging from the care of the mother during her labour to the supervision of milk and food supplies.[66] All of these would become central to the maternity debate in the ensuing years; the first five dealt exclusively with the mother's health and her economic position and social surroundings.[67] Bigger argued that all social factors were interrelated and that 'poverty, by means of the influence which it exerts on the parents, the food and the environment of the infant, is a serious factor in the causation of infant mortality'.[68] Although Bigger considered the realities of impoverished motherhood, his primary focus was the infant. Imbued by the atmosphere of war, Bigger drew attention to the high infant-mortality rate in Dublin by placing the death rate in the context of war casualties:

> If the public can only be made to realise that the newly born infant has less chance of living till this time next year than his father who is fighting in France, surely something must be done, but we have a burden of apathy and ignorance to contend with, and these foes are so dangerous as they are insidious.[69]

The Weekly Irish Times made the same comparison, declaring that 'the death of Irish babies exceeds the casualties of war so far as Irish soldiers are concerned'. This it attributed to 'Ireland's neglect', noting that it was deeply unpopular even to suggest such communal negligence.[70] However, poignant juxtapositions of infant corpses and military body bags did not lead to comprehensive provision for the protection of infant life. The Notification of Births Act, 1915 and the Midwives Act, 1918 marked the only legislative initiatives prompted by the raised awareness of war. Both were mandatory but involved the regulation of procedures and the fortification of professionalism rather than any brave new measures in the field of infant and maternal welfare.

Historians have argued that up until the late 1920s the high infant-mortality rate in Ireland was accepted with a curious mix of apathy and stoicism.[71] Concern was slow to emerge, owing primarily to a sense of fatalism and an underlying suspicion that debility was the cause. The notion of debility was frequently used to defend the high infant-mortality rate among illegitimate babies.[72] The Eugenics movement did not take hold in any major way in Catholic Ireland[73] Nonetheless, social commentators and doctors did indulge in eugenic semantics and it was often hinted that a belief in the 'survival of the fittest' was a reason for the tardy response of many in positions of responsibility. Furthermore, some of the leading public health campaigners were associated with the eugenic movement, for example Lady Aberdeen and Dr Marion Andrews of the WNHA.[74] It was, however, the fatalistic attitude, resultant, in part, from the long-standing history of high mortality rates among the poorer sections of Irish society, which lead to the conviction that these deaths were inevitable. Prunty noted that in the fight against tuberculosis 'the biggest obstacle was fatalism', and this defeatism was apparent generally when it came to confronting the social problems of slum living.[75]

The notable exception was the WNHA, which worked tirelessly to counteract the latent apathy regarding public health.[76] It was a pioneering public health organisation established by Countess Aberdeen, the wife of the Lord Lieutenant of Ireland, in 1907 in response to the appalling social conditions she witnessed in Dublin.[77] By 1911 the WNHA had 155 branches and almost 18,000 members.[78] The organisation sought to educate and energise the public in relation to health and welfare. Its activists focused on subjects particularly relevant to the poor: tuberculosis, clean milk, the implications of poor hygiene, and maternal and child welfare.[79] They were instrumental in raising awareness regarding tuberculosis and instigating the campaign for school meals.[80] Although the organisation operated nationwide, Dublin was the focus of initial campaigns to establish clubs for infant welfare. On extension of the 1915 Notification Act the WNHA began negotiations with Dublin Corporation and secured the first grant to establish baby clubs in the city in 1916.[81] The clubs were created with the intention of fostering co-operation between official and voluntary bodies.[82] In the long run this was perhaps the most beneficial aspect of the association's work for Dublin mothers, as they encouraged the authorities to enter the field of maternity services, a process which became irreversible. In 1927 a model child care centre was established at Lord Edward's Street with

Carnegie UK Trust funds.[83] By 1932 there were twelve such baby clubs in the city.

While the notion that 'war is good for babies' was broadly true in the Irish context in relation to public health awareness, it was a theory hotly contested by Irish nationalists.[84] Sinn Féin's public health circulars issued occasionally during and after the First World War warned of the negative impact of the war on civilian life in Ireland. Dr Kathleen Lynn, a Sinn Féin director of public health, warned of the impending 'social evil which threatens us individually and racially at the termination of the war': that is, the spread of syphilis. Referring to the thousands of Irish servicemen who would inevitably return to Ireland infected, which would lead 'to enormous yearly loss of children's lives', she urged the Irish people to call on the British authorities to control the disease.[85] Female members of Sinn Féin established Cumann na dTeachtaire (League of Women Delegates) to campaign on issues relevant to women and children.[86] The Cumann's minutes reveal that they were largely interested in medico-political issues such as venereal diseases, public hygiene and sanitation (for example, clean public toilets) rather than infant mortality.[87] Nonetheless, the members were influential in the establishment of the first and only hospital in Ireland managed entirely by women for infants: Saint Ultan's Hospital for Infants (Teach Ultáin) in 1919.[88] Kathleen Lynn and Madeleine ffrench-Mullen[89] established St Ultan's in response to the appalling conditions in Dublin, in particular the threat of venereal disease.[90]

For Lynn, Irish public health had a particular political resonance. As Ó hÓgartaigh argues, Lynn and the St Ultan's committee were concerned with revitalising the nation just as the Gaelic League was concerned with reviving the Irish language.[91] The St Ultan's committee was part of a group known as Sláinte na nGaedheal which was interested in promoting national health and advocated the establishment of children's clinics.[92] While Sinn Féin public health literature was often embellished with calls to rejuvenate racial health, there was no great emphasis on infant and maternal health.

Interestingly, despite the nationalist convictions of many of its members, the St Ultan's committee co-operated with the WNHA in the training of health visitors and the teaching of mothercraft. It sought to become a 'university for mothers'.[93] The WNHA was certainly not a nationalist organisation, and the co-operation between its members and the St Ultan's committee reflected the strength of the ties between women working in the interests of other women and their children. St Ultan's saw itself as part of an international movement to train mothers and promote infant protection. These concerns crossed national and religious boundaries,[94] therefore, St Ultan's was a rarity in the Ireland of the twentieth century. Furthermore, St Ultan's, unlike the National Children's Hospital (Harcourt St., Dublin), and Temple St. Children's Hospital, accepted infants with infectious diseases. As gastroenteritis was one of the biggest killers of infants, this was a significant step in tackling infant mortality.[95] However, its multidenominational make-up made it the target of suspicion and a smear campaign by members of the Catholic hierarchy, as well as certain Catholic activists who were prominent medical practitioners, such as Dr Marie (Monica) Lea-Wilson and Dr Stafford-Johnson, a close personal friend of Dr (later Archbishop) John Charles McQuaid.[96]

Pre-Independence Ireland was hugely influenced by the imperialist ideology that informed anxieties regarding infant survival in Britain, but the debate was situated in the Irish political context whereby Irish nationalist groups used public health to contest the legitimacy of the British Empire and British rule in Ireland. While nationalist groups frequently alleged that many of the social ills of Ireland were indictments of British rule, infant mortality was not central to this argument. There was the consistent implication that Irish rule would reduce poverty and its consequent effects. *The Democratic Programme of the First Dáil* in 1919 articulated this contention by placing the care of children as 'the first duty of the republic'. Stressing the negative impact of the 'alien system' imposed by British rule, the Dáil promised reform in the interest of society's most vulnerable: children and the aged.[97] Nevertheless, there was a reluctance to advocate state responsibility for child welfare, as this brought with it implications of socialism and fears regarding the religious sanctity of the Irish family. Schemes to support or assist the children of working-class Dubliners during the lock-out of 1913[98] met with fierce opposition from nationalist quarters and the Roman Catholic hierarchy.[99] A plan was conceived by the leader of the Irish Transport and General Workers' Union, James Larkin, and others to send the children of lock-out families to England on holiday. Infuriated by the threat of proselytism, the Roman Catholic Archbishop of Dublin, William Walsh, wrote to all the main newspapers warning Dublin mothers that they would 'be no longer worthy of the name of Catholic mothers if they so far forget that duty as to send away their children to be cared for in a strange land, without security of any kind that those to whom the poor children are to be handed over are Catholics, or, indeed, are persons of any faith at all'.[100]

The scheme may have been intended as a mere act of 'worker solidarity', but in the Irish political context it was perceived as a threat to Catholicism and nationalism. The cocktail of religion, nationalism and anti-Larkinism led the *Irish Catholic* to decry the holiday scheme as tantamount to 'satanism and socialism'. This neatly combined anti-Catholicism with socialism.[101] The Archbishop's response to pleas to reconsider was indicative of the Catholic response to welfare: those, he argued, genuinely concerned should donate money to charities dedicated to the welfare of Catholic children, not break up the family by 'deportation'.[102] Walsh's concerns were sufficient to generate port vigils to stop the children leaving, and led to the withdrawal of consent by many parents. In the face of such opposition, the scheme wilted.[103] Likewise, the food committee established by Maud Gonne to feed the hungry children of Dublin had to seek Walsh's approval or risk similar opprobrium and failure.[104]

Thus, despite the work of Lynn and others, infant mortality was not central to the nationalist agenda. Those who expounded on the wastage of human life that infant mortality wrought were usually of a socialist disposition, leading, of course, to suspicion from other quarters, principally the Roman Catholic Church, which viewed any collective or state initiatives in relation to mothers and children as a threat to its authority. The 'Worker' who contributed to the 'Labour Notes' section in the nationalist journal *Bean na hÉireann* pointed to this apparently bizarre oversight in Ireland: 'here in Ireland where we have so many public spirits and patriotic men, both lay and clerical, we seem to lack the possession of a single champion to plead for the lives of these innocent units of society, who are sacrificed yearly to enrich sweating manufacturers, slum owners, and publicans'.[105]

While the 'Worker' was perhaps overly pessimistic regarding the lack of any champion for Irish infants, he/she was highlighting a resignation when it came to the high levels of Irish infant mortality. It was women, nationalist, unionist and apolitical, who championed the cause of Irish infants. Neither the Catholic clergy nor nationalists who had decried the holiday scheme for working-class Dublin children were prominent in the early initiatives to combat infant mortality. Nor did the reality of infant mortality in Ireland gain any prominent position in the propaganda war against British rule. There was, at best, the lazy conviction that self-rule would resolve the problem. As the 'Worker' noted, in relation to Dublin's infant mortality rate,

> The existing social and economic conditions are the cause of this lamentable state of affairs, and if Ireland had the making of her own laws, the duty of protecting these helpless infants would naturally devolve on our representatives in our native Parliament. It would be necessary to have Acts framed whereby mothers should be nourished and protected, and children supported. Any far seeing state must recognise that each child born into the state is an asset, and as such should be protected and educated, so that the state will gain as much profit as possible from its citizenship.[106]

Conclusion

Ironically, largely as a result of financial, social and cultural constraints, maternal and infant welfare would continue to ignite ideological passions in Independent Ireland, leaving activists like Lynn and the WNHA struggling for legitimacy, and often survival, in the sectarian minefield of Irish public health culture.[107] It would be far from straightforward for the new Irish Free State to recognise the value of its citizens and legislate for the welfare and protection of mothers and children. The spectres of socialism and proselytism remained powerful arguments against state interference in family welfare and non-Catholic assistance of poor mothers and children for the first half of the twentieth century. In fact, the central lines of debate were essentially sketched prior to 1922. In the wake of Independence certain issues were intensified as a result of cultural and financial dictates but concerns regarding infectious diseases, the role of the state and voluntary bodies, and the intersection of religion and public health were evident before the birth of the Irish Free State.[108]

Notes

1 Quoted in M. Ó hÓgartaigh, 'St Ultan's: a women's hospital for infants', *History Ireland*, (July/Aug., 2005), 38. See M. Keane, *Ishbel, Lady Aberdeen in Ireland* (Newtownards, 1999). Jones noted that the WNHA was born of the nineteenth-century voluntary philanthropic tradition. See G. Jones, *'Captain of All these Men of Death': The History of Tuberculosis in Nineteenth and Twentieth Century Ireland* (New York, 2001), p. 101.

2 R. D. Cassell, *Medical Charities, Medical Politics: The Irish Dispensary System and the Poor Law, 1836–1872* (Woodbridge: Boydell, 1997), p. 17; Fleetwood referred to this period as the 'Golden Age of Irish medicine', in J. F. Fleetwood, *The History of Medicine in Ireland* (Dublin, 1983), p. 132; B. Hensey, *The Health Services of Ireland* (Dublin, 1988), pp. 3–4; L. M. Geary, *Medicine and Charity in Ireland, 1718–1851* (Dublin, 2004).

3 The dispensary was intended for the necessitous and among its objectives was the assistance of lying-in women. See Geary, *Medicine and Charity*, p. 61.

4 R. Barrington, *Health, Medicine and Politics in Ireland 1900–1970* (Dublin, 1987), p. 7.

5 Cassell, *Medical Charities*, p. 57. Geary points out that the Poor Law Inquiry of 1836 concluded that state intervention was necessary to address the issue of poverty. However, he notes that this was not accepted without controversy, as members of the Irish medical profession were largely horrified at the notion of placing medical charities under the control of the Poor Law Commission. The Irish medical profession engaged in poisonous 'medical politics' underscored by sectarianism to prevent the government's Medical Charities Bill of 1842. See Geary, *Medicine and Charity*, pp. 157, 159–61.

6 The act was restricted to dispensaries and did not address the broader medical charities network. It divided the poor law unions into 723 dispensary districts, with a minimum of one dispensary in each district. See Geary, *Medicine and Charity*, p. 210.

7 Cassell, *Medical Charities*, p. 78.

8 *Ibid.*, p. 93.

9 *Ibid.*, p. 95.

10 Geary, *Medicine and Charity*, p. 211.

11 *Annual Report of the Department of Local Government and Public Health, 1922–25*, p. 74.

12 Barrington, *Health, Medicine and Politics*, p. 5.

13 Cassell, *Medical Charities*, p. 160.

14 Hensey, *The Health Services of Ireland*, p. 5; Cousins, *The Birth of Social Welfare in Ireland*, p. 21.

15 The grounds for objection are illuminating in the light of future twentieth-century health controversies. The doctors objected to the vaccination act on the grounds that it was unjust to oblige parents to submit their children to medical treatment and invasive to punish them for non-compliance. Catholic clergy, forbidden by law

to celebrate mixed marriages, were opposed to the civil registration of births, deaths and marriages. See Cassell, *Medical Charities*, p. 123.

16 D. Porter, *Health, Civilization and the State: A History of Public Health from Ancient to Modern Times* (London, 1999), p. 112.

17 Department of Health, *White Paper on Health Services: Outline of the Improvement of the Health Services* (Dublin, 1947), p. 6.

18 Only Dublin and Belfast adopted the tenets of the 1907 Act in Ireland. See W. Lawson, 'Infant mortality and the Notification of Births Act, 1907, 1915', *JSSISI*, 13 (Oct. 1919), 482.

19 C. A. Cameron, *Report Upon the State of Public Health in the City of Dublin for the Year 1915* (Dublin, 1916), p. 195.

20 Each of the Lady Sanitary Officers' reports stated that only 'poor mothers' were visited. See, for example, the public health reports of the corporation for 1915 and 1916.

21 Barrington, *Health, Medicine and Politics*, p. 76.

22 Cameron, *Report Upon the State of Public Health in the City of Dublin for the Year 1915*, p. 202.

23 Lawson, 'Infant mortality', 483.

24 Barrington, *Health, Medicine and Politics*, p. 76.

25 Lawson, 'Infant mortality,' 484; Dwork noted that this act opened up a new profession to women who became officially associated with maternal welfare. See D. Dwork, *War is Good for Babies and Other Young Children: A History of the Infant and Child Welfare Movement in England, 1898–1918* (London, 1987), p. 156.

26 Lawson noted that there were separate reports attached to Bigger's report by Drs Ella Webb, Marion Andrews and Alice Barry on the work carried out in relation to maternal and infant welfare in Dublin, Belfast and Cork. See Lawson, 'Infant mortality', 484, 487.

27 M. Ó hÓgartaigh, 'Dr Dorothy Price and the elimination of childhood tuberculosis', in J. Augusteijn (ed.), *Ireland in the 1930s: New Perspectives* (Dublin, 1999), p. 71. Finn makes the same point regarding the 'lady doctor' and the Babies' Clubs. She notes that their response was practical rather than political, which may account for their virtual eclipse in Irish historiography that has largely focused on the political to the detriment of the social. See I. Finn, 'Women in the medical profession in Ireland, 1876–1919', in B. Whelan (ed.), *Women and Paid Work in Ireland, 1500–1930* (Dublin, 2000), p. 116.

28 Ó hÓgartaigh, 'Dr Dorothy Price'; M. Ó hÓgartaigh, 'Flower power and "mental grooviness": Nurses and midwives in Ireland in the early twentieth century', pp. 133–47; and Finn, 'Women in the medical profession', pp. 102–19.

29 See *Annual Report of the Department of Local Government and Public Health, 1922–25* (Dublin, 1925), p. 33. This act is often confused with the Maternity and Child Welfare Act, 1918, which was not extended to Ireland.

30 Cameron, *Report upon the State of Public Health in the City of Dublin for the Year 1916*, p. 94.

31 G. Kiely, 'From colonial paternalism to national partnership: An overview of Irish social policy', in G. Kiely, A. O'Donnell, P. Kennedy and S. Quinn (eds), *Irish Social Policy in Context* (Dublin, 1999), p. 3.

32 H. Burke, 'Foundation stones of Irish social policy, 1831–1951', in Kiely, O'Donnell, Kennedy and Quinn (eds), *Irish Social Policy*, p. 11.

33 C. Ó Grada, '"The greatest blessing of all": The old age pension', *Past and Present*, (May, 2002), 124–61, 175.

34 A brief history of this opposition is given from a post-Independence perspective in

Committee of Inquiry into Health Insurance and Medical Services. Interim Report, (Dublin, 1925), pp. 1–3. See also Cousins, *The Birth of Social Welfare in Ireland,* p. 20; Burke, 'Foundation stones of Irish social policy, p. 23.

35 For contemporary criticism of the act in relation to women, see, Anon., 'Women under the Insurance Act', *Irish Citizen* (21 Mar. 1914).

36 Barrington, *Health, Medicine and Politics,* pp. 37–8.

37 *Ibid.,* p. 42.

38 T. Farmar, *Holles Street 1894–1994: The National Maternity Hospital Centenary History* (Dublin, 1994), p. 45.

39 A. Browne (ed.), *Masters, Midwives and Ladies-in-Waiting: The Rotunda Hospital 1745–1995* (Dublin, 1995)

40 J. K. Feeney, *The Coombe Lying-in Hospital* (Dublin, c. 1980).

41 Farmar, *Holles Street.*

42 *Ibid.*

43 *Ibid.*

44 *Ibid.*

45 Barrington, *Health, Medicine and Politics,* p. 76. Major inroads were made into this gain for women when an Irish administration took charge. See F. W. Powell, *The Politics of Irish Social Policy, 1600–1990* (New York, 1992), pp. 172–3.

46 Cameron, *Report upon the State of Public Health in the City of Dublin for the year 1915* (Dublin, 1916), p. 218.

47 The Women's Cooperative Guild worked to make the needs of working-class mothers central to social policy. In 1916 it published 160 letters by working-class mothers in order to highlight the physical and national cost of deprived motherhood. The Guild demanded trained midwives in 1914 and easy access to a doctor for all mothers in 1917. See I. Loudon, *Death in Childbirth: An International Study of Maternal Care and Maternal Mortality 1800–1950* (Oxford, 1992), p. 223; M. Llewelyn Davies, *Maternity: Letters from Working Women* (London, 1984, 1st edition, 1915).

48 Anon., 'Maternity benefit', *Irish Citizen* (16 Aug. 1913).

49 Signed 'B', 'The cry of the mothers', *Irish Citizen* (16 May 1914).

50 Helen Hayes, 'Feed the children', *Irish Citizen* (18 Oct. 1913).

51 Barrington, *Health, Medicine and Politics,* p. 80.

52 Dáil Éireann 'Committee on Finance – Debate on Estimates Resumed', *Official Reports of the Debates of Dáil Éireann,* vol. 7, col. 1978, (5 June 1924)

53 Anon., 'How to save the babies', *Irish Citizen* (25 July 1914).

54 Porter, *Health, Civilization and the State,* p. 177; J. V. O'Brien, *'Dear Dirty Dublin': A City in Distress, 1899–1916* (Berkley and Los Angeles, CA, 1982), p. 102.

55 The Boer War led to the establishment of the Inter-Departmental Committee on Physical Deterioration. It encouraged the emerging mothercraft movement in Britain. See R. A. Soloway, *Demography and Degeneration: Eugenics and the Declining Birthrate in Twentieth-Century Britain* (Durham, NC, 1995), p. 44; Lewis, *The Politics of Motherhood,* p. 15.

56 B. Harrison 'Women and health', in J. Purvis (ed.), *Women's History in Britain, 1850–1945: An Introduction* (London, 1995), p. 58; Loudon, *Death in Childbirth,* p. 210.

57 Lawson, 'Infant mortality', 479.

58 J. Dunwoody, 'Child welfare', in D. Fitzpatrick (ed.), *Ireland, the First World War* (Dublin, 1986), p. 75.

59 E. Corey Bigger, *Welfare of Mothers and Children,* vol. 4 (Carnegie UK Trust, 1917).

60 Edward Coey Bigger was a member of the Vice-regal Commission of 1903–6. He was the Chairman of the Central Midwives Board of Ireland from its inception in 1918 until his death in 1942.

61 Porter, *Health, Civilization and the State,* p. 177.
62 Carnegie, *Report on the Physical Welfare of Mothers and Children,* p. 1.
63 Lawson, 'Infant mortality', 491–2.
64 *Ibid.,* p. 82.
65 *Ibid.,* p. 25.
66 1. The care of the mother before, during and after labour, and the advice given as to the care of the child. 2. The economic conditions of the family. 3. The domestic surroundings of the infant and child. 4. The extra-domestic surroundings of the home. 5. The Health and habits of the mother and father. 6. The affection of the mother for the child; her education and fitness for motherhood. 7. Legitimacy and illegitimacy of the offspring. 8. The size of the family. 9. The ages of the mother and father at marriage. 10. The supervision of milk and food supplies, p. 26.
67 WNHA of Ireland, *Infantile Mortality and Infant Milk Depots* (Dublin, 1908), p. 8.
68 Coey Bigger, *Welfare of Mothers and Children,* p. 34.
69 *Ibid.,* p. 2.
70 Cited in Dunwoody, 'Child welfare', p. 69.
71 M. E. Daly, *Dublin: The Deposed Capital. A Social and Economic History, 1860–1914* (Cork, 1984), p. 276; Barrington, *Health, Medicine, and Politics,* p. 75, Clear, *Women of the House,* pp. 128–9.
72 *Annual Report of the Department of Local Government and Public Health, 1932–3,* p. 55.
73 G. Jones, 'Eugenics in Ireland: The Belfast Eugenics Society, 1911–15', *Irish Historical Studies,* 28:109 (May 1992), 80–95. For further discussion, see Chapter 3.
74 M. Ó hÓgartaigh, *Kathleen Lynn: Irishwoman, Patriot, Doctor* (Dublin, 2006), p. 70.
75 J. Prunty, *Dublin Slums, 1800–1925: A Study in Urban Geography* (Dublin, 1998), p. 163.
76 Ó hÓgartaigh noted that the WNHA was associated with eugenics, and certain members were involved in the Belfast Eugenic Society. Ó hÓgartaigh, *Kathleen Lynn,* pp. 65–70.
77 For an account of the work of the WNHA in combating TB, see Prunty, *Dublin Slums,* pp. 163–7.
78 M. Ó hÓgartaigh, 'Women, politics, and public health: The babies' clubs in Ireland and the Children's Bureau in the US', in C. Burns, Y. V. O'Neill, P. Albou, J. G. Rigáu-Pérez (eds), *Proceedings of the 37th International Congress on the History of Medicine* (Texas, 2001), pp. 99–103, 100.
79 In 1919 the organisation established a committee on legislation affecting child welfare and public health. *Ibid.,* pp. 100–1.
80 *Ibid.* See also WNHA of Ireland, *The Golden Jubilee 1907–1957: The Women's National Health Association of Ireland* (Dublin, 1957).
81 WNHA of Ireland, *The Golden Jubilee,* p. 7. Ó hÓgartaigh noted that women's involvement with baby clubs helped to place public health on the political agenda. See Ó hÓgartaigh, 'Women, politics, and public health', p. 99.
82 Dr Alice Barry was in charge of the Dublin Baby Clubs between 1912 and 1929. See Ó hÓgartaigh, 'Dr Dorothy Price', p. 70.
83 The Carnegie UK Trust gave £25,000 to fund the centre. *Annual Report of the Department of Local Government and Public Health, 1927–8,* p. 42.
84 Dwork, *War is Good for Babies.* However, Jones has argued that in Dublin the economic situation showed no improvement during the First World War and actually worsened for the poorest. See Jones, *'Captain of All These Men of Death',* p. 129.
85 K. Lynn and R. Hayes, *Sinn Fein Public Health Department: Public Health Circular,*

No. 1 (Dublin, 1918). I am grateful to M. Ó hÓgartaigh for this reference.

86 M. Ward, 'The League of Women Delegates and Sinn Féin', *History Ireland*, 4:3 (Autumn, 1996), 37–41.

87 Cumann na dTeachtaire Minute Book, National Library of Ireland (NLI), Ms. Dept. 21, 194 (47).

88 Ó hÓgartaigh, 'St Ultan's: a women's hospital for infants', p. 36.

89 Ó hÓgartaigh, *Kathleen Lynn*, p. 68.

90 *Ibid.*

91 *Ibid.*, p. 37.

92 *Ibid.*

93 *St Ultan's Annual Report*, 1923. Cited in Ó hÓgartaigh, *Kathleen Lynn*, p. 75.

94 Ó hÓgartaigh, *Kathleen Lynn*, pp. 65–91.

95 *Ibid.*, p. 106.

96 I am grateful to M. Ó hÓgartaigh for information relating to M. Lea-Wilson.

97 See Dáil Éireann, *The Democratic Programme of the First Dáil*, 1919.

98 Labour dispute in Dublin between a group of employers, headed by William Martin Murphy and the workers of the Irish Transport and General Workers' Union, which resulted in 20,000 workers on strike or lockout between August 1913 and January 1914.

99 T. J. Morrissey, *William J. Walsh, Archbishop of Dublin: No Uncertain Voice* (Dublin, 2000), pp. 249–60.

100 Quoted in Morrissey, *William J. Walsh*, p. 249.

101 *Ibid.*, p. 253.

102 *Ibid.*, p. 251.

103 *Ibid.*, p. 254.

104 According to Morrissey, Walsh did approve of the feeding scheme upon consultation with Gonne. *Ibid.*, p. 261.

105 'Labour notes', *Bean na hÉireann*, 1:19 (June 1910), 3–15.

106 *Ibid.*

107 Finn notes that religion was possibly of more significance in the Irish medical world than gender. See Finn, 'Women in the medical profession', p. 113.

108 See, for example, Prunty, *Dublin Slums*, p. 61; Jones also argues that the 'denominational rivalry' that preceded partition (1921) increased after it. See Jones, *Captain of All these Men of Death*, p. 134.

2

Maternity and child welfare: setting the agenda, 1922–39

Ireland has been cursed with permissive Acts of Parliament[1]

The fight for national independence between 1919 and 1921, followed by a civil war from 1922 to 1923, threw the Irish public health system into chaos. Cumann na nGaedheal, the first Irish administration,[2] battled between 1923 and 1932 to reinstall law and order, prioritising (largely out of necessity) issues such as security, and political and financial reconstruction.[3] Inexperience, conservatism and financial realities meant that the first social policy initiatives were regressive welfare cuts; symbolically the popular old age pension was reduced by 10 per cent, which impacted on the less-well-off, whereas income tax was reduced, benefiting the better-off.[4] Throughout the first decade of Independence there was an atmosphere of crisis management, infused with defeatism, in relation to welfare and public health. It was a question of containing expenditure, streamlining chaos and encouraging voluntary effort to fill the gaps in state services. It is hardly surprising that, as the provision of maternity services was not mandatory, 'the comprehensive mother and child service for needy persons envisaged before independence hardly existed'.[5] The services provided depended hugely on voluntary effort, and in Dublin the system based around maternity hospitals and voluntary groups remained largely intact until the 1940s. Sectarianism, a long-standing source of tension in Irish life, became increasingly prominent in relation to maternity and child welfare as the Roman Catholic Church began to organise itself in response to its new responsibility to guide the Irish Free State in relation to public welfare, both spiritual and temporal. The Catholic Church became one of the central lobbying forces in Irish public life and sought to assume the power of veto on matters regarding health and morality.

A divided service: Dublin and 'outside Dublin'

The Minister for Local Government and Public Health, Séamus Burke, lamented that his department was in a 'chaotic condition', and it was 'absolutely impossible to get in touch with every detail of administration'. The Minister complained, 'We have got none of these health services centralised. They are all divided up between local authorities and voluntary agencies and agencies. It is really a very difficult task to keep in touch with them all.'[6] By 1925 there was a 'gradual recovery from the confused administrative conditions', and the areas of most concern were the 'normal functions of the Public Health control, notably in the directions of renewed medical inspection, and of the methodical collection of particulars of the incidence of infectious disease'.[7] The authors of the 1927 *Report of the Commission on the Relief of the Sick and Destitute Poor, including the Insane Poor* explained:

> It will, we think, be generally admitted that during the year 1920 and the following three or four years, whether in those counties where schemes had been adopted or in those where the old law was supposed to operate, that it was difficult if not impossible for either the poor or those interested on their behalf to know what law, if any, was being administered.[8]

While the report pointed out that the Local Government Act of 1923 lent some sense of order to the chaos by legalising schemes adopted by county councils, the situation was still unsatisfactory, with the standard of care varying hugely from county to county.[9]

A constant theme throughout the 1920s, 1930s and 1940s was how the standard of maternity and child welfare services varied throughout the country.[10] In an attempt to raise the standard of county-based care, the Local Government Act of 1925, which refashioned the old Local Government Board into the Department of Local Government and Public Health, allowed the appointment of county medical officers. The medical officers were given jurisdiction in urban and rural areas and were responsible for, among other things, the operation of maternity and child welfare services, such as the school medical service and a programme of school meals. The cornerstone of the maternity and child welfare services was the County Medical Officer (CMO) of health as both overseer and instigator. However, the theory did not readily translate into practice. The main problem was ensuring that every county had at least one medical officer. In 1928 the Rockefeller Foundation offered 'generous financial assistance' for the appointment of medical officers of health in Cork and Kildare.[11] The department continued to put pressure on local authorities to appoint CMOs, pointing out in 1929, for example, that the high maternal mortality in Kerry was attributed to the lack of a CMO.[12] The following year Kerry appointed its first CMO.[13] By 1932, eighteen counties, comprising 75 per cent of the entire population, possessed a CMO.[14] By 1934 the department appeared to have met implacable resistance, with the CMO campaign bemoaning that it failed to induce more local authorities to appoint CMOs. The reason given by local authorities was finance, but the department argued strongly that this attitude constituted a false economy.[15] However, in 1935 there were still nine counties out of twenty-six with no CMO, which, in view of the pivotal role of the medical officer, did not bode well for the establishment of a comprehensive maternity and child welfare service.[16]

The bulk of maternity and child welfare services were carried out by women as health visitors, midwives (private and/or dispensary) and voluntary or public health (known as district) nurses. Apart from the assistant medical officer, the medical officer's second-in-command was the public health nurse. The public health nurse was needed to extract the most from the system, as she could be assigned 'routine work' of the school medical service, the inspection of midwives, health visiting and 'other matters connected with the arrangements for promoting the welfare of expectant and nursing mothers and young children'.[17] In 1931 there were only thirteen public health nurses employed nationwide: in Cork, Kildare, Louth and Offaly.[18] By 1938 the figure had increased dramatically to forty-six. The district nurse ultimately carried out much of the work of the maternity and child welfare services at a county level as the CMOs became more occupied with diversifying services and compiling annual reports.

For necessitous women the dispensary midwife was crucial, as she was obliged to attend free of charge to the sick poor. In 1925 for the 588 dispensary districts there were 656 dispensary midwives employed, by 1938 there were 580 dispensary districts with 686 dispensary midwives[19] and by 1952 there were 724 such midwives. This system, however paltry, was specifically for poor women, and any case where a dispensary midwife was suspected of giving priority to private cases resulted in public condemnation and reprimand. In 1935 a dispensary midwife was reprimanded for refusing to attend a dispensary patient on the grounds that she was attending a private case and she was informed that she was 'not at liberty to neglect the poor for the purposes of attending a private patient'. [20]

There is no way of knowing how widespread this practice was, given that the majority of dispensary midwives also functioned as private midwives. However, the dispensary system was the main organ of assistance at birth for many necessitous women in rural areas. In cases of emergency, where a woman was not entitled to free care, the midwife was obliged to call on a doctor whose fees were then paid by the local supervising authority.

Until 1953 the maternity and child welfare grant was largely used to fund health visiting/voluntary nursing schemes, maternity centres, hospital treatment, the provision of milk and food to expectant and nursing necessitous mothers, and arrangements for widowed, deserted or unmarried mothers and their children. In 1922, the first year of Irish administration, the maternity and child welfare grant amounted to £12,915.[21] By the mid-1940s, when the issue of maternity and child welfare services became increasingly controversial, the grant was £32,473 7s. 9d. Of this sum, £17,767 0s. 2d. was recouped by local authorities for their efforts; the rest was given to voluntary agencies.[22] The degree to which the maternity and child welfare services were beholden to voluntary effort was a constant theme up to, and including, the years of contentious debate in the late 1940s and early 1950s. The department repeatedly paid homage to this voluntary army of welfare workers and hinted at the intransigence of local authorities. Making a virtue of necessity, the department claimed that it was 'policy' to 'encourage and assist voluntary agencies and voluntary effort', which was of course a cheaper option than providing the services without such assistance. By casting the indispensable work of voluntary agencies as part of its wider plan, the department effectively claimed credit for keeping voluntary effort alive. In 1927 it boasted that in making such encouragement a policy, 'District Nursing Societies [sic] have been kept alive in many parts of the Saorstát.'[23] In 1935 the CMO of Cavan declared that the Lady Dudley Nursing scheme had visited 2,908 infants in the area and prevented many probable deaths.[24] In the same year the Roscommon report noted that it was a pity more nurses were not available 'as they do very useful work among the sick poor and make the work of the doctors much more effective'.[25]

As elsewhere, the health visitor was crucial in the development of the Irish maternity and child welfare services. Great hopes were placed on the health visiting system: the health visitor was to enlighten mothers and enlist their help in the battle against infant mortality. They were also the crucial link between medical and welfare services. She arrived, as a health propagandist, at the site of battle, the home, and observed, educated and reported or referred the special cases to other centres of assistance or authority. In 1931 the Public Health Department acknowledged, 'The benefits conferred on a neighbourhood by the activities of a Nursing Association are not easily estimated but can be appreciated from the popularity which the nurse usually enjoys amongst the families she visits and by the way in which her instructions are carried out.'[26] Her qualifications were quite exact and gendered: she should be of an age to advise a mother but not so old as to alienate her; she should view herself as a helper to mother and child not merely as a bureaucrat that 'fills in forms and piles up statistics'; she should be kind, tactful and good-natured. Essentially she was, as Dr Kerry Reddin, who was in charge of the maternity and child welfare service for Dublin Corporation, put it, 'a perfect woman'.[27]

Health visiting received the lion's share of funding and accounted for the bulk of work carried out in the name of maternity and child welfare in Ireland, a fact acknowledged by the public health authorities.[28] In 1925 there were 130 district nurses employed by the various voluntary nursing associations. There was, even in this respect, a rural/urban divide, with these nurses operating on a full-time basis in 'larger centres of population' and on a part-time basis elsewhere.[29] Most of these nursing associations were affiliated with the Queen's Institute of District Nursing which provided a uniform system.[30] The Lady Dudley's Nursing scheme was also prominent in the early development of nursing services in Ireland.[31] These women functioned primarily as health visitors but also performed 'ordinary nursing duties' in the congested districts of the west of Ireland.[32] In 1928 the department extended 'no stinted praise ... to those early propagandists who without proper machinery or organisation spread the gospel of health'.[33] The implication was that the 'proper machinery' was now in place. Voluntary effort, however, remained the mainstay of services until the 1950s.

In 1927 the department explained how the health visitor was created: initially trained in medical and surgical nursing, these 'girls intended as Health Visitors attend a special course of lectures on social subjects, Child Welfare and Hygiene [sic] and are given practical training in district visiting'.[34] Apart from the patronising tone, the department freely admitted its dependency on these women and expressed the intention of utilising their services to the 'fullest extent' in the future. The health visitor was the link in the often weak chain of services: she kept in touch with expectant mothers and mothers of children under five years of age.[35] These women gave advice on maternal health and 'the care of and management of young children'. The official hope was that she would 'forestall the development of conditions of health'.[36] She was also crucial in the official campaign against 'handy women'. The health visitor was supposed to 'exert a valuable influence' by encouraging mothers, particularly in rural areas, to decline the kind assistance of their neighbours in favour of the professional attendance of a midwife either private or dispensary, depending on the client.[37]

Outside Dublin, the chief centres of development were Cork, Limerick and Waterford, where maternity and child welfare clinics were established by the early 1930s. As in Dublin, services were linked to the main maternity hospitals: in Cork, the Erinville Hospital; in Limerick, the Bedford Row Hospital; in Drogheda, the Lourdes Hospital. These clinics dealt with thousands of mothers and children and co-ordinated the health visits of many more and the supply of milk and food. In 1934 there were approved maternity and child welfare schemes in operation in four county boroughs, Cork, Dublin, Limerick and Waterford, in the boroughs of Clonmel, Dun Laoghaire and Wexford, and in fifteen urban districts and three county health districts. In addition, there were 103 voluntary associations engaged in maternity and child welfare services operating in every county except Leitrim.[38]

In spite of the publicity and the obvious official awareness with regard to the benefits of antenatal care for both mother and child, the inadequacy of services was still a central theme by 1940. In 1941 Dr J. G. Gallagher emphasised the need for 'widespread, adequate antenatal care and better all-round standard of nutrition amongst the poorer members of the population'.[39] Lighting on what was to become a familiar theme, he isolated the lack of services outside Dublin as a key factor in many cases of maternal mortality, lamenting that 'neglected and moribund patients arrive from all over the country for whom little can be done: a lethal blow has been dealt to the patient before admission'.[40] Clear noted that as late as 1956, 28 per cent of women delivered in Holles St. hospital in Dublin had received no antenatal care.[41]

By the end of 1944, little had changed with regard to the geography of

services. The Master of the National Maternity Hospital (Holles St.), Dr
Alex Spain, conducted a survey of services available outside Dublin. He
noted that with 'the exception of such limited services as are available in
Cork, Limerick and Drogheda, there is not a maternity service in the rest of
Éire comparable to that of Dublin'.[42] He complained that the system outside
Dublin was one layered in administrative confusion: 'our maternity service
is based upon (a) the district midwife, who in difficulty may call upon (b)
the dispensary doctor, who in turn may call in the help of (c) another practitioner, or may refer the case to (d) one of the hospitals provided by the
local authority, or in certain circumstances to special hospitals'. In relation
to antenatal care, the only statement of intent he unearthed was the declaration that it was one of the duties of the physician to a county hospital to
attend any antenatal clinics which 'may be established in, or attached to the
hospital at any time'.[43] Parallel with this Poor Law service, there operated a
private service based 'in its essentials upon the same structure' except that
many of these private patients could afford to avail themselves of private
antenatal supervision and private midwifery care or confinement in a registered nursing home.[44] Class was a key determinant in the standard of care
available. When services were so haphazard and inconsistent, money alone
could secure attention.

The government did not dispute Spain's assessment of the development
of Irish maternity and child welfare services. The uneven geographical development was acknowledged as a central flaw in the system. As the newly
founded Department of Health explained in its controversial 1947 White
Paper, the system 'developed unevenly over the country as a whole and has
not grown beyond the health visitor stage save in the cities and a few urban
centres. In the cities the service is for all practical purposes confined to the
poorer classes.'[45]

The influence of the Dublin maternity hospitals

Dublin was exceptional for its highly advanced maternity services centred
on the three voluntary maternity hospitals: the Rotunda, the Coombe and
the National Maternity Hospital.[46] Each of these hospitals serviced traditional areas in Dublin City: the Rotunda drew its patients from north Dublin,
the Coombe from Dublin south-west, and the National Maternity Hospital
the south-east of the city and Ringsend, Irishtown and Sandymount. Religious affiliation was as important to the client list as geography; each hospital played its role in the religious segregation of Irish health care. The Rotunda was the Protestant, largely working-class, mother's hospital; the National Maternity Hospital and the Coombe catered for the overwhelmingly
Roman Catholic population of the city. These hospitals administered to
mothers during parturition, in the hospital and on their district service,
which supervised domiciliary births. The hospitals catered, without charge,

for a proportion of mothers who qualified under the medical charities acts; a significant number of women were treated in return for voluntary contributions.[47] Each institution also catered for mothers from outside Dublin City.

The role of hospitals grew first out of a tendency to cater for the poorest cases, then dealing with the complicated cases until finally it was the aim of state health policy to provide hospital facilities for all women at childbirth. In 1927 the Department of Local Government and Public Health noted that provision was made at county and district hospitals and county homes for all classes of maternity cases. The national policy was to refer cases 'requiring more specialised care' to maternity hospitals in Dublin or Cork.[48] The conviction that complicated maternal cases were best served in 'centres of excellence' influenced the hospital policy in succeeding decades.[49] The main voluntary maternity hospitals in the country took on an increasingly central role in maternity welfare.[50] They were involved in some way in most of the births in the country and they extended their remit from the supervision of childbirth to the management of pregnancy. Through their antenatal clinics and almoner departments, the hospitals co-ordinated their services with the municipal maternity and child welfare schemes and frequently acted as referral agents, sending women to charitable organisations.

An Irish administration did not protect the nation from the rising costs of health care and the dilemma posed by the need for increased state intervention. By 1930 the voluntary maternity hospitals were finding it impossible to survive, as costs had increased by 50 per cent between 1911 and 1930.[51] In 1930 the Public Charitable Hospitals Act gave the named hospitals a right to funds raised from the horse-racing sweepstakes, which within its first year had raised £1 million.[52] The Public Hospitals Act of 1933 gave the Minister for Local Government and Public Health responsibility for the allocation of the Hospitals Trust Fund (sweepstakes fund).[53] The same act established the Hospitals' Commission to aid the Minister in assessing the needs of various local authority and voluntary institutions.[54] The Hospitals' Commission, with its demands for reports and audits, signalled a fundamental change in the status of the voluntary hospitals. Once the hospitals accepted the 'Hospitals' Commission's shilling', 'true independence was gone'.[55] In the succeeding decades the lines of co-operation with, and dependence on, the state became increasingly blurred and consequently all the more ferociously guarded.

In the short term, however, the Hospitals' Commission proved to be an excellent tool of inspection, providing a clearer idea of the needs for improvement and the quality of services available. The commission paid due tribute to the central role of the Dublin maternity hospitals, while drawing attention to the growing problem of overcrowding.[56] In 1932 there were 11,828 births in the city: the Rotunda catered for 2,258 intern births and 1,724 extern births, the Coombe dealt with 1,138 intern and 1,460 extern cases, and the National Maternity Hospital recorded 1,030 intern births and 569 extern deliveries (see Table 2.1).[57] Owing to the central role these maternity hospitals played in the provision of maternity services for working-class mothers, the medical practitioners began to consider pregnancy beyond confinement.[58] Imbued by the socio-medical approach to health care, the hospitals began to focus on the influence of the prenatal and postnatal periods. By 1937, 60 per cent of Dublin maternity cases were seen at the maternity hospitals' prenatal departments.[59] By 1933 the antenatal clinics in all three of the Dublin maternity hospitals were co-ordinated with the county borough maternity and child welfare scheme, and subsidised by Dublin Corporation.[60] This co-operative approach afforded the hospitals extra financial aid, and the corporation was able to refer needy cases to the hospitals for treatment and supervision. In the prenatal departments both the mothers and the doctors learned more about each other; the latter were forced to admit that the rate of anaemia was considerable among these women, that their clothing was frequently inadequate, and that their breast milk was insufficient owing, primarily, to malnutrition.[61]

The hospitals also played an important part in home births, many of which were supervised by the district service. In 1932, 4,298 district births were attended by staff members of the three maternity hospitals in the city, a practice that brought medical personnel into the homes of many of their poorest patients, awakening them to the social circumstances of their clients.[62] An anonymous contributor to the *Journal of the Medical Association of Éire* (*JMAÉ*) in 1943 articulated the sense of frustration felt by those who cared for the poor: 'To preach health to the underfed or overcrowded is a hypocrisy.'[63]

A strong indication that maternity hospitals appreciated the impact of social environment on maternal and infant health was the increased demand for almoners, who, in time, were more appropriately known as social workers.[64] The *First General Report 1933–34 of the Hospitals' Commission* decried the slow development of social services in connection with hospitals.[65] The report described it as 'noteworthy' that

> in connection with the Maternity Service, very close co-operation exists between the Public Health Department and the three Dublin Maternity Hospitals: similar co-operation between the almonery departments of the other hospitals and the health activities of the Corporation, on the one hand, and the voluntary Social Service organisations which already exist outside the hospital, on the other, is essential, if hospitals are to take their rightful place as the centres from which all Public Health activities relating to preventive medicine should radiate.[66]

The report argued that the absence of an almoner system in Ireland was due to the fact that Irish universities had only that year begun to provide courses for social workers and almoners.[67] Notwithstanding this, it stressed that the development of an almoner system was crucial to any comprehensive maternity service, confirming the connection between health and welfare.

The report drew attention to the increased demand in Dublin for hospital services in relation to pregnancy and childbirth, and recommended that the development of the maternity hospitals should take priority over general hospitals 'in view of the obvious deficiencies in maternity accommodation'.[68] In 1933 the Coombe lamented having to refuse the admission of thirty expectant mothers as a result of overcrowding, for the first time in the history of the hospital.[69] The Hospitals' Commission report argued that by 1944 there should be enough maternity beds to accommodate 50 per cent of all births in the capital.[70] In fact, in 1933, 40 per cent of Dublin births took place in hospital, and by 1942 this had risen to 54 per cent, which meant that the 287 maternity beds in the city were coping with 8,188 births.[71] The number of Dublin hospital births increased considerably during the Second World War, from 6,699 intern births in 1938 to 9,181 in 1945, while the number of extern district births dropped from 4,207 to 3,407. During the same period the number of births registered in Dublin City rose from 11,633 in 1938 to 12,528 in 1942. The shift from district (home) births to hospital births was undoubtedly prompted by wartime conditions – primarily the shortage of turf.[72] Nonetheless, the rate of intern and extern hospital births never returned to pre-war levels.

The 1933–34 Hospitals' Commission report claimed that mothers were opting for hospital births in the 1930s because the maternity and child welfare clinics provided by the corporation and the Dublin Board of Health encouraged mothers to seek medical advice in the early stages of pregnancy. Furthermore, the report expressed the belief that the preference for hospital births among mothers was motivated by economic factors and the convenience of hospital care.[73] The hospitalisation of childbirth in Ireland began gradually in the 1930s and increased markedly during the 1950s when domiciliary births began their steady and relentless decline.[74] In 1955 one-third of births in Ireland were domiciliary; in 1973, 85 per cent of births took place in hospital, 14 per cent in private maternity homes, and 1 per cent were classed as domiciliary.[75] This trend was influenced by social and medical factors but was copper-fastened by the introduction of the Maternity and Child Health Services (Amendment) Regulations in 1956, which allowed for free hospital treatment in many cases.[76]

There has been much debate about the hospitalisation of childbirth in terms of its impact both on infant and maternal mortality and on the experience of birth for women.[77] Loudon pointed out that, in terms of safety, 'the place of delivery' was only a matter of serious importance in complicated cases.[78] He concluded that what mattered most 'was the morale and the standard of co-operation and integration between all concerned in maternal care'.[79] Hence, in Ireland, the uneven geographical development of services played a crucial role in inflating maternal mortality figures at least until the late 1930s when drug therapy helped reduce puerperal deaths. However, 'other accidents of pregnancy' remained higher in rural areas. In terms of maternity services in Dublin City the role of the hospitals was central in terms of both co-operation and integration. The hospitals served as a link not only between local and central government but also between the medical and the social welfare of mothers, by referring many women to the various voluntary initiatives in the city. Moreover, the hospitals were training grounds for the country's midwives and obstetricians, and they played a

Table 2.1 Numbers of internal and external births managed by the three Dublin maternity hospitals, 1930–55

Year	Dublin city	Rotunda		Coombe		Holles St	
		Intern	Extern	Intern	Extern	Intern	Extern
1930	11,893	2,258	1,724	1,138	1,807	1,030	569
1931	11,647	2,169	1,814	1,172	1,500	1,141	613
1932	11,828	2,239	1,553	1,289	1,478	1,118	601
1933	12,054	2,376	——	1,279	1,517	1,163	692
1934	12,653	2,773	1,915	1,254	1,491	1,327	692
1935	13,264	2,777	1,903	1,188	1,316	2,025	672
1936	13,511	2,871	1,920	1,184	1,870	2,259	733
1937	13,558	2,851	1,944	1,449	1,935	2,281	735
1938	11,633	3,864	1,889	1,531	1,949	2,568	705
1939	11,558	3,121	1,706	1,963	1,876	2,819	598
1940	11,276	3,293	1,574	1,931	1,850	2,869	543
1941	11,301	3,536	1,530	2,047	1,462	2,957	494
1942	12,528	3,750	1,554	1,840	1,481	3,024	494
1943	12,673	3,884	1,536	1,877	1,433	3,002	458
1944	12,74	3,975	1,438	1,926	1,265	3,187	472
1945	12,508	4,033	1,602	1,808	1,378	3,371	428
1946	13,159	3,724	1,902	1,811	1,473	3,668	476
1947	13,643	3,910	2,067	1,804	1,354	3,710	478
1948	13,580	3,918	1,880	1,783	1,489	3,747	404
1949	12,768	3,928	——	1,788	1,549	3,886	422
1950	12,691	3,954	1,699	2,002	1,553	4,147	408
1951	12,841	4128	1,555	2,113	1,751	4,162	376
1952	16,739	4,276	1,598	2,250	1,495	4,638	495
1953	16,155	3,998	1,635	2,554	1,460	4,803	589
1954	16,452	4,367	——	2,400	1,130	4,673	625
1955	18,566	4,177	1,560	2,555	787	4,885	547

Note: When considering the increase in intern hospital births it is important to keep in mind other external influences, such as the number of women moving to suburbs like Crumlin. These women were no longer in the hospital district catchment area, and therefore had to opt for intern births. Furthermore, the three Dublin voluntary maternity hospitals increased in size during the period under review.

Sources: Figures for hospital births for the Rotunda and the National Maternity Hospital, Holles St., taken from the annual hospital reports printed in the Irish Journal of Medical Science. Figures for the Coombe Hospital taken from J. K. Feeney, *The Coombe Lying-in Hospital* (Dublin, c. 1980), p. 279.

crucial role in political negotiations regarding the future of maternity services throughout the twentieth century.[80] Therefore, whatever the final analysis regarding the hospitalisation of childbirth, in terms of the history of maternity care in Ireland, the three voluntary maternity hospitals in Dublin were pivotal to the canopy of services that developed during the 1930s and 1940s.[81]

Maternal mortality: beyond the scope of services

Maternity and child welfare was gauged by mortality statistics: figures were anxiously calculated, increases decried and decreases gratefully acknowledged and analysed (see Table 2.2). During the 1920s there was a growing conviction that maternal mortality could be reduced with more efficient prenatal care. In 1922, Dr W. G. MacKenzi of the Ulster Medical Society noted that 14 per cent of maternal deaths in Ireland during 1920 were due to albuminuria and convulsions – conditions which, he believed, with 'efficient ante-natal care should not be operative in swelling the mortality figures'.[82] By 1928 the 'unyielding character' of maternal mortality dismayed the Department of Local Government and Public Health who observed that despite 'better equipped hospitals, the better educated physician and the more numerous and better trained Midwives, the problem of safety in child birth remains unsolved'.[83] Maternal mortality figures were broken down into those caused by puerperal infections and 'other accidents of pregnancy'. Morbidity, which was rarely documented, would probably provide a much more accurate picture of the costs of poverty, neglect and cases of negligence.[84] Mortality was the primary focus: puerperal deaths accounted for the majority of deaths until the late 1930s and other conditions such as haemorrhage, albuminuria convulsions, toxaemias of pregnancy, abortion, embolism and thrombosis made up the rest. The higher rural death toll was attributed to difficulties in 'procuring skilled aid promptly owing to distance and lack of facilities for communication'.[85] While this may have been the case in complicated births or protracted labour, Loudon cautions against the huge and widespread assumption that increased medical attention led automatically to a reduction in maternal deaths.[86] Nonetheless, the ultimate goal of maternity services was to provide hospital treatment to all women during parturition. The practice was to refer complicated cases to hospital care when possible, but the department noted that, in recent years, the 'care of normal pregnant women' had become an important part of 'obstetric practice'.[87] In view of the growing conviction that certain complications of pregnancy and childbirth were preventable if detected at the prenatal stage, the hospital system had been reorganised to accommodate certain maternity cases: 'women anticipating difficult labour' or those whose home circumstances were 'unsuitable for confinement'.[88] The problem was anticipation, as 'too often the doctor and midwife see the patient for the

Table 2.2 Number and rate of maternal deaths per annum in Ireland, 1923–54

Year	Maternal mortality	
	No.	Rate
1923	32	5.23
1924	33	5.21
1925	31	5.03
1926	32	5.38
1927	29	4.80
1928	318	5.37
1929	283	4.85
1930	294	5.04
1931	272	4.75
1932	280	4.98
1933	296	5.16
1934	304	5.25
1935	297	5.10
1936	299	5.14
1937	237	4.19
1938	267	4.69
1939	218	3.89
1940	227	4.01
1941	209	3.68
1942	163	2.86
1943	162	2.51
1944	176	2.69
1945	176	2.63
1946	163	2.39
1947	148	2.39
1948	124	1.88
1949	129	2.01
1950	99	1.56
1951	103	1.20
1952	92	1.42
1953	83	1.33
1954	69	1.10
1955	70	1.14
1956	52	0.86
1957	132	1.32
1958	103	1.03
1959	65	0.65
1960	58	0.58

Source: Compiled from summaries in Department of Local Government and Public Health Department of Health, *Annual Reports of the Registrar-General*, 1922–52 and Central Statistics Office, *Report on Vital Statistics*, 1973, p. xxxv. These figures include all three categories of maternal death returned by the Registrar-General: (1) septic conditions, (2) intrinsic accidents of childbirth, and (3) diseases or causes associated with pregnancy and childbirth. These changed in 1933 to (1) septic deaths, (2) deaths from accidents and diseases of pregnancy and (3) deaths not classed to pregnancy and childbirth but returned as associated therewith. Figures for major causes of maternal death for the years 1923–61 are given in Clear, 'Women in de Valera's Ireland, 1932–48', p. 205; see also Clear, *Women of the House*, p. 115.

first time after the onset of labour, when it is too late to use any correction methods'.[89] If women were not routinely seen during pregnancy, then it was unlikely that difficult cases could be earmarked for obstetric delivery. In this regard, geography was crucial.

The difference between maternal mortality in urban and rural areas was evident from the foundation of the state (and before). In 1923 the respective rates were 4.38 and 5.04 per 1,000 births; by 1938 the rates were 3.49 versus 4.51.[90] The divergence was attributed to the lack of services in rural areas, isolation, and delays in receiving attention. The official line was to promote 'medical supervision' and to encourage both the establishment of antenatal clinics in centres of population and close co-operation between health personnel in order to complete the circle of care in even the remotest spots of Ireland.[91] The mother was an essential convert to this logic: she must be 'taught the importance of seeking medical advice at an early stage, and of keeping in touch with the midwife.'[92]

The role of the midwife was considered crucial in combating maternal deaths as a result of puerperal infection. The regulation of midwifery and the prosecution of the unqualified and/or unregistered 'handy women', or 'careless' registered midwives, formed the main strategy against the puerperal infection which levied 'a substantial toll on maternal life' and resulted in 'long periods of illness and incapacity'.[93] In January 1924 the statutory prohibition against the unqualified practice of midwifery became operative. The intention was to examine every case of puerperal sepsis which involved a 'careful inquiry ... as to the character of the attendance, so that if there were a *prima-facie* proof of an offence' a local authority would be 'called to the matter'.[94] Consequently, combating the 'custom of the country' whereby assistance at childbirth was 'rendered gratuitously by a neighbour' became the department's main strategy against maternal mortality.[95] There was little official consideration of the social realities that often led to the kindness of neighbours being seen as a lifeline because the assistance of the qualified midwife was either unavailable or viewed as foreign and/or hostile.[96]

In 1932 the Department of Local Government and Public Health noted with some relief that 'except in Mayo there has been no substantial evidence of any widespread practice of midwifery by unqualified women'.[97] It was hoped that the fear of prosecution would help to 'stamp out this objectionable practice which is fraught with danger to the mother'.[98] In 1934 there were four prosecutions of unqualified midwives in Mayo but, due to lack of evidence, no convictions were secured.[99] Both the 1918 and the 1931 midwives acts were primarily introduced to control the practice of midwifery in Ireland,[100] as it was believed that so-called 'handy women' were responsible for the spread of infection in childbirth.[101] Loudon noted that 'handy women' became the 'scapegoats for high maternal mortality', when in fact there was no 'direct evidence' that they were an important cause of maternal mortality. On the contrary, he argued that these women provided 'certain menial and essential services for the poor at a time when publicly provided nursing and midwifery care was inadequate and inconsistent'.[102] Farmar concurred that 'handy women' were more likely to treat the family as a whole, offering the mother a more comprehensive service than merely assistance during the birth.[103]

The 1918 act established the Irish Central Midwives Board which supervised the regulation of midwifery in the country until it was replaced by the Midwives Committee of An Bord Altranais (the Nursing Board) in 1950.[104] The acts indicated the persuasive power of infectious diseases to stimulate legislative action, and the tendency to respond to maternity care from the perspective of the professional. The role of socio-economic disadvantage was conspicuously avoided.[105] It was accepted that outside the key urban areas there was no maternity service other than the midwife. Thus the department placed all the onus and expectation on the midwife, who was regarded as more important than the 'ordinary medical or surgical nurse' as she was 'often employed in remote districts and in circumstances where no doctor is readily available'.[106]

In 1921 the maternal mortality rate from puerperal sepsis was 1.66 per 1,000 births; by 1933 it had declined slightly to 1.39 (see Table 2.3). The disease remained much more 'prevalent in rural than in urban districts': the respective rates for 1933 were 1.54 and 1.14 per 1,000 births.[107] The situation was beginning to cause official alarm by 1935:

> It is a matter of some concern for this country that while a substantial improvement has been effected in other directions, as evidenced by the decline in infant mortality, the reduced incidence of certain infectious diseases, and the decrease in the general death rate, the present position as regards the risks associated with motherhood does not warrant a claim that any definite advance has been made towards reducing maternal mortality.[108]

This negative tone from the department is partially explained by the increase in puerperal deaths that year from 1.39 in 1933 to 1.80 in 1934: an increase of twenty-four deaths.[109] The maternal death rate was up nationwide in urban and rural areas with even Dublin County Borough, which had recorded a continuous decline since 1928, registering an increase from 0.86 to 1.2 per 1,000 births. The highest urban death toll came in Wexford Urban District with 10.3 per 1,000 births, which was due to the admission of a maternity patient with scarlet fever.[110] These statistics indicated the volatility of maternal mortality, with one admission resulting in six deaths.[111]

A considerable amount of pressure was taken off the issue of maternal mortality with the introduction and success of sulphonamide drugs.[112] Loudon cites evidence that hospitals in London, Edinburgh, Glasgow, Belfast and Liverpool had supplies of sulphonamide by 1936. He was certain by 1937 that the drugs were widely used in hospitals and general practice.[113] Statistical evidence confirms this finding in Ireland, with maternal mortality beginning its consistent downward descent from 1937 onwards. The

Table 2.3 Puerperal sepsis deaths per 1,000 registered births for Dublin County and Dublin County Borough (from 1930 Dublin City), 1923–49

	Puerperal sepsis deaths	
Year	Dublin County	Dublin County Borough
1923	1.67	1.89
1924	1.27	1.56
1925	1.32	1.83
1926	1.60	1.70
1927	0.28	1.05
1928	0.84	1.75
1929	1.67	1.51
1930*	1.04	1.54
1931	2.17	1.16
1932	1.06	1.06
1933	——	0.86
1934	1.78	1.20
1935	——	1.25
1936	1.71	1.92
1937	0.46	0.94
1938	0.82	0.61
1939	1.66	0.53
1940	0.42	0.36
1941	——	0.88
1942	1.14	0.48
1943	0.39	0.24
1944	0.40	0.30
1945	0.40	0.30
1946	0.70	0.40
1947	——	0.30
1948	0.4	0.40
1949	——	0.60

Note: From 1930 Dublin County Borough was relabelled in tables Dublin City

Source: Figures compiled from Department of Local Government and Public Health, *Annual Reports of the Registrar-General*, 1923–49

following year the lowest rate ever was recorded for puerperal sepsis deaths.[114] The 1939 figure of thirty-eight deaths from puerperal sepsis represented a 50 per cent reduction on the average figure for the period from 1929 to 1938.[115] In 1939 the Minister for Public Health and Local Government basked in the glow of the 'gratifying decline in mortality from puerperal sepsis'.[116] The average mortality from puerperal sepsis for the decade 1926 to 1936 (the year when sulphonamide was introduced into Ireland) was 1.49 per 1,000 births, whereas it fell dramatically in 1937 to 0.9 and again in 1938 to 0.7.[117] The Master of the National Maternity Hospital, Alex

Spain, concluded that the reduction was as a result of sulphonamide drugs and the 'more frequent resort to institutional midwifery for the abnormal case'.[118] In 1941 the department reluctantly conceded that 'the widespread use of the Sulphonamide group of drugs ... probably played a very important part'.[119]

The 1941 Public Health (Infectious Diseases) Regulation order made it compulsory to notify the health authorities of every case of puerperal infection.[120] This was the ultimate official act of regulation and control. While the decline in Irish maternal mortality was less impressive than in Britain, by 1950 the rate was one-third of the 1935 figure.[121] As Clear argues, the significance of this improvement in maternal survival is frequently overlooked when assessing Irish social history, and in particular when analysing women's lives in de Valera's Ireland.[122] For a comparison of the infant mortality rates for Ireland, Northern Ireland, England and Wales, and Scotland from 1901 to 1973, see Table 2.4.

Maternal health and birth control

The issue of birth control or family limitation was consciously avoided in relation to maternity care in Ireland. Many health workers, including members of the Protestant community like Lynn, believed that even to consider maternal health and contraception in the same breath would tarnish the good work of the prenatal clinics and the mother and baby clubs.[123] Both Clear and Ó hÓgartaigh have revealed that the issue of 'voluntary motherhood' was complicated and tainted by association with eugenic principles.[124] Some of the more vocal champions of contraception framed their argument in eugenic terms. For example the Regius Professor of Medicine in Trinity College Dublin, T. G. Moorhead, advocated the sterilisation of the 'unfit'.[125] As Roman Catholic doctrine did not permit eugenic principles, this association made it difficult for any non-eugenic advocates of birth control to build their case on health grounds. The Censorship of Publications Act of 1929 banned the sale of literature advocated the use of birth control.[126] The Fianna Fáil government[127] completed the task of prohibition and criminalised the sale of contraceptives under the Criminal Law Amendments Act of 1935.[128] Consequently, Pauline Conroy argued, the issue of fertility control was driven underground in Ireland for much of the period between 1930 and 1970, leading to the importation of illegal contraceptives, back-street abortions and prosecutions against those who broke the law.[129] The only acceptable place for a debate on contraception in Ireland was in the context of social morality and censorship.

During the early years of the Irish Free State there was considerable pressure exerted by religious and other interest groups to have moral codes enshrined in legislation that reflected the Roman Catholic ethos of the new state. Immoral literature, divorce and contraception were all important target

Table 2.4 Infant mortality rates for Ireland, Northern Ireland, England and Wales, and Scotland, 1901–73

Period	Ireland	Northern Ireland	England and Wales	Scotland
1901–11	91	107	128	116
1911–20	84	99	100	106
1921–30	70	81	72	89
1931–40	68	78	59	78
1941–50	66	60	43	57
1941	74	77	60	83
1942	69	76	51	69
1943	83	78	49	65
1944	79	67	45	65
1945	71	68	46	56
1946	65	54	43	54
1947	68	53	41	56
1948	50	46	34	45
1949	53	45	32	41
1950	46	40	30	39
1951	46	41	30	37
1952	41	39	28	35
1953	39	38	27	31
1954	38	33	25	31
1955	37	32	25	30
1956	36	29	24	29
1957	33	29	23	29
1958	35	28	23	28
1959	32	28	22	28
1960	29	27	22	26
1961	31	27	22	26
1962	29	27	21	27
1963	27	27	21	26
1964	27	26	20	24
1965	25	25	19	25
1966	25	26	19	23
1967	24	23	18	21
1968	21	24	18	21
1969	21	24	18	21
1970	19	23	18	20
1971	18	23	18	20
1972	18	21	18	19
1973	18	21	18	19

Source: Compiled from Department of Health, *Annual Reports of the Registrar-General*, 1950, 1951, 1952 and Central Statistics Office, *Report on Vital Statistics*, 1953–73

areas. Birth control was potentially the most fraught question, as it crossed the line between health and morality. For those wishing to see a total ban, therefore, it was essential that the subject be seen in absolute terms. While the general consensus (which crossed all religious divides) was that contraception was morally wrong, a fundamental cleavage emerged between Roman Catholic doctrine and the Church of Ireland around the idea of maternal health as a mitigating reason for the practice of birth control.

In November 1923, Revd Vincent McNabb, OP gave a speech to the Irish Guild of SS Luke, Cosmas and Damian,[130] outlining the Catholic medical perspective on birth control:

> No doctor has the right to say to a married couple: 'You *ought* not to have any children at all; or if at all, then, only after a long interval.' All that may be said is a bare statement of the medical fact, in such words as: 'In my opinion, if you have another pregnancy at any time, or soon, you will die, or be ill, or risk the life of the child etc., etc.'[131]

In 1930, at the Lambeth conference in England, the Anglican hierarchy, including the Church of Ireland bishops, accepted that birth control was morally justifiable in certain circumstances. In Ireland, the Bishop of Ossory, Dr Day, accepted the use of birth control in 'hard cases'.[132] Revd M. P. Cleary condemned the Church of Ireland's stance: 'They have proclaimed a doctrine of race-suicide that would empty the cradle, and close the maternity home and sap the vitals of the nation.'[133] Cleary's response to the Lambeth conference reflected not just the Catholic doctrine of moral absolutism but also the association between birth control and eugenics.

The papal encyclical *Casti Connubii*, 'On Christian Marriage', issued in December 1930, was taken very seriously in Ireland. It was seen as a validation of the majority opinion and as a spur to ensure that all legal loopholes were closed in relation to birth control.[134] The encyclical outlined the purpose of conjugal relations: 'Since, therefore, the conjugal act is destined primarily by nature for the begetting of children, those who in exercising it deliberately frustrate its natural power and purpose sin against nature and commit a deed which is shameful and intrinsically vicious.'[135] The language bespoke a wartime offensive rather than a moral instruction. The encyclical also addressed the issue of 'hard cases' and condemned the argument that the mother's health should justify the use of birth control as 'shameful', 'false and exaggerated'. It explained the Catholic position: 'Who is not filled with the greatest admiration when he sees a mother risking her life with heroic fortitude, that she may preserve the life of the offspring which she has conceived? God alone ... can reward her for the fulfilment of the office allotted to her by nature, and will assuredly repay her in a measure full of overflowing.'[136]

It was considerably easier to negotiate the complicated topic of family limitation from a purely moral perspective. However, it was in the arena of maternal health that the price for such piety was paid. Sandra McAvoy pointed out that the 'women's health issue was perceived as subordinate to the public morality question'.[137] This was substantiated with chilling consequences in the Rotunda hospital in 1932. A twenty-five-year-old woman was admitted after swallowing a large amount of abortifacients. After three weeks of procrastination, hyperglycaemia was diagnosed and she was given a minor section. She died. The Master, Bethel Solomons, candidly admitted, 'This woman might have been saved by an earlier minor section, but her desire for abortion rather cloaked the gravity of her case and probably warped judgment.'[138]

The issue of birth control and maternal health copper-fastened the emerging alliance between the Catholic members of the medical profession and the Catholic hierarchy. Following *Casti Connubii*, the Irish Catholic hierarchy made their concerns known to the Cumann na nGaedheal government regarding the appointment of Protestant doctors to state dispensary posts.[139] It was the Archbishop of Tuam, Revd Gilmartin, who first raised the issue in his Lenten pastoral of 1931, in which he explained,

> In the light of the Papal Encyclical there is revealed a deep cleavage between the Christian idea of marriage and the views of some non-Catholics on this most important subject. Hence a Catholic people have a right that medical practitioners to whom they must have recourse should have been trained in schools where Catholic principles about childbirth and kindred subjects are taught, and whose views on the errors and vices condemned by the Pope would be above all suspicion.[140]

The objection was directed at doctors educated at Trinity College Dublin: in effect, social code for Protestant doctors.[141] In theory a Protestant doctor educated in a Catholic school was exempt from Gilmartin's suspicions. However, the objections were in fact a mixture of sectarianism and medical ethics (which were often indistinguishable).[142] Dispensary jobs were highly sought after for the security they offered, and there was a long history of corruption and politics in relation to medical appointments in general in Ireland.[143] The dispensary appointments often involved ingredients of localism, politics and religion, and in the early years of the Free State there were frequent, unabashed declarations that such jobs, which involved administering to the largely Catholic poor, should only go to 'safe' Catholic hands.[144] Gilmartin finally declared himself satisfied with the government's appointment procedures if all prospective dispensary doctors were asked their opinion on contraception and craniotomy.[145] Gilmartin reflected nervousness amongst the Catholic hierarchy following the 1930 Lambeth conference. The hierarchy feared that if Protestants were administering health care to the poorest sections of society, they could use the position to issue birth control advice.[146] Furthermore, in 1930, under pressure from the Society for the Provision of Birth Control Clinics, the British Ministry for Health finally permitted birth control instruction in maternity welfare clinics in 'cases where further pregnancy would be detrimental to health'.[147] This development, coupled with the Lambeth conference declaration, served to harden the resolve of the Catholic community in Ireland to disassociate maternity services from such immorality. Although the potential crisis regarding Protestant dispensary doctors was settled by private negotiations, it was an augury of future objections to the ever-increasing role of the state in health care, and indicative of the territorial response to the care of the poor.[148]

In June 1932, armed with the clarity of *Casti Connubii*, Dr J. Stafford Johnson, Master of the Irish Guild of SS Luke, Cosmas and Damian, confronted the League of Nations.[149] He wrote to object to the insertion of a passage in the League of Nations report, *Maternal Welfare and the Hygiene of Infants and Children*, about giving 'anti-conception' advice to mothers suffering from heart disease, tuberculosis or nephritis. The offending passage specified that it was not sufficient to tell the mother not to become pregnant – it was necessary that she be told how to avoid pregnancy, if not by the doctor then at a health care centre. This unambiguous instruction crossed the more obscure line between medical care and morality, which the Catholic doctor was anxious to construct. Stafford Johnson wrote to 'Monsieur le Directeur' that the line between health and morality was drawn by conscience. He was quite clear that beyond the claim of conscience the health of a mother did not entitle the doctor to transgress his medical remit as, he believed, the issue of contraception was moral not medical.[150]

In directing the attention of the Department of External Affairs to the passage, Stafford Johnson referred to birth control as 'repugnant to the feelings of the vast majority of the citizens of Saorstát Eireann'.[151] This spirit of revulsion, he believed, was represented in the Censorship of Publications Act of 1929 and the state should speak up for all Catholic countries. One month after contacting the department, apparently dissatisfied with the rate of progress, Stafford Johnson wrote again to explain that the Irish Guild of SS Luke, Cosmas and Damian Society: an organisation representing opinions of Catholic doctors in Ireland with the 'unanimous approval of the Irish hierarchy'.[152] The Department would become very well acquainted with the Guild, as one of its founding members, Dr Edward McPolin, would play a central role in the medical campaign against the mother-and-child scheme in the late 1940s and early 1950s. Stafford Johnson and John Charles McQuaid, the future Archbishop of Dublin, sought to ensure the alliance between the Roman Catholic Church and the medical profession. Both were influential in directing government policy in relation to health generally, and maternal and child welfare in particular.[153] To that end, Stafford Johnson urged the Irish government, as the rulers of a 'Catholic Nation and as a member of the League of Nations', to vocalise national convictions and 'take the protest into a quite different plane'.[154] His faith in the government's convictions was not misplaced, as the Minister for Local Government and Public Health, Séan T. O'Kelly, believed that objections should be made on moral grounds, despite the fact that:

Eminent authorities in the fields of gynaecology and obstetrics have borne evidence to the ill effects of the use of contraceptives. Permanent sterility and many neuroses and illnesses, are attributable to this practice, and some authorities consider that all contraceptives are inimical to the health of both husband and wife.[155]

In the light of future controversy it is interesting to note that the Department of Local Government and Public Health had also considered the damage that such an association between contraception and maternal health might cause to the development of maternity services in Ireland. O'Kelly pointed out that:

> the practice of contraception is contrary to Catholic doctrine and is abhorrent to the people of Saorstat Eireann and that the association of such teaching with arrangements for maternal welfare would be calculated to bring the health centres into disrepute and to neutralize the efforts that are being made by the state to reduce maternal mortality and morbidity.[156]

Sentient of the intimate connection between health and morality, the department had also anticipated future arguments for limiting state intervention in maternal care. Cognisant of and sympathetic to public opinion, it was determined that morality must not become a pretext for inaction or limitation with regard to maternal morality.

The League of Nations was also anxious that moral sensibilities should not interfere with the medical health of mothers. It clarified that it had not intended to support the 'indiscriminate use of contraception', but merely to ensure that women, whose lives would be endangered by pregnancy, be given a choice and not 'called upon to sacrifice their lives'. It had deliberately left the methods of birth control vague in order not to 'cause offence to any government or religious body'.[157] The Secretary of the Department of External Affairs, Joseph Walshe, a devout Catholic, suggested the following wording:

> Nevertheless it may be necessary to avoid pregnancy on account of the mother's own health. But it is not sufficient merely to tell a married woman suffering from tuberculosis or heart disease or nephritis that she should not become pregnant. The dangers, which might arise from pregnancy in such cases, should be fully explained by a doctor to the husband and wife.[158]

The response to the dilemma of maternal health and Catholic morality was to place the onus on the husband and wife. The only concession that the Irish state was willing to make to the international concern regarding maternal health was to agree that the couple could be advised to avoid pregnancy, and should be told just how devastating the consequences would be to the mother if she did not heed the advice. How man and wife avoided pregnancy was their responsibility. As one doctor, who wrote to the Department on 28 July 1932, explained, it was a doctor's duty to inform a woman of the risk to her life, 'but it should be left to the patient as to what steps they would take to avoid the possibility of becoming pregnant'.[159]

The League of Nations took on board the concern regarding the morality of contraceptive advice, and the offending passage was reworded to accommodate each country's moral outlook: 'It is necessary further that the steps to be taken to avoid this should be explained to the husband and wife by a doctor, either privately or at a health centre, due account being taken of the individual's religious beliefs and moral principles, as well as of national legislation.'[160]

Ireland responded that it did not satiate the moral qualms of the Irish Free State, and was still 'entirely contrary to Catholic teaching'.[161] In reality, however, de Valera, as Minister for External Affairs, regarded the rewording as a 'success' in the face of 'very considerable opposition'.[162] Interestingly, Finnane discovered that the Carrigan Committee, established to review the Criminal Law Amendment Acts of 1880 and 1885, also dealt with the issue of contraception in late 1932 at its final meeting. The Minister for Justice, James Geoghan, was present at this meeting when it was recommended that (while there would be a general prohibition of contraceptive appliances) 'qualified medical practitioners might have the power to prescribe and supply such appliances'.[163] The committee's recommendations, which clearly made the distinction between the moral and medical uses of contraceptive devices, were not followed when contraception was unequivocally banned in 1935.

The disassociation of birth control and health was significant in Ireland for two major reasons: the demographic profile of late marriages and large families, and the high rate of tuberculosis. Ireland had the highest rate in Western Europe of older women having large families. Furthermore, tuberculosis was one of the conditions that made pregnancy an increased risk to female health. Nevertheless, the *status quo* in relation to birth control was rarely challenged publicly in Ireland. Even Bethel Solomons, who was a champion of poor mothers and worked at the forefront of maternity care in the Rotunda hospital, implied his dissent by criticising the impact of regular pregnancy on poor women.[164] Solomons acknowledged the physical and mental cost of multiple pregnancies on Dublin's poorest and most ill-equipped mothers. His allusions to the 'quality of life' contained implicit criticism of a state and society that allowed *laissez-faire* morality to settle the question of family survival. He coined the phrase 'dangerous multipara' to describe a mother who had given birth more than seven times. He first used this expression in *The Lancet* in 1934 when he cautioned that 'it is altogether a mistake to suppose that in childbearing practice makes perfect'.[165] He noted that 'from the fifth pregnancy the rate of mortality is over average by an amount which increases steadily and speedily until in women bearing their tenth child or more the mortality is five times as high as for all women bearing children'.[166] In 1933 he cautioned that '[w]omen with decompensated cardiac disease should not marry, and if they do, they should not become pregnant, or they will surely die'.[167] The Department of Local Government and Public Health concurred, starkly declaring that it was 'a fact that pregnancy is a grave complication in the case of a woman suffering from any form of tuberculosis ... tubercular patients should not marry'.[168]

The few who tried to make a case on the grounds of maternal health, like Sir John Keane, were silenced by claims of eugenism. Senator Dr John Gogarty articulated this sentiment during the Séanad debate on the Censorship of Publications Bill in 1929: 'No one who has any care for a nation's welfare can for one moment countenance contraceptive practices, which are a contradiction of a nation's life ... The English government has practically told the unemployed that they should not cumber the earth. That is in the land in which heroes are contra-conceived.'[169] Objections to the criminalisation of contraception were also muted. As Hug argued, the refusal to legislate for the issue of maternal health was not due to a lack of awareness. The Committee on the Criminal Law Amendment Acts (1880–85) and Juvenile Prostitution (Carrigan Committee), in recommendation 16 of the final report, advised legislation that catered for birth control in the event of maternal risk.[170] The Department of Justice, when reviewing the Carrigan Committee's findings, also accepted this point and inscribed it in article 16 of the original draft of the Criminal Amendment Bill. However, article 16 disappeared from the final draft the bill. It is not clear at what stage this deletion occurred or why. However, it is likely that a keen sense of Catholic social teaching played a role in the decision to delete.[171]

The argument expressed by Deputy Dr Rowlette during Dáil debates on the Criminal Law Amendment Bill in 1934 was too risqué and nuanced, calling as it did for the right of conscience. Rowlette presented the case of a 'respectable married woman' in ill health who would endanger her life by pregnancy.[172] He was careful to express agreement with the 'common moral judgment and feeling in this country' which was against the practice of birth control. He argued, however, that, while abstinence was an alternative for these women, 'there are very considerable practical difficulties in many households ... with narrow accommodation, where wife and her husband are living on affectionate and proper terms'. He argued that such a practice could lead to 'grave nervous disorders' in the wife, 'infidelity on the part of the husband' and 'marital unhappiness' all round.[173] This was a particularly valid point considering that the Catholic Church believed that a wife 'must resist the intercourse of a husband who uses a condom, as a virgin must resist a man who attacks her virtue'. According to the adviser of the *Irish Ecclesiastical Record* this meant 'active, forceful resistance which may be discontinued only in the face of the gravest actual danger – and provided there is no proximate fear of consent to the illicit intercourse'.[174] Apparently, female health and safety was an acceptable price to pay (according to Catholic doctrine) to prevent the use of birth control.

Raising the thorny issue of individual conscience, Rowlette noted that there were many people in the state 'who do not adopt the view that the use of contraceptives in such a position is contrary to morality'.[175] Rowlette was virtually a lone warrior: a total ban on contraception irrespective of maternal health remained in force in Ireland until 1979, when contraceptives were legalised for married couples under the Health (Family Planning) Act, 1979.[176]

Birth control was a moral and not a medical issue in Ireland. The argument against family limitation was quite consciously restricted to the arena of morality, precisely because it was feared that any association between preventive health work and contraception would negatively impact on the work of maternity and child welfare services.[177] The idea that birth control in certain cases might constitute a positive health intervention was not countenanced on the grounds of Catholic doctrine, which rested obstinately on the belief of moral absolutism.

Infant mortality: the motivating factor

While maternal mortality remained a major issue throughout the 1920s and 1930s, infant mortality began to supersede it in the hierarchy of official concern.[178] The 'discovery of the fetus' was not unique to Ireland: it reflected a European anxiety concerning population growth, which manifested itself in, amongst other things, a focus on infant mortality.[179] Lewis argued that, in Britain, antenatal care of the mother originated from a desire to protect her unborn child.[180] The concentration on the unborn child's survival did not mean that the mother's life was disregarded or denigrated, rather that the elevation of the infant's life in health and social care led to a more comprehensive treatment of pregnancy and motherhood.

The rural/urban divide effected different mortality tolls in relation to infant and maternal mortality: the infant was more at risk in an urban environment than a rural one (see Table 2.5).[181] The national infant-mortality rate for the decennial period 1920 to 1929 was 71 deaths per 1,000 live births.[182] The Department of Local Government and Public Health noted the 'adverse influence of urban conditions on infant life', which was illustrated 'by the substantial excess of the infant death rate in the towns of 10,000 inhabitants and over which was returned as 93 per 1,000 births in comparison with the rate of 56 rural areas'.[183] The department clearly believed that antenatal care was responsible for a reduction in infant mortality rates. It cited Dublin County Borough with its well-developed maternity and child welfare scheme and continuous decrease in infant mortality rate from 127 per 1,000 births in 1926 to 97 in 1929 (see Table 2.6).

However, the cadences of infant mortality levelled an even more damning indictment of the social make-up of Irish society than unevenly distributed medical services. In 1933 a higher percentage of infants died in the first month of life (the neonatal period) in rural areas than in urban areas. In urban areas 37 per cent of deaths occurred in the first month, as opposed to 44 per cent in rural areas. This indicated that 'better facilities for obtaining prompt medical and midwifery services in towns gave the urban infants a better chance of surviving the dangers attendant on delivery'.[184] However, it also exposed the toll of poverty after the first month of life when the 'unfavourable urban home conditions' began to 'play a sinister role' and the benefits of services were outweighed by the disadvantages of congestion and poverty, environmental factors that facilitated the easy spread of infectious diseases. The deaths of urban infants in the second half of the first year of life accounted for 23 per cent of the total mortality count, compared to 17 per cent in rural areas.[185] In 1936 the aggregate for urban infant mortality was 99 per 1,000 live births compared to 59 in rural areas.[186] The 'unenviable prominence'[187] of urban districts in infant-mortality statistics continued until the 1940s when maternity and child welfare services were re-examined.[188]

Table 2.5 National rural and urban infant deaths per 1,000 registered births

Year	Rural	Urban
1923	50	99
1924	55	104
1925	53	97
1926	56	110
1927	56	99
1928	56	91
1929	58	93
1930	56	90
1931	58	88
1932	59	95
1933	85	54
1934	78	55
1935	87	57
1936	59	99
1937	61	91
1938	55	84
1939	55	83
1940	55	85
1941	58	99
1942	58	90
1943	67	110
1944	65	105
1945	58	93
1946	58	93
1947	60	80
1948	49	52
1949	48	62

Source: Figures compiled from Department of Local Government and Public Health, *Annual Reports of the Registrar-General*, 1923–49

Table 2.6 Deaths of infants under one per 1,000 registered births for Dublin County and Dublin County Borough (from 1930 Dublin City), 1923–49

Year	Dublin County	Dublin County Borough
1923	82	125
1924	72	91
1925	92	119
1926	102	127
1927	86	123
1928	83	102
1929	69	106
1930*	81	97
1931	91	94
1932	86	100
1933	81	83
1934	72	80
1935	76	94
1936	93	114
1937	109	102
1938	77	96
1939	75	90
1940	80	91
1941	74	114
1942	88	98
1943	85	126
1944	95	117
1945	94	111
1946	77	92
1947	71	85
1948	53	46
1949	51	64

Note: From 1930 Dublin County Borough was relabelled in tables Dublin City

Source: Figures compiled from Department of Local Government and Public Health *Annual Reports of the Registrar-General*, 1923–49

It was clear in the official mind that in 'Urban Districts unemployment, bad housing, defective sanitary conveniences and indifferent scavenging arrangements are attended with baneful consequences to infant life'.[189] In the case of infant mortality, the largest determinant was social class: poverty was the greatest killer of infants in the first year of life, particularly of those infants who died during the post-neonatal period.[190] This fact was repeatedly acknowledged by contemporaries who linked Dublin's urban poverty with its high infant mortality. Thus health and welfare were intimately associated with the earliest stages of maternity and child welfare in the city.

Dublin quickly became the focus of attention because it held the unenviable distinction of being the most dangerous place for infants under the age of one. Much of the work carried out by the Dublin maternity hospitals and various voluntary organisations focused on completing the circle of family health and reducing the carnage among Dublin's youngest inhabitants. However, the multiplicity of services available in Dublin was central to the difficulties in co-ordination and, increasingly, contemporaries believed that closer co-operation would extract the maximum from limited resources. To this end, the committee of St Ultan's Hospital began negotiations with the National Children's Hospital at Harcourt St. in Dublin to amalgamate the two hospitals to create a centre of excellence in child health.[191] However, the prospect of a central children's hospital not under Roman Catholic control galvanised the agents of sectarianism. The Roman Catholic Archbishop of Dublin, Dr Edward Byrne,[192] made it clear through his acolytes that he did not approve of the proposed amalgamation.[193] In a statement dated 20 December 1935, he opposed the venture on the grounds of 'religious principles solely'.[194] He believed that the 'Faith of Catholic children (who will be 99% of the total treated) would not be safe' at such a hospital.[195] Crucially, he argued that such an amalgamation would 'create a virtual monopoly in the medical treatment of children on the south side of the city'. He referred to remarks made by Professor Moorhead of Trinity College Dublin challenging the Archbishop's authority in the matter and the resignation of the Catholic doctor, Dr Alice Barry, from St Ultan's medical committee.[196]

The Archbishop's objections to the amalgamation contained all the ingredients of future controversies regarding the health and welfare of Irish mothers and children. In many respects, his statement foreshadowed the statement issued by the Catholic hierarchy in 1950 in response to the proposed free mother-and-child scheme.[197] Byrne feared that, in catering for children up to sixteen years of age, the new institution would deal with 'many serious and delicate problems of puberty and pre-adolescent stage. The danger of naturalistic and wrong teachings on sex instruction or adolescent problems is a powerful argument for retaining the custody of children in Catholic hands.' Highlighting Dr Moorhead's public pronouncements on the sterilisation of the unfit and alleging that Trinity College Dublin would be the 'dominating influence' behind the proposed hospital, Byrne concluded that the outpatient department would provide a perfect basis for promotion of 'contraceptive practices'.[198]

Byrne enlisted the president of Blackrock College, Fr. John Charles McQuaid, in his campaign to stamp out 'activity by many non-Catholics directed towards the care of children'.[199] McQuaid became one of Byrne's chief informants and orchestrated an often covert operation to control health and welfare in Dublin.[200] McQuaid became instrumental in quashing the amalgamation plans and ensuring that the new children's hospital would be firmly in Catholic hands. This he achieved with Our Lady's Children's Hospital, Crumlin, established in 1956. Clearly McQuaid intended on using his office and influence to shore up the Dublin welfare market for Catholicism.

Conclusion

By the 1920s, the official consensus was that the fatalities of childbirth and early life could no longer be left to fate and old custom. The Irish Free State, with its inherited public health apparatus, had a duty to rally voluntary effort and co-ordinate it with local authority initiatives. Central to this emerging picture was the rise of professionalism: the regulated professional midwife, the official CMO, the general practitioner (family doctor) and finally, the hospital-based obstetrician. Woven into the fabric of the development of maternity and child welfare in Dublin was religion and the power struggles it contained. Religion and the cultural conceptualisation of morality influenced not only the possibilities for co-operation between various groups but also definitions of health. Birth control was categorically relegated to the arena of morality and consciously excluded from any health debate. Archbishop Byrne's campaign against plans for a non-denominational children's hospital set the tone for Catholic involvement in maternal and child welfare. Henceforth, the Roman Catholic Church regarded maternal and child welfare as a crucial issue to control in the face of either other religious or non-denominational groups or state encroachment.

Notes

1 Sir James Craig speaking about the necessity to provide school meals. See *Dáil Debates,* vol. 7, col. 1973 (5 June 1924).
2 A provisional government was in place between January and December 1922.
3 A. Jackson, *Ireland, 1798–1998* (Oxford, 1999), p. 276.
4 Cousins, *The Birth of Social Welfare in Ireland,* pp. 31–3; Jackson, *Ireland,* pp. 283–4.
5 Barrington, *Health, Medicine and Politics,* p. 104.
6 *Dáil Debates,* vol. 7, col. 1986 (5 June 1924).
7 *Annual Report of the Department of Local Government and Public Health, 1922–25,* p. 26.
8 *Report of the Commission on the Relief of the Sick and Destitute Poor, Including the Insane Poor* (Dublin, 1927), pp. 10–11.
9 *Ibid.,* p. 1.
10 *Departmental Committee on Health Services Report* (September 1945), National Archives of Ireland (NAI), Dept. Taoiseach, S13444 (B).
11 *Annual Report of the Department of Local Government and Public Health, 1927–8,* p. 38.
12 *Ibid., 1828–9,* p. 46.
13 *Ibid., 1930–1,* p. 57.
14 *Ibid., 1932–3,* p. 49.
15 *Ibid., 1933–4,* p. 59.
16 *Ibid., 1934–5,* p. 87.
17 *Ibid., 1933–4,* p. 61.
18 *Ibid., 1930–1,* p. 57.
19 *Ibid., 1937–8,* p. 53.
20 *Ibid., 1934–5,* p. 129.

21 *Ibid., 1922–5*, p. 34.

22 *Ibid., 1944–5*, p. 48.

23 *Ibid., 1925–7*, p. 66.

24 *Ibid., 1934–5*, p. 104.

25 *Ibid.*

26 *Ibid., 1930–1*, p. 65.

27 K. Reddin, 'The maternity and child welfare clinic – its origin, scope and trend', *Irish Journal of Medical Science (IJMSc.)*, 77 (May 1932), 222.

28 *Annual Report of the Department of Local Government and Public Health, 1922–5*, p. 34.

29 *Ibid.*

30 Originally the Queen Victoria's Jubilee Institute for Nurses, renamed the Queen's Institute of District Nursing in 1928. See P. Scanlan, *The Irish Nurse. A Study in Nursing in Ireland: History and Education, 1718–1981* (Drumlín, 1991), p. 133, n. 125.

31 Lady Dudley, wife of the Viceroy, founded the Dudley in 1902 . By 1910 it operated in nineteen districts. For older people in the West of Ireland, the district nurses are still known as Dudleys. The Dudley scheme was disbanded in the 1970s. Scanlan, *The Irish Nurse*, p. 104. I am grateful to M. Ó hÓgartaigh for information relating to the Dudley nurses.

32 *Annual Report of the Department of Local Government and Public Health, 1925–7*, p. 66.

33 *Ibid., 1927–8*, p. 37.

34 *Ibid., 1925–7*, p. 66.

35 The Notification of Births Act, 1915 empowered local authorities to provide services for mothers and children up to the age of five.

36 *Annual Report of the Department of Local Government and Public Health, 1925–7*, p. 66.

37 *Ibid., 1922–5*, p. 34.

38 *Ibid., 1933–4*, p. 72.

39 J. G. Gallagher, 'Causes of maternal mortality', *IJMSc.,* 188 (Aug. 1941), 499.

40 *Ibid.*, p. 500.

41 C. Clear, 'Women in de Valera's Ireland, 1932–48: a reappraisal', in G. Doherty and D. Keogh (eds), *De Valera's Irelands* (Cork, 2003), p. 112.

42 A. Spain, 'Maternity services in Éire', *IJMSc*, 229 (Jan. 1945), 1–11.

43 *Ibid.*

44 *Ibid.*, p. 7.

45 Department of Health, *White Paper on Health services*, p. 15.

46 Philanthropic bodies founded voluntary hospitals. See M. E. Daly, '"An atmosphere of sturdy independence": the state and the Dublin hospitals in the 1930s', in E. Malcom and G. Jones (eds), *Medicine, Disease and the State in Ireland, 1650–1940* (Cork, 1999), p. 235.

47 All three hospitals had been the recipients of government and corporation grants since the late nineteenth century in order to facilitate the treatment of poorer-class patients. See G. D. Williams, *Dublin Charities: Being a Handbook of Dublin Philanthropic Organisation and Charities* (Dublin, 1902), pp. 68, 72–4.

48 *Annual Report of the Department of Local Government and Public Health, 1927–8*, p. 41.

49 Spain, 'Maternity services in Éire,' p. 1.

50 The Cork Erinville Lying-in Hospital and the Limerick Lying-in Hospital, Bedford Row Hospital, Limerick.

51 Farmar, *Holles Street*, p. 75.

52 NAI, Dept. Taoiseach, S13774 A. See also Hensey, *The Health Services of Ireland*, p. 22; Barrington, *Health, Medicine and Politics*, pp. 108–10. Between 1930 and 1939 there were twenty-eight sweeps held, yielding £17,146,980 in ticket sales, £13,479,605 of which went directly to the hospitals, NAI, Dept. Taoiseach, S13775; Daly, 'An atmosphere of sturdy independence', p. 238. M. Coleman, 'The origins of the Irish Hospitals' Sweepstake', *Irish Economic and Social History (IESH)*, 29 (Nov. 2002), 40–55.
53 Department of Health, *White Paper on Health Services*, p. 2.
54 *First General Report of the Hospitals' Commission 1933–34* (Dublin, 1936)
55 Farmar, *Holles Street*, p. 94.
56 *Ibid.*
57 *IJMSc.*, 90 (Aug. 1933), 329, 387, 434.
58 This is in line with practices elsewhere. See Lewis, *The Politics of Motherhood*; A. Oakley, *The Captured Womb* (Oxford, 1984)
59 M. J. Russell, 'The health of Dublin', *Journal of the Irish Free State Medical Union (JIFSMU)*, 3:17 (Nov. 1938), 56. Russell (1876–1956) was Medical Officer of Health to Dublin Corporation between 1921 and 1947.
60 *Annual Report of the Department of Local Government and Public Health, 1932–3*, p. 58.
61 Prunty, *Dublin Slums*, p. 162.
62 *Report of the Department of Local Government and Public Health, 1932–3*, p. 53.
63 'Some social aspects of an improved medical service', *(JMAÉ)* 13 (Aug. 1943), 20.
64 The almoner also served the less altruistic purpose of ascertaining who could afford to pay for services and was instrumental in gathering funds owed to the hospitals.
65 Hospitals' Commission, *First General Report 1933–34*, p. 70.
66 *Ibid.*
67 Religion also dogged this aspect of social medicine. See NAI, Dept. Health, A114/21.
68 *Ibid.*, p. 24.
69 'Report of the Coombe', *IJMSc.*, 92 (Aug. 1934), 387.
70 *Ibid.*
71 'Events of the month: maternity hospitals report', *JMAÉ*, 13:77 (Nov. 1943), 56.
72 Farmar noted that due to the lack of fuel and light in patients' homes, many women had to be brought to hospital to complete the birth. See Farmar, *Holles Street*, p. 120. See J. Robins, 'Public policy and the maternity services in Ireland during the twentieth century', in Browne (ed.), *Masters, Midwives and Ladies-in-Waiting*, p. 289.
73 Dr John O'Connell noted that while home births allowed the family to feel involved in a 'family event', it usually meant that the mother was back to work within days, whereas a hospital birth gave her a period of 'enforced rest'. See J. O'Connell, *Doctor John: A Crusading Doctor and Politician* (Dublin, 1989), p. 26.
74 J. F. Cunningham, 'Mother and child service: the medical problem', *Studies: An Irish Quarterly Review of Letters, Philosophy and Science*, 40 (June 1951), 150.
75 I. O'Dwyer and A. L. Mulhall, ' Midwifery', in J. Robins (ed.), *Nursing and Midwifery in Ireland in the Twentieth Century: Fifty Years of an Board Altranais (The Nursing Board) 1950–2000* (Dublin, 2000), p. 115. The proportion of domiciliary births remained constant between 1973 and 1999. In 1999 only 1 per cent of births were domiciliary. P. Kennedy, 'Childbirth in Ireland', in Kennedy (ed.), *Motherhood in Ireland*, p. 82.
76 O'Dwyer and Mulhall, 'Midwifery', p. 116.
77 The issue of the hospitalisation of birth has been dealt with in many international essays concerning motherhood. See Loudon, *Death in Childbirth*, pp. 224–9; J. C.

Bogdan, 'Childbirth in America, 1650–1900', in R. D. Apple (ed.), *Women, Health, and Medicine in America: A Historical Handbook* (New York, 1990), p. 114; J. W. Leavitt, *Brought to Bed: Childbearing in America, 1750–1950* (Oxford, 1986); Lewis, *The Politics of Motherhood*, pp. 117–34; Clear, *Women of the House*, pp. 96–122; J. Murphy-Lawless, *Reading Birth and Death: A History of Obstetric Thinking* (Cork, 1998).

78 This was a code of practice supported by the Masters of the maternity hospitals. See Spain, 'Maternity services in Éire', p. 1.

79 Loudon, *Death in Childbirth*, p. 227.

80 Prior to 1918, the Central Midwives Board in London had been the chief agency of regulation for Irish midwifery. For details of approved training hospitals, see *Annual Report of the Department of Local Government and Public Health, 1933–4*, p. 110 and O'Dwyer and Mulhall, ' Midwifery', pp. 102–3.

81 In 1988 these three hospitals catered for 36 per cent of the nations births per annum. This increased to 40 per cent by 2000. See Kennedy, 'Childbirth in Ireland', p. 82.

82 W. G. MacKenzi, 'Ulster Medical Society', *The Lancet*, 1, (1922), 158.

83 *Annual Report of the Department of Local Government and Public Health, 1927–8*, p. 41.

84 Loudon, *Death in Childbirth*, p. 496.

85 *Annual Report of the Department of Local Government and Public Health, 1930–1*, p. 60.

86 A doctor delivery was believed to be the safest for the mother. Loudon questions this conviction and points out the increased tendency of the medical profession during the 1930s to intervene unnecessarily in normal births. See Loudon, *Death in Childbirth*, p. 494.

87 *Annual Report of the Department of Local Government and Public Health, 1930–1*, p. 60.

88 *Ibid.*

89 *Ibid.*

90 'Memo from Department of Local Government and Public Health: Population of the country', NAI, Dept. Taoiseach, S9684.

91 *Annual Report of the Department of Local Government and Public Health, 1933–4*, p. 64.

92 *Ibid.*, p. 65.

93 *Ibid.*, *1933–4*, p. 64.

94 *Ibid.*, *1922–5*, p. 34.

95 *Ibid.*

96 Clear points out that there was a shortage of midwives during the Second World War when Irish midwives were attracted by better pay in Britain, which meant that friends or relatives were often the only option. See Clear, 'Women in de Valera's Ireland, 1932–48', p. 112.

97 *Annual Report of the Department of Local Government and Public Health, 1932–3*, p. 53.

98 *Ibid.*

99 *Annual Report of the Department of Local Government and Public Health, 1933–4*, p. 66.

100 See, for example, *Annual Report of the Local Government of Public Health, 1927–8*, p. 40. See also *Annual Report of the Department of Local Government and Public Health, 1933–4*, p. 66.

101 *Annual Report of the Department of Local Government and Public Health, 1932–3*, p. 53.

102 Loudon, *Death in Childbirth*, pp. 216–18;

103 Farmar, *Holles Street*, p. 20; Robins, 'Public policy and the maternity services in Ireland during the twentieth century', pp. 280–1; See also T. Mcintosh, 'Profession, skill, or domestic duty? Midwifery in Sheffield, 1881–1936', *Social History of Medicine*, 11:3 (Dec. 1998), 403–20.

104 O'Dwyer and Mulhall, 'Midwifery', pp. 102–3.

105 *Annual Report of the Department of Local Government and Public Health, 1922–5*, p. 33.

106 *Ibid.*

107 *Annual Report of the Department of Local Government and Public Health, 1933–4*, p. 64

108 *Annual Report of the Department of Local Government and Public Health, 1934–5*, p. 92.

109 *Ibid.*

110 *Ibid.*, p. 93.

111 *Ibid.*

112 The Master of the National Maternity Hospital, Alex Spain, made reference to the impact of sulphonamide drugs in Ireland. See Spain, 'Maternity services in Éire', p. 1. Robins notes that sulphonamide became available in 1935. Robins, J., 'Public policy and the maternity services in Ireland during the twentieth-century,' p. 292; However, Clear cautions against the overemphasis of the impact of sulphonamide drugs on maternal mortality rates as the drug was often not available to women either owing to shortages, particularly during the Second World War, or because so many women still gave birth at home. Clear, 'Women in de Valera's Ireland, 1932–48', p. 112.

113 Loudon, *Death in Childbirth*, p. 259.

114 *Annual Report of the Department of Local Government and Public Health, 1937–8*, p. 52.

115 *Ibid., 1939–40*, p. 39.

116 'Health of the country: Debate in the Dáil,' *JIFSMU*, 4:23 (May 1939), 52.

117 *Ibid.*

118 Spain, 'Maternity services in Éire', p. 1.

119 *Annual Report of the Department of Local Government and Public Health, 1941–2*, p. 54.

120 *Ibid.*, p. 53.

121 In England, by 1950 the maternal mortality rate was 20 per cent of its 1935 rate. See Loudon, *Death in Childbirth*, p. 254.

122 Clear, 'Women in de Valera's Ireland 1932–48', pp. 110–14.

123 See Lynn to Archbishop Byrne, 27 January 1936, Dublin Diocesan Archives (DDA), Byrne Papers, Hospital General. Cited in Ó hÓgartaigh, *Kathleen Lynn*, p. 103.

124 Clear, 'Women in de Valera's Ireland 1932–48', p. 113; Ó hÓgartaigh, *Kathleen Lynn*, pp. 96–106.

125 *Irish Times* (16 Nov. 1935), cited in Ó hÓgartaigh, *Kathleen Lynn*, p. 101.

126 Hug notes the divergences in English and Irish legislation in this respect, as in the same year the Infant Life (Preservation) Act was passed in England, which allowed for abortion to save a mother's life. See C. Hug, *The Politics of Sexual Morality in Ireland* (New York, 1999), p. 79.

127 Fianna Fáil, under the leadership of Eamon de Valera, held power between 1932 and 1948.

128 J. H. Whyte, *Church and State in Modern Ireland 1923–1979* (Dublin, 1980), p. 49.

129 Conroy noted that between 1926 and 1974 there were fifty-eight cases of back-

street abortion investigated or prosecuted by the authorities. P. Conroy, 'Maternity confined – The struggle for fertility control,' in Kennedy (ed.), *Motherhood in Ireland,* p. 131; Kennedy noted that the subject was rarely mentioned in Ireland but that the case of Nurse Cadden, a back-street abortionist, brought the issue to public attention in the 1950s. See F. Kennedy, *Cottage to Crèche: Family Change in Ireland* (Dublin, 2001), p. 39. For a review of the case of Nurse Cadden, see NAI Dept. Taoiseach, S16116. S. McAvoy, 'Before Cadden: abortion in mid-twentieth-century Ireland', in D. Keogh, F. O'Shea, and C. Quinlan (eds), *Ireland in the 1950s: The Lost Decade* (Cork, 2004), pp. 147–63.

130 Dr Stafford Johnson wrote to Archbishop Byrne in 1931 to inform him of this Roman Catholic organisation of doctors established to ensure 'the application of Christian Virtue in the practice of their profession and life'. See DDA, Byrne Papers Box One: Lay Organisations, Stafford Johnson to Archbishop Byrne, 31 November 1931. See also the inaugural address delivered before the Guild of SS Luke, Cosmas and Damian, Dublin, 21 April 1932: 'The True Idea and Outlook of a Catholic Medical Guild' by Dr J. Stafford Johnson. Reprinted from the *Catholic Medical Guardian* (July 1932).

131 Cited in Catholic Truth Society, *The Problem of Undesirable Printed Matter: Suggested Remedies: Evidence of the Catholic Truth Society of Ireland Presented to the Departmental Committee of Inquiry 1926* (Dublin, 1926), p. 11. (Author's emphasis.)

132 *Kilkenny People*, 31 August 1930.

133 Revd M. P. Cleary, 'The Church of Ireland and birth control', *(IER)* 38 (1931), 624.

134 See the 1929 Censorship Act and section 17 of the 1935 Criminal Law Amendment Act.

135 *Casti Connubii*, quoted in A. Fremantle, *The Papal Encyclicals in their Historical Context* (New York, 1956), p. 239.

136 *Ibid.*

137 S. McAvoy, 'Regulation of sexuality in the Irish Free State', in Malcom and Jones (eds), *Medicine, Disease and the State in Ireland*, p. 257.

138 'The annual report of the Rotunda', *IJMSc.*, 92 (Aug. 1933), 334.

139 NAI, Dept. Taoiseach, S 2547A.

140 *Ibid.*

141 Archbishop McQuaid prohibited Catholics from attending Trinity College in 1944, claiming that to do so was a 'mortal sin'. See D. Keogh, *Twentieth-Century Ireland: Nation and State* (Dublin, 1994), p. 146.

142 Minister's note regarding interview with the archbishop of Tuam, 11 February 1931.

143 Geary, *Medicine and Charity*, pp. 123–51; M. Ó hÓgartaigh, 'A medical appointment in County Meath', *Ríocht na Midhe: Records of the Meath Archaeological and Historical Society*, xvii, 2006, pp. 266–70.

144 Ó hÓgartaigh, 'A medical appointment in Meath: controversy in Kilskyre', pp. 266–70.

145 *Ibid.*, Memorandum of conversation between the Archbishop of Tuam and Sir Joseph Glynn, 26 February 1931. Craniotomy involved the surgical removal of part of the skull of the foetus to ease delivery.

146 McAvoy, 'Regulation of sexuality in the Irish Free State', p. 256; D. Keogh, *The Vatican, the Bishops and Irish Politics 1919–1939* (Cambridge, 1986), pp. 169–76.

147 Memorandum 153/MCW, cited in L. Hoggart, 'The campaign for birth control in Britain in the 1920s', in A. Digby, and J. Stewart (eds), *Gender, Health, and Welfare* (London, 1996), p. 144; R. Soloway, *Demography*, pp. 182–8.

148 NAI, Dept. Taoiseach, S2547A.

149 Dr J. Stafford Johnson was Supreme Knight of the Knights of Columbanus, a Catholic,

masonic organisation, between 1942 and 1948.

150 Letter from Stafford Johnson to League of Nations, 6 June 1932, International League of Nations legislation relating to maternity and child welfare, NAI, Dept. Health, B130/59.

151 *Ibid.*

152 Letter from Stafford Johnson to Minister for External Affairs, 26 July 1932, NAI, Dept. Health, B130/59.

153 According to David Sheehy, Stafford Johnson was a close personal friend of John Charles McQuaid, Archbishop of Dublin, (1941–72) frequently dining with him at his private residence in Killiney, Co. Dublin. See D. Sheehy, 'Archbishop McQuaid: The diocesan administrator', *Doctrine and Life,* 53:3 (Mar. 2003), 166–9.

154 NAI, Dept. Health, B130/59.

155 Note signed by ED, 23 August 1932, NAI, Dept. Health, B130/59.

156 Letter from the Department of Local Government and Public Health to the Department of External Affairs, 8 September 1932, NAI, Dept. Health, B130/59.

157 Extract of Coyne's report: Confidential statement re section on contraception, issued by the League of Nations, *c.* 1932, NAI, Dept. Health, B130/59.

158 Secretary of Department of External Affairs, 17 November 1932, NAI, Dept. Health, B130/59.

159 Dr McDonald to Department of Local Government and Public Health, 28 July 1932, NAI, Dept. Health, B130/59.

160 *Report of the Council on the Work of the Nineteenth Session of the Committee,* 15 October 1932, NAI, Dept. Health, B130/59.

161 *2nd Committee of 14th Assembly of the League of Nations,* 28 September 1933, NAI, Dept. Health, B130/59.

162 Memo from Department of External Affairs, 8 September 1933 NAI, Dept. Health, B130/59.

163 Cited in M. Finnane, 'The Carrigan committee of 1930–1 and the "moral condition of the Saorstát"', *IHS,* 33:128 (Nov. 2001), 529.

164 B. Solomons, 'The dangerous multipara', *The Lancet,* 2 (7 July 1934), 8–11.

165 *Ibid.*

166 *Ibid.*

167 B. Solomons, 'The prevention of maternal morbidity and mortality', *IJMSc.,* 88 (Apr. 1933), 175.

168 Memo Department of Local Government and Public Health, *c.* 1932, NAI, Dept. Health, B130/59.

169 Seanad Éireann, *Seanad Debates,* vol. 12, col. 87 (Apr. 1929).

170 Hug, *The Politics of Sexual Morality in Ireland,* p. 82; Keogh, *The Vatican, the Bishops,* p. 206. For a copy of this see NAI, Dept. Taoiseach, S6489A. This file also contains the 'Department of Justice Memorandum,' 10 November 1933.

171 Hug, *The Politics of Sexual Morality,* p. 82.

172 Cited in Kennedy, *Cottage to Crèche,* p. 163.

173 Dáil Éireann, *Official Reports of the Debates of Dáil Éireann,* vol. 53, col. 2019 (1 Aug., 1934)

174 'Notes and queries: the excusing cause for "passivity" in onanism. Counselling the lesser sin of onanism', *IER,* 70 (Jan.–June, 1948), 245.

175 *Ibid.*

176 Hug, *The Politics of Sexual Morality,* p. 114.

177 Letter from the Department of Local Government and Public Health to the Department of External Affairs, 8 September 1932, NAI, Dept. Health, B130/59.

178 Powell also noted the tendency to stress infant mortality rates rather than maternal

mortality and morbidity. See Powell, *The Politics of Irish Social Policy*, p. 130; Loudon, *Death in Childbirth*, p. 483.

179 E. Shorter, *A History of Women's Bodies* (London, 1983), p. 164; Lewis, *The Politics of Motherhood*, p. 35.

180 Lewis, *The Politics of Motherhood*, p. 35; B. Harrison, 'Women and health', p. 174.

181 For figures relating to the rural/urban divide in relation to infant mortality from 1901 to 1938, see NAI, Dept. Taoiseach, S9684 A.

182 *Annual Report of the Department of Local Government and Public Health, 1930–1*, p. 63.

183 *Ibid.*

184 *Ibid.*, p. 67.

185 *Ibid., 1933–4*, p. 67.

186 *Ibid., 1936–7*, p. 75.

187 *Ibid., 1932–3*, p. 54.

188 Department of Local Government and Public Health, Report of the Departmental Committee on Health Services (Sept. 1945), unpublished, copy in NAI, Dept. Taoiseach, S13444B. (September 1945). In 1940 the infant mortality rate for infants in urban areas was 83 and in rural areas 55 per 1,000 live births. *Annual Report of the Department of Local Government and Public Health, 1939–40*, p. 40.

189 *Ibid., 1927–8*, p. 41.

190 Loudon, *Death in Childbirth*, p. 492.

191 Ó hÓgartaigh, 'Dr Dorothy Price', p. 79.

192 Dr Edward J. Byrne (1872–1940) served as archbishop from 1921 until 1940. See B. J. Canning, *Bishops of Ireland 1870–1987* (Ballyshannon, 1987), pp. 181–2.

193 Ó hÓgartaigh, *Kathleen Lynn*, pp. 101–2.

194 Statement of His Grace, the Archbishop of Dublin, to Members of the Deputation of the Committee of St Ultan's Hospital, 20th December 1935. St Ultan's Archives, Royal College of Physicians of Ireland. I am grateful to Ó hÓgartaigh for the provision of a copy of this. There is also a draft copy of the same statement in the Byrne Papers. DDA, Byrne Papers, Hospital General.

195 *Ibid.* Cited in Ó hÓgartaigh, 'Dr Dorothy Price', p. 79.

196 Ó hÓgartaigh, *Kathleen Lynn*, pp. 101–2.

197 See Dr James Staunton, Secretary to the Hierarchy to Taoiseach, 10 October 1950, DDA, McQuaid Papers, AB8/B/XVIII/15.

198 Statement of His Grace, the Archbishop of Dublin.

199 *Ibid.*

200 See, for example, 'Memo on the New Catholic Children's Hospital, Crumlin' signed by McQuaid, 19 September 1938, DDA, Byrne Papers, Hospital General.

3

The Dublin mother:
maternal welfare and child health, 1920–40

> Without doubt, apart from the special needy cases, ignorance on the part of young mothers is one of the greatest factors in the production of our high infant mortality rates; and, it is the wide-spread teaching of the simple rules of mothercraft we must rely upon if we are to save the babies and reduce the high death-rates ... The mother has now every opportunity at her door for obtaining the necessary advice as to how to rear her infant, but the Treasury ... has not provided adequately to give practical aid to the mother and her child, which ... makes it almost impossible for the mother to provide the necessaries of life for herself, much less an adequate milk supply for her infant.[1]

By the beginning of the twentieth century, international concern regarding the 'quality of national stock'[2] was focusing attention on the issue of maternity and child welfare as a potential area of social service and national regeneration.[3] In Ireland, mothers became the target of health propaganda and mothercraft philosophies in a bid to improve infant mortality figures and family health. This campaign was primarily aimed at working-class mothers whose infants were most at risk from premature death and who, it was argued, were most in need of domestic guidance. The theory of mothercraft, however, was stretched by the harsh realities of working-class poverty, which often meant that good intentions were dashed on the rocks of financial necessity. While modifications were made to the rigid theories first expounded, working-class mothers were still held accountable for the deaths of their infants. In reality, much of a working-class mother's time and energy was spent mapping survival via the various charities and services available. Independent Ireland drew heavily on the nineteenth-century tradition of charitable assistance to cater for the welfare of mothers and children.[4] Poor mothers had to negotiate a web of charitable organisations and voluntary welfare projects and maximise the limited state services available, in order to secure family survival.[5] The contemporary desire to support mothers and their children became enmeshed in cultural concerns regarding the sanctity of the family and the role of religion and charity in society. In the wake of national independence, the moral ethos of the Free State made the task of maternal support extremely difficult as religion took on a heightened national significance and moral qualms about intervention in family life led to a degree of social inaction. It is important to examine the ways in which working-class mothers became the targets of various social and medical campaigns and to contrast these campaigns with the social reality for many of these mothers. However, this study also questions the assumption that these women were always the passive recipients of either advice or charity and investigates the ways in which they derived power and influence in their own right. In analysing the ways in which working-class mothers negotiated the services and charities available, an attempt is made to contextualise the importance of sectarianism in Ireland to the formation of an *ad hoc* support network for Irish mothers.

Mothercraft: teaching motherhood

Coey Bigger had identified the lack of instructive mothercraft as an important failing in the Irish approach to preventive health. 'Mothercraft,' he wrote, 'is not instinctive any more than is reading or writing.'[6] This move away from, or loss of faith in, instinct formed part of a wider shift in the public health domain toward the expert: 'handy women' were the source of all infection, maternal ignorance was the cause of infant death, family-based knowledge or tradition regarding birth and mothering was to be superseded by 'enlightenment'.[7] Innate skills, or those passed down through the generations, were seen as dangerous as well as the source of suspicion or worse.[8] The professional was meant to promote scientific rather than instinctual motherhood. Consequently, mothers were lectured by health visitors or at baby clubs on their responsibility and provided with practical domestic advice. Expectant and nursing mothers were instructed in mothering skills, and their children supervised from birth to the age of five. The WNHA modelled itself on St Pancras, the school for mothers in London, and the Dublin baby clubs introduced the notion of 'mothercraft' to working-class mothers.[9] Lady Aberdeen presented silver shields to the best mothers at the clubs. These shields were ostensibly a reward but also a manifestation of the belief that motherhood could be taught.[10] Both Michael Anderson and Edward Shorter claimed that 'good motherhood' was an invention of modernisation. In the Irish context, the growing belief in preventive medicine led to a new emphasis on the education of mothers.[11]

In 1906, the first National Conference of Infant Mortality in Britain declared, 'At the bottom of infant mortality, high or low, is good or bad motherhood.'[12] Lewis reaffirmed that in Britain infant mortality was seen as a 'failure of motherhood', and consequently the aim of maternity services was to 'promote a greater sense of moral responsibility on the part of the mother'.[13] In Ireland, too, by the 1920s there were calls for a more proactive response to infant mortality by targeting the mother in the home. Mary E. Daly noted that in the early part of the twentieth century the ignorance of Dublin mothers was blamed for the high rate of infant mortality in the city. Very little consideration was given to the impossible conditions under which many were expected to mother.[14] All of the available services stressed the importance of the maternal influence and the need to enlist that influence in the fight against infant death. The Department of Local Government and Public Health frequently reiterated the need to enlighten mothers regarding the risks of 'handy women' and the need for proper hygiene and culinary standards.[15] In 1932, Dr Kerry Reddin, reporting on the maternity services of Dublin Corporation, commended mothers for their high rate of breastfeeding (which he claimed was higher than in many comparable cities in England). However, he also linked infant mortality to maternal ignorance:

> Many of these deaths are also directly attributable to ignorance in the care of baby on the mother's part, and we could surprise you by a recital of some diets, and foods that have been given to young babies by some of our Dublin mothers.[16]

Catholic clerical opinion was largely in agreement with the official view but was equally anxious to keep the aspect of religion to the forefront of any new maternity welfare initiatives. Revd Lambert McKenna, for example, concerned himself with a myriad of the most pressing social issues in Lenten pastorals. Foremost among his concerns was encouraging Catholic 'ladies' to busy themselves with 'social charity' by forming a Catholic Ladies' League to fight poverty and child mortality and, crucially, to ensure that their Protestant counterparts were not using the Catholic gap in the social services market to proselytise working-class mothers. He was cognisant of the pressures under which working-class mothers operated, conceding, 'Whole holocausts of children die because their mothers have to work too hard or too long, or cannot give them proper care.' While McKenna implicitly acknowledged the toll of poverty, multiple pregnancies, and the hazards of the practice, borne of necessity, of older siblings or 'wee mummies'[17] caring for younger children, he still believed that 'Thousands of children, too, are killed by their mothers' ignorance.'[18]

Even when it came to the issue of maternal death, the women themselves were viewed as culpable by the patronising, if learned, medics. In 1930, Dr G. J. Tierney noted that six women a week died in the Irish Free State as a direct result of pregnancy or childbirth.[19] He listed three medical reasons for this: the omission or inadequacy of antenatal examinations, errors of judgement in the management of cases, and the lack of reasonable facilities. However, despite these outside factors, he believed that the overriding responsibility lay with 'the patient herself'. Tierney urged a 'systematised campaign of enlightenment' to impress on mothers-to-be the risks to both themselves and their children of such resistance to available services. Yet he neglected to note that the available services were insufficient, overtaxed and poorly publicised and that the evidence of maternal 'resistance' was minimal.

The Master of the Rotunda, Bethel Solomons, went even further in 1932 in his condemnation of ignorant mothers, when he suggested that patients who initially resisted treatment should be refused treatment at the last hour, but he conceded that 'the ignorant *must* be treated'.[20] Solomons's exasperation was indicative of the powerlessness felt by many medical practitioners in the face of stubborn mortality statistics and the slack response from public representatives, as well as their own impatience with the impoverished.[21] To view the chastisement of maternal ignorance as merely misogynistic or unsympathetic is to ignore an element of truth in the charge. Many mothers were ignorant as to the causes of both maternal and infant mortality, but then so too were many of the experts.

The mother was targeted because she was considered the key to social health, in terms of both her biological and her emotional role as a mother. The mother's physical health was not just crucial to the health of the un-born, but was also necessary to enable her to care for the children and the family. She was expected to make a pittance suffice and to allocate time for emotional nurture and moral vigilance. There was, however, a genuine problem in reaching mothers in order to educate them in relation to basic hygiene and domestic skills. Not only were the resources lacking and publicity shied away from, but also mothers themselves frequently displayed a suspicion of such clinical intervention. The Department of Local Government and Public Health noted with regret that women did not always avail themselves of the existing services, which hindered the effectiveness of child welfare schemes.[22] In 1938 the medical officer of health for County Louth, Dr Musgrave, lamented the 'hush-hush policy of many mothers in regard to their children. They look on all attempts at de-lousing as futile, and still shrug expressively when told that lice do not rise spontaneously from the skin.'[23] In this area, as in many others, an ambiguous view of 'intervention' was apparent: on the one hand, official intervention in family life was seen as a threat to personal privacy and morality; on the other, it was perceived as an antidote to the traditional superstition that cost lives.

The medical superintendent officer for Cork County Borough Council, Dr J. C. Saunders, believed that modern legislation, while less spectacular than the public health acts of the previous century, had helped to improve individual health, but he also lamented the fact that:

> One of the greatest stumbling blocks to public health administration is the fact that legislation is generally years ahead of public opinion. So far as the general public is concerned knowledge of health matters is based very largely on tradition and superstition while the idea of prevention in the sphere of health appears only just now to have taken a slight hold on the imagination of the people.[24]

This conclusion was not atypical and indicates that there were problems in the dissemination of health information. Moreover, it reveals the problematic relationship between tradition and modernity. Parents were chastised for their reluctance to submit their children to outside examination,[25] one of the advances in modern health care, at the same time as being exhorted to protect the traditional sanctity of their home. Bigger was again perceptive in observing the dilemma of modern urban motherhood:

> The Irish mother is celebrated throughout the world for the affection she has for her offspring. It is only among the most drunken and debased in the towns that there is any wilful neglect or cruelty to children. But affection, unfortunately, is not sufficient. Love teaches much, but it does not teach all that it behoves a mother to know in cities and towns to-day. The truth is that although she loves her child, she is not fitted for motherhood. The fault is not hers, but is that of the system of education in this country. All that she knows about her functions, childbearing and child nurture is what she has learned from her mother; it has been handed down from generation to generation and is a blend of good and bad, a mingling of useful knowledge and harmful superstition. Though she went to national school, she was taught nothing that would fit her for her work of bringing into the world and rearing a strong and healthy family of sons and daughters.[26]

The traditional view of motherhood was encouraged in relation to the role of the mother in the family, but discouraged in terms of health. The degree of mysticism that still surrounded the 'delicate condition' (the term 'pregnant' was rarely used by women themselves) was both deprecated and facilitated.[27] The 'orthodoxy of privacy' that shrouded female sexuality left many women unprepared for the realities of parturition and reluctant to seek help or advice.[28] Women were supposed to embrace the new social medicine and submit themselves to antenatal clinics and attend baby clubs where they were meant to absorb the information deemed suitable for their ears.[29] At the same time, a detailed understanding of pregnancy was discouraged as immodest and, in terms of potential birth control, dangerous.[30] Public discourse on sexuality and reproduction in Ireland between 1920 and 1960 was centred on the 'potential evil of sex' and rarely allowed for the discussion of the 'lived reality of individual sexuality'.[31] The mother had a *duty* with regard to the traditional understanding of her position in the family and a modern *responsibility* for the health of herself and her offspring. The need to maintain duty and curtail the definition of responsibility was to prove the central dilemma in succeeding years of increasing social service and welfare provision.

The feeding mothers: malnutrition and maternal health

In the light of the emphasis on foetal health, pregnancy could no longer be regarded in isolation from its social context. Lewis noted that in England the promotion of breastfeeding and 'mothercraft' became central to maternity and child welfare services.[32] This was true in Ireland also. However, the drive for better medical or welfare provision was not motivated by either pronatalism or eugenics, but by a desire to see a decline in the infant mortality rate.[33] The WNHA believed that infant mortality was the result of hereditary and environmental influences and that the solution was good mothering. The most essential aspect of good mothering, in their view, was a basic understanding of hygiene and good feeding:

> Whether or not he will emerge safely from the troubles that beset that critical period, the first year of life, depends above all things on the way he is mothered and of the many qualities that go to make up good mothering the most important is the proper administration of suitable food.[34]

The WNHA identified the failure to breastfeed as a negative outcome of urban existence.[35] It acknowledged that economic and social circumstances had made it difficult for many mothers to breastfeed.[36] The association lamented that the middle-class mother, bound by the duties of her class, found breastfeeding incompatible with the structure of her day, whereas the working-class mother was often out of the house earning her family's dinner.[37] Hence it recommended that a law should be introduced to standardise the quality of milk sold, particularly in the capital.[38] Coey Bigger reiterated the conviction that breastfeeding was crucial in the battle against infant death. However, he also stressed the interrelationship between maternal nourishment and breastfeeding. He explained:

> An ill-nourished mother may, at the expense of her own resources, bring forth a well nourished baby, but she will not generally be able to supply it with a sufficient quantity or quality of breast milk. It has been shown fairly clearly that the nourishment of the mother during pregnancy has a definite effect on her capacity to suckle her infant.[39]

However, it was not until the late 1930s that a breastfeeding drive began in earnest and the real complications involved in encouraging women to breastfeed were acknowledged: to feed her infant, a mother must be properly fed herself. In 1933 the Fianna Fáil government inaugurated a free milk scheme, which was run by the voluntary Infant Aid Association.[40] The association distributed free milk to expectant or nursing mothers on the Dublin Corporation register. Outside Dublin milk, was distributed via the various maternity and child welfare clinics and on the recommendation of the health visitor. By 1941, free milk schemes were in operation in four county boroughs, fifty-nine urban districts, and twenty-nine county health districts.[41] The milk scheme aimed at ensuring that mothers received sufficient nourishment to breastfeed. However, there was ample evidence that this scheme was not sufficient to combat the adverse social conditions in which many mothers were living and mothering. In 1938 the Department of Local Government and Public Health bemoaned the fact that:

> very little progress has been made in the reduction in infant mortality, and strikes and economic stress are large factors in keeping the rate high. There still remain large numbers of bad housing areas where the toll on infant life is

very heavy. A causative factor of the high infant mortality rate in Dublin is the failure to breastfeed. A survey amongst 1,414 mothers showed that 580 breastfed and 359 partially breastfed their infants, whilst in 475 cases artificial feeding was resorted to. The survey suggests that 60 per cent of Dublin mothers are unable to breastfeed their infants.[42]

The reasons why so many women could not breastfeed varied, but in the lower income group the two main factors were malnutrition and the constraints of an outside job. The issue of breastfeeding was particularly contentious in Dublin, where it was considered that the supply and standard of milk was most unsatisfactory and, in this context, breast milk was deemed safer for the infant. However, the issue of breastfeeding and infant survival was fast becoming a national issue. In 1937 the Cork Medical Superintendent Officer of Health noted that two main causes of infant death were diarrhoea and broncho-pneumonia. In relation to the former, he isolated the cause as 'improper feeding'. He explained that the

enormous preponderance of deaths of artificially-fed babies leads to the conclusion that this is the main factor which determines the death of infants from this condition. Of the 45 deaths from gastro-enteritis in infants under one year, no less than 42 were artificially-fed babies.[43]

By the early 1940s breastfeeding became the main focus in combating infant mortality and was to prove pivotal in the campaign to involve the mother in her newborn's survival. The issue of breastfeeding in Ireland resulted in a constant reassessment of social conditions and attitudes, forcing health officials to acknowledge the role of poverty in ill health.

In 1925 the St John Ambulance Brigade began to branch out into maternity welfare, making it the only organisation to cater specifically for mothers.[44] The St John Ambulance Brigade was a non-denominational voluntary organisation involved in first aid and other civic activities. The brigade's focus on the mother was unique: it ran maternity kitchens to cater for, and protect, the welfare of the impoverished and undernourished mother who was expected to carry the burden of family life in adverse conditions.[45] The mothers were offered sit-down meals, as it was believed that if they took the food home they would share it with the family.[46] This was the prime motivation of the organisation, which noted in 1950, 'The Brigade were pioneers in this work and started the first dining room when it was proved that by no other means could it be guaranteed that a semi-starving mother actually ate the necessary nourishment freely given.'[47]

The fact that starvation was a common sacrifice made by mothers was observed as late as 1945 by the professor of medicine at University College Dublin, T. W. T. Dillon, who noted, '[T]he mother starves herself to feed her children and, in a very high percentage of cases, is found on examination to be suffering from nutritional anaemia.'[48] The distribution of food within the family context was often a sign of status or power; the father was usually served first and often ate separately, what was left went next to the children. There was also a practical reason for self-denial on the part of the mother: she wished the breadwinner to remain healthy and able to provide. Self-denial was therefore also a form of self-preservation. This was confirmed by Pember Reeves's study of working-class wives in Britain between 1909 and 1913. She noted that the practice of the working-class mother feeding herself less was not 'thought-out self-sacrifice on her part. It is the pressure of circumstances. The wage-earner must be fed.'[49] Margaret Spring Rice's study of working-class women in Britain in the late 1930s revealed that working-class women often budgeted by denying themselves a proper meal.[50] It saved money and time if she did not eat properly. Furthermore, women often stood while the rest of the family dined, meaning that they were unable to eat a proper hot meal. Women frequently remarked that they waited until the family was finished and ate whatever 'scraps that may be left'.[51] Charles Cameron, Chief Medical Officer, and the secretary of the Public Health Department of Dublin Corporation, noted that when the poor had meat it was 'generally for the use of the breadwinner of the family'.[52] The Lady Sanitary Officers in Dublin City observed, 'it is almost impossible to feed a family of children and leave a fair share for the mother, who usually is the last to be considered'.[53] Thus, as a rule, the mother ate last and least. This she considered her duty: in denying herself she appropriated the brunt of poverty and hopefully spared her children. It was important therefore that, at the charitable dining halls throughout Dublin, mothers were offered not only a chance to eat, but also an opportunity to sit down and chat with other mothers – a luxury to women accustomed to rearing families in one-room tenements. Under the corporation's maternity and child welfare scheme, the St John Ambulance Brigade was given a grant from the very beginning of its project in 1925.[54] Commendable though this work was, it was still insufficient: there were only two dining halls which catered for a maximum of eighty mothers and therefore only a small fraction of maternal appetites were satisfied in this way.

International research into nutrition and its impact on resistance to disease and overall life expectancy prompted much of the debate on public health and helped expand the notion of social medicine.[55] Nutritional research, begun in the 1920s, intensified in the 1930s. In Ireland it was reflected in the medical journals of the day, and in studies conducted by the St John Ambulance Brigade. By the close of the decade, nutrition was a central plank of the public health campaign, which was inextricably linked with the battle against infant mortality. Nutritional advice became part of antenatal care. In 1938 Dublin Corporation and Dr Sterling Barry of the Department of Local Government and Public Health held a joint inquiry into the causes of infant mortality in the city. The inquiry pointed out that 'many expectant mothers were suffering from malnutrition', which stimulated an interest in the connection between maternal malnutrition and infant mortality.[56] In the same year the corporation noted that Dr G. C. Dockerlay had started research at the Rotunda into the impact of maternal anaemia and infant mortality.[57] As a result of his research, Dockerlay, a dietician and the professor of biochemistry at Trinity College Dublin, along with William R. Fearon, declared, 'It is the duty of the civilised state to anticipate the nutritional needs of its future citizens.'[58] The shift of attention to 'future citizens', together with the principles of preventive medicine, led indirectly to greater concern for the welfare of the mother. As the child-bearer, the mother became a vital component in any campaign to reduce infant mortality. In 1938, Fearon noted that during pregnancy the human body is in need of extra nourishment: 'Under these conditions the maternal organism is bearing a double burden, often amid very unfavourable circumstances, and the effects of malnutrition during these critical periods are doubly unfortunate in that they affect the health of two individuals.'[59] In the same year, M. J. Russell noted that in slum areas in Dublin there was a considerable amount of anaemia in expectant mothers.[60] Combating anaemia and thus fortifying the expectant mother and the unborn child was the chief aim of the maternity kitchens established throughout Dublin City. It was observed that, amongst the mothers, the most popular gift was a jug of soup each day for the young children at home, two sets of baby clothes, and a set of underclothes for the mother herself.[61] The daily meal served at these maternity kitchens was planned by Fearon and Dockerlay, who carried out a survey of fifty expectant mothers whose husbands were unemployed. They discovered that all 'were definitely anaemic' and that this anaemia was the iron-deficiency type, indicating that it was as a direct result of malnutrition during pregnancy.[62] In fact, the diet that these women were surviving on was shown to W. R. Aykroyd of the Koonoor Laboratories and he noted that they were 'as deficient as some he had seen in badly nourished villages in India'.[63] According to Fearon only 6 per cent of the mothers surveyed consumed an adequate amount of protein and only 8 per cent showed an adequate calorie intake.[64] He informed the Royal Academy of Medicine in Ireland that 'The averages of the entire group were about half the quantities advocated by the Committee on Nutrition set up by the British Medical Association.'[65] In the face of voluntary effort, medical opinion and nutritional research, the state was increasingly appearing in dereliction of its duty with regard to the mother and child.

Fearon argued for a national nutritional policy. He pointed out that the League of Nations had published a report in 1936 dealing with the issue of nutrition and its impact on public health. Reflecting the emerging twentieth-century conviction that citizens were assets worthy of investment, Fearon lamented the absence of any systematic investigation into the nutritional situation in Ireland. Making reference to the study carried out by Dockerlay into the prevalence of nutritional anaemia among antenatal patients in Dublin, Fearon noted that the problem in Ireland was 'most obvious among the mothers, many of whom are sacrificed to the super-tax that poverty imposes on maternity'.[66] The connection between preventive medicine and the science of nutrition was understood by medical contemporaries, as one doctor noted in response to Fearon's paper: 'Maintenance of good health, which is more important than its restoration, is the aspect of life with which the science of nutrition is most intimately associated.'[67] However, the professor of economics and national economy at University College Dublin, George O'Brien, pointed out that there were 'less altruistic' reasons for the increased interest in nutrition, primarily the concern regarding the tendency for the birth rate to fall, and the desire to improve the 'quality' of populations. This, he believed, resulted in a 'growing realization that the social services may constitute the soundest form of national investment, and that no object of public expenditure is more truly productive than money spent on improving the health and strength of people'.[68] According to contemporaries, therefore, it was a mix of humanitarian conscience and social necessity that resulted in the desire to invest in public health and to extend social services. In 1930 the Minister for Local Government and Public Health, General Richard Mulcahy, grasped the silver lining of preventive health care: 'Prevention is better than cure. It is also cheaper. The wise development of the preventive side of public health work is an investment more than a mere outlay.'[69] In order to yield the best return on the public health investment, the most sensible targets were the unborn and the very young. This had the added advantage of reaching the wider family by example. If the mother was present at all child welfare examinations, was visited in her home and was instructed on how best to feed herself and baby, this information would then, it was hoped, filter down to the wider family. The Minister succinctly concluded, 'Our hope is in the children.'[70]

The sponsorship of motherhood and the role of charity in the Irish Free State

Revd McKenna, arguing in fact for greater Catholic involvement in charitable welfare projects, highlighted the contemporary conviction that the mother was central to family welfare. He argued that there were 'countless social works aiming at the preservation of family life among the poor. Naturally these works are interested first in the mother.'[71] Perceptible amid the general anxiety regarding the moral and spiritual health of the nation throughout the 1920s and 1930s, was a particular reliance on, and a simultaneous loss of, faith in the traditional Irish family.[72] The dilemma facing contemporaries, it was argued, was how to achieve a balance between the desire to protect the family, 'assaulted' by immorality, modernity and poverty, and the need to safeguard it from undue intervention. The central role of the mother in terms of both family health and morality meant that her physical and spiritual welfare became the vital link in the chain of family survival. The general assumption was that physical health and moral well-being were inextricably linked. However, any attempt actively to support motherhood invariably raised questions about the perceived notions of family power, most notably the role of fatherhood. Therefore, in developing social services it was believed that the least socially disruptive policy would be one that offered help only in cases of need and primarily on the basis of moral compliance. The contemporary debate that ensued, and that lasted in some shape or form well into the 1950s, centred on ascertaining the appropriate level of charitable aid in relation to state assistance both in terms of medical care and welfare assistance. This debate was accompanied on the ground by an ongoing denominational battle for control of the charity market.

Much of the historical focus has been on restrictive legislation introduced in the Free State to reinforce a conservative gender ideology and prevailing Roman Catholic creed.[73] From the compulsory retirement of married women primary teachers in 1934[74] to Article 41 of the 1937 constitution, historical writing on women's history has emphasised the degree to which Church and State sought to create a restrictive society that locked women into a specific role. While there is truth in this conclusion, there is a certain irony in the fact that most poor mothers would have been only too glad had the state kept its promise to 'endeavour to ensure that mothers shall not be obliged by economic necessity to engage in labour to the neglect of their duties in the home'.[75] As J. J. Lee astutely observed, Article 41 was 'honoured more in the breach than in the observance'.[76] Of more practical relevance to poor Irish mothers, battling in the filth and hunger of poverty, was the limited extent of positive support offered to them on the ground. In a letter to de Valera in 1937, Reginald Roper expressed the conviction that, without financial support, the rhetoric sanctifying domestic motherhood was worthless. He explained:

> Were there any guarantee that this should be interpreted to mean that a woman who chooses to bear a child should be sure of a state grant to secure her economic independence during the period in which she might be incapacitated from work, there might to something to be said in its favour.[77]

In reality, despite the constitutional promise, the lack of state aid left many mothers to seek work and, when that failed, assistance from an informal network of charities and voluntary organisations. Prior to the Second World War, maternity social services were initiated by voluntary workers and medical campaigners. As Patricia Harkin argued:

> The gap in social services in Ireland resulting from the reluctance to endorse state intervention was filled firstly by the subordination of the rights of individuals – mainly the right of women to work outside the home – to the duties inherent in the institution of the family, and secondly by a heavy reliance on the informal private sphere.[78]

Outdoor relief was available to certain 'hard cases' in the form of home assistance,[79] but this was frequently a humiliating process for the widowed or necessitous mother, and the relief was not sufficient to support herself or her family.[80] Institutional relief was available in the county home, which was, in effect, the old workhouse renamed after independence. The county home, however, only offered refuge to those who were not accommodated within the conventional family, such as the unmarried mother, the deserted wife, the insane and the elderly. In view of the parsimonious state welfare provisions, it is hardly surprising that many poor mothers relied on the 'private sphere' to supplement either the meagre family income or the paltry state assistance.

References had been made to the financial support of mothers much earlier than 1937, although they remained isolated until debates surrounding children's allowances in the early 1940s. The turbulent early years of independence raised many questions regarding not only the legitimacy of the state and the morality of the race, but also the urgent need to institute a better system of care for the citizens of the Irish Free State. In pursuit of this aim, a commission was established in 1925 to review the national situation and suggest remedial measures.[81] The commission considered public health and poor relief as part and parcel of the same problem, thereby providing a more inclusive framework for discussion. The commission was made up of parliamentary representatives, senators, charity workers and religious representatives. The Right Revd Monsignor Dunne, Archbishop Edward Byrne's vicar general, Sir Joseph Glynn of the Society of St Vincent de Paul, senators Sir John Keane and Jennifer Wyse-Power, and TDs Alderman Corish, Dr Thomas Hennessy and Major Myles were among the members appointed in March 1925. Given the array of social, political and religious representatives, it is interesting to note that the report dealt confidently with two issues that were to prove controversial in the following years: the role of charity in welfare and the sponsorship of motherhood.

Charitable organisations were engaged in delicately balancing financial assistance with moral and social supervision and encouragement. The *Report of the Commission on the Relief of the Sick and Destitute Poor* recommended that the

> relations between the Poor Law authorities and all charitable agencies should be that of cordial co-operation in achieving a common end. If Home Assistance is measured with reference to the help granted by the charitable societies we fear it will tend to place public and private agencies in antagonism. We suggest that the converse should hold good instead, and that it is the charitable societies who might measure their assistance having regard to the amount granted by the public authority, and that in this way a fair balance will be maintained and the poor will feel that the charitable societies are interested in them from motives other than the bringing of mere material relief.[82]

The commission declared it did not believe that it was desirable for private charities to administer public funds like home assistance, as it was a state subsidy.[83] This objection was based on the premise that charitable workers should foster a different relationship with those they assist than public administrators.[84] The mission to 'uplift' the poor in both a moral and a social sense was paramount, and it was feared that this unique role of charity would be jeopardised by 'conjoining' charity with public administration.[85] This was reiterated in the 1928 *Annual Report of the Society of St Vincent de Paul*: 'we do not regard as our proper function the continued relief of very large numbers of families suffering as a result of unemployment. Such a task can be effectively undertaken only by the public authorities whose action we can supplement but cannot undertake to replace.' The society was adamant that it would not 'suffer [it] to be turned into a relief organisation'.[86] In reality the Society of St Vincent de Paul served as a social net for many Irish families when employment and relief assistance failed them. The passing of the Poor Relief (Dublin) Act in 1931 was greeted with enthusiasm, as the society was relieved of the 'onus of providing against actual starvation for workless families'. With this responsibility passing to the public authorities, the society could 'select its cases in accordance with its rules and traditions'.[87] The various charitable organisations perceived state assistance as tantamount to secular aid, whereas they were concerned with the business of alms primarily in relation to moral and spiritual welfare. This conviction Revd McKenna articulated when he noted that the secret of success for Catholic charitable works was that they were 'done for supernatural motives'.[88] Hence, despite the best efforts of 'non-sectarian' or multidenominational organisations like the WNHA and St John Ambulance Brigade, who both worked tirelessly in the interests of public health and maternity welfare, the emphasis on moral supervision meant that welfare provision was often carved up according to creed. The support of motherhood was, therefore, a particularly contentious issue.

The *Report of the Commission on the Relief of the Sick and Destitute Poor*, respecting social mores, dealt with the Irish mother in terms of her marital status; the unmarried mother received separate attention as a complicated case requiring relief and reform, whereas the widowed mother simply deserved assistance. Lamenting the fact that Irish widows had to 'parade their poverty' at the office of public assistance, the report pointed out that many American states paid 'mother's pensions' to widowed or deserted wives.[89] Between 1911 and 1920, legislation had been passed in 40 US states providing payments for needy widows.[90] The commission declared itself in favour of the introduction of mother's pensions payable by the state in Ireland.[91] This open declaration in favour of state support for necessitous mothers was supported by many social and medical commentators who viewed married mothers left alone through bereavement or desertion as the responsibility of the state. The plight of widowed mothers was often highlighted and the 'abnormally high proportion of widows and of fatherless children' in the Free State was interpreted as another indication of the decline of the conventional family structure.[92] As long as welfare provision was restricted to poor widowed mothers, it provoked few objections because this approach to welfare carried with it an element of charity. Furthermore, it facilitated the protection of infant life and alleviated the most visible manifestations of poverty, while conforming to the contemporary assumption that women were essentially needy and dependent. Morality was a principal ingredient of the earliest welfare initiatives: the family was considered the cornerstone of moral living.[93] It was essential, therefore, that public or charitable assistance did not disrupt the balance of power within the family structure, and the way of avoiding this was through moral control.[94] Anne Coakley argued that gender inequality was the 'organising concept of the Irish social welfare system from its foundation'.[95] She attributes this underlying concept in Irish social welfare to 'an institutionalisation of the male breadwinner model of welfare provision for the family', noting that this relegated women to a 'dependent status'.[96] In this 'discourse of familism' Coakley concludes that a married woman's social rights were obtained via her husband. In the Irish context this 'discourse of familism' explains the degree of reluctance to destabilise through welfare the 'proper family structure': father as head of household and breadwinner, and mother as dependent carer.

Not surprisingly, therefore, the first welfare legislation directed at mothers concerned widowed mothers with dependent children. Widows were viewed as particularly needy cases and helping them was more straightforward, as the traditional provider, the father, was dead and therefore could not be undermined by any assistance that was offered to his family.[97] In 1933 the Committee of Inquiry into Widows' and Orphans' Pensions carried a clear moral agenda, noting, under the subtitle of 'moral conditions,' that

> seeing that the welfare of the children is a matter of prime importance, it is necessary to provide that the widowed mother to whom a pension is paid should be a fit and proper person to bring up her children. In our opinion, therefore, a scheme of non-contributory widowed mothers' pensions should provide that the pensioner must be of sober habits and of good moral character.[98]

The committee reflected the tendency to deal with infant health and protection through maternal welfare by clearly stating that the children were of 'prime importance'. On the grounds that fifty-five laws in other countries provided for payment of widows' pensions only to widows with dependent children, the pensions committee decided that a widow should only qualify as necessitous on the basis of her motherhood, and only as long as she had children under the age of sixteen years. Furthermore, it was considered legitimate that the state should concern itself with the moral character of a mother if her husband was dead, the implication being that assistance was judged on moral merit and the husband was usually the judge of his wife's character.[99] In the absence of the husband, the intervention of the state was legitimated by a clear moral agenda. The idea of moral qualifications was largely drawn from similar legislation in Great Britain, America and New Zealand where the view of the mother as 'trustee of the State' was often given even greater weight than in Ireland.[100] Significantly, the Fianna Fáil government did not in fact adopt the moral clause.[101]

Susan Pedersen astutely observed that 'policies were often based on normative rather than actual patterns of familial dependence'.[102] In the case of Irish widows the moral assumptions of the day informed the policy-making process. Consequently, a widowed mother with an illegitimate child did not qualify under the Widows' and Orphans' Pensions Act of 1935.[103] The 1935 act was divided into two schemes: a contributory pension and a non-contributory pension.[104] The former was to cover those widows whose husbands had paid sufficient insurance contributions, and this class of widow was entitled to a pension whether or not she had dependent children. As Luke Duffy, the Labour party secretary noted, 'Primarily, non-contributory pensions are for the benefit of the children rather than the widow.'[105] Thus the non-contributory pension, aimed at those widows not covered by the contributory scheme (largely the poorer widows) was only paid to widows with at least one dependent child. If the widow's child was born after the husband's death she did not qualify and once an only child (or the last dependent child) turned fourteen the widow's pension was cut off if she was under sixty years of age. This non-contributory pension was also stringently means-tested. The mother who had reared her children and 'devoted herself to home-making' but whose children were over fourteen at the time of her bereavement was expected, if not eligible for a contributory pension, to enter the work-force. The difficulties this might pose after decades of domesticity (however frugal) were simply not acknowledged and the society and state that valued and 'imposed' this role did not honour it in the legislation introduced to cater for widows.[106] In truth, just as with public health policy, welfare policy focused on the child rather than the mother. The 1935 Widows' and Orphans' Pensions Act respected the Irish cultural interpretation of family dynamics. However, it failed to enshrine in welfare legislation, as it had done and would do in industrial law, the publicly valued notion of female domesticity, at least for the poor widow.

In the case of necessitous widowed mothers it was generally accepted, without controversy, that local charity should not bear the burden 'which should be equally poised on the shoulders of all members of the State'.[107] In every other respect, maternal welfare was dogged by anxiety regarding the role of charity and religion. The relationship between charity and public assistance became increasingly complex and political as the fears of state control increased.[108] In response to the modern world, the Catholic Church sought, through Catholic Action,[109] to 'counteract by suitable measures in harmony with the teachings of the church, the poverty, insecurity and material misery of the labouring populations'.[110] Since the nineteenth century the Irish Catholic Church had laid claims 'to prerogatives which, in modern Europe, are normally reserved to the State alone'.[111] The Catholic Church was wary of any attempt to alter the landscape of charitable assistance either from non-Catholic voluntary bodies or by increased state interference, fearing that this might lead to the evils of secularism or socialism.[112] In fact, Eamonn Dunne argued that Catholic social action intentionally helped to limit the 'ground available for revolutionary mobilisation' in Dublin.[113]

The Catholic Church's voice was certainly foremost in the cry for 'national' restoration, as it had a vested interest in how Ireland, as a 'free state', would negotiate power between religious and lay leaders. This balance between Church and State was to form the framework for much of the social and political debate on how Ireland would provide for its people. The fear that the state could outgrow its remit and crush individual liberty and threaten spirituality was heightened by developments in Europe, particularly during the 1930s. Hence, even though hindsight has proven that communism was 'never even a shadow-threat in Ireland', the Roman Catholic Church's warnings about state control were credible in an era of growing communism.[114] Furthermore, the Irish debate on the role of the state in civic life was understandably limited and influenced by the international debates on the subject. The dual threat of communism and socialism formed the backdrop for the discussion in most Western European states of the period, albeit more pertinent to some domestic realities than others. Had Ireland ignored the debate, it would no doubt have been accused of complacency and/or isolationism.[115] Moreover, the evidence of anticlericalism in many of the European states assailed by communism naturally struck a cord with the predominantly Roman Catholic Ireland.[116] A brief glance at the papal encyclicals of the period revealed that the Irish Church was in keeping with Roman preoccupation. From *Quadragesimo Anno* (15 May 1931) on the function of the state to *Divini Redemptoris* (28 March 1937) on atheistic communism, each of the papal encyclicals of the period addressed in some way the role and potential of the state.[117] The latter specifically identified motherhood as the testing-ground, noting that communism was 'characterised by the rejection of any link that binds woman to the family and the home, and her emancipation is proclaimed as a basic principle ... The care of the home and children then devolves upon the collectivity.'[118]

Apart from genuinely desiring to protect Irish society from the ravages of an 'octopus' state, the Roman Catholic Church was also ensuring its essential role in the future of the country. The Jesuit priest Fr. Edward Cahill, whom Dermot Keogh described as the 'founder of Catholic Action in Ireland and the scourge of freemasonry',[119] explained,

> rulers are bound [so] to adjust the laws regulating public morality, family life, property rights, finance, industry, income, etc., and so to regulate the administration of these laws that each and all of the subjects may have a fair opportunity of securing temporal happiness, viz., the due development of their physical, intellectual, and moral faculties.[120]

However, he subsequently pointed out that the less the state intervened in the domain of charity the better.[121] By 1933 the future Bishop of Cork, Revd Cornelius Lucey,[122] was warning that the nation was 'beginning to look too much to the state as a universal provider, a sort of never-failing Aunt in whose hands we may safely leave, at least, the future. That is wrong.'[123]

Michael Peillon observed that religions 'prosper as long as they are seen to accomplish tasks felt as essential to the community, but decline as soon as their functions are perceived as inessential'.[124] It is too simplistic to suggest that the Irish Catholic church was motivated only by a desire to survive. However, it was certainly true that for many contemporaries the survival of the Roman Catholic Church and the well-being of the nation were perceived as one and the same. There was a very real fear that the era of the state would spell the end of the Church, and there was also a general belief that a successful society was one that managed to strike an 'appropriate' balance between the two. It was the definition of 'appropriate' that would cause general anxiety and many future problems. The landscape of welfarism in Ireland was marked by religious protectionism and antagonism but this was also crucially mixed with a distrust and fear of the potential of the state and of modernity. It was believed that whoever controlled welfare, or at least whoever influenced welfare policy, controlled Ireland's moral and spiritual future. In this respect, Catholicism, owing as much to its preponderance as to its war strategy, was dominant by the mid–1940s, but the previous decades were crucial.

Poor Irish mothers: active agents or charity cases?

The nineteenth-century legacy of the fear of proselytism lent itself comfortably to the growing conviction that the moral integrity of the country depended on the Catholic charities outwitting their Protestant or 'non-sectarian' contenders. The tales of famine 'soupers' still abounded in early twentieth-century Ireland,[125] and the belief that Protestant or 'non-sectarian' charities were only interested in helping Catholics in order to convert them was a potent motivation for the creation of equivalent Catholic charities.[126] As Revd McKenna argued, the onus was on Catholics to 'checkmate' Protestants with 'designs' on the Catholic poor.[127] In 1929 the Bishop of Galway, Dr O'Doherty, was not alone in his belief that while 'souperism' had been eradicated from Galway it was still at large in Dublin. In the slums of Dublin, he warned, '[T]here are soul-snatchers who descend upon the homes of poverty and prowl around hospitals'.[128] Indeed, the handbook of Dublin charities, published in 1902, bears witness to the degree of religious segregation, recording a number of charities providing denominationally based support for everything from the relief of widows to institutional care for 'fallen women'.[129] So strong was the nineteenth-century legacy of sectarian assistance that those organisations which did not subscribe to denominational ethics made this clear in the handbook, such as the Police-Aided Children's Clothing Society, which noted that it was run on 'strictly non-sectarian lines'.[130]

A conspicuous feature of the voluntary assistance landscape in the early twentieth century was the lack of Roman Catholic initiatives in the area of

maternal welfare. While the religious communities of women were promi-
nently represented in the institutional care of women and children, there
was remarkably little provided in terms of support for mothers within the
home structure.[131] Specifically, Roman Catholic relief tended to operate only
when the legitimate family structure had failed as a result of illegitimacy,
prostitution, infirmity or death. An anxiety that Protestants were excelling
in the Catholic charity vacuum began to emerge by the 1920s:

> It has been said that Protestants in Ireland do more social work than Catholics
> … We have recourse to the poor excuse that those who do such work among
> us become priests or nuns. Certainly Irish Catholic layfolk leave charitable
> work for the most part to religious, and think that they have done enough
> when they have supplied the necessary funds [sic].[132]

The question of Roman Catholic involvement in the new era of social
services was an issue that Revd McKenna took on as his own, defining a
new form of charity – 'social charity' or social work – which aimed at encouraging the Catholic laity to practice charity rather than merely donating
money.[133] For him, the Catholics were failing to exercise 'constructive' charity, providing an opportunity for unscrupulous Protestants:

> We have the Vincent de Paul Society … We have some ladies who visit the sick
> … We have raffles or bazaars in which charity is copiously watered with frivolity
> and amusement. We have, I say, a certain amount of charitable personal work
> done by lay folk … but of the more constructive forms of charitable endeavour,
> of Catholic social work properly so called, there is little, very little indeed, in
> Catholic Ireland.[134]

Joseph Robins attributed the lack of Catholic initiative to a long-standing
distrust of the aims of certain societies with regard to religious conversion.[135]
While there is little doubt that this fear of proselytism existed, it appears
that this concern acted as a spur rather than an inhibitor.[136] Catholic
organisations were guided by the belief that charity should respect religious
conviction, but also by a desire to protect the faithful from the temptation
of assistance offered by other Protestant or non-sectarian organisations.[137]
The Catholic Protection and Rescue Society,[138] the Legion of Mary[139] and
the Saint Patrick's Guild[140] targeted families and children threatened by
proselytism. 'Checkmating' Protestant charity was, if not their raison d'être,
a crucial driving force.

However, there is another important feature of the sectarian dimension
of charitable work in Ireland. The fear of proselytism offered the poor something to bargain with: their souls. There is ample evidence that poor mothers were well aware of the Catholic horror of proselytisers threatening to
steal their children for the Protestant faith. Neither the fear nor the exploitation of it was fanciful or ridiculous: souls were a very serious, long-term
business. The contemporary understanding was that charity and faith were
two sides of the same spiritual coin; to divide them would be to reduce
charity to mere financial assistance and the recipient to a beggar. The element

of religion, it was believed, lent the whole business dignity and purpose. Faith was hard to maintain if one lived in rat-infested slums but essential if one wanted bread and boots. It was a system that poor Irish mothers understood; religion was the only currency most of them had with which to bargain. [141]

Ascertaining the genuine religious conviction of Irish Catholic mothers is impossible and unnecessary. Religious obedience is a complicated phenomenon and much has been written about the Irish brand of Catholicism.[142] It is possible both to believe and manipulate as it is to love and do the same. Undoubtedly, many Dublin mothers believed whole-heartedly in their religion, but evidently many also believed that they were better Catholics alive than dead. As Mrs C. of Talbot Place candidly explained to Archbishop Byrne in 1937, 'I can see now that Religion is only a Cloke [sic] what matters which side your on onse [sic] you have enough to eat.'[143] This admission concluded a begging letter in which the mother of six children warned the Archbishop that Protestants had offered to clothe and educate her brood. Whether or not she relied on the Roman Catholic Church for 'moral power' in the home, the Irish mother frequently relied on her religion for financial support.[144]

All the domestic advice and mothering skills were wasted as long as mothers were not given the means of implementation. 'Good mothering' and slum living were not comfortable bedfellows. As the doctor in charge of the School Medical Service for Dublin City noted in 1938, 'While whole families continue to be housed in one-roomed dwellings, even to reside in basements, the water supply one tap and sink in the tenement yard, or landing, it is, perhaps fantastic to consider even the question of cleanliness.'[145] In order to supplement the family income, it was more often than not the mother who did the begging: it was the negotiation of poverty that made good mothering a reality. This maternal attribute was not unique to Ireland, as Porter pointed out: 'Poor wives are often the main family agents who sought relief either from the state or private charity in times of economic stress ... For wives and mothers, managing access of relief was an extension of managing the household economy.'[146] Susan Pedersen described the mother as 'the nexus of the complex system of negotiations and obligations by which working class families survived'.[147] Similarly, in Ireland it was the mother who had the most contact with various charity organisations; she was the crucial link between family and care agencies. Consequently, when those care agencies were not sufficient, adequate or directly available to her family, it was she who sought other alternatives.

While there is anecdotal evidence and a growing body of oral history that can testify to the efforts that these women made for their families, there are few contemporary sources which allow the mothers themselves to tell their tale.[148] Given the weight of shame attached to seeking assistance beyond the remit of the extended family, a prized source of support in working-class communities, help sought elsewhere was rarely spoken of.

Consequently, the thousands of letters written to the Archbishop of Dublin, Dr Byrne, between 1921 and 1939, are an exceptionally valuable source as they bear witness not merely to the level of need in the country but to the relationship many mothers had with their society and church.[149] The majority of these letters, known as 'charity cases', were penned by desperate mothers. These women called from the cracks of society; their life was about survival.

Catholic social teaching discouraged the long-term subsidisation of families, as it was believed that this policy would stymie the dynamism of the family network. This was to become a central argument against state aid. Owing to the short-term policy of most relief agencies, mothers were accustomed to shopping for assistance, and the Archbishop was usually the last port of call. The 'charity case' letters were, in fact, specifically 'cases with which alone it is possible for the Archbishop to deal', and in order to ensure compliance with this rule each letter had to be accompanied by a reference from a parish priest.[150]

There were approximately 3,500 letters written to the Archbishop during his tenure, almost 2,500 of which were sent between 1932 and 1939.[151] The majority of mothers who wrote to the Archbishop did not place their case in a political context; instead their accounts were usually highly personalised and extremely articulate. These women were aware that their greatest hold on the Church was their motherhood: Mrs F. explained, when she wrote for the second time, that she had been told by her parish priest that she would need a house full of children before she would receive any charity.[152] While she complained that two starving people should be enough to engender charity, the reality was that without children she fell way down a long list of needy cases. All of these women were surrounded by cases as bad, if not worse, than their own. Consequently, they needed to pitch their case in the context of their children's welfare. They usually began by telling the Archbishop how many starving souls they had produced. Mrs Q. of Dorset St. was a classic example:

> I write these few lines to ask you if you can for God Sake give me a little help as I have four young children starving with the hunger my husband is out of work for the past 5 months and I am expecting to be confined on my fifth baby any day this week as I appeal, to you Father for God Sake for a little help and I shall pray for your intentions if you can grant me this little favour trusting you will do something in your power for me [sic].[153]

The justification for their entreaties was motherhood: 'I the respective mother take this liberty of tresspassing [sic] on your valuable time', a mother from Gardiner St. began.[154] Another mother from Temple St. assured the Archbishop that she had 'always been a good mother'[155] and in 1930 a pregnant mother of five concluded, 'I place myself and my family on your mercy.'[156] Indeed, the parish priests who vetted the letters clearly believed that a 'deserving mother' was a worthy recipient of charity and repeatedly described the women in terms of their sense of maternal responsibility. The 'deserving mother' was one who protected her children's religious upbringing and made sure that they attended school. She displayed no 'worldly' characteristics or undue wilfulness. Mrs P. of Ringsend, who had been in receipt of 2s. 6d. from the Society of St Vincent de Paul up until three months prior to writing, was described as 'very deserving. The children are sent to school regularly and are very well educated.'[157] Mrs McD., a widowed mother of four, was given £5 in 1924 when her parish priest confirmed that she was 'an exceptionally good woman and mother',[158] as was Mrs R. Although married to a Protestant, she made sure he 'never interfered with the childrens [sic] training'. The priest commented, 'there is a slight *suppressio veri* in her not mentioning her husband's intemperance', but he concluded 'she has done her best and succeeded in looking after her children and provided them with an admirable education'.[159]

The parish priest could also act as censor, indicating not only the power of the priest as 'moral policeman', but also the concerns and priorities of the Catholic Church.[160] For example, though it was admitted that Mrs G. was in 'distress', she was considered 'self-willed in regard to the two children she has'.[161] What is meant by 'self-willed' is not clear. It was probably one of two things: either the mother was not willing to put her children in to care until she got back on her feet, or she had her own ideas regarding their religious instruction. Mrs G. of Ranelagh committed the gravest sin of all for a mother by being 'worldly'. The parish priest went into great detail in order to explain her worldly activities: 'She goes to the pictures on an average of six times a week, the seventh evening being devoted to cards. She has not been to the sacraments for at least three years and she sends her children to a Protestant school.'[162]

These women often expressed a sense of abandonment and frustration; as one woman put it, they were left in the 'lost corner'.[163] Consequently, the tone of these letters vacillated from the obsequious to the aggressive, but sheer need was the thread that linked most of the writers. The mothers were quite frank in articulating the burden of motherhood. Mrs D., a mother of five, in 1932 wrote, 'I my self is only after getting out of a very sick bed after child birth which I am glad to say is gone to god *above* [sic].'[164] Another mother of five wrote in 1930, 'my confinement to take place shortly and this is a constant worry'.[165] The toll of the large family was apparent in letter after letter, and while some women undoubtedly used their maternity to engender pathos they were merely exploiting the system in which they were trapped.

If pathos was not seductive enough, veiled or explicit threats of conversion were common and effective.[166] The parish priest of Drumcondra, in a letter in 1931, described the B. family as 'rather Black in their duty as Catholics, but perhaps an act of clemency might awaken them to their responsibilities in this matter'.[167] Mothers appeared to be aware of this priestly conviction and time and again implied or threatened conversion to the 'black faith'.[168]

Mrs B. of Kimmage was by no means atypical when she wrote in 1935:

> I owe rent and has received a writ for the court my children are like little
> Pagans don't know what School or Chapel is owing to them been barefooted
> and naked in Clothes … It is very hard to look at your own Children Half
> Starved and naked and to know that in such a distress Case your own Religion
> could help … Should I take myself and Family to another Religion [sic]?[169]

Mrs C. of Kimmage, who wrote in 1938, employed almost exactly the same
tone, describing herself as a 'sorrowful mother'. She made no bones about
her intention to get help regardless of the donor's denomination:

> Me and my six children are in a desperate state of distress and were noticed
> to quit our home we are to be Summoned to court for non payment of rent.
> This is no great fault of myself or my husband. If something is not done for us
> I will have to seek help from some other religion. For Gods his holy mothers
> Sake help us [sic].[170]

There were countless pleas for help framed in this way, varying in tone
but not in message: mothers wanted to be good Catholics but the welfare of
their children came first. As one mother put it, 'we are trying to bring up
our children in the best way we can in the Catholic religion, as I don't wish
to reply to any other religion, like others for help [sic]'.[171] Mothering tested
not just these women's negotiating skills but their spiritual reserve. Due to
their poverty they were locked into a paradoxical relationship with their
religion; they relied on their religious conviction for spiritual and financial
support but, as mothers, they had to be willing to sacrifice their religion for
the welfare of their children. 'I love my Catholic religion,' Mrs J., a widowed
mother of three, wrote in 1935 begging for assistance and pleading to the
Archbishop, 'don't drive me to the Church of England with my 3 orphans.'[172]
In working-class Ireland, 'good mothering' required religious tenacity and
social ingenuity: when children were ill-clad and underfed, principles offered cold comfort.

Not surprisingly in this climate, mixed marriages elicited considerable
attention. Catholic women who married Protestants were rarely denied assistance, as there was always the implicit, if not explicit, threat of the Protestant relatives who were only too willing to provide for the children. The
clearest indication of how seriously these cases were taken is the amount of
money paid out by the Archbishop. The average mother from a working-
class area could expect to receive, if proved a *bona fide* case, anything from
£1 to £5. However, the mother married to a Protestant whose children were
considered at risk could receive anything from £6 to £30. Mrs C., who was
married to a convert, and was a mother of six, received £6 in 1935 and was
given ongoing support.[173] In 1923, Fr. Farrell wrote on behalf of Mrs B.,
who was the mother of six and married to a Protestant. The priest explained,

> The mother is not of the same social standing as her deceased husband was,
> and is a weak Catholic. Though two children are in the Sacred Heart home

and two are in Lakelands Industrial School she had made arrangements to take them out, to allow them to be put into a Protestant school on doing which she would be helped financially.[174]

Fr. Farrell put the case convincingly: Mrs B. was sent £30 in order to continue her husband's business. There was a system, however, in place to weed out those who were considered to be 'touchers' or professional beggars. Mrs W. was denied help on the grounds that she frequently used her marriage to a 'convert' to elicit financial assistance, and she had been given £5 by the Archbishop on a previous occasion.[175]

The fear of proselytism exposed more than religious bigotry; it revealed the intimate connection between charity and religion and the understanding that desperation was fertile ground for religious manipulation. This fear also formed part of the general concern regarding modernity and the deconstruction of faith and family. However, in these women's otherwise empty hands, proselytism became a bargaining tool. They knew the only thing more precious than their souls was the souls of their children. They were bartering souls for sustenance and they had correctly judged the assistance market. Both women's letters and the priests' responses revealed all the anxieties in the face of uncertainty and a rapidly changing world: proselytism, religious disobedience, immorality, incest and family breakdown. The confessional nature of the relationship between the mother and her Church is recorded with pathos, anger, exasperation and honesty.

The sheer volume of correspondence indicated that many cases of want were not catered for by existing organisations. The charity case letters also revealed the pressing need for someone to take decisive action and responsibility for maternal and child welfare. In 1938, a Mrs M. D. from Dublin wrote to the Archbishop, 'I have always recognised that we owe to both church and state. Is there no reciprocal duty.'[176] A mother of seven, Mrs D. had honoured her part of the bargain as a prolific mother, but received no active Church or State support in return. It was noted also by contemporaries in the medical profession that the Roman Catholic Church was virtually unrepresented in maternity and child welfare projects in the city, in stark contrast to their involvement in so many other areas.[177] Indeed, there were murmurs within the Dublin diocese itself. As a result, several members of the flock suggested organising a Catholic congress to co-ordinate and strengthen Catholic action in society.[178] They were told by Dr Byrne's secretary, 'Archbishop not consulted about Catholic Congress and does not want to know anything about it considers such congresses dangerous [sic]'.[179]

Conclusion

The sponsorship of motherhood was to present an ongoing challenge to the Irish state and society. In particular, it disturbed the long-standing equilibrium between Church and State in the provision of assistance to the poor. Independence failed to solve the obdurate problem of poverty, nor did it bring sweeping changes to maternity welfare. On the contrary, the Irish Free State relied almost completely on the public health foundations laid by an 'alien administration' in the nineteenth century and on the voluntary energies of the Protestant community. In fact, independence appeared only to exacerbate sectarian tensions, making interdenominational co-operation even more difficult than before. The intimate association between physical and spiritual welfare meant that the debate concerning maternal welfare inevitably became embroiled in cultural preoccupations regarding the sanctity of the family and religious anxieties with respect to sectarian manipulation and state power.

Notes

1 Report of the Lady Sanitary Officer, Mrs M. O'Brien, in C. A. Cameron, *Report upon the State of Public Health in the City of Dublin for the year 1916* (Dublin, 1917), pp. 88–90.

2 Porter, *Health, Civilization and the State*, p.99; L. Hall, *Sex, Gender and Social Change in Britain since 1880* (London, 2000), pp. 65–81 and 116–32.

3 For example, see Bock and Thane (eds), *Maternity and Gender Policies*; M. S. Quine, *Population Politics in Twentieth-Century Europe: Fascist Dictatorships and Liberal Democracies* (London, 1996); J. R. Gillis, A. L. Tilly, and D. Levine, *The European Experience of Declining Fertility, 1850–1970: A Quiet Revolution* (Oxford, 1992).

4 Prunty, *Dublin Slums*, pp. 234–73.

5 In this study, poor mothers are defined as those who qualified for public assistance and free maternity care under the Medical Charities Act, and/or received assistance regularly from charitable organisations such as the Society of the St Vincent de Paul. Many families dipped in and out of the poverty trap, relying on public assistance or charity during particularly lean periods but often managing to be self-sufficient during periods of employment etc. Often a bereavement, abandonment or eviction could result in a previously self-sufficient family needing assistance and qualifying as poor for the purposes of public assistance or charity.

6 E. Coey Bigger, *Welfare of Mothers and Children*, p. 46.

7 The phrase enlightenment was repeatedly used in public health reports when referring to the need to educate mothers regarding infant health and the dangers of handywomen. See, for example, *Annual Reports of the Department of Local Government and Public Health, 1922–5*, p. 34; *Ibid., 1927–8*, p. 40.

8 Murphy-Lawless, *Reading Birth and Death*, pp. 6–7.

9 WNHA of Ireland, *The Golden Jubilee*, p. 6. Skocpol noted a similar emphasis on 'educated motherhood' emerging in 1920s America. See T. Skocpol, *Protecting Soldiers and Mothers: The Political Origins of Social Policy in the United States* (Boston, MA, 1992), p. 333; Cruze also observed a focus on 'maternal competence' in Britain during the same period. See S. Cruze, 'Women and the family', in Purvis (ed.), *Women's History in Britain, 1850–1945*, pp. 51–76, p.74.

10 WNHA, *The Golden Jubilee*, p. 7.

11 M. Anderson, *Approaches to the History of the Western Family 1500–1914* (London, 1980), p. 59.

12 John Burns, President of the Local Government Board, cited in M. Pember Reeves, *Round About a Pound a Week* (London, 1979, 1st edition 1939), p. x.

13 Lewis, *The Politics of Motherhood*, p. 18.

14 Daly, *Dublin*, p. 265.

15 *Annual Report of the Department of Local Government and Public Health, 1922–5*, p. 34.

16 Reddin, 'The maternity and child welfare clinic', p. 218.

17 Little mothers referred to elder daughters who looked after younger siblings when the mother worked or upon her death. This practice was observed in Dublin City by many voluntary workers and health officials. See K. Kearns, *Dublin's Lost Heroines: Mammies and Grannies in a Vanished City* (Dublin, 2004), pp. 126–37. 'Wee mummies' was the term used in Belfast. See J. Hamill, 'Childcare arrangements within the Belfast linen industry', in Whelan (ed.), *Women and Paid Work in Ireland*, p. 124.

18 Revd L. McKenna, *The Church and Social Work* (Dublin, 1928), p. 117.

19 G. J. Tierney, 'Maternal mortality', *IJMSc.*, 82 (Oct. 1930), 603.

20 'Annual report of the Rotunda', *IJMSc.*, 88 (Aug. 1933), 329.

21 B. Solomons, *One Doctor in His Time* (London, 1956), p. 54.

22 *Annual Report of the Department of Local Government and Public Health, 1931–2*, p. 54.

23 Anon., 'The education of the public', *JIFSMU*, 3:14 (Aug. 1938), 33; Farmar noted that the belief that lice came from water was held by the public and certain professionals. T. Farmar, *Patients, Potions and Physicians: A Social History of Medicine in Ireland* (Dublin, 2004), p. 141.

24 Department of Local Government and Public Health, *Report of the Conference on Public Health and Social Services, 1930* (Dublin, 1930), p. 15.

25 *Ibid.*, p. 14.

26 E. Coey Bigger, *Welfare of Mothers and Children*, p. 45.

27 Women who wrote begging letters to Archbishop Byrne between 1921 and 1940 frequently referred to their 'condition' as a 'delicate' one or described themselves as waiting or expecting a child. Ethna McCarthy noted in 1948 that the superstition that washing weakened the constitution was still prevalent among Irish mothers, 'Public health problems created by louse infestation', *IJMSc.*, 266 (Feb. 1948), 67; Clear noted the same reluctance on the part of mothers to engage in conversations regarding the details of pregnancy in Clear, *Women of the House*, p. 97.

28 Harrison, 'Women and health', p. 170.

29 For a photograph of mothers attending a health talk at the Carnegie Welfare Centre, Lord Edward Street, Dublin, see Russell, *Report on the State of Public Health in the City of Dublin for the Year 1938* (Dublin, 1939), p. 103.

30 Betty Hilliard noted that among the women she interviewed regarding their experiences of motherhood during the 1950s and 1960s the most 'striking feature of the sexual dimensions of respondents' lives was the lack of any knowledge regarding sex and reproduction which they brought to their marriages'. See B. Hilliard, 'Motherhood, sexuality and the Catholic church', in Kennedy (ed.), *Motherhood in Ireland*, pp. 140–1.

31 *Ibid.*

32 Lewis, *The Politics of Motherhood*, pp. 69, 89. In France, breastfeeding in the late nineteenth and early twentieth centuries was an indication of the depth of maternal love. See R. Fuchs, 'Morality and poverty', 301.

33 Jones, 'Eugenics in Ireland', pp. 81–95; NAI, Dept. Taoiseach, S9684a. MacEntee made it clear that any intervention in the welfare of mothers would not be motivated by a desire to increase the birth rate, but rather to reduce the death rate of

infants.

34 WNHA, *Infantile Mortality and Infant Milk Depots* (Dublin, 1908), p. 5.

35 *Ibid.*, p. 8.

36 Breastfeeding, through the infant imbibing the mother's immune system, helped to protect the infant from infection. See Loudon, *Death in Childbirth*, p. 486.

37 *Ibid.*

38 The Milk Commission in 1911 noted the poor quality of Dublin's milk. The Milk and Dairies Act (1936) regulated the quality of milk by stipulating that milk producers had to comply with certain sanitary standards. However, problems persisted and in March 1945 a tribunal of inquiry into the supply of milk to Dublin was established. It is interesting to note that, in keeping with the traditions laid down by the WNHA, the Irish Housewives' Association made the quality of milk a key issue when lobbying for social improvements and was crucial in the foundation of the Milk Tribunal. Members also presented themselves as key witnesses. See H. Tweedy, *A Link in the Chain: The Story of the Irish Housewives Association 1942–1992* (Dublin, 1992).

39 Carnegie United Kingdom Trust, *Report on the Physical Welfare of Mothers and Children*, p. 28.

40 The Infant Aid Society was a voluntary organisation, originally named the Dublin Committee for the Prevention of Infantile Mortality, which was established in 1910 'to protect and preserve Infant Life, in the very poorest quarters'. See Cameron, *Report Upon the State of Public Health in the City of Dublin for the year 1915*, p. 198.

41 'Report of the Department of Local Government and Public Health', *JIFSMU*, 8:44 (Feb. 1941), 19.

42 *Annual Report of the Department of Local Government and Public Health, 1938–9*, p. 37.

43 *Ibid., 1937–8*, p. 56.

44 For a photograph of a midday meal at the St John Ambulance Brigade kitchen in Merrion Square, see Russell, *Report on the State of Public Health in the City of Dublin for the Year 1938*, p. 87.

45 *St John Ambulance Brigade: Official Handbook of the St John Ambulance Brigade, 1950* (Dublin, 1951), p. 17.

46 B. S. Anderson and J. P. Zinsser, *A History of Their Own. Women in Europe from Prehistory to the Present, Volume 2* (New York, 1988), p. 241; K. C. Kearns, *Dublin Tenement Life: An Oral History* (Dublin, 1994), p. 175.

47 *St John Ambulance Brigade: Official Handbook of the St John Ambulance Brigade, 1950*, p. 17. The first Brigade maternity kitchen was in Merrion Square, Dublin.

48 T. W. T. Dillon, 'The social services in Éire', *Studies*, 34 (Sept. 1945), 331.

49 Pember Reeves, *Round About a Pound A Week*, p. 156.

50 Coakley notes that recent research reveals that mothers still 'police the family food supply'. See A. Coakley, 'Mothers and poverty in Kennedy, *Motherhood in Ireland*,' p. 215.

51 M. Spring Rice, *Working-Class Wives: Their Health and Conditions* (London, 1981, 1st edition, 1939), p. 157.

52 C. A. Cameron, *How the Poor Live* (Dublin, 1904), p. 11.

53 Report of the Lady Sanitary Officer, Mrs M. Lucas, in Cameron, *Report upon the State of Public Health in the City of Dublin for the year 1916*, p. 91.

54 NAI, Dept. Health, M34/7, vol. 2.

55 Macnicol noted that the 'newer knowledge of nutrition' had gained such attention that in 1933 there were as many as 5,000 papers on the subject in the world's literature. See J. Macnicol, *The Movement for Family Allowances, 1918–1945: A Study in Social Policy Development* (London, 1980), p. 46. See, for example, E.

Mellanby, 'Nutrition and childbearing', *The Lancet,* 2 (1933), 1131–7.

56 M. J. Russell, *Report on the State of Public Health in the City of Dublin for the Year 1938* (Dublin, 1939), p. 67.

57 *Ibid.,* p. 68.

58 G. C. Dockerlay and W. R. Fearon, 'Ante-natal nutrition in Dublin: A preliminary survey', *IJMSc.,*128 (Aug. 1939), 80.

59 W. Fearon, 'The national problem of nutrition', *Studies,* 27: 105 (Mar. 1938), 17.

60 M. J. Russell, 'The health of Dublin', *JIFSMU,* 3:17 (Nov. 1938), 56–8.

61 M. J. Russell, 'The health of Dublin,' *JIFSMU,* 5: 29 (Nov. 1939), 54–6.

62 *Ibid.*

63 G. C. Dockerlay, 'Diet in pregnancy', *JMAÉ,* 12:70 (Apr. 1943), 39.

64 Cited in Russell, *Report on the State of Public Health in the City of Dublin for the Year 1938,* p. 88.

65 *Ibid.*

66 *Ibid.,* p. 23.

67 *Ibid.,* p. 26.

68 Anon., 'Comments on the foregoing article', *Studies,* 27:105 (Mar. 1938), 24.

69 *Ibid.,* p. 13.

70 *Ibid.*

71 McKenna, *The Church and Social Work,* p. 117.

72 For examples of this moral anxiety and fear regarding the family, see the *Report of the Commission on the Relief of the Sick and Destitute Poor, including the Insane Poor* (Dublin, 1927) and the *Report of the Committee on the Criminal Law Amendment Acts (1880–85) and Juvenile Prostitution* (unpub. 1931), NAI, Attorney General 2000/10/1235.

73 For an interesting appraisal of the focus of women's historical research, see L. Connolly, *The Women's Movement: From Revolution to Devolution* (New York, 2002), pp. 57–71.

74 NAI, Dept. Taoiseach, S7985a. This retirement policy only applied to women who married after the introduction of the act.

75 Government Publication, Bunreacht na hÉireann (Constitution of Ireland) 1937 (Dublin, 1997), p. 138.

76 J. J. Lee, *Ireland 1912–1985: Politics and Society* (Cambridge, 1989), p. 207.

77 Reginald Roper, Drayton Hse., Gordon St, WC1 London to de Valera, 23 May 1937, NAI, Dept. Taoiseach, S9880.

78 P. Harkin, '*La famille, fruit du passé, germe de l'avenir*: family policy in Ireland and Vichy France', MA, University College Dublin, 1991, pp. 30–1.

79 S. Ó Cinnéide, 'The development of the home assistance service', *Administration,* 17 (1969), 284–308.

80 *Report of the Commission on the Relief of the Sick and Destitute Poor, Including the Insane Poor* (Dublin, 1927), p. 56.

81 *Ibid*

82 *Ibid.,* p. 86.

83 Home assistance was paid to the neediest in society who were unable to work for reasons of disability, age or ill health. In 1932 there were 126,035 people in receipt of home assistance. See *Annual Report of the Department of Local Government and Public Health, 1932–3,* p. 125.

84 Powell noted that, from the beginning of social policy in Ireland, poverty was viewed as a social issue and charity as a means of regulation. See Powell, *The Politics of Irish Social Policy,* p. 1.

85 *Ibid.,* p. 59.

86 Society of St Vincent de Paul, *Annual Report of the Society of St Vincent de Paul* (Dublin, 1928), pp. 4–5.

87 Society of St Vincent de Paul, *Report of the Council of Ireland 1933*, p. 51.

88 McKenna, *The Church and Social Work*, p. 5.

89 Commission on the Relief of the Sick and Destitute Poor, *Report*, p. 57.

90 T. Skocpol, *Protecting Soldiers and Mothers*, p.10.

91 Commission on the Relief of the Sick and Destitute Poor, *Report*, p. 57.

92 J. Meenan, 'Some causes and consequences of the low Irish marriage rate', *JSSISI*, 86 (1932–3), 24.

93 Skocpol noted that similar moral criteria existed in most of the provisions for widows in the US. See Skocpol, *Protecting Soldiers and Mothers*, p. 32.

94 In Dublin, for example, all the charitable assistance for widows ran along religious lines: the Dill's Widows' Fund (Presbyterian widows), the Church of Ireland Widows' and Orphans' Society and the Dublin Hebrew Board of Guardians also dealt with widows' assistance. There was no specifically Catholic fund recorded, as Roman Catholic widows were either aided by the Society of St Vincent de Paul or survived purely on home assistance. Alternatively they surrendered themselves and their children, or were forcibly admitted, to institutional care.

95 Coakley, 'Mothers and poverty', p. 208.

96 *Ibid.*

97 Daly noted that the Widows' and Orphans' Pension Act upheld the social conventions of father as breadwinner and the wife as dependant. See M. E. Daly, 'The Irish family since the Famine', *Irish Journal of Feminist Studies,* 3:2 (Autumn, 1999), 11.

98 Committee of Inquiry into Widows' and Orphans' Pensions, *Committee of Inquiry into Widows' and Orphans' Pensions Reports,* 1933, p. 28. Note also that a lack of temperance was considered grounds for disqualification with regard to the Old Age Pension Act, 1908. See Powell, *The Politics of Irish Social Policy*, p. 138.

99 This social assumption underlined the response of the courts in relation to infanticide cases. Often judges would release women convicted of infanticide from prison or detention if they could provide a marriage certificate. They were released into the 'custody of their husbands'. See A. Guilbride, 'Infanticide: the crime of motherhood', in Kennedy (ed.), *Motherhood in Ireland*, p. 179.

100 Committee of Inquiry into Widows' and Orphans' Pensions, *Reports*, p. 129. Skocpol noted that few unmarried mothers benefited under the assistance schemes in the US. See Skocpol, *Protecting Soldiers and Mothers*, p. 467.

101 M. Cousins, *The Birth of Social Welfare in Ireland, 1922–1952* (Dublin, 2003), p. 77.

102 Pedersen, *Family Dependence, and the Origins of the Welfare State*, p. 10.

103 *Widows' and Orphans' Pensions Act 1935* (Dublin, 1936). This was based on a recommendation made by the committee of inquiry and was in keeping with poverty legislation of the nineteenth century. See Committee of Inquiry into Widows' and Orphans' Pensions, *Reports*, p. 27.

104 For a detailed explanation of the scheme, see *Widows' and Orphans' Pensions Act 1935* (Dublin, 1936) and Luke Duffy, *Pensions for Widows in Saorstát Éireann: A Popular Guide to the Widows' and Orphans' Pensions Act, 1935* (Dublin, 1936).

105 Duffy, *Pensions for Widows in Saorstát Éireann*, p. 21.

106 *Ibid.*, p. 5.

107 Dunne, *'Waiting The Verdict': Pensions or Pauperism: Necessitous Widows and Orphans in the Free State* (Dublin, *c.* 1930), p. 3.

108 See, for example, Cardinal O'Connell, *The Reasonable Limits of State Activity* (Dublin, 1920).

109 Catholic Action was a movement to encourage the involvement of the laity in the

propagating of social Catholicism. According to Eamonn Dunne, Catholic Action reached its 'zenith' during the inter-war pontificate of Pius XI. See E. Dunne, 'Action and reaction: Catholic lay organisations in Dublin in the 1920s and 1930s', *Archivium Hibernicum*, 48 (1994), 108. See also M. Hartigan, 'The Catholic laity of Dublin, 1914–1939, Ph.D., National University of Ireland, Maynooth, 1992.

110 Revd E. Cahill, *The Framework of a Christian State: An Introduction to Social Science* (Dublin, 1932) p. 250.

111 D. W. Miller, *Church, State and Nation in Ireland 1989–1921* (Dublin, 1973), p. 3.

112 Dunne, 'Action and reaction', 109.

113 *Ibid.*, p. 115.

114 B. Fallon, *An Age of Innocence: Irish Culture 1930–1960* (Dublin, 1998), p. 258.

115 *Ibid.*, p. 6.

116 P. Corish, *The Irish Catholic Experience: A Historical Survey* (Dublin, 1985), p. 241.

117 Fremantle, *The Papal Encyclicals*.

118 *Ibid.*, p. 255; *Quadragismo Anno* was issued in 1931 to celebrate the fortieth anniversary of *Rerum Novarum* and excited much interest in Ireland in social Catholicism. *Rerum Novarum* laid, according to O'Leary, the foundation of the modern social teaching of the Roman Catholic Church. See D. O'Leary, *Vocationalism and Social Catholicism in Twentieth-Century Ireland* (Dublin, 2000), pp. 5–20.

119 Keogh, *The Vatican, the Bishops*, p. 208.

120 E. Cahill, 'The social bond: a study in Christian sociology', *IER*, 26 (1925), 58.

121 E. Cahill, 'The social bond: a study in Christian sociology', *IER*, 27 (1926), 295.

122 Revd Cornelius Lucey (1902–82) was appointed coadjutor bishop of Cork with right of succession on 14 November 1950. He succeeded to the see on 24 August 1952. He was named the apostolic administrator of Ross 20 February 1954 and became its bishop in April 1958. See Canning, *Bishops of Ireland,* pp. 255–8.

123 Revd Lucey, 'On a recent study in social science', *IER*, 41 (1933), 375.

124 M. Peillon, *Contemporary Irish Society: An Introduction* (Dublin, 1982), p. 90.

125 Souperism referred to the soup kitchens run during the famine by Protestant philanthropic organisations. It was believed that Catholics who accepted soup did so in return for conversion to the Protestant faith. Several letters in the Charity Case boxes (Byrne's Papers, DDA) refer to neighbours as 'soupers', meaning that they had accepted charity in exchange for converting to Protestantism.

126 Dunne, 'Action and reaction', p. 110.

127 Revd MacKenna, *An Irish Catholic Women's League* (Dublin, 1917), p. 15.

128 Catholic Protection and Rescue Society, *16th Report of Catholic Protection and Rescue Society 1929* (Dublin, n.d.) p. 3.

129 Williams, *Dublin Charities*.

130 *Ibid.*, p. 35; See also M. Preston, *Charitable Words: Women, Philanthropy, and the Language of Charity in Nineteenth-Century Dublin* (Westport, CT, 2004), pp. 67–100.

131 In Dublin alone there was the St Mary's Asylum and Reformatory, High Park Convent, Drumcondra (1833) run by the Srs of Our Lady of Charity and Refuge; St Mary's Asylum for Female Penitents, Donnybrook (1798) run by the Srs of Charity; St Mary's Magdalens Asylum, 104 Gloucester St, (1822) run by the Srs of Mercy and St Patrick's, Crofton Rd., Kingstown (1798) also in the hands of the Srs of Mercy.

132 Revd McKenna, *The Church and Social Work*, p. 111.

133 *Ibid.*, p. 121.

134 *Ibid.*

135 J. Robins, *The Lost Children: A Study of Charity Children in Ireland 1700–1900* (Dublin,

1980), p. 308; Prunty, *Dublin Slums*, p. 9.

136 Prunty, *Dublin Slums*, p. 11.

137 See, for example, *Irish Catholic Directory and Almanac for 1920* (Dublin 1920).

138 The Catholic Protection and Rescue Society of Ireland was founded in 1913 and based in South Anne St., Dublin. The aim of the organisation was to protect the Catholic poor against the evils of proselytism and to deal with cases of unmarried mothers and their children.

139 The Legion of Mary was founded by Frank Duff in September 1921 and based in North Brunswick St., Dublin. The aim of the organisation was to enkindle the apostolic spirit in the laity. Although the legion was made up primarily of female workers, Duff was generally considered the leader until his death in 1980. The legion opened a hostel, the Sancta Maria, for the reformation of prostitutes in 1922, and by 1930 they had opened another hostel, Regina Coeli, for unmarried mothers. See L. Ó Broin, *Frank Duff: A Biography* (Dublin, 1982).

140 The Saint Patrick's Guild was founded in 1910 by Canon Robert Fagan and administered by Mary Josephine Cruice. The Guild sought to combat proselytising by non-Catholic organisations. In 1919 it opened the St Patrick's home for the care of unmarried mothers and their children in Mountjoy Square, which later relocated to Herbert Avenue. In 1930, in Blackrock Co. Dublin, it opened Temple Hill Hospital for sick children. See the annual reports of the Guild of Saint Patrick, 1922–38.

141 The passivity of the poor has been increasingly questioned in social history. See A. Digby, 'Poverty, health, and the politics of gender in Britain, 1870–1948', in A. Digby and J. Stewart (eds), *Gender, Health and Welfare* (London, 1996), p. 69.

142 See, for example, Corish, *The Irish Catholic Experience*; T. Inglis, *Moral Monopoly: The Catholic Church in Modern Irish Society* (Dublin, 1987); M. Kenny, *Goodbye to Catholic Ireland* (London, 1997).

143 Mrs C. to Archbishop Byrne, 5 May 1937, DDA, Byrne Papers, AB 7, Charity Cases, Box 5 1931–35. All the names of the authors of these 'charity case' letters have been changed.

144 Inglis, *Moral Monopoly*, p. 4.

145 Dr Catherine O'Brien's observations are contained in the annual report of the Medical Officer of Health for Dublin City in *JIFSMU*, 3:17 (Nov. 1938), 57.

146 Porter, *Health, Civilization and the State*, p. 174.

147 Pedersen, *Family, Dependence and the Origins of the Welfare State*, p. 39; Digby, 'Poverty, health, and the politics of gender', p. 69.

148 See, for example, Kearns, *Dublin Tenement Life*, and *Dublin's Lost Heroines*.

149 The charity case letters continued under Archbishop John Charles McQuaid but have not yet been released for public access.

150 A card was issued to those who wrote without a parish priest's reference copy in index.

151 Some mothers like a Mrs B. of Glasnevin wrote about how the 'tariff war' had impacted on her family life. Mrs B. to Byrne, 31 September 1933, DDA, Byrne Papers, AB 7, Charity Cases, Box 5, 1931–35.

152 Mrs F. to Byrne, February 1924, DDA, Byrne Papers, AB 7, Charity Cases, Box 1, 1921–26.

153 Mrs M. Q., Dorset St., to Byrne, c. 1928, DDA, Byrne Papers, AB 7, Charity Cases, Box 2, 1926–29.

154 Mrs O'R., Lr. Gardiner St., to Byrne, c. 1925, DDA, Byrne Papers, AB 7, Charity Cases, Box 1, 1921–26.

155 Mrs S., Temple St., to Byrne, c. 1926, DDA, Byrne Papers, AB 7, Charity Cases, Box 1, 1921–26.

156 Mrs F., Francis St. to Byrne, 4 March 1930, DDA, Byrne Papers, AB 7, Charity Cases, Box 3, 1929–32.
157 Mrs P., Ringsend to Byrne, 27 June 1925, DDA, Byrne Papers, AB 7, Charity Cases, Box 1, 1921–26.
158 Mrs McD., Mountjoy Sq., to Byrne, c. 1924, DDA, Byrne Papers, AB 7, Charity Cases, Box 1, 1921–26.
159 Ibid., Mrs O'R., Clonlife, to Byrne, 10 November 1923, DDA, Byrne Papers, AB 7, Charity Cases, Box 1, 1921–26.
160 Inglis, *Moral Monopoly,* p. 42.
161 J. Young CC, of Presbytery, 117 North Circular St. on behalf of Mrs G., to Byrne, DDA, Byrne Papers, AB 7, Charity Cases, Box 3, 1926–29.
162 Mrs G., Ranelagh, to Byrne, 3 April 1934, DDA, Byrne Papers, AB 7, Charity Cases, Box 5, 1931–35.
163 Mrs M.G., Foxrock, to Byrne, c, 1926, DDA, Byrne Papers, AB 7, Charity Cases, Box 1, 1921–6.
164 Mrs D., Foley St., Dublin, to Byrne, 14 November 1932, DDA, Byrne Papers, AB 7, Charity Cases, Box 3, 1929–32.
165 Mrs F., Bow St., Dublin, to Byrne, 10 January 1930, DDA, Byrne Papers, AB 7, Charity Cases, Box 3, 1929–32.
166 Fuchs notes a similar pattern of supplication whereby single mothers in Paris resorted to threats of suicide or infanticide. See Fuchs, 'Morality and poverty', p. 294.
167 PP Drumcondra to Byrne, 1931, DDA, Byrne Papers, AB 7, Charity Cases, Box 3, 1929–32.
168 The 'black faith' was a common term used by Catholics to describe Protestantism.
169 Mrs B., Kimmage, to Byrne, December 1935, DDA, Byrne Papers, AB 7, Charity Cases, Box 6 July 1935–May 1937.
170 Mrs C., Kimmage, to Byrne, 1938, DDA, Byrne Papers, AB 7, Charity Cases, Box 7, May 1937–December 1939.
171 Mrs R., Mountjoy Sq., (Basement) to Byrne, c. 1936, DDA, Byrne Papers, AB 7, Charity Cases, Box 5, 1935–37.
172 Mrs J., Forest St., Swords, to Byrne, 7 February 1935, DDA, Byrne Papers, AB 7, Charity Cases, Box 5, 1935–37.
173 Mrs C., to Byrne, January 1935, DDA, Byrne Papers, AB 7, Charity Cases, Box 5, 1935–37
174 Fr. Farrell of Pro-Cathedral on behalf of Mrs B., of NCR, to Byrne, March 1923, DDA, Byrne Papers, AB 7, Charity Cases, Box 1, 1921–26.
175 Mrs G. W., Dundrum to Byrne, February 1924. Mrs W. had been given £5 on 20 March 1923, DDA, Byrne Papers, AB 7, Charity Cases, Box 1, 1921–26.
176 Mrs M. D. to Byrne, 21 September 1938, DDA, Byrne Papers, AB 7, Charity Cases, Box 7, May 1937-December 1939.
177 C. J. MacSweeney, 'A public health programme for Éire', *IJMSc.,* 170 (Feb. 1940), 54.
178 Catholic Action, *Catholic Action: Principles and Practice* (Dublin, 1934). For an indication of the level of intellectual interest in the issue of a Catholic social movement in Ireland, see E. Cahill, 'The Catholic social movement', *IER*, 36 (1930), 572–87.
179 Revd P. Dunne to J. F. Flanagan of Catholic Truth Society, 8 March 1931, DDA, Byrne Papers, Lay organisations (4). It should be noted that Byrne was ill for so long before his actual death that many of the clergy believed that the running of the diocese was taken care of by his 'strong-willed' priest secretaries. See, Sheehy, 'Archbishop McQuaid: The diocesan administrator', 164.

4

The Emergency: the war, the poor, the Church and the state, 1939–45

A very common sight in the Dublin dispensaries is a poor slum mother, about forty years of age, with pale face and colourless lips – tired and lifeless. She frequently lives on a diet consisting of tea and a small amount of milk in it, and possibly bread dipped in dripping.[1]

The Second World War was defined as the Emergency by the Irish Free State, which maintained a policy of 'benevolent neutrality'.[2] While the state was spared the direct carnage of war, it nevertheless faced a number of social problems caused by increased levels of tuberculosis, infant mortality and emigration.[3] During the war Irish industrial production fell by 25 per cent, the supply situation became critical and the government was forced to introduce rationing, and price and wage controls.[4] The war highlighted the appalling social conditions in which many Irish citizens lived.[5] Much of the social and medical evidence relating to health and poverty, emerging since the turn of the century, was brought into high relief during the Emergency period when infant mortality rates soared and infectious diseases impacted on the public consciousness and legislation. The communal response to adversity facilitated initiatives such as community kitchens, the introduction of children's allowances and a re-examination of the role of charity versus state responsibility.

This extraordinary period also introduced into positions of power crucial personalities such as McQuaid, who launched a welfare offensive in Dublin, Dr Conn Ward, Parliamentary Secretary to the Department of Local Government and Public Health with the responsibility for the health services, and Dr James Deeny, Chief Medical Adviser to the Department of Local Government and Public. These personalities also represented different ideological standpoints which competed, intersected and influenced each other. This was a period when the ideologies of Catholic action and the developing welfare state underwent 'strenuous development' and the dialogue between both ultimately fed into the development of social and medical services for Irish families in general, and Irish mothers and infants in particular.[6]

Catholic action: the agenda of charity

Archbishop Byrne had been very slow to give his official recognition to the few lay organisations that dealt with mothers in 'moral danger', such as the Legion of Mary or the Catholic Rescue Society.[7] He was nervous of excessive lay zeal and he suffered from poor health, which, in many respects, inhibited both what he was able to achieve and the perception of his tenure as Archbishop of Dublin. As the 1930s progressed, he was virtually unable to move because of Parkinson's disease.[8] In 1939, Fr. McQuaid wrote to him to voice his concern about the lack of a Roman Catholic presence in maternity and child welfare. He warned Byrne about the Civics Institute and other 'non-sectarian' organisations in Dublin that were involved in child guidance, home visiting, playgrounds and nurseries. This correspondence offers a revealing insight into the future Archbishop McQuaid's motives for establishing comprehensive social services in the 1940s for Dublin mothers and their children. McQuaid recommended a committee to keep the Archbishop informed. This Catholic committee 'could make effective the directions decided on for various branches of social activity, and thus maintain a loyal co-ordination with the Archbishop'.[9] Only one year later, as Archbishop of Dublin, McQuaid established just such a committee, calling it the Catholic Social Service Conference (CSSC).

McQuaid was consecrated Archbishop of Dublin on 27 December 1940 in Dublin's pro-cathedral. On the day that he was officially welcomed as the new spiritual leader of the diocese he received a visit from members of Dublin Corporation, among them the city manager, P. J. Hernon, who promised to help build harmonious relations between the Catholic Church and the civic authorities.[10] In the course of the following ten years, McQuaid sought to build a 'network of divine charity' in the city, which would operate in conjunction with state services and co-ordinate Catholic charities.[11] McQuaid intended to counteract non-Catholic influences in social services, and establish an indispensable place in welfare provision for the Catholic Church. In this respect, McQuaid gave teeth to Catholic Action in Dublin and played his part in ensuring that Catholic social teaching 'became a very significant part of the debate on Irish social policy'.[12] An essential part of this story is the relationship forged between certain members of the Department of Local Government and Public Health and the Archbishop of Dublin. In this context it is possible to analyse the changing relationship between the Irish state and the Irish Catholic Church in the era of modern welfare provision that prefigured the mother-and-child controversy of the 1950s.

There is little doubt that McQuaid entered the field of social services in general, and maternity services in particular, in order to counteract the activities of other 'non-sectarian' organisations. The protection of poor Catholic children was the prime motive behind the social work that McQuaid sponsored during the 1940s and 1950s. McQuaid believed that Catholics should administer charity to Catholics, and Protestants to Protestants; he was convinced that the shared administration of care would lead to a confusion of principle. The Catholic principles of social justice and moral supremacy were the central tenets of Catholic Action and, therefore, formed the basis of Catholic social services. In 1942, the Archbishop explained his views clearly with regard to the CSSC in the preamble to its constitution:

> We set up our own system of Charity because it is part of the mission of Catholic Social Service to bring home to the minds of all, our benefactors as well as our beneficiaries, a true appreciation of the principles of Charity and Social Justice ... It would be utterly wrong to acquiesce in, recommend or accept economic or social teachings that are not in harmony with our religious principles. Hence we can best fulfil the work we have set out to do by pursuing the age-old policy of the Church of developing our own machinery of Social Service.[13]

Archbishop McQuaid eschewed the use of the word humanitarian, drawing a clear distinction between 'humanitarian' endeavour and 'Catholic Charity', and he insisted that his apostolate do the same: the Catholic Church undertook charity for the good of the faith not for the benefit of humanity *per se*. In 1944, McQuaid went to great pains to explain his views on 'supernatural charity' to the president of the Society of St Vincent de Paul, Mr Lonan Murphy. The Archbishop refused to attend a meeting under the auspices of the Council of Ireland of the Society of St Vincent de Paul, as he would have to share the platform with non-Catholics. He explained to Murphy, 'I wish my reason to be clearly grasped – that, if such a Meeting is addressed by non-Catholics, my presence would reinforce the error that your Society has for a purpose humanitarian well-doing, not supernatural exercise of charity.'[14]

The Archbishop wished to create a specifically Catholic organisation to consolidate existing Catholic charitable and social work and to expand into other areas vital to the moral and social well-being of the Catholic faith, such as maternal welfare. The CSSC was, in essence, a federation of some thirty-nine existing Catholic charities, which attempted to co-ordinate services and reduce overlap. The pretext given for such a federalisation of Catholic charities was 'the extreme conditions'[15] created by the Second World War and the fact that existing services were not sufficient.[16]

The CSSC, as the 'paragon of Catholic Action', sought to harness the latent zeal for social action in the face of adversity and direct it in a bid both to co-operate with state action and to protect society against state intervention.[17] The conference dealt initially with social issues that were brought to crisis point by the wartime atmosphere.[18] The Emergency provided a sincere rally call, with rationing starting in 1942 on bread and petrol, and a wages standstill order in effect from May 1941, while the cost of living index rose by 70 per cent between 1938 and 1944.[19] Nonetheless, it is clear from McQuaid's papers that he intended to co-ordinate the Roman Catholic effort in relation to social services regardless of the war. For McQuaid and

for many Catholic theologians, Catholic social teaching only permitted assistance based on need. A system of co-operation between Church and State
was, therefore, central to securing the type of social justice that the Catholic
Church encouraged. In March 1941 Owen Cowley, the president of the Catholic Social Service Conference,[20] explained to an informal gathering of various Catholic charities[21] that the 'Conference set out to devise a national
solution, in accordance with Catholic principles, sufficiently adequate to
meet the situation caused by the rapidly increasing poverty and distress
among our people and to consider the need for the co-operation of all Social Welfare Activities'.[22]

While the claim of devising a 'national solution' was somewhat exaggerated, given that the conference was restricted to the Dublin diocese, it is
significant that Cowley stressed the need to incorporate Catholic principles
in the development of 'Social Welfare Activities'. Clearly the CSSC was devised and developed with the intention of securing the place of Catholic
social teaching in the developing welfare policy of the Irish state.[23] During
the first meeting, Cowley explained to the various charities that the conference would 'supplement' government and local authority efforts by co-
ordinating Catholic charities.[24] However, there was an explicit aim to create a 'long-term Social Policy on Catholic principles' which would give an
outlet to Catholic Action and encourage voluntary effort in the face of social
need.[25] By 15 April 1941 the name was officially changed to the Catholic
Social Service Conference, and it was accepted as a 'fundamental principle'
that the conference would co-operate with and support the state and the
local authorities, while intensifying the specifically Catholic contributions
to social services in the city.[26]

The apparent confusion over the title for this conference is relevant as it
was rooted in the fact that McQuaid wished also to create a central Catholic
secretariat or bureau to act as a referral agency for all cases of need in the
diocese.[27] This he finally achieved in 1942 with the creation of the Catholic
Social Welfare Bureau (CSWB), through which he hoped to tackle neglected
social problems like the protection of Irish emigrants.[28] The CSWB was
officially opened on 17 June 1942 and operated by the Legion of Mary. Its
first task was the protection of female emigrants.[29] The CSWB eventually
comprised an Emigrants Section (1942), a Playground Section (1943),[30] a
Primary Schools Welfare Section (1944), and a Family Welfare Section
(1945). By 1967 the CSWB had dealt with the moral welfare of 200,000
emigrants, finding relatives who had emigrated and lost contact with their
family, and ensuring that others maintained their faith abroad.[31] The Family Welfare Section was established as an agency for the training of hospital
almoners and other social science students. McQuaid recognised the vital
role played by almoners/social workers in linking physical, medical and
moral welfare, and he was anxious that Irish almoners should be trained in
a Catholic environment. He was instrumental in ensuring the creation of a
social science diploma in University College Dublin and he offered his CSWB

as a practical training-ground for these students.[32] The Archbishop was determined to stamp out 'non-Irish, non-Catholic control' in the Dublin Committee of the London Institute of Almoners, and in 1945 his Family Welfare Section was officially recognised by the institute as a training centre.[33] The object of this section was

> to provide a supply of trained social workers who will be familiar with social legislation and social services of a modern state, and who will know how to apply them in all the varying circumstances of individual cases in complete accordance with the unchanging principles of Christian Morality and Christian Charity.[34]

The first striking feature of the original plans for the CSSC and the CSWB was the degree to which McQuaid sought to mirror the state structure. In one draft programme Cowley referred to a health department which, he explained, would work in partnership with the state Department of Local Government and Public Health to 'promote and help, through social action, the cause of health and the prevention and cure of disease'.[35] It was obvious from the beginning of the planning process that McQuaid and Cowley regarded health and welfare as intimately connected. The health department never materialised. However, the fundamental convictions expressed in this draft informed the creation of the Pre-Natal and Post-Natal Welfare Department of the CSSC and the Family Section of the CSWB. McQuaid believed that the Church could provide assistance without disrupting the family unit by employing state and charitable services in accordance with Catholic doctrine. There was, Cowley argued,

> a great need for a Catholic body having the confidence of the community and prepared to interpret the Catholic point of view towards social problems. Positions in public welfare work are often held by people whose training and philosophic outlook are not in harmony with Catholic principles. Hence Catholics are sometimes exposed to doctrines which may prove hazardous for them.[36]

'Our own poor': setting the boundaries between Church and state

The belief that Catholics, through their need, could be exposed to potentially hazardous influences was based not on merely bigotry, but also on a profound understanding of the trends in welfare provision. Cowley, as a devout Catholic, viewed with understanding the good intentions of many social workers, but he was concerned at the tendency to view morality as objective and, therefore, separate or irrelevant to welfare provision:

> Family social workers are becoming increasingly objective in their study of the behaviour problems of their clients. This does not mean that they are becoming less human but more scientific. As a corollary they are often pragmatists in morals, believing in their evolution rather than that rules of

conduct are fixed, unchangeable, absolute.[37]

For the Catholic Church, the rules were absolute. Consequently, it was necessary for the Church to provide efficient alternative forms of care, and to direct the use of public assistance in accordance with an absolute moral code. The Catholic objectives in welfare provision were clearly articulated: self-realisation, family integrity and moral supremacy. For that reason the official handbook of the CSSC, published in 1945, was at pains to stress the appropriate relationship between Church and State services:

> It was, from the beginning, a primary plank in the Conference's policy to co-operate with Public Authorities ... We would not, indeed, wish to destroy the charitable character of our social services, to make them merely another form of state dole or public assistance. They must remain true to the charitable inspiration which created them ... If the state subsequently helps so much the better, for thereby funds are liberated for use in yet further fields of charitable endeavour.[38]

McQuaid was determined to strike a balance between co-operation with state services and the preservation of religious autonomy in the running of his Catholic social services. He argued that the voluntary and statutory services could complement one another; according to his philosophy, state aid was only a problem if it was not restricted to remedial care and was allowed to become all-encompassing.

McQuaid was keenly aware of developments in England in relation to state responsibility. He was familiar with the English hierarchy's reservations regarding the growing role of the state in social services and the risks that this posed to the autonomy of the family. The Archbishop studied a joint pastoral issued by the Catholic hierarchy of England and Wales on the 'Social Question' in June 1942. This pastoral asserted the Catholic vision of society based on natural law and founded on the two communities of the family and the state.[39] The English hierarchy stressed the duty of the family unit to provide for itself, insisting that any state intervention into family life should be 'remedial'.[40] Foreshadowing McQuaid's objection to the 1947 Health Act and the mother-and-child scheme of 1950, the Catholic Church in England and Wales asserted that Catholic doctrine insisted that the state should act as facilitator rather than provider. They argued that the state should ensure that parenthood did not become a burden by creating a social system that was family-orientated and respected the family as an independent unit.[41]

In 1943, Fr. E. J. Coyne SJ, a moral theologian and one of the founding members of the CSSC, voiced the Irish Catholic Church's concerns regarding social services.[42] In considering the impact of the Beveridge Report, he asked, 'do such services and such plans tend to sacrifice specifically human values, moral values, for other values, say, purely economic or political or material ones?'[43] Coyne's fears, steeped in middle-class assumption and bias, were threefold: first that the citizen would become a 'slave' to an 'impersonal bureaucracy', secondly that such services would 'sap and weaken the moral fibre of citizens',[44] and thirdly that universal state welfare would result in the destruction of charity.[45] He warned that once the moral aspect of need-based social services was undermined by universal entitlement, man's 'moral stamina' would be jeopardised. He explained, 'Hunger or its fear, the love of wife and family, the hope of a secure old age are Nature's own ways of calling forth the best that is in man.'[46] Coyne believed that the solution rested in a 'just wage'[47] rather than 'clumsy' state restitution, and he advocated a balanced system of co-operation between state services and voluntary effort. Coyne was not merely flexing his rhetorical muscles; through the CSSC he was involved in realising the Catholic ambition of creating a system of social services that could cater for need. Moreover, he was not alone in warning against any system that broadened the criteria of entitlement beyond necessity to one based on rights irrespective of income.

The CSSC and maternity policy during the Emergency

Gastro-enteritis reached epidemic proportions in the first few years of the war.[48] In 1942 465 infants died in Dublin of gastro-enteritis, by 1943 that had risen to 609 and by 1944 the case fatality rate had more than doubled to 40.03 per cent (see Table 4.1).[49] From the outset it was acknowledged that artificially fed infants were infected and died at a much higher rate. Consequently, voluntary initiatives began to focus on enabling the mother to breastfeed her infant by supplying her with sufficient nutrients. Although organisations like the St John Ambulance Brigade had been feeding the poor since the early 1920s, the Emergency witnessed a proliferation of feeding centres for poor Dubliners.[50] Judge Wylie's 'Good Will restaurants' supplied hot meals, the Society of Friends recruited the staff of the Dublin Bewley's café in feeding initiatives, and the Marrowbone Lane Project[51] highlighted the level of malnutrition among poor Dublin children and established the Samaritan Fund to finance feeding schemes.[52] *The Irish Times* did much to publicise the issue of communal feeding in 1941, referring to food centres and voluntary kitchens as Dublin's 'first line of defence against hunger'.[53]

Mary E. Daly noted that the government investigated the issue of communal feeding during the Emergency. The Department of Local Government and Public Health, however, urged against this intervention on the grounds that there were 'strong moral and social reasons for refraining as far as possible from interfering even in very difficult circumstances with the normal family regime of the people'.[54] Dublin Corporation established a cooked meal service under the chairmanship of the secretary of the Infant Aid Society, Patricia Byrne.[55] Byrne was in contact with the CSSC in November 1941.[56] However, not all the conference's food centres were willing to co-operate under the Corporation's scheme owing to a fear of undue interference.[57]

Table 4.1 Cases of gastro-enteritis in infants in Dublin city, 1942–47

Year	Total no. of cases	Deaths	Case fatality rate
1942	2,657	465	17.50
1943	2,031	609	29.98
1944	1,279	513	40.03
1945	1,837	557	30.32
1946	1,837	461	24.87
1947	1,868	280	14.90

Note: The average for the peak years of 1942 to 1946 was 521 deaths or a case fatality rate of 28.54

Source: Consultative Child Health Council, Report of the Consultative Child Health Council, 1949, NAI, Department of Health, A116/167

Mothers rapidly became the targets of these feeding initiatives. In February 1942, the St John Ambulance Brigade conducted a study of Irish mothers in conjunction with the Rotunda hospital.[58] The results of this study confirmed that malnourished mothers were often subject to anaemia. Anaemia, long suspected a contributory factor, was clearly identified in 1941 as a cause in 20 per cent of the seventy-four maternal deaths, described as 'obstetric shock', in the Dublin maternity hospitals between the years 1935 and 1940.[59] Anaemia was a debilitating 'poor mother's disease'.[60] The professor of biochemistry in Trinity College, W. R. Fearon, was employed by the St John Ambulance Brigade to design an ideal diet for mothers. Fearon warned that the 'calorie starvation' of Dublin mothers was short-sighted, as 'in any long-term policy of social architecture, it leads to the ante-natal disablement and disendows the children of the health that is their natural birthright'.[61] In 1943, Dr Denis K. O'Donovan,[62] a member of the CSSC's Food Committee, gave a lecture to the Pre-Natal and Post-Natal Welfare Department in which he drew explicit attention to the importance of maternal diet:

> The proper diet for pregnant and nursing mothers is so necessary that this aspect of Social Welfare should take priority over any dietary schemes for other groups of the population. The mother during this period must ... eat sufficient not only to maintain herself in good health for her own sake and for future pregnancies, but in addition eat sufficient for the infant. If the infant is exposed to even a slight dietary deficiency at this time it fails to get that 'flying start' in life which is so essential for its future well-being.[63]

The CSSC continuously underlined the connection between health and nutrition, regarding the preservation of health as one of their key functions, while respecting the Catholic understanding of the association between health and morality. In this respect, the CSSC's maternity policy was quite at variance with that of the other non-Catholic organisations. The multidenominational Marrowbone Lane project clearly expressed the opinion that maternity welfare should not be left to charity and instead should be a 'right' of all mothers:

> This work is of such absolute national importance that there is no doubt that it should not be treated in any way as a charity. Every expectant mother should be able to obtain as her right a proper balanced meal a day, the necessary funds being supplied by organized society (i.e. the City of Central Health body).[64]

The CSSC established its maternity section in order to ensure that the charitable principle was maintained and that 'organized society' did not interfere in the welfare of all mothers.

In November 1941 the Legion of Mary was given the responsibility of directing the CSSC's prenatal work.[65] In terms of its maternity policy, the CSSC focused on the health of the unborn infant. While the maternity committee displayed an understanding that it was generally the mother who bore the strain of family poverty, they were anxious not to disrupt internal family politics. The conference was careful to organise its maternity work in harmony with the Catholic vision of family life; it reiterated in its official handbook that it was 'fully alive to the importance of safeguarding the ties of home life, so rightly cherished by the poor'.[66] There was, in fact, very little effort made to discover what 'poor Catholic mothers' actually felt about either the charity available or 'the ties of home life'.

By the end of 1943 the CSSC had established sixteen Pre-Natal and Post-Natal Department welfare centres, which supplied 480 expectant and nursing mothers with 'a substantial meal and pint of milk each day'.[67] From the outset the Conference attempted to integrate the almoners of each of the maternity hospitals into their system of care.[68] The members of the maternity welfare team were instructed to approach the Rotunda's almoner, Miss Murphy, the medical secretary of the National Maternity Hospital, Miss Pope, and the matron of the Coombe to inform them that they were 'prepared and anxious' to help 'necessitous Pre-Natal cases.'[69] The conference volunteers received a list of necessitous cases from the social workers of the hospitals and then visited these homes. During this phase of the work the volunteers were warned to employ 'sympathy, tact and understanding' and to inform the mother that the food available to them would be 'supplied free and that it is not for the use of the family but for her own use personally.'[70] The conference was practical in its approach to maternal and child welfare, employing its clothing guilds to supply underwear and suitable clothing for the mothers to ensure that they would attend the centres and the hospitals' antenatal clinics. In 1944 a maternity ambulance was introduced to cater for mothers isolated in the new suburban estates of Cabra, Whitehall and East Wall.[71] The introduction of a maternity ambulance in 1944 was seen as a positive step to meet the demands of these suburban poorer communities. The Rotunda noted that while the ambulance was chiefly used for women attending the CSSC maternity centres, it was also available to transport other necessitous patients recommended by the maternity hospitals.[72]

By 1945 all the maternity centres provided sit-down meals in order to counteract the 'maternal instinct' to divide the food received with the family.[73] The conference's maternity work soon became its central activity, and by 1943 it was noted that 'practically the whole of the expenditure was incurred in our Food, Clothing and Pre-Natal Welfare Services'.[74] While the necessitous mother received aid and advice, the dignity of family was consistently defended. The reiteration of this theme was political: the intention was to characterise the CSSC as the appropriate method of family support rather than a bureaucratic state version. A draft article submitted by a Catholic weekly paper, *The Standard*, for McQuaid's approval, stressed these issues:

> [T]he room set apart for these women is generally a quiet place, cheery and well-lighted. They can come in and slip away without being conspicuous. The nun in charge takes a gentle interest in them and nothing is ever said or done that does not make these decent women realise the dignity of motherhood.[75]

The piece that was published in *The Standard* a few days later was introduced as a comment by an 'American visitor' and entitled 'A charity that grew out of war': 'There is no cold "institutionalism" about the food centres, nor do the poor suffer any loss of self-respect in frequenting them. This applies with added force to the mothers' dining rooms, which are really pleasant clubs.'[76] The article was sanctimonious and the intention was to advertise the CSSC maternity kitchens as the epitome of Catholic charity and to stress that the poor were enriched by the experience of Catholic charity.

The CSSC justified its maternity work in terms of infant health, and the official handbook outlined, 'The health of the newborn infant depends very much on the mother's condition, and this depends largely on a proper diet.'[77] As a result, mothers who attended the conference's maternity centres were fed for the three months before childbirth and up to six months afterwards in order to ensure lactation.[78] This emphasis on natural feeding was spurred on by co-operation with the Department of Local Government and Public Health, and the three maternity hospitals that were all stressing the value of natural milk against infectious disease.

The issue of breastfeeding has for a century been highly controversial on both medical and cultural grounds.[79] Many of the issues still pertinent to public debate at the end of the twentieth century could be traced back to the early twentieth century: class, poverty, commercial advertising, the role of hospitals and health care professionals, the benefits to infant and maternal health, cultural reluctance to accept and promote breastfeeding, and apparent maternal reluctance. Initially, in the late 1930s and the 1940s, the primary focus of debate was on breastfeeding as a weapon against infant mortality and illness and the secondary focus was on the impact of poverty on the maternal ability to breastfeed.[80]

In 1938 the medical officer of the maternity and child welfare scheme in Dublin County Borough, Dr M. J. Russell, reported that the 'enormous pre-ponderance of deaths of artificially-fed babies leads to the conclusion that this is the main factor which determines the deaths of infants from this condition'.[81] The following year Russell identified the failure to breastfeed in Dublin as a 'causative factor of the high infant mortality rate'. Moreover, he went on to suggest that 60 per cent of Dublin mothers were unable to breastfeed.[82] This was a particularly serious admission in terms of national health as the Medical Officer explained: 'The invariable conclusion is that the breastfed infant not only has the higher survivorship, but having sur-vived, it is on all points of its health record the better placed in every phase of its later life.'[83] The role of malnutrition was highlighted when he con-cluded in 1940 that 85 per cent of mothers surveyed failed to breastfeed their infants after three months, which he believed was largely due 'to some form of malnutrition or diet deficiency and to the increased pace of life conditions in the city'.[84]

By the 1940s increased attention was paid to encouraging and training mothers to breastfeed by both health visitors and nursing staff in the vari-ous maternity hospitals or maternity wards throughout the country as a result of the link between breastfeeding and the prevention of gastro-en-teritis.[85] In relation to maternal malnutrition, the work of the maternity kitchens was seen as central. As the Master of the Rotunda, Ninian Falkiner, acknowledged, 'splendid work was again done in the campaign to encour-age breastfeeding of babies'. With the aid of the Marrowbone Lane Samari-tan Fund, the St John Ambulance was able to supply dinners to 200 nursing mothers, 'thus enabling them to breastfeed their babies up to the age of six months'.[86] It was increasingly accepted that women who were not properly nourished failed to maintain breastfeeding. In 1941, when thirty-five ex-pectant Dublin mothers were given a balanced meal a day for three months before and two months after confinement, it was discovered that the moth-ers began losing milk once taken off the meals.[87]

The issue of nutrition and breastfeeding was the primary health agenda behind the maternity kitchens established by the CSSC throughout the 1940s. Dr O'Donovan clearly outlined the cost of maternal poverty to the CSSC:

> A poor diet for this class results in a very high infant mortality rate as well as in a whole series of other illnesses, maybe years later, in the mother. It is stated that in certain parts of Dublin approximately 160 infants, out of every 1,000 born alive, die during the first twelve months of life. With a properly controlled health service it is estimated that about 120 of these deaths could be prevented, or that the infant mortality could be reduced to 40 per 1,000 live births.[88]

O'Donovan argued that 'the artificially fed infant of the slums is the major sufferer from the prevailing gastro-enteritis.'[89] He concluded that breastfeeding was one weapon against infant mortality. The CSSC's annual appeal of 1943 acknowledged that it was a public health issue to ensure that poor mothers received sufficient nourishment to breastfeed their own infants.[90]

The issue of maternal malnutrition highlighted the connection between poverty and ill health. As one doctor noted in 1943, 'Whilst many well-to-do women take unsuitable diets, poverty is undoubtedly the chief obstacle in preventing a larger number of women from taking a sufficient and suitable diet.'[91] Morgan Crowe, the acting medical officer in charge of child welfare for Dublin Corporation, also argued that it was class rather than breastfeeding *per se* that was the crucial factor in infant death.[92] In 1945, it was in working-class Dublin homes that 75 per cent of deaths from gastro-enteritis were recorded. It was because these mothers could not breastfeed, as a result of malnourishment or demands on their time, and were also denied safer alternatives, that their infants were more prone to death. Thus for the working-class infant the implications of not breastfeeding were potentially lethal. As Morgan explained,

> emancipation has brought little change to the working-class mother in this country. Her large young family will demand her presence at home, and she will not be unwilling to breastfeed her child if she is able, and understands how, to do so. However, when artificial feeding is employed, circumstances do not permit the hygienic preparation possible in the more wealthy home, and, in this stratum gastro-enteritis is a relatively frequent cause of death.[93]

He did not challenge the 'inherent advantages in breastfeeding', but was anxious that breastfeeding should not be viewed as a panacea to all social ills and/or used to obscure serious social questions that underlay principle issues of child health.[94]

In 1942, despite the best efforts of the various charitable agencies, the almoner of the Rotunda hospital claimed that the wives of unemployed men were still not receiving sufficient food during pregnancy.[95] In 1944, James Quin addressed the Biological Society of the Royal College of Physicians and Surgeons of Ireland on the issue of a new maternity service for Ireland. In this speech he stressed the importance of breastfeeding and the inhibiting impact of poverty. Quin's speech reveals not only the importance of the issue of breastfeeding as an impetus for change but also the firm connection between poverty and infant death.[96] Quin noted that in 1943 in the Rotunda hospital not one of the infants who perished from gastro-enteritis was either wholly or partially breastfed, citing Dr Collis's conviction that the importance of breastfeeding in terms of infant survival could not be 'over-emphasised'.[97] Quin contended that 'in the vast majority of cases failure of breastfeeding is due either to a lack of desire to do so on the part of the mother or to insufficient nutrition'.[98]

The connection between breastfeeding and infant survival was the largest single factor that brought the Department of Local Government and Public Health into the arena of maternal health. Medical evidence that gastro-enteritis was the largest single killer of infants under six months old allowed the department to justify intervention in the intimate arena of maternal health on the grounds of community welfare. During the Emergency the department began to flex its muscles in relation to infectious disease by way of the Emergency Powers (no. 26) Order 1940, which gave the department the powers to detain and isolate probable sources of infection.[99]

In June 1943 the Department of Local Government and Public Health officially requested McQuaid's assistance in its campaign to encourage breastfeeding. Dr Conn Ward, Parliamentary Secretary to the Department of Local Government and Public Health between 1932 and 1946, informed the Archbishop of the preliminary findings of a departmental committee established to 'investigate the causation and prevention of diarrhoea and enteritis in Dublin'.[100] The committee's report drew attention to the fact that 'diarrhoea and enteritis was responsible for over one-third of all infant deaths. It was also the greatest single cause of infant mortality.'[101] The committee discovered that all deaths of infants from gastro-enteritis, with few exceptions, occurred in the first year and 80 per cent in the first six months. The report noted that the incidence of gastro-enteritis in breastfed infants was 'much lower than in artificially fed infants'.[102] However, it was noted that the Department of Local Government and Public Health believed that there had been a marked decline in breastfeeding in recent years. Figures from the Child Welfare Department revealed that in 1938 41 per cent of infants were breastfed in the first month of life. By 1942 this figure had dropped to 19 per cent for the first year of life.[103] Although the committee admitted that the 1938 survey had only investigated breastfeeding in the first month of life, whereas the 1942 survey had considered the first year of life, it concluded that these surveys were still representative of 'the city as a whole at the time'.

The committee recommended that mothers be induced to breastfeed their infants for a period of six months.[104] The three maternity hospitals were approached with a view to gaining their support. However, the hospitals had pointed out that there were few facilities to instruct extern cases and that many women were too badly nourished to feed their infants naturally. Ward explained that he had been instructed by the committee to enlist McQuaid's 'invaluable aid',[105] as it accepted that 'mothers who are ill-nourished cannot be expected to feed their infants' and these mothers should be advised to make full use of the opportunities for free meals.[106] McQuaid declared himself 'happy to cooperate with the Department in its efforts to reduce infant mortality', and he sent the Parliamentary Secretary a list of all his maternity centres.[107]

The following month the director of the maternity section, Dr Conor Martin, reported that there was an increase in the number of mothers attending at all the centres, and that 'satisfactory opinions have been expressed as to the improvement in the health of the mothers and also the babies for the short time we have been in existence.'[108]

Respecting a partnership: co-operation between the religious and secular powers

The Department of Local Government and Public Health made it clear that it wished the CSSC to corner the market in maternity welfare, in preference to the St John Ambulance Brigade, which had been working in that field since 1925. McQuaid recorded a meeting with Dr Ward in January 1943 during which Ward clarified that he 'wished Cath. [sic] Society to get both credit and probable money-grant for such services, as Cath. [sic] Approach to problems is very much more necessary and desirable'.[109] Ward alerted McQuaid to correspondence he had had with Dr Ninian Falkiner, a 'non-Catholic', urging the development of prenatal work by the St John Ambulance Brigade.[110] The Master praised the maternity work carried out by the Brigade as one of the 'most valuable' services in the battle against infant death. Falkiner concluded his letter by stressing that this aspect of maternal care should not be left to charitable endeavour. He explained that this was 'obviously not a matter which can be left indefinitely to charity. Indeed, it seems to me one of national importance, which should be taken by the state or the Municipal Authorities.'[111] Within ten days Falkiner wrote again, urging that the 'Department should shoulder this responsibility without delay'.[112]

In response to this letter, the department's general inspector, Alice Litster, informed Ward that the cost of providing hot meals for mothers would be greatly increased if the Dublin Corporation had to take over the operation.[113] Imbued by Catholic principles and financial realism, Ward sought the advice of McQuaid and sent him a draft copy of the departmental response to Falkiner.[114] In his response, Ward agreed with Falkiner's suggestion that the maternity clinics be extended, but stated that he wished to correct the mistaken impression of the Master of the Rotunda that the St John Ambulance Brigade was the only voluntary organisation 'shouldering the burden'. He pointed out that the Brigade was subsidised not only by Dublin Corporation but also by the CSSC. Ward proceeded to explain that the department was not prepared

> to accept the view that it is solely a matter for the state or the Municipal Authorities. On the contrary, they believe that this is essentially the type of service which can be best administered by those who feel that they have a Christian obligation towards the less fortunate of their brethren. Accordingly while they would be prepared to encourage the Local Authority to assist such existing organisations in extending their activities in this regard, they would strongly deprecate any attempt to impose sole responsibility for the work on the Municipality or the state.[115]

McQuaid approved the letter as 'comprehensive, accurate and, in its insistence on principle, excellent'.[116] Ward's response to Falkiner's concerns was indeed consistent with Catholic principles, insisting that the state should subsidise voluntary effort and endeavour to preserve the Christian impulse to care for those in need. However, by giving preference to one organisation over another on religious grounds, Ward was not consistent with the state's obligations expressed in Article 43.2, paragraph 3 of the 1937 Constitution.[117]

In February 1943 McQuaid wrote again to Ward to update him on the progress made by the maternity welfare section of the conference. He referred to a comment made by the Master of the Rotunda that the services provided by the CSSC were 'slight', however, the Archbishop wished to assure Ward that the CSSC could provide a 'comprehensive scheme'.[118] McQuaid had every reason to feel confident; he knew that the Department of Local Government and Public Health would prefer his Catholic organisation to receive the credit and the funding. Moreover, the department had made it clear that they believed as much as the Archbishop in a system of subsidisation and co-operation. The Archbishop could have been forgiven for believing that the Department had no intention of assuming the 'sole responsibility' for maternal welfare, nor any inclination to extend free medical care beyond those in need.

Consequently, McQuaid, anxious to protect poor mothers from the hazardous influences of 'non-sectarian' organisations, and bolstered by departmental support, deliberately placed his maternity clinics in the same area as those of the St John Ambulance Brigade. When the Brigade was forced to shut down one of its kitchens,[119] the Archbishop noted in an internal memo that they had been forced to 'give way a little'.[120] Thus, while the Archbishop of Dublin encouraged the Catholic Church to take its place in the development of maternity services, he did so at the expense of other multi-denominational organisations already working in the field. Had the conference's maternity centres been used to extend existing services, all mothers would have benefited; instead valuable resources were used to compete along religious lines. Government officials did not only tacitly accept this denominational strategy; the Parliamentary Secretary, Dr Ward, actively encouraged it. He, according to McQuaid, was willing to use the department's subvention policy to the benefit of Catholic organisations. While both McQuaid and Ward were careful to express themselves in denominational rather than sectarian terms – in other words, neither man articulated a prejudice *against* Protestant organisations but rather a bias *in favour of* the 'Catholic approach' – the result was the same. In order to ensure that Catholic mothers received aid from Catholic volunteers, the CSSC was virtually allowed to supplant the St John Ambulance Brigade after years of service.[121]

The denominational element caused problems for both Protestant and Catholic workers who had worked in co-operation to protect Dublin's mothers and children. A volunteer at one of the Brigade's maternity kitchens, Mrs Nora Reddin, describing herself as a 'Catholic worker', wrote to *The Irish Times* in 1943 to express her dismay at the conference's decision to open centres where others already existed.[122] This policy had caused the closure of successfully operating centres, and Reddin took it as a 'personal affront' and believed that it was as a result of 'either sectarianism – which undoubtedly needs no further encouragement – or else an unwitting overlapping of services'.[123] She noted that such voluntary effort had facilitated 'a spirit of comradeship between Catholics and Protestants working together', expressing the humanitarian interpretation of citizenship, 'surely co-operation between people of different creeds makes for true citizenship'.[124] While there is evidence that McQuaid knew about this letter, he gave no answer to the question posed. [125] For McQuaid, ignorance or anti-Catholicism motivated any such reaction to the CSSC. In an address to his Pre-Natal and Post-Natal Welfare Department that year, he explained,

> I need not remind you that we have not wished to put out of existence any institutions and organisations, but this fact has not been understood and some persons have looked and still look askance at us, but after all we in the CSSC are only entering into a sphere proper to ourselves, caring for our own poor.[126]

According to McQuaid, one of the main reasons for insisting that such welfare provision rested in the hands of voluntary organisations was that under that system each religion could provide for its flock. It was very much a question of territory. McQuaid was utterly convinced that any charity offered to Catholics by non-Catholics was in fact proselytism. He regarded proselytism as a form of spiritual blackmail perpetrated against the most vulnerable of any community – the poor. He appeared not to consider the fact that he was perpetuating a system that manipulated need and poverty by associating charity with religious allegiance. McQuaid put the Brigade kitchen out of business by forcing his flock to choose. Once he placed his kitchen next to the Brigade's centre, for many loyal Catholics that choice was a foregone conclusion: like Mrs Reddin, they would have understood the implicit message in McQuaid's choice of location for his maternity centre.

The obvious preference that Ward expressed for the 'Catholic approach' had a quite devastating impact on the fate of the maternity scheme run by the St John Ambulance Brigade, a non-denominational organisation. Since 1929, Dublin Corporation had approved the Brigade's scheme for an annual grant, grateful that such an efficient voluntary organisation was willing to tackle such a vital and neglected area of social service.[127] When the CSSC began to operate a similar scheme in 1941, the need for feeding initiatives was even greater, and the corporation recognised that there was plenty of room for more voluntary effort. In 1943 the conference received recognition under the Dublin Corporation maternity and child welfare scheme. However, the conference employed a policy of obstruction when it came to co-ordinating their services with other non-Catholic maternity centres. An internal memo from the corporation to the Department of Local Government and Public Health explained, 'As regards the suggestion by the St J [sic] that there should be a re-distribution of the dining halls operated by them and by the CSSC to prevent overlapping it appears that any such *re-distribution would not be acceptable*. The whole difficulty is seemingly an insuperable religious one.'[128] The Corporation made the decision not to find alternative duties for the Brigade on the grounds that it '*would not be acceptable* to the Ecclesiastical Authorities'.[129] As a result, the organisation that had been one of the first to rise to the challenge of preventive maternal health care was sidelined in order to appease the members of the Catholic hierarchy.

The treatment of the St John Ambulance Brigade was poor recompense for the years during which they had relieved Dublin Corporation of the responsibility of running maternity services. Primarily for reasons of finance, it was corporation policy to encourage voluntary agencies in this field.[130] The Brigade came to their assistance and the corporation was both well aware of and anxious to conceal this fact. The County Medical Officer, Russell, wrote to the Secretary of the Department of Local Government and Public Health in 1937, in relation to paying an increased grant to the Brigade: 'The only fear I have is that when it is realized that this is a Corporation function, it is only a matter of time until a demand is received from some Trade Union for very much increased wages for these employees.'[131] The General Inspector of the department, Alice Litster, was also convinced that the voluntary administration saved the department a considerable amount in terms of finance and health. In 1941 she noted that while the administrative costs were high they would not necessarily be reduced if run by the corporation. She feared that the contrary was the most likely outcome if the St John Ambulance Brigade abandoned the work.[132]

Although McQuaid promoted the subsidiary principle by encouraging co-operation between the Catholic Church and the Irish state, he was determined that co-operation would not entail capitulation. Despite accepting a grant from Dublin Corporation, McQuaid refused to co-operate with any aspect of the corporation maternity and child welfare scheme that he regarded as needlessly interventionist. In fact, McQuaid wished the corporation to supplement his operation – not the other way around. For him to integrate his operation into the existing corporation scheme would have meant accepting a subservient role. Furthermore, the aim of McQuaid's social services was to liberate welfare from state or municipal control by co-operating but not capitulating. It was a fine line and one that McQuaid continuously sought to assert. He refused to insist that mothers first attend the corporation's maternity clinic on the grounds that this 'implied a certain degree of compulsion on mothers'.[133] The fact that each mother who received a meal at the CSSC's centres had to be certified by the corporation's maternity centre as eligible had been made clear to the conference before it was given official recognition. The various conference maternity centres were also reluctant to supply roll books[134] for audit, as this too was seen as interference.[135]

Dublin Corporation allowed McQuaid to manage welfare as he saw fit during the Emergency, but when it came to recouping their investment from the Department of Finance, they faced serious questions. A 1946 auditor's report found that the corporation was not entitled to reimbursement, as the CSSC scheme had not complied with the rules. The Auditor reported:

> I may add that there appears to be a reluctance on the part of the CSSC to conform to control under the approved scheme, although all Voluntary Organisations at present operating have willingly complied and have not regarded such control as vexatious. Public monies are concerned and such monies if administered by public officials would be subject to very close control and audit, in comparison with which the simple requirements in the scheme bear no comparison [sic]. Rolls when requested at audit were at first refused, and such as reached me were only produced after pressure.[136]

The auditor's decision may have been objective and accurate, but it was nevertheless overruled. On 13 August 1946, thanks to an Emergency Powers Order, the corporation received its recoupment on the grounds that the Emergency had 'clouded judgement.'[137]

For the first five years of McQuaid's reign as Archbishop, he successfully operated a policy of collaboration with government departments in relation to the welfare of Catholic mothers and children, while simultaneously eschewing interdenominational co-operation. Any attempt to merge Catholic interests with other non-sectarian projects encountered his opprobrium, as he sought to protect the territory of Catholic social services from interference by other religious or non-religious organisations. The delineation of religious jurisdictions formed the backbone of McQuaid's understanding of Catholic charity; moral and physical welfare were inseparable according to the Catholic principles of social justice and moral absolutism. A recent biographer referred to Archbishop McQuaid as the 'ecclesiastical Taoiseach'.[138] McQuaid was frequently given this impression by individual members of various Irish governments. Ward cultivated a working relationship with McQuaid, one in which the Archbishop was not only given the impression but also, on one occasion at least, told that the issue of maternity care was a religious one. In view of this history, it is little wonder that any attempt by the state to legislate in areas previously negotiated by private agreement with the Catholic Church would be greeted with reluctance, if not censure.

Barrington placed the revision of the Irish health services within the context of the 'stimulating' effect of war,[139] which established the climate of extremity, allowing the government to exercise greater powers of compulsion with regard to infectious diseases such as tuberculosis and typhus.[140] In 1943, as a direct result of his committee's findings on gastro-enteritis, Ward sequestered the old Claremount Protestant deaf and dumb training school for the isolation of babies with gastro-enteritis and renamed it St Clare's Hospital.[141] Action at a departmental level had finally been taken, but only after the connection between infant mortality and infectious disease was established: infection broadened the issue of infant mortality from one of domestic responsibility to one of communal concern. Séan MacEntee had been appointed Minister to the Department of Local Government and Public Health in 1942, and he was profoundly affected by Ward's findings on gastro-enteritis. In January 1944 he handed over his functions with regard to health to Dr Ward, and a month later he promised a 'root-and-branch reorganisation of his Department'.[142] MacEntee's interest in maternal welfare was most definitely motivated by the connection between maternal health, natural feeding and gastro-enteritis.[143] In March 1944 he informed the Cabinet that there was an 'urgent need, not only for the provision of additional institutional accommodation for the treatment of the disease [gastro-enteritis], but also for a great expansion in and more vigorous administration of our local Maternity and Child Welfare Services, together with a widespread campaign to educate mothers in the care of themselves and their babies'.[144] It is somewhat ironic that McQuaid had assisted in the breastfeeding campaign that was to prove the most convincing reason for the government to intervene in maternal health in a more comprehensive fashion.

A children's allowance: child protection versus family privacy

> From the maternity grant, payable when he is born, to the funeral grant payable when he dies, a man will be beholden to the state.[145]

The social and medical evidence raised by the various voluntary initiatives during the Emergency, coupled with developments across the water, forced the Irish state to deal with the issue of child protection in a more comprehensive fashion. The Beveridge Report[146] loomed large in the Irish consciousness and was frequently referred to in debates on the adequacy of Irish social services.[147] J. J. Lee noted that many of the debates within the government on social and economic policy 'were constructed largely in terms of recent English thought'.[148] Séan MacEntee engaged in the rhetoric of denial, denouncing the Beveridge report as 'closely akin in every characteristic to those totalitarian organisations which once we were told the world was being devastated to destroy'.[149] Nonetheless, while affirming that the Irish state would also confront its responsibility in relation to the health and welfare of its citizens, he was careful to specify that the Irish fight against poverty would not give the state a licence to smother the admirable instincts of charity:

> If those who believe Beveridgism can eradicate poverty, sickness, unemployment from human society, so can we. And to the utmost of our capacity this we shall try to do for our people. But we shall be careful that whatever be the consequences the state that will function here will be constituted by a community of free men and women, who the state will exist to serve, and not they to serve the state. We want no stamp licking Irish serfs.[150]

It was one thing to intervene in family life when the conventional structure had broken down through death, desertion, unemployment or illegitimacy; it was quite another issue to intervene as a right in the lives of all families. Opponents of state intervention argued that universal family allowances, proposed in the early 1940s, threatened to undermine the role of the father as breadwinner and provider by replacing the principle of 'need' with that of 'rights'.[151] Powell was correct in assessing the introduction of children's allowances in 1944 as a 'major step on the road to the welfare state'.[152] However, his contention that the introduction of children's allowances was intended to 'augment the population' and was therefore a pronatalist measure highlighted by the title 'children's allowances' rather than 'family allowances' is not borne out by contemporary evidence.[153] It is true that concern regarding the population decline revealed by the 1936 census prompted the initial considerations of some type of family allowance scheme.[154] However, very early in the investigation phase it was acknowledged that such a measure was not likely to increase the birth rate and that such a pronatalist policy was not even desirable in the Irish case. The focus during all the major debates and the final phase of design was on child protection and assisting large families. Cousins confirms that this rationale for the introduction of children's allowances, first put forward by the interdepartmental committee established to examine the question, was ultimately accepted by the government.[155] In fact, the title 'children's allowances' was selected to emphasise the measure as a child-protection issue and to underline that there was no intention on the part of the state to interfere with or to finance the family. Furthermore, Cousins concluded that the purpose of the scheme ultimately broadened from the relief of poverty in large families to general family support.[156] Lemass himself claimed that it was 'not contemplated that the ... establishment of children's allowances will influence either the birth rate or the marriage rate'.[157]

Professor T. A. Smiddy, de Valera's private economic adviser, pointed out during the early stages of consideration that the argument that a family allowance system would increase the population was unsustainable in view of contemporary demographic trends elsewhere. He noted that in those countries in which the standard of living and of social services was highest there was a tendency to population decline.[158] He noted that 'where family allowances have been adopted as a means to increase the population they have not produced clear results'.[159] Although, Smiddy clearly believed that spending any available funds on social services was preferable to cash payouts to families, he concluded his report by clearly ruling out any pronatalist motivations for the introduction of family allowances in Ireland.[160]

MacEntee was the chief cabinet opponent of family allowances, so it is little wonder that he discredited any motives for their introduction. However, his scepticism in relation to the potential pronatalist impact of such allowances was largely shared. In Ireland any references to pronatalism were usually rhetorical flourishes and little more; the underlying cultural tendency to steer clear of the bedroom at all costs predominated. There was

at no time a strong political (or social) will to implement pronatalist policies. Political anxiety regarding fertility rates, although evident following
the 1936 census, was not sustained as the years 1942–43 witnessed a sharp
rise in the birth rate.[161] In a demographic sense, the main concern expressed
consistently during this period was the desire to redistribute the burden of
large families and child protection.[162] While this was a tenet of other
pronatalist regimes, in the Irish context it was more about alleviating poverty than punishing the infertile.[163]

As Powell observed, de Valera faced intense opposition from his own
Cabinet on the grounds of cost and the risks to family autonomy.[164] Cousins
argued that de Valera and Lemass were important in pushing through
children's allowances. This was interesting in view of the central role that
both politicians played in ensuring the passage of the mother-and-child
scheme in 1953.[165] The Department of Local Government and Public Health
was not in favour of children's allowances on the grounds that they failed to
observe the following principles: (a) the responsibilities of the wage earner
himself as a present or potential parent; (b) the employer in his use of
human capital requiring replacement; (c) the state towards parents for the
conservation of the race. Finally, the department argued that it had already
done much to provide for families by way of the school medical service, the
free milk scheme and the mother and child welfare services.[166] The department did subsequently raise the issue of Catholic social teaching, claiming
that the children's allowances scheme might be objected to by Catholic so-
ciologists, as the scheme was 'based on the assumption that a man has an
inherent right to make himself and his dependants a charge on society'.[167]

The Department of Industry and Commerce pointed out that the Swedish commission on the birth rate had found that social services were a better use of resources than cash benefits to families.[168] The Department of
Finance pointed out that there were 'numerous charitable institutions and
organisations which through voluntary effort and subscription of money
cater most efficiently for the poor and the sick'.[169] The climate of concern
was not lost on the department, which astutely manipulated the general
nervousness regarding state power by claiming that any such organised
interference would destroy the primary unit of Irish society: the family.
Anxious about the cost of any such scheme, the Department of Finance
raised the emotive threat of socialism, arguing that such a scheme would
lead to the 'nationalisation of mother and offspring and the break-up of the
ordinary ideas of family ties and responsibility'.[170] Evidently, the *ideas* of
family ties' were considered more important than the reality of family life.
It was acknowledged by all who worked at the coalface that mothers shoul-
dered the brunt of poverty. Nonetheless, it was generally believed that if
allowances were paid, this payment should be to the father, in order to
preserve as much of his dignity as possible and to reinforce traditional views
regarding the male breadwinner.

The central anxiety during the debates on the Children's Allowance Bill involved the role of the state in relation to the family. Even those in favour of allowances were anxious that they be designed and administered so as to minimise the role of the state in family life. Those who argued against any form of allowance stressed the much more benign role of either social services or charity. The arguments for and against payment to the mother are well versed and analysed by Clear, Cousins and Kennedy. All three concur that the arguments in favour of paying the father were largely based on notional concepts of family power and a desire not to interfere with the private running of Irish households.[171] The decision to make family allowances payable to the father confirmed that it was more important to safeguard the perceived roles of familial dependence than to reflect social reality. The allowance did not, therefore, necessarily represent 'a welcome respite from total dependency'[172] as it was not made payable directly to the mother until 1974. Before that date the ultimate decision regarding the family budget still lay with the patriarchal head of the family.[173] The decision to make the allowance payable to the father was not, however, a move against female autonomy *per se;* women's rights were infringed insofar as they were ignored. The emphasis was on the father and the protection of a cultural and social understanding of the 'true order of the family'.

The initial children's allowance was a paltry sum and only payable on the birth of the third child as long as all three children remained under the age of sixteen. These stipulations were both cost- *and* policy-related. The intention was to keep the scheme affordable but also to target large families, as statistical evidence revealed that children in large families were most at risk from poverty, childhood illnesses and death. The Children's Allowances Act of 1944 respected the social concerns regarding the role of the father by making the allowances payable to the father as the head of the family. While the act allowed for general family support rather than merely the alleviation of poverty, thanks largely to the role of de Valera and Lemass,[174] it also respected Catholic social teaching insofar as it supplemented rather than supplanted the family wage – it was too paltry to have pretensions to the latter.[175] It was also consistent with the 1937 Constitution, which vowed to protect the 'Family' both from undue interference and undue strain.[176] Thus the debates surrounding the act and its ultimate design reflected a political anxiety about striking a balance between the increasing responsibility of the state and the survival of charity, and family privacy. Many contemporaries believed that the careful balance of charitable endeavour and state subsidy would protect Irish society from the pitfall of socialism and communism. Though the debate on welfare was frequently clouded by words of warning and dogged by predictions of communist invasion and the end of Christianity, the essence of the controversy was not about whether welfare should be provided, but rather about who should ultimately control its deliverance. Owing to the centrality of the mother in any discussion on population growth, infant mortality and welfare provision, it was hardly surprising that motherhood would provide the axis on which the debate regarding state aid and voluntary assistance would ultimately hinge.

Conclusion

Gerard Fee, who explored the impact of the Emergency on Dublin's working class, argued that the social realities of the war period led the Irish state to reconsider its responsibilities in relation to the welfare of Irish citizens, which resulted in an 'internal social reaction that has left its mark to the present day'.[177] This is evidenced in concrete ways with, for example, the introduction of children's allowances and compulsory powers relating to the control of infectious disease. However, in the long term the Emergency witnessed a change in state mentality. In the post-Second-World-War era, the Irish state had to contend with the enduring social deprivation caused by war, along with demands for more adequate social services, and was thus forced to rethink its remit of responsibility. Extending state responsibility was a complex process that had to take account of financial realities, social mores, religious qualms and the capricious tide of politics. The decade 1945–55 witnessed the interplay of all these factors, resulting in social, religious and political controversy and finally a maternity service.

Notes

1 Dr Oliver Fitzgerald, *A Balanced Diet* (10 Feb. 1943), p. 3, DDA, McQuaid Papers, AB8/B/XIX, (CSSC). Fitzgerald was editor of the *JMAÉ* between 1944 and 1952, and the professor of therapeutics at St Vincent's Hospital, Dublin between 1950 and 1983.

2 Ireland operated a policy of co-operation with Britain, while adhering strictly to the formalities of neutrality. See Lee, *Ireland, 1912–1985*, p. 244.

3 M. E. Daly, *The Buffer State: The Historical Roots of the Department of the Environment* (Dublin, 1997), p. 249.

4 Lee, *Ireland 1912–1985*, p. 233.

5 D. Ferriter, *The Transformation of Ireland, 1900–2000* (London, 2004), pp. 391–2.

6 A. Kelly, 'Catholic Action and the development of the Irish welfare state in the 1930s and 1940s', *Archivium Hibernicum*, 53 (1999), 109.

7 DDA, Byrne papers, Lay Organisations (1).

8 *Ibid.*, p. 9.

9 John Charles McQuaid to Archbishop Byrne, 17 March 1939. DDA, Byrne papers, Hospital General.

10 J. Cooney, *John Charles McQuaid: Ruler of Catholic Ireland* (Dublin, 1999), p. 132.

11 Opening of the Catholic Social Welfare Bureau, 17 June 1942, DDA, AB8/B/XIX.

12 Kelly, 'Catholic action and the development of the Irish welfare state', p. 109.

13 'Catholic Social Service Conference, Draft Constitution (v), preamble', DDA, McQuaid Papers, AB8/B/XIX.

14 McQuaid to Lonan Murphy, 17 March 1944, DDA, McQuaid Papers, Lay Organisations: St Vincent de Paul.

15 'Catholic Social Service Conference Appeal', September 1943, DDA, McQuaid Papers, AB8/B/XIX.

16 *Ibid.*

17 G. Fee, 'The effects of World War II on Dublin's low-income families, 1939–1945', Ph.D., University College Dublin, 1996, p. 61; Catholic Action was based on the papal encyclicals *Rerum Novarum* (1891) and *Quadragesimo Anno* (1931). The former rejected the excessive state intervention except in cases of 'extreme necessity' and stressed the importance of Christian charity, while the latter again stressed the centrality of Christian charity and advocated corporatism instead of state interference. See Kelly, 'Catholic Action and the development of the Irish welfare state', pp. 109–10.

18 See Cowley's memo to McQuaid regarding the informal conference held on 12 and 13 March 1941, during which the 'immediate objectives' were outlined, Cowley to McQuaid, 31 March 1941, DDA, McQuaid Papers, AB8/B/XIX.

19 Daly, *The Buffer State*, p. 260; Lee, *Ireland, 1912–1985*, p. 233.

20 Cowley worked closely with McQuaid in developing the conference and was president until his death in 1950.

21 For a list of Catholic organisations invited to join the CSSC, see DDA, McQuaid Papers, AB8/B/XIX.

22 Memo by Owen Cowley, 31 March 1941, DDA, McQuaid Papers, AB8/B/XIX.

23 *Ibid.*

24 *Ibid.*

25 *Ibid.*

26 'Report of the provisional executive of the Catholic Social Service Conference, April 1941', DDA, McQuaid Papers, AB8/B/XIX.

27 McQuaid was obviously influenced by the Liverpool Catholic Social Service Bureau, which was a federation of Catholic charities organised as a relief agency. See Cowley to McQuaid, 21 November 1941, DDA, McQuaid Papers, AB8/B/XIX; M. Purcell, *Catholic Social Service Conference, Golden Jubilee 1941–1991* (Dublin, 1991), p. 2. McQuaid correspondence with the Professor of Systemic Medicine at University College Dublin, Henry Moore, and his wife indicates that he was also heavily influenced by the organisation of charity in New York City. See Henry Moore to McQuaid, 24 February 1942, DDA, McQuaid Papers, AB8/B/XIX (CSWB); *Irish Times*, (24 Feb. 1942).

28 McQuaid's speech at the opening of the Catholic Social Welfare Bureau, 17 June 1942, DDA, McQuaid Papers, AB8/B/XIX.

29 McQuaid's opening speech, 17 June 1943, DDA, McQuaid Papers, AB8/B/XIX.

30 The Playground Section was McQuaid's attempt to counteract the playgrounds run by the non-denominational Civics Institute.

31 *Catholic Social Welfare Bureau: Twenty-Five Years of Service, 1942–1967* (Dublin, 1968), p. 11, DDA, McQuaid Papers, AB8/B/XIX.

32 McQuaid to MacEntee, 24 September 1942, NAI, Dept. Health, A114/21.

33 *Catholic Social Welfare Bureau Annual Report, 1946*, DDA, McQuaid Papers, AB8/B/XIX.

34 *Catholic Social Welfare Bureau Annual Report, 1955*, DDA, McQuaid Papers, AB8/B/XIX.

35 Cowley to McQuaid, 5 August 1943, Notes on the Conference's Health Department, p. 1, DDA, McQuaid Papers, AB8/B/XIX.

36 Document entitled 'Family welfare', p. 4. DDA, McQuaid Papers, AB8/B/XIX.

37 *Ibid.*

38 *Handbook of the Catholic Social Service Conference* (Dublin, 1945), p. 14, DDA,

McQuaid Papers, AB8/B/XIX.

39 *Joint Pastoral by the Hierarchy of England and Wales,* June 1942, p. 6, DDA, McQuaid Papers, AB8/B/XIX.

40 *Ibid.,* p. 7.

41 *Ibid.,* p. 9.

42 E. J. Coyne, 'The ethical aspect', *Journal of the Statistical and Social Society of Ireland, (JSSSI)* 96 (1942–43), 107–10.

43 *Ibid.,* p. 107.

44 *Ibid.,* p. 109.

45 *Ibid.,* p. 110.

46 *Ibid.,* p. 108.

47 The issue of a 'just wage' or 'family wage' formed part of the welfare debate in many states such as Norway, England, Italy, Germany and France. See Bock and Thane (eds), *Maternity and Gender Policies;* E. Rathbone, *The Disinherited Family* (London, 1927); Lewis (ed.), *Women's Welfare, Women's Rights;* Macnicol, *The Movement for Family Allowances, 1918–1945;* Pedersen, *Family, Dependence, and the Origins of the Welfare State.*

48 'Editorial: the lost town', *JMAÉ,* 19:112 (Oct. 1946), 145.

49 Consultative Child Health Council, *Report of the Consultative Child Health Council, 1949,* NAI, Department of Health, A116/167.

50 St John Ambulance Brigade, *Official Handbook of the St John's Ambulance Brigade, 1950* (Dublin, 1950) p. 17.

51 The Marrowbone Lane Project was founded in 1941 by Dr William R. F. Collis. The project established the Samaritan Fund, which endeavoured to finance feeding centres for children. The project was greatly aided by Bewley's Cafés, who offered their Westmoreland St. premises as a feeding centre for fifty children of unemployed men. These children were fed and examined during 1941 in order to ascertain the impact of malnutrition on child health. See *The Irish Times,* 'Feeding mothers' (12 Aug. 1941); R. Collis, *Marrowbone Lane, A Play in Three Acts* (Dublin, 1943)

52 Samaritan Fund, *Marrowbone Lane: Samaritan Fund* (Dublin, c. 1943); M. Purcell, *Catholic Social Service Conference Golden Jubilee 1941–1991* (Dublin, 1991), p. 1.

53 The paper ran a series of ten articles on communal feeding in August 1941; NAI, Dept. Finance, S72/9/41.

54 Secretary of the Department of Local Government and Public Health, Hurson, cited in Daly, *The Buffer State,* p. 255.

55 'Community kitchens Dublin plans are underway', *The Irish Times* (22 Aug. 1941).

56 Cowley to McQuaid, 14 November 1941; Minutes of the conference executive, 18 November 1941, DDA, McQuaid Papers, AB8/B/XIX.

57 Minutes of the food centres, 27 November 1941; Cowley to McQuaid, 31 December 1941, DDA, McQuaid Papers, AB8/B/XIX.

58 Samaritan Fund, *Marrowbone Lane,* p. 7; 'Some aspects of an improved medical service', *JMAÉ,* 13:74 (Aug. 1943), 19–20; W. Collis and N. Sheehan, 'Investigation into the condition of malnutrition in the children and wives of unemployed men in Dublin: Children I', *JMAÉ,* 11:63 (Sept. 1942), 31–4; W. Collis and D. M. Minabbawy, 'Investigation into the condition of malnutrition in children and wives of unemployed men in Dublin: Expectant mother', *JMAÉ,* 11:64 (Oct. 1942), 43–5.

59 Gallagher, 'Causes of maternal mortality', pp. 497–500. The influence of anaemia in the pregnant mother on infant mortality rates was also stressed in medical circles. See W. J. S. Reid and J. MacKintosh, 'The influence of anaemia and poor social circumstances during pregnancy', *The Lancet,* 2 (1937), 1389–92.

60 Shorter, *A History of Women's Bodies,* p. 252.

61 W. R. Fearon, 'Deficiency diseases: nutritional problems of to-day', *JMAÉ,* 9:49 (July

1941), 5; St John Ambulance Brigade, *St John Ambulance Brigade in Ireland: Welfare Department 15 Years of Work 1920–1935* (Dublin, 1935)

62 D. K. O'Donovan was Professor of Medicine at St Vincent's Hospital between 1943 and 1976.

63 O'Donovan, 'Diet in relation to pre and post natal care', *c*. March 1943. For a published copy of this lecture, see Catholic Social Service Conference, *Handbook of the Catholic Social Service Conference, 1945*, p. 37, McQuaid Papers, AB8/B/XIX.

64 Samaritan Fund, *Marrowbone Lane*, p. 7

65 'Minutes of meeting of executive, 3 November 1941', DDA, McQuaid Papers, AB8/B/XIX.

66 Catholic Social Service Conference, *Handbook of the Catholic Social Service Conference, 1945*, p. 17.

67 *The Annual General Report, 1942/43*, DDA, McQuaid Papers, AB8/B/XIX.

68 Cowley, 'Confidential report on pre-natal welfare work', 26 February 1942, DDA, McQuaid Papers, AB8/B/XIX; Purcell, *Catholic Social Service Conference*, p. 11.

69 Cowley, 'Confidential report on pre-natal welfare work', p. 1. All italicised sections were underlined in the original report.

70 *Ibid.*, p. 2.

71 *Annual Report of the Catholic Social Service Conference, 1944–5* DDA, McQuaid Papers, AB8/B/XIX.

72 'Maternity hospital clinical reports. Rotunda', *IJMSc.*, 212 (Aug. 1945), 233–422.

73 *Annual Report of the Catholic Social Service Conference, 1945–6*, DDA, McQuaid Papers, AB8/B/XIX.

74 The financial report noted that £23,249 was received by the CSSC and £24,497 was spent. See *Financial Statement, 1942/43*, DDA, McQuaid Papers, AB8/B/XIX.

75 Draft article submitted by the news editor of *The Standard*, in a letter dated 23 September 1946, DDA, McQuaid Papers, AB8/B/XIX.

76 *The Standard*, 27 Sept. 1946.

77 *Handbook of the Catholic Social Service Conference*, 1945, p. 23, DDA, McQuaid Papers, AB8/B/XIX.

78 St. John Ambulance Brigade had initiated this feed policy in 1925; Purcell, *Catholic Social Service Conference*, p. 11.

79 For example, Pember Reeves remarks that poorer working-class women breastfed their infants for too long. See Pember Reeves, *Round About a Pound a Week*, p. 102. Patricia Kennedy's analysis of the various reasons why breastfeeding was so controversial in Ireland during the twentieth century is fascinating. See P. Kennedy, *Maternity in Ireland: a woman-centred perspective* (Dublin, 2002), pp. 166–80.

80 Michael Curtain cited a volume of literature regarding the issue of breastfeeding and the protection of infants from certain diseases dating back to 1919. See M. Curtain, 'Failure to breastfeed: a review of the feeding history of 1,007 infants', *IJMSc.*, 346 (Oct. 1954), 447.

81 *Annual Report of the Department of Local Government and Public Health, 1937–8*, p. 56.

82 *Ibid.*, *1938–9*, p. 37.

83 Russell, 'The health of Dublin', p. 55.

84 The corporation surveyed 1,549 mothers, 413 of whom breastfed, while 662 partially breastfed and 474 fed artificially their babies. See *Annual Report of the Department of Local Government and Public Health, 1939–40*, p. 41; See also M. J. Russell, *Report on the State of Public Health in the City of Dublin for the Two Years Ending December 31st 1940* (Dublin, 1941), pp. 92–3.

85 Falkiner stressed this policy of encouraging breastfeeding in his clinical report. See N. Falkiner, 'Maternity hospital clinical reports: Rotunda', *IJMSc.*, 212 (Aug. 1943),

233–376.

86 *Ibid.*

87 R. Collis and D. M. Minabbawy, 'Investigation into the condition of malnutrition in wives and children of unemployed men in Dublin', *JMAÉ*, 11:64 (Oct. 1942), 43–5.

88 O'Donovan, 'Diet in relation to pre and post natal care,'

89 *Ibid.*

90 'Catholic Social Service Conference Appeal', September 1943, p. 2, DDA, McQuaid Papers, AB8/B/XIX.

91 G. C. Dockeray, 'Diet in pregnancy', *JMAÉ*, 12:70 (Apr. 1943), 39.

92 M. Crowe, 'Conditions affecting child health in Éire', *IJMSc.*, 255 (Mar. 1947), 96.

93 Crowe, 'Conditions affecting child health in Éire', p. 94.

94 *Ibid.*

95 *Ibid.*, p. 140.

96 J. Quin, 'A suggested maternity service for Eire', *IJMSc.*, 229 (Jan. 1945), 11–23. (President's Address to Biological Soc of the Royal College of Physicians and Surgeons in Ireland, 4 Nov. 1944.)

97 *Ibid.*, p. 20.

98 *Ibid.* See also *Annual Report of the Department of Local Government and Public Health, 1930–1*, pp. 55–8. Interestingly, both Quin and Crowe were among the few champions of child health to promote maternity leave. See Quin, 'A suggested maternity service for Eire', p. 19; Crowe, 'Conditions affecting child health in Éire', p. 96. For a historical analysis of the decline in breastfeeding in Ireland, see Clear, *Women of the House*, pp. 129–42; C. Clear, 'The decline of breastfeeding in twentieth-century Ireland', in A. Hayes and D.Urquhart (eds), *Irish Women's History* (Dublin, 2004), pp. 187–98.

99 Barrington, *Health, Medicine and Politics*, p. 138.

100 Dr Ward to McQuaid, 9 June 1943, DDA, McQuaid Papers, AB8/B/XIX.

101 *Ibid.*, p. 1.

102 *Ibid.*, p. 2.

103 *Ibid.*, p. 4.

104 *Ibid.*

105 *Ibid.*, p. 2.

106 *Ibid.*, p. 5.

107 McQuaid to Ward, 28 July 1943, DDA, McQuaid Papers, AB8/B/XIX.

108 Dr Conor Martin, MO, reporting on 19 November 1943, DDA, McQuaid Papers, AB8/B/XIX.

109 Notes written by McQuaid on a copy of the Catholic Social Service Conference programme, regarding a meeting with Dr Ward on 15 January 1943, DDA, McQuaid Papers, AB8/B/XIX.

110 *Ibid.*

111 Falkiner to MacEntee, Minister of Local Government and Public Health, 8 December 1942, NAI, Dept. Health, M34/7, vol. II.

112 Falkiner to Ward, 18 December 1942, NAI, Dept. Health, M34/7, vol. II.

113 Memo from chief medical adviser to Ward, December 1942, NAI, Dept. Health, M34/7, vol. II.

114 Dr Ward to McQuaid, 19 January 1943, DDA, McQuaid Papers, AB8/B/XIX.

115 The Secretary of the Department to Dr N. Falkiner, 22 January 1943, NAI, Dept. Health, M34/7, vol. II.

116 McQuaid to Dr Ward, 20 January 1943, DDA, McQuaid Papers, AB8/B/XIX.

117 'The State shall not impose any disabilities or make any discrimination on the grounds of religious profession, belief or status.' Government Publication, *Bunreacht na hÉireann (Constitution of Ireland) 1937* (Dublin, 1997), p. 144.

118 McQuaid to Ward, 15 February, 1943, DDA, McQuaid Papers, AB8/B/XIX. This was
     an extremely important development, as previously mothers had been getting a
     tram from Crumlin and Cabra to the Brigade kitchens. See St John Ambulance
     Brigade, *Annual Report, 1935*. See also M. Craft, 'The development of Dublin: the
     southern suburbs, *Studies* (Spring 1971), 79.

119 Hilda Nolan, a Catholic member of the St John Ambulance Brigade, wrote in Octo-
     ber 1943 to explain to the Archbishop the Brigade's decision to close its maternity
     kitchen in Merrion Square. Hilda Nolan, Pembroke Mansions to McQuaid, 17 Octo-
     ber 1943, DDA, McQuaid Papers, AB8/B/XIX.

120 This was noted in his handwriting on the minutes for the meeting of the executive
     committee, 6 November 1943, DDA, McQuaid Papers, AB8/B/XIX.

121 L. Earner-Byrne, '"Managing motherhood": negotiating a maternity service for catho-
     lic mothers in Dublin, 1930–54', *Social History of Medicine*, 20:2 (Aug. 2006).

122 N. Reddin, 'Lost to Rathmines', *The Irish Times* (30 Dec. 1943) noted that the food
     centre in Rathmines was closing for no apparent reason. The article went on to
     point out that a new kitchen was opening in the area under the auspices of the
     Catholic Social Service Conference. The article implies that the two events were
     not accidental.

123 *Irish Times* (3 Jan. 1944).

124 *Ibid.*

125 There is a copy in his papers, DDA, McQuaid Papers, AB8/B/XIX.

126 Transcript of an address by His Grace, at Pre-Natal and Post-Natal Welfare meeting,
     9 June 1943, DDA, McQuaid Papers, AB8/B/XIX.

127 Russell of the Public Health Committee, to Secretary of the Department of Local
     Government and Public Health, February 1928, NAI, Dept Health, M34/7, vol. II.

128 Mr O'Nuallain of the Public Health Section of Dublin Corporation was quoted in a
     memo regarding a meeting between the department and the corporation, dated 14
     June 1948, NAI, Dept Health, M34/7, ol. II.

129 *Ibid.*

130 *Annual Report of Department of Local Government and Public Health, 1932–3*, p. 55.

131 Dr Russell to the Secretary of the Department of Local Government and Public
     Health, 9 August 1937, NAI, Dept Health, M34/7, vol. II.

132 General Inspector of the Department of Local Government and Public Health, A.
     Litster to the Principal Officer of the Department of Local Government and Public
     Health, M. A. Lang, 30 June 1941, NAI, Dept. Health, M34/7, vol. II.

133 Auditor's Report, 19 June 1946, NAI, Dept. Health, M34/7 vol. I.

134 Public Health Department of Dublin Corporation to Cowley, President of the CSSC,
     7 October 1943, DDA, McQuaid Papers, AB8/B/XIX.

135 Auditor's Report, 16 June 1946, NAI, Dept. Health, M34/7, vol. I.

136 Auditor's Report, 8 January 1946, NAI, Dept. Health, M34/7, vol. I.

137 Mr Dowling to T. J. Barrington; Emergency Powers (No. 389) Order, 1946, NAI,
     Dept Health, M34/7 vol. I.; *The Irish Times* (30 Aug. 1946).

138 Cooney, *John Charles McQuaid*, p. 288.

139 *Ibid.*, p. 137.

140 *Ibid.*, p. 138.

141 Memo of Department of Local Government and Public Health, 'Epidemic of children's
     diseases, 1942', 31 March 1943, NAI, Dept. Taoiseach, S13066.

142 *The Irish Times* (25 Feb. 1944).

143 E. McKee, 'Church-state relations and the development of Irish health policy: and
     the mother-and-child scheme, 1944–1953', *Irish Historical Studies (IHS)*, 25 (1986),
     160.

144 'Memo regarding the Minister for Local Government and Public Health request on

4 January 1944 to delegate powers to Parliamentary Secretary', 22 March 1944, NAI, Dept. Taoiseach, S13444A.

145 Revd P. McKevitt, 'The Beveridge plan reviewed', *IER*, 61 (1943), 150.

146 'Social insurance and allied services: Beveridge report, 1944–45', NAI, Dept. Taoiseach, S13053.

147 NAI, Dept. Taoiseach, S13053A; Kelly, 'Catholic Action and the development of the Irish welfare state', p. 108; Cousins, *The Birth of Social Welfare in Ireland*, p. 116, pp. 128–47.

148 Lee, *Ireland 1912–1985*, p. 261.

149 MacEntee, 'Address on Beveridge and full employment, 1945', University College Dublin Archives (UCDA), MacEntee papers, P67/276.

150 *Ibid.*

151 Kennedy notes that the issue was raised as early as 1938 and there were isolated references to child or maternal endowment early in the century in, for example, Bigger's report of 1917. See Kennedy, *Cottage to Crèche*, p. 212.

152 Powell, *The Politics of Irish Social Policy*, p. 213; Clear, *Women of the House*, pp. 51–6; M. Cousins, 'The introduction of children's allowances in Ireland, 1939–1944', *IESH*, 26 (1999), 34.

153 Cousins, 'The introduction of children's allowances', p. 39.

154 The 1936 census revealed an overall population decline of 114,000. The majority of the decline was in those under 21 years and there was a decline in overall fertility. Despite the decline in fertility, the census revealed that Irish fertility rates for females were still 'much greater than in other countries'. See 'Observations on the population problem of this country: analysis of results contained in volume v., part i, of Report on Census of Population, 1936', NAI, Dept. Taoiseach, S9684 A.

155 Cousins, 'The introduction of family allowances', p. 42; Cousins, *The Birth of Social Welfare in Ireland*, p. 121.

156 *Ibid.*, p. 47.

157 Cited in Cousins, 'The introduction of children's allowances', p. 47.

158 T. A. Smiddy, 'Appraisal of Deputy Dillon's proposal for family allowances', NAI, Dept. Taoiseach, S11265 B.

159 Smiddy's 'Appraisal of Deputy Dillon's proposal for family allowances'. A form of family allowances had been introduced in France, Germany, Italy and Spain by the end of the 1930s: France introduced the *allocations familiales* in 1932, Germany the *Kinderbeihilfen* in 1935, Italy the *assegni familiari* in 1936 and Spain the *subsidio familiar* in 1938. See Bock and Thane (eds), *Maternity and Gender Policies*, p. 5.

160 See also Smiddy, 'Possibility of increased population', 13 December 1939, NAI, Dept. Taoiseach, S9684A. As Daly noted, Smiddy had interesting views on the issue of the burden of large families on the working-class poor which he regarded as 'grossly exaggerated'. His views were important as he was de Valera's economic adviser. See Daly, 'The Irish family since the Famine', p. 20, n. 48.

161 This was most likely as a result of the Emergency. The department noted that Ireland had followed the same trend as 'belligerent countries during the war' in relation to marriage patterns. The department noted that whereas in other countries the cause of population decline was fertility rates, in Ireland it was principally declining marriage rates. See Department of Industry and Commerce, 'The current trend in the birth and marriage rates in Éire', May 1944, NAI, Dept. Taoiseach, S9684 (A). However, the general increase in the birth rate continued in 1943–44. See *Annual Report of the Department of Local Government and Public Health, 1943–4*, p. 36.

162 The interdepartmental committee on family allowances noted that considerable poverty existed in large families and that family allowances would be an effective

way of militating against this disadvantage. See *Report of the Inter-departmental Committee on Family Allowances*, 14 October 1942, NAI, Dept. Taoiseach, S12117B. Cited in Cousins, 'The introduction of family allowances', p. 41.

163 Italy, France and Germany took measures to penalise those who did not marry or reproduce, by means of tax and employment opportunities. See, for example, C. Saraceno, 'Redefining maternity and paternity: gender, pronatalism and social policies in Fascist Italy', in Bock and Thane (eds), *Maternity and Gender Policies,* pp. 204–5; in 1920, the French Government introduced a tax law which penalised celibates over 30 by 25 per cent surcharge on income tax, and childless couples married for longer than ten years were liable for a 10 per cent surcharge. See Quine, *Population Politics*, p. 74.

164 Powell, *The Politics of Irish Social Policy*, p. 214.

165 Cousins, *The Birth of Social Welfare*, pp. 122, 126.

166 'Summary of views of three departments', 5 September 1940, NAI, Dept. Taoiseach, S11265B.

167 'Department of Local Government and Public Health: Summary of observations on memo on children's allowances submitted by the Department of Industry and Commerce.' The Department of Finance reiterated this concern regarding Catholic social teaching, pointing out that the three encyclicals *Rerum Novarum, Casti Connubii* and *Quadragesimo Anno* advocated family allowances only as a palliative in instances where a father or a breadwinner of a family was not in receipt of a just wage. The department also noted objections from Irish theologians like Coyne and the Professor of Catholic Sociology at Maynooth, P. McKevitt, who believed that Beveridge brought the 'omnipotent State closer'. See 'Further memo submitted by the Department of Finance', 11 March 1943, NAI, Dept. Taoiseach, S11265B. See also McKevitt, 'The Beveridge plan reviewed', pp. 145–50.

168 'Summary of views of three departments', 5 September 1940, p. 5. The Swedish commission to investigate the birth rate reported in 1936.

169 Memo submitted by Department of Finance, 11 March 1943, NAI, Dept Taoiseach, S11265B.

170 'Observations of the Minister for Finance on scheme of family allowances', p. 13. See also Clear, *Women of the House*, pp. 52–6.

171 Clear, *Women of the House*, pp. 51–4; C. Clear, '"A living saint if ever there was one": work, austerity and authority in the lives of Irish women of the house, 1921–1961', pp. 215–16; Kennedy, *Cottage to Crèche*, pp. 217–18. See also Cousins, 'The introduction of children's allowances', p. 47; Cousins, *The Birth of Welfare*, pp. 112–13.

172 Powell, *The Politics of Irish Social Policy*, p. 214.

173 Kennedy, *Cottage to Crèche*, p. 217. Clear has noted that the in many cases the father nominated the mother as recipient of the allowance. However, this was still discretionary and the law gave this power of decision to the father. See Clear, 'Women in de Valera's Ireland', p. 112.

174 Cousins, *The Birth of Welfare*, pp. 122, 126.

175 *Ibid.*

176 *Ibid*, p. 123.

177 Fee, 'The effects of World War II on Dublin's low-income families, 1939–1945', p. 14.

5

Cracks in the 'cordial collaboration':
political reality and religious principle, 1945–56

> The State does not exist to do for individuals and families ... what they can do
> reasonably well themselves; the State should not supplant them when they
> can partly do things but should supplement their efforts; finally the State is
> there to do for them what they cannot at all do for themselves.[1]

The stringency of the Emergency period, the sustained atmosphere of deprivation throughout the 1940s and the British White Paper, *A National
Health Service* (1944) stimulated debate in Ireland regarding the public
health services.[2] In 1944 the Minister for Local Government and Public
Health, Séan MacEntee, announced his intention to create a public health
system 'commensurate with modern requirement'.[3] This aspiration signalled a fundamental shift in state health and welfare policy. The new
Department of Health, created in 1947, was designed not only to reorganise
existing health services but also to take a more official and legislative
approach to health care. Essentially this involved the central government
taking control of an area of public welfare that had been left largely to
private practitioners, local authority initiative and charitable endeavour.
The attempts to implement the mother-and-child scheme in the early 1950s
became entangled in a web of political, professional and religious power
struggles. The original 'free-for-all' scheme fell victim to internal political
wranglings, attempts by a section of the medical profession to protect
private practice from state interference, and clumsy defence of the *status
quo* by the Irish Catholic hierarchy. Motherhood was a test case for the
Irish state, the medical profession and the Catholic hierarchy. The battle
that ensued became known as the 'mother and child controversy' and was
heralded as the first Church–State clash in the history of the state.[4] Consequently, the dilemma between assistance and intervention in the Irish
context became shrouded in the rhetoric of Church–State conflict, somewhat obscuring the complexities generated by social change.

More than a change in procedure: from public assistance to a public health service

In June 1945, an assistant principal officer of the public health section of the Department of Local Government and Public Health, C. F. Dowling, telephoned the Archbishop of Dublin to inquire if he would be available to be interviewed by the chief medical adviser with regard to repairs in certain Dublin schools. McQuaid was furious and drafted his response: '[T]he Archbishop at once took exception to the procedure by which the Archbishop of Dublin is rung up on the telephone and asked to see a subordinate official.'[5] In a letter to Dr Ward, McQuaid explained that the upkeep and running of Dublin schools was the 'subject of continuous and cordial collaboration between the Ministers already mentioned [Ministers for Education and Industry and Commerce] and the Archbishop'. Dowling apologised for 'adopting the wrong procedure' and business resumed its usual 'cordial collaboration'.[6]

The 'subordinate official' in question, Dr James Deeny, was credited by the historian John Whyte as the individual who was most 'responsible for the shape which health legislation took in Ireland'.[7] The fact that Deeny should first come to the Archbishop's attention in connection with a breach of procedure was symbolic of the role he would play in subverting all previously accepted limits and protocol. Deeny, a Roman Catholic, was born in Lurgan, Northern Ireland in 1906, the son of a medical doctor. He graduated in 1927 with an honours degree in medicine from Queen's University Belfast.[8] Both he and his father had realised the impact of social conditions on pregnancy and infant survival, and by 1929 they had opened an antenatal clinic in Lurgan.[9] Deeny was awarded a master's degree in 1939 for his study, 'Poverty as the cause of ill-health'.[10] By 1941 he was tackling the issue of infant mortality,[11] and by 1943 he had entered the Customs House (the Department of Local and Government and Public Health building) as the Chief Medical Adviser.[12] Timing was, of course, as crucial as personality, and the fact that Deeny entered a department already re-evaluating its role in public health meant that his talents were well exploited and occasionally frustrated.[13]

In June 1944, as a direct result of his work on gastro-enteritis and experiences in the delousing programme under the embarkation scheme, Ward decided to introduce a new public health bill to deal with the problem of infectious disease.[14] The association between infant mortality and infectious disease meant that an extension of maternity and child welfare services was included in the bill.[15] The department was analysing four schemes for reshaping the Irish health services: the Dignan plan, Dr John Shanley's plan, the official plan of the Irish Medical Association (IMA) and its own health bill.[16] Dr Dignan, the Bishop of Clonfert, was the chairman of the Unified Health Insurance Society,[17] and his plan was an attempt to apply Catholic social teaching to the area of social services.[18] There was much attention afforded to the publication of the Dignan plan, primarily due to MacEntee's hostile response to it.[19] He was irritated because the Dignan plan had been submitted to the government on the same day that it was released to the press.[20] The Dignan plan had obvious defects: it was very idealistic, assuming that an adherence to the tenets of Catholic social teaching would absorb human egotisms. Consequently, it failed to consider the aspect of finance and was 'rife with antipathy towards the services administered by the Department of Local Government and Public Health'.[21] However, the publicity surrounding the publication of Dignan's plan added to the atmosphere of controversy, and intensified the general sense that a change in the health services was imminent.

The President of the IMA, Dr Shanley, submitted his scheme without the approval of the IMA. He recommended the creation of a medical council to assist the Minister for Health, which would have powers to override his decisions in matters of 'major policy'. Shanley envisaged four regional health areas for administrative purposes. He recommended that people earning less than £550 per annum would be entitled to medical care free of 'direct payment'. Shanley's scheme was rejected by the IMA as too radical, and by the dispensary doctors as an attempt to continue the dispensary system in private practitioners' hands.[22] The IMA's official proposals excluded any serious consideration of the maternity services, noting only that it would be unwise to situate 'large maternity hospitals outside the main teaching centres' and that the conditions of employment for district midwives should be improved.[23] The department considered the IMA's scheme to be 'carelessly thrown together' and 'not the product of a clear realisation of existing deficiencies, and a genuine desire to remedy them by means adapted to conditions in this country'.[24]

A departmental committee was set up in early 1944, headed by Deeny, to assess all the plans and to draw up a coherent official plan for the Irish health services.[25] It reported in September 1945, condemning both the Dignan plan and the IMA's suggestions as

> open to the accusation that spade work is scamped, problems and difficulties are neither adequately realised nor squarely faced; their objects and the means of securing them are stated with vagueness with a view to escaping as long as possible from indictment on the ground of impracticability. Neither is what it purports to be. They both show what the objective is but not how it is to be reached.[26]

The department intended to integrate existing services and fortify their preventive aspects.[27] Deeny laid the blame for the continued failure to increase breastfeeding levels, for example, at the door of the existing preventive services which, he argued, were hampered by 'inadequate organisation and an uncoordinated approach'.[28]

The departmental committee examined trends in health care for mothers and children in Austria, Belgium, Canada, Czechoslovakia, Denmark,

France, Greece, Holland, New Zealand, Norway, Poland, South Africa, Spain, Sweden, Turkey, the USA, Yugoslavia, Northern Ireland, Great Britain and Scotland.[29] It deduced two broad streams of development: the insurance method and the social services funded by taxation. The committee noted that the former system was generally in use in continental countries: the latter was confined to Great Britain and the British Dominions.[30] By examining the various international approaches to public health services, the committee sought to find a solution that would be appropriate for Ireland. The Irish public health system varied considerably from area to area, and it was based on a dual system of public assistance and public health services. Irish citizens qualified on the basis of need: those earning only slightly above the poverty line had to fund their own health care either through the National Health Insurance Society or by paying from personal funds for private practice services. There was an acknowledged need to regulate the system to create a national service, and to co-ordinate services to provide a comprehensive system. The departmental report envisaged a public health service for all within ten years, irrespective of income.

Barrington described the departmental report as the 'most radical document ever produced on the Irish health services' and the 'root of later controversies'.[31] It was most definitely the clearest indication that the department was determined to regulate existing health services, especially maternity services. The departmental committee placed maternity services high on the list of priorities, making the provision of adequate services a main part of the medical officers' portfolio.[32] The most potentially controversial element of the report was the commitment to remove the distinction between public assistance and public health services. The committee decried the existing maternity services as 'confined to the poor classes' and 'more in the nature of a medical assistance than a public health service'.[33] By criticising the existing maternity services for being 'rudimentary' and restricted to the poor, it implicitly signalled a desire to find a universal and comprehensive approach to maternity and child welfare.[34] This policy shift was the basis of future controversy, as it meant, in effect, the formation of a health service based on right rather than need.

Acknowledging the *ad hoc* development of maternity services in the country, the authors noted that the system in Dublin was quite different to that in the rest of the country. The report noted that Dublin was dominated by the three voluntary maternity hospitals and, as a result, 'generations of Dubliners were used to seeking attention from institutions and the doctor–patient relationship ... does not exist here to the same extent as elsewhere in Ireland'.[35] As, by the 1940s, 80 per cent of Dublin births were catered for by the three maternity hospitals, either within the hospitals or by means of their district service it was decided that these institutions should be responsible for antenatal care and care of the infant for at least the first nine months of life. This was an extension of the system already in operation, whereby the three maternity hospitals operated antenatal clinics. There was also a desire to rationalise the system in Dublin, in order to create a 'unified service' for the city and county of Dublin, by linking the public health services run by the corporation, the voluntary hospitals, the private practitioner group and the public assistance dispensaries.[36] Dublin became the focus of initial developments in relation to maternal and child welfare from this point on, primarily because of the positive infrastructure available in the city and the tradition of co-operation between Dublin Corporation and the hospitals. These factors led to the experimental neonatal scheme organised in the city by the new Department of Health, which it was hoped would be a forerunner for a national scheme.[37]

On the basis of the 1945 report, the department began to prepare a draft White Paper on the reorganisation of the health services. There is no evidence that the Catholic hierarchy was consulted regarding any of this preparatory work, which was significant, given the relationship that existed between Ward and McQuaid. It is possible that Ward, under the influence of Deeny, whom he regarded as a genius, knew that he was allowing the governmental responsibility for public health to go beyond McQuaid's interpretation of subsidisation.[38] However, it is unlikely that Ward ever intended that an extension of state services would impinge on the work of voluntary organisations like the CSSC. On the contrary, the government repeatedly acknowledged its debt to such voluntary organisations; it was aware of the cost-saving aspect of this relationship.[39] The Department of Local Government and Public Health planned the more efficient medicalisation of childbirth in Dublin, but it did not envisage that this would impact on the work of voluntary organisations that dealt with the social aspects of maternal and child welfare. For this reason, the emphasis was laid on the better co-ordination of existing services and a broadening of the concept of entitlement in relation to medical services. There was no expressed intention to change the nature of the advice centres or maternity kitchens in operation in the city, simply a desire to complete the circle of care by ensuring that all women seen at the various clinics and clubs would be entitled to free medical care 'in respect of motherhood'.[40]

The Public Health Bill, the product of almost two years' gestation, was finally ready by the end of 1945. It was primarily concerned with the control of infectious diseases and it legalised powers of detention and isolation afforded by the Emergency Powers (no. 26) Order 1940. In the miscellaneous section, the bill proposed the introduction of a compulsory inspection of schoolchildren, and free care for mothers and for children up to sixteen years of age.[41] The opposition, particularly Fine Gael (the main opposition party), objected to this compulsory examination of schoolchildren on the grounds that it infringed parental rights.[42] The same level of concern regarding 'parental rights' was not voiced when it concerned primarily working-class or disadvantaged sections of society, for example unmarried mothers or working-class children institutionalised in industrial schools. Nonetheless, the same argument was made by members of the

Roman Catholic Church in January 1946 when Sister Alberta, a Dominican nun and member of the standing committee of the Conference of Convent Secondary Schools, contacted the Archbishop of Dublin to request his permission to protest to de Valera against sections of the bill affecting schoolchildren.[43] The conference objected to sections 12, 22, 86, 87 and 88 concerning the compulsory medical inspection of all schoolchildren. McQuaid sanctioned the conference's protest, and protested in his own right on 24 January 1946. It appears that McQuaid was particularly concerned regarding the medical inspection of adolescent girls, which he noted as 'inadvisable'.[44]

De Valera responded by sending Ward to see the Archbishop to discuss the matter further.[45] McQuaid had enlisted his own theologians to review the bill,[46] and they had expressed concern about the compulsory nature of the bill in relation to infectious persons and schoolchildren. They argued that these proposals invaded the rights of parents and individuals.[47] In February 1946, Dr Ward wrote to McQuaid describing the Public Health Bill of 1945 as 'one of the greatest social measures ever introduced in this country'.[48] However, he concluded that, despite Fine Gael's attempt to gain 'political publicity' by objecting to the bill, if he were able to 'satisfy the Church on any points that may be causing uneasiness I shall not worry too much about the lay theologians'.[49] While McQuaid had marked the section concerning maternity services in his copy of the bill, he did not voice any concerns to Ward when they met on 7 February 1946. At this meeting, Ward agreed to certain amendments concerning the medical inspection of children, which he sent to the Archbishop in March.[50] McQuaid appeared satisfied with the concessions made to Catholic social teaching regarding the sanctity of the family. Ward had ensured that children would not be examined at school if parents produced a medical certificate to show that they had taken care of their child's health elsewhere, as was their right. Although none of these amendments concerned the maternity section, McQuaid declared them sufficient to 'allay anxiety in respect of personal and family rights'.[51] The anxiety here was primarily for middle-class-family rights; the working-class poor were already subjected to a system that did not afford choice. The focus was not on maternal welfare, because this scheme had not yet been finalised, and, given his relationship with Ward, McQuaid had every reason to believe that his concerns would be catered for as they arose. However, the Public Health Bill of 1945 was not proceeded with on account of the resignation of Ward on 26 May 1946 owing to minor irregularities in his tax affairs.[52]

In March 1946 MacEntee, who had resumed responsibilities for health, sought government approval for the proposals he intended on announcing in his White Paper to reform the health services. He clearly articulated his intention to provide 'free medical treatment detached from public assistance administration'.[53] The Department of Finance reacted to this document in characteristically conservative style, expressing many of the concerns subsequently aired with vehemence by the IMA and members of the Catholic hierarchy. The Secretary of the Department of Finance, J. J. McElligott, warned the government that the proposals were, 'no matter how disguised', tantamount to 'the socialisation of medicine, and would entail an extension of benefit at the expense of individual liberty'.[54] MacElligott also married the fear of state medicine with the risks to private medical practice and voluntary initiative.[55] Barrington notes that de Valera also considered the proposals 'very far reaching' and the government had not agreed any outline by early 1947.[56] In view of the level of internal debate regarding the future of the Irish health services and the recent 1945 Public Health Bill, it was little wonder that rumours began to abound that fundamental change was imminent.[57]

The impact of Ward's departure was further compounded by the creation of two new departments in 1947: a Department of Health and a Department of Social Welfare. The new departments signalled not only the end of a *laissez-faire* approach to public health and social welfare, but a statutory separation between health and welfare provision.[58] This was more than a symbolic change, as it indicated a completely new understanding of welfare provision in Ireland, and a more proactive approach to health care. Welfare provision was administratively separated from public health, which facilitated an increasingly bureaucratic approach to both and an increasing emphasis on the impact of services on public health and welfare.

In January 1947, Dr James Ryan was appointed the first Minister for Health.[59] This author could find no evidence that Dr Ryan contacted the Archbishop before the publication of the 1947 Public Health Bill, which included a separate section entitled 'mother and child section', as opposed to the miscellaneous section in the 1945 bill.[60] The 1947 bill reiterated the departmental commitment to 'make arrangements for safe-guarding the health of women in respect of motherhood and for their education in that respect'. The bill also made provision for the care of all children under sixteen years of age.[61] Dr Ryan was primarily preoccupied with the medical reaction to his bill, as most attention was directed towards its potential impact on private practice. The bill was enacted in August 1947. In September 1947 the White Paper, *Outline of Proposals for the Improvement of the Health Services* was published. The White Paper made it clear that the provisions for mothers and children outlined in the Public Health Act were just the start of an ultimate programme to provide free medical care to all sections of society.[62]

Deeny summed up the events of 1946 and early 1947 to his friend Dr Smith of the Rockefeller Foundation in New York, explaining that Ward 'had been impeached in good old fashioned manner by a doctor who in the interests of public morality and because his brother had been fired, called the Government's attention to certain irregularities in the Parliamentary Secretary's business'.[63] Deeny went on in an optimistic fashion to fill Smith in on the state of play:

Anyway the PS [Parliamentary Secretary] lost his job and for six months we had no Ministerial head and things were in a mess. Eventually the object for which we had been fighting so long was achieved and the Health Section was divorced from Local Government and we now have a separate Ministry of Health and a new Minister [Ryan] who is, thank God, a decent, honest and an able man. As a result, progress has been exceptionally good during the last three or four months. The Public Health Bill which had become a political football and which had been suspended as a result of the former parliamentary secretary's departure was re-introduced and is going through beautifully ... Apart from other features the main advance is a clause enabling us to set up a free service for all mothers before, during and after childbirth and a similar free service for children up to the age of 16 years.[64]

Members of the medical profession had been calling for a separate Ministry of Health since the establishment of an English Ministry of Health in 1919, and the new Department of Health was greeted with enthusiasm by the main body of the medical profession.[65] The editorial of the *JMAÉ* reported with apparent relief, 'At last we are to have a Minister for Health and the uncongenial marriage of Local Government and Public Health is to come to an end.'[66] However, that enthusiasm was soon to wane. Deeny's correspondence made it clear that the general consensus of the new Department of Health was that this was the first phase of an overall strategy of conversion that would lead to a complete system of preventive health care available to the entire population:

> Our plan is, to make the family doctor the health officer of the family and to swing the whole service towards prevention ... Our idea is to concentrate on producing a really healthy normal race of children and we propose to concern ourselves with things like posture, nutrition etc., rather than the diseases of children. This is the first step towards development of a comprehensive service available to the whole population on a similar preventative basis.[67]

This letter captures a rare moment in time between one phase and the next when Deeny was still enthused and optimistic and before the issue of the new health services became mired in controversy.

Deeny was unprepared for any future objections by the Catholic hierarchy and was exceedingly pleased with his new minister's approach. As he explained to Dr Morris Fishbein, the editor of the *Journal of the American Medical Association*, 'we are trying to slant the whole medical services towards prevention, and we will commence with free services for women in child-birth and children up to 16 years'. However, he stressed repeatedly that there was no intention on the part of the government to 'alter the autonomy of voluntary hospitals even though they are mostly state financed'.[68] It was the hope of the government to 'achieve a balance between organised or state medicine and obtain what is good from such an approach, and at the same time preserve the voluntary system and the individual person element so necessary in Ireland'.[69] When thanking the editor of the *British Medical Journal* for his treatment of the White Paper, Deeny remarked, 'it is a bit "statish" nevertheless it is not nearly so bad as on your side of the water and you can rest assured that the Irish temperament and the treatment it will receive from public opinion in this country before it is implemented, will take a lot of the starch out of it'. Deeny was referring to the National Health Service in the United Kingdom, the reality of which had struck terror in the hearts of many members of the IMA. His focus was on political not clerical opposition, as he informed Clegg: 'In the meantime democracy is at work here and our Health Act, which after superhuman efforts over three years we got through the Dail (600 amendments from the Opposition) has now been challenged in the High Courts by Deputy Dillon on the grounds that certain sections are repugnant to the Constitution'.[70] James Dillon, of Fine Gael, spearheaded the opposition to the reform of the health services in relation to the Public Health Bills of 1945 and 1947 on the grounds that they were not in accordance with Catholic social teaching.[71] While democracy was at work, so too were other forces.

On 7 October 1947, after a meeting of the hierarchy's standing committee, the joint secretary to the committee, the Bishop of Ferns, Dr James Staunton, sent a statement to de Valera on the new health act.[72] The hierarchy argued that the minister 'in the Health Act assumes certain absolute, unlimited powers where, according to Catholic principles, his powers are derivative and subsidiary, and therefore qualified by the prior rights of the persons and institutions'.[73] The hierarchy believed that the rights of the family and the Church were violated by the educative intention of the act with regard to mothers, as it was 'precisely in this sphere of health education, where so many moral questions arise'.[74] Barrington was correct in concluding that the moral concerns expressed in this protest (the first formal protest from the hierarchy regarding a specific piece of legislation) were indicative of the deep fears regarding the introduction of birth control in Ireland.[75] She also noted that the principle of public authorities advising women with regard to health had been introduced in the Notification of Births Act, 1915 and the Public Health (Medical Treatment of Children) Act, 1919.[76] Barrington is correct to highlight the inconsistency in the Irish hierarchy's position. However, the objections raised with regard to a national 'free-for-all' maternity service were based less on any profound principle than on a desire to prevent change. Furthermore, two things must be said in relation to the aforementioned acts: first, they were not introduced by an Irish administration, secondly, the 1915 Act was permissive.

In the 1930s the Irish hierarchy had objected to dispensary doctors, not versed in Catholic social teaching, instructing mothers about family planning.[77] On that occasion the Archbishop of Tuam, Thomas Gilmartin, had explained that his objection concerned dispensary doctors, as they were the only doctors available to the poor.[78] The new maternity services proposed in the 1947 Health Act provided for the education of all mothers in respect of health without allowing for a choice of doctor, and the educative clause was vague enough to cause alarm regarding the possible provision of birth control. While the issue of a free maternity service was not raised at this stage, it was evident that the underlying fear was the same as that expressed in the 1950s, that morality and health were being separated by a statutory approach to maternity care. The hierarchy was nervous of any change in the *status quo*. The context of these objections is also crucial: the National Health Service in Britain and its proposed introduction into Northern Ireland in August 1947 caused alarm regarding the potential for state medicine.[79]

Ryan took his time drafting his response to the hierarchy's statement, and the final response was not sent to the hierarchy until a few days before the Fianna Fáil government fell from power in February 1948. Interestingly, his initial reply was cognisant of Catholic principles. However, when de Valera reviewed Dr Ryan's draft, he removed any references to Catholic doctrine, rendering the document more of an objective statement on human rights. Dr Ryan's draft read,

> According to Catholic teaching the individual person, the family, the professions and voluntary institutions have certain fundamental rights which the State must respect. It is contended that in the Health Act the Minister assumes certain absolute, unlimited powers which, if exercised, would violate Catholic principles.[80]

The version received by the hierarchy following de Valera's redrafting was subtly and significantly different:

> It is fully recognised that the individual person, the family, the profession and voluntary institutions have certain fundamental rights which the State must respect. The question is whether certain powers assumed by the Minister in the Health Act are such, that, if exercised, they would violate these principles.[81]

The government's response included a memorandum on the points raised by the hierarchy, in which the Minister for Health explained that the powers of the Minister cited in the act could only be implemented through regulations, and hence the power was not absolute but subject to Oireachtas approval.[82] Thus, he pointed out it was 'hardly conceivable that any Minister could, even if he so desired, flout public opinion in face of these safeguards'.[83] Furthermore, he argued, the 'powers under review which the Minister assumes in this Act are in nearly all cases either continuing powers which he already held or extending to a larger part of the population powers which he already held. He is not therefore, introducing any new principles.'[84] The power of the health authority to educate women in 'respect of motherhood' was not a shift in principle or an increase in power as far as the Minister was concerned. However, by making these provisions mandatory and available free of charge, the Department of Health had most definitely changed its policy from a permissive, assistance-based system to a more comprehensive national service. The CSSC had endeavoured to ensure the maintenance of the fine balance between Catholic social justice and state aid. The *ad hoc* arrangements arrived at between Church and State with regard to motherhood suited the contemporary reticence to deal directly and explicitly with any issues that crossed the line between the private and public spheres. The essence of this working relationship was one of balance; the state would 'supplement not supplant' Church effort. Consequently, any attempt to standardise or universalise entitlement would destroy the very basis of that system. The new governmental approach was not only upfront and mandatory, it was the first step in rendering the days of *ad hoc* arrangements unacceptable.

Prevention in principle: starting with the mother and child

McKee, in his comprehensive article on the mother-and-child scheme, puts a considerable emphasis on the role of a section of the IMA in fuelling the apparent 'clash' between Church and State.[85] He claims that what 'brought the hierarchy into the conflict was the successful demonstration of the innate connexion between the survival of private practitioners in public health and the safeguarding of catholic morality and social teaching'.[86] An analysis of the arguments presented by the members of the medical profession between 1943 and 1947 certainly lends credence to McKee's conviction. The most vocal members of the IMA consciously attempted to marry their professional concerns with the wider issue of Catholic social teaching and state power. In 1943, at the inaugural address of the Medical Society in University College Dublin, Dr Séan McCann of the IMA invoked the papal encyclical *Rerum Novarum* as a guide to the proper role of the state in welfare provision.[87] He went on to express the growing sense of concern within the IMA regarding the future of state involvement in health care:

> The modern idea is now growing, especially since the beginning of the war, that if a country in the field of medical health wishes to progress, then the State must become a positive instrument of service in most fields where individual action is not enough, or is leading to chaos. What does all this mean? In the field of medical health it implies that the State is entering many fields formerly cultivated by voluntary organisations. It is also widening its sphere of influence and is tending to convert the health services from a mainly preventive service which it is now into a positive health service with the aim of improving the general health and well-being.[88]

McCann, while representing the sense of fear within the profession regarding the threat of state medicine, also admitted that there were many people in need who would benefit from a free service. Nonetheless, he concluded his article by turning to religion for the final say: 'While the medical profession can confidently condemn the socialisation of medicine from the point of view of medicine and efficiency one could look at it from the Christian prospect and find other reasons for objection.'[89] Quoting *Quadragesimo Anno*, McCann argued the 'fundamental principle of social philosophy': voluntary effort should not be absorbed by a state service.[90]

McCann's article prefigured Dr James McPolin's arguments against a state medical service, which he repeated with admirable insistence from 1946 until the early 1950s. McPolin, as a founding member of the Irish Guild of SS Luke, Cosmos and Damian Society, and county medical officer of Limerick until 1946, was versed in Catholic doctrine and experienced in state administration.[91] While he conceded that the world had changed, and 'the State is now compelled to deal more and more with matters of a purely sociological character',[92] he blamed the state for the condition of the existing health service which he admitted was inadequate.[93] McPolin also used papal encyclicals to ascertain the 'correct relationship between the family and the State', and repeatedly warned that the development of free state-run services would obliterate Christian charity. In fact, in July 1947 McPolin submitted extracts from the relevant papal encyclicals to the Department of Health as proof that the Health Bill of 1947 would 'damage family life'.[94]

McPolin's arguments formed the basis of the medico-moral opposition to *any* new maternity scheme that was designed and controlled by the state. The objections expressed by the medical profession and the Catholic hierarchy were based on concerns regarding professional territory: the basis on which health care was administered was fundamental in ascertaining the integrity of that service in moral and, more importantly from their point of view, professional terms. Consequently, the arguments used against a mandatory state maternity scheme ranged from the potential risks to the father, to the 'family doctor' and to social morality. The impact of such a scheme on the physical welfare of mothers and their children was not the primary concern. Nor was it appreciated by the critics that the desire to ensure that *all* mothers received the same standard of care was a basic requirement of the preventive health care, which everybody involved – doctors, clergymen and government officials – had been advocating for years. The essence of the controversy was not that preventive health care should be administered, but who should control it.

The medical profession had been drawing attention to the social dimensions of health since the beginning of the century, particularly in relation to maternal and child welfare. The examiner for midwifery at the Royal College of Physicians, Dr James Quin, explained in 1944, 'The prosperity of any nation must ultimately rest on the health of its citizens, and the basic structure of any scheme to improve the national health must be a good maternity and infant health service.'[95] The medical profession believed that when change came, it *should* come in the shape of maternity services, because this was the key to the nation's health. Nonetheless, there were many members of the profession, such as Professor John A. Ryle of the Nuffield Foundation, who had reservations: 'Social medicine, as we conceive it, is concerned with scientific disciplines and improvements of preventive and remedial practice based thereon, and not with political planning.'[96]

In July 1947 the International Congress of Obstetricians and Gynaecologists was held in the Rotunda hospital in Dublin. Delayed as a result of the Second World War, the congress took place at a highly pertinent time in the history of Irish public health policy. The majority of the papers presented not only acknowledged the symbolic timing, but also reflected the mentality and convictions that had informed the changes in Irish health care. Falkiner was the chairman, and, as an outspoken advocate of organised maternity care and integrated antenatal services, he was an appropriate, if partisan, surveyor. Many other central figures in the history of maternity care such as Dr Bethel Solomons and the Masters of the Coombe and Holles Street, Drs Edward Keelan and Alex Spain,[97] were among the organisers.[98] This congress revealed the complexity of social medicine with its medical dimensions and social considerations, and it served as an informative reflection on the developments in preventive medicine during the Second World War. Many of the papers explored in a medical context the changing approach to pregnancy, referring to the need for antenatal care and proper management. Although the speakers stressed the management of pregnancy in medical terms, the social element of maternal care was repeatedly mentioned, and it was acknowledged to form part of any programme of prevention.[99]

Dr Deeny spoke on behalf of the new Department of Health from 'the standpoint of administrative and social medicine'.[100] Stressing the need for 'ante-natal supervision' in the battle against infant death, he noted with pleasure that the obstetrical profession was considering the 'social side of medicine'.[101] Deeny sought to establish a case for state action, and he pointed out that while poverty was a definite factor in ill health, its relief was not the answer to all ills. He argued that preventive health care must be based on 'an effective and comprehensive organisation of maternal and infant welfare services'.[102] He suggested that there were few places in the world where every member of the society could afford adequate care and that, therefore, any scheme should be operated on a 'community basis'.[103] Throughout his paper the chief medical adviser stressed the need for continuity of care, arguing that the mother and baby should be treated as a 'unit'.[104] He decried the tendency to separate services, urging that 'community antenatal, obstetrical and infant health services should be closely integrated'.[105] Deeny's hyphenated approach to maternity care was the basis of the mother-and-child service, which considered the health of mother and baby as inseparable. In the interests of child safety, he pointed out that the education of mothers in health matters should be a 'major feature and should be dealt with in a systematic way'.[106]

Deeny was answering criticism that had been voiced about the proposals for the care of mothers and children during the previous months revealing the degree to which the Irish state was considering involving itself in the care of its citizens. Much of what Deeny recommended had already been implemented in Dublin in conjunction with the three maternity hospitals, which were in the early stages of co-operating with the department in establishing a neonatal scheme. He was therefore quite confident that the path would shortly be cleared for a national scheme. By placing the emphasis on child care, Deeny sought to downplay the notion that 'everyone should be regimented under a State Service', stressing that the aim was 'that those responsible should know that every child is receiving proper attention, whether this is provided privately or through the community services'.[107]

Capitalising on the spirit of the congress, Deeny stressed the preventive nature of the department's mother-and-child scheme, which he believed would close the gaps of the haphazard system that existed for mothers and their babies:

> Although such care has always been available, it has not been on a proper foundation, but has been provided either on a public charitable basis or secured privately. As regards infants, it has largely been a matter of treating, but not preventing, illness; and where infant welfare services have developed they have been operated by public health personnel and have lacked the proper association with the family doctor or the family.[108]

The reorganisation was less a matter of a radical shift in principle than an improvement of existing structures. Deeny concluded by reiterating the increasingly familiar departmental line: maternal and child welfare was just the beginning of a fundamental reorganisation of public health services.[109] He emphasised, ' it is considered that we must proceed cautiously, step by step, and gain experience in the Mother-and-Child Service before further developments are attempted'.[110]

In July 1947 the IMA reported 'friendly relations' with the new Minister for Health, Dr James Ryan. However, the publication of the more radical White Paper later that year ended the brief period of optimism.[111] The IMA expressed concern for the fate of charitable initiatives, claiming that 'the undue consideration of the evolution of the public health services in this country tends to cast a veil over the large services which have long been given to the Irish poor and needy by voluntary organisations'.[112] By January 1948 the IMA described the 1947 Health Act as 'a compromise of nationalism and a vague socialism – a not very happy mixture'.[113] The IMA drew heavily on Catholic social teaching, insisting not only that health and morality were intimately connected, but also that this understanding of health and welfare would save the country from socialism or communism. McPolin, by far the most able and polemical advocate of this mixed defence of Catholic teaching and medical professional ethics, explained clearly, 'the only true object of law and medical activity is the promotion of virtue and any other view of law and medicine will eventually corrupt health as well as virtue'.[114] There was precious little consideration of the medical or physical welfare of mothers.

The Irish medical profession was also keenly aware of the fate of their colleagues in Britain and Northern Ireland who were facing a National Health Service which allowed for free medical treatment for all. The NHS was introduced in Northern Ireland in July 1948 to the dismay of the medical profession there, who feared that they would be swamped and held to ransom by patients.[115] Dr D. J. Cannon published an article of warning in late 1948 in the *IER* with the opening words: 'There can be no doubt that the medical profession in these islands has reached a crisis in its history.'[116] He opposed the very notion that a state should dictate the evolution of the health services, believing that development should be 'gradual' and 'from below'. The state should provide the funds necessary for 'technically poor patients', but if the state imposed a 'state-salaried system' on the medical profession it would destroy 'the confidential relationship between the doctor and the patient'. While Cannon claimed that the medical profession supported the 'mother and child-welfare scheme', he stressed, 'it insists that families who can afford to pay a fee should do so and should have, in consequence, the choice of doctor'.[117] The article was full of the horrors of the situation in Britain and concluded with the hope: 'Being a Catholic country, we have an excellent opportunity of applying the principles of social philosophy outlined by the Papal Encyclicals.'[118]

Motherhood was a test case for the department, the medical profession and the Catholic hierarchy. Dr Ryan insisted that the maternity section of the 1947 act was vital, and while he was open to compromise on details of the act, he made it clear that the principle of state responsibility had to be honoured. This was the *raison d'être* of the new department, which laid an emphasis on organisation and integration, and on a more official and legislative approach to health care. Deeny was determined to focus on the medical aspects of maternal and infant welfare, and he interpreted the 1947 act as a mandate to begin the first phase of the scheme in Dublin, where the doctor–patient relationship was not as central in view of the hospitalisation of maternity care.[119]

The mother-and-child scheme: a political casualty

Fianna Fáil did not respond to the hierarchy's official protest of October 1947 until a few days before the party left government in February 1948. Fianna Fáil, led by de Valera, had a 'virtual hegemonic status' and the departure marked the end of sixteen years in power.[120] As a result of this delay, the issue of a comprehensive maternity service lay in abeyance until the new Minister for Health, Dr Noël Browne, was well installed. The succeeding government was the first interparty government under the leadership of John A. Costello: a coalition constructed as much out of the desire to keep Fianna Fáil out of power as out of any genuine political creed.[121] The youthful and politically inexperienced Noël Browne of Clann na Poblachta showed even less respect for both the sensibilities of the medical profession and the history of co-operation between Church and State than his predecessor. Dr Browne proved to be difficult to work with, was not fully supported by either his own party or the cabinet and was prone to bouts of ill health.[122] He did not handle either the opposition of the medical profession or the hierarchy very skilfully, provoking the former and underestimating the latter, which finally lost him the support of his chief medical adviser, Dr Deeny, who was 'seconded out' of the department in early 1950.[123] Hogan noted that the controversy which ensued was 'testament to obduracy on the part of the doctors and their clerical allies, but also the fact that this obduracy collided, head-on, with a Minister who was temperamentally opposed to consensus and motivated not only by ideology but by personal feelings of extraordinary depth and power'.[124]

The proposals for a free and comprehensive maternity scheme became mired in political rivalries, professional power and religious territory. However, access to Archbishop McQuaid's archives confirms not only McKee's belief that the hierarchy was influenced by the medical profession, but also his contention that much of the 'controversy' lay in the 'complex arena of inter-party cabinet politics'.[125] As early as 19 August 1948 Dr J. P. Delaney, the Secretary of the IMA, sent McQuaid a copy of a letter he had received from the Department of Health. The letter informed the IMA that 'the provision free of charge of a Mother and Child Health Service has been fully considered and the government had decided against making any change in that respect in the Health Act, 1947'.[126] The outline of the mother-and-child scheme was not completed for another year primarily as a result of financial anxieties.[127] When McQuaid received the draft of Browne's new 'mother-and-child scheme' in June 1950, he asked Fr. James Kavanagh, an expert in social ethics, to analyse the document.[128] Browne's scheme offered a free maternity and infant service to all mothers, and free medical services to children up to sixteen years of age. The Minister stressed that women 'could avail or not as they saw fit, without payment, without contribution and without means test'.[129] Kavanagh pointed out the dangers it posed to voluntary hospitals which might become subsumed under a state system, and the burden on taxpayers of any such scheme. He believed that it would be more 'burdensome financially' to the community than a 'non-State-controlled method'.[130] Referring to the British experience of 'State Welfare Schemes' as not a happy one, Kavanagh warned that it was frequently the 'poor citizen' who paid via 'indirect taxation'.[131] It was also Kavanagh who alerted McQuaid to the 'moral considerations' of the 'free-for-all' aspect of Browne's scheme: 'Why take from a great many individuals their own innate initiative in looking after the members of their families?' he asked, clearly considering the position of the family provider. Kavanagh believed that the role of the state should be to help the organisations 'already doing such sterling work in the matter of Maternity & Child Welfare'. According to Kavanagh, the problem was not the medical services but the social conditions. Consequently, it was after the child left the hospital that it faced the greatest dangers.[132] Kavanagh concluded, 'It is at least doubtful if men will gain materially, but there is no doubt that the Welfare state leads to a dire impoverishment of the spirit.'[133] It is essential to understand that the Catholic

Church, if forced, chose physical rather than spiritual impoverishment for its people. Kavanagh's analysis formed the basis of the hierarchy's subsequent objections to the mother-and-child scheme.

In order to ensure that the relationship between morality and health was maintained, the Church needed to defend the 'subsidiary capacity' of state intervention, as the hierarchy explained in its protest concerning the maternity scheme in 1950.[134] In describing the scheme as 'a ready-made instrument for future totalitarian aggression', they were effectively (and unintentionally) paraphrasing the response of the former Minister for Local Government and Public Health, Sean MacEntee to Beveridgism. While the development of a more comprehensive maternity service was a logical step for the Department of Health, it was quite a shocking one for the hierarchy, who had become accustomed to a relationship of close co-operation whereby the state fostered charitable endeavour. Their objections to the clause promising 'education in respect of motherhood' was based on the premise that it could 'include provision for birth limitation and abortion'.[135] This was never on the agenda, but by raising the spectre of such a possibility, the Catholic hierarchy would have expected a favourable response from a state that banned such practices. The hierarchy claimed that they had no 'guarantee that State officials will respect Catholic principles'. This complaint certainly marked the difference in the relationship between the new Department of Health and the old Department of Local Government and Public Health. If the new department was determined to legislate for a mandatory state public health system, then the hierarchy also required legal guarantees.

Browne met with the members of the hierarchy prior to receiving the letter of 10 October 1950, and it was from that point that a series of misunderstandings, miscalculations and confusion detracted from the establishment of a comprehensive maternity service.[136] Browne apparently believed that he had satisfied the hierarchy's qualms with regard to the scheme by firstly insisting that the scheme was not compulsory.[137] With regard to the concerns expressed associated with the education of mothers in 'respect of motherhood', the Minister admitted that this

> may include instruction in sex relationship, chastity and marriage. It also includes, however, such matters as correct diet during pregnancy, an avoidance of certain forms of work and certain social habits, for example, smoking during that time. It is only the latter type of education which is to be provided under the Scheme and care will be taken to ensure that the regulations governing its operation will include nothing of an objectionable nature under this heading.[138]

By emphasising foetal health issues, such as smoking during pregnancy, Browne sought to allay fears of moral intrusion on the part of the state. However, by suggesting that issues of sexual health 'might' form part of the instruction given to mothers, he had virtually guaranteed a negative response from the Irish Catholic hierarchy. It was not surprising that the hierarchy took Browne up on his offer of a veto on this section of the maternity scheme, as papal teaching expressly forbade birth control education, even in the interests of maternal health.[139] To allow even the risk of such a moral transgression would be tantamount to a dereliction of duty as far as the standing committee of the Irish hierarchy was concerned.

Testimony to the fact that Browne had underestimated the importance that these men attached to the lack of a means test in the scheme[140] was his confident assertion that the 'only fundamental difference in principle between the existing Public Assistance system of medical relief and the proposed Mother and Child Service is that there was a means test for the former and that it will be eliminated in the latter'.[141] Regarding the absence of income criteria for qualification, the Minister referred to the Children's Allowances Act of 1944, which was paid to all fathers of three or more children, irrespective of income.[142]

Browne sent this memorandum to the Taoiseach, J. A. Costello, who decided to retain it rather than passing it on to the hierarchy. Instead, unbeknownst to Browne, Costello adopted a policy of direct contact with McQuaid.[143] Costello's tactic played a major part in creating the impression that the controversy that ensued was merely a 'church-state clash', detracting attention from the internal political reasons for Browne's resignation and the central role of the IMA.[144] Browne, unaware of Costello's dealings with McQuaid, focused his attention on the IMA. However, in this respect his own naiveté, the lack of political unity within the coalition government and the strength of the medical opposition conspired against a workable solution. Dr McCann, a member of the deputation that met with Browne in October 1950, clearly explained the IMA's concerns that 'which ever doctor gets the mother and children almost invariably gets the remainder of the family practice'.[145] McCann predicted the 'almost total abolition' of private practice.[146] Browne did little other than confirm the doctors' suspicions when he informed the doctors that 'his own view was that the country should have a whole-time salaried service for doctors'.[147] The doctors were insistent that without a means test they would never co-operate with the scheme. In their resistance to the threat of 'state medicine', the Irish medical profession was not exceptional. Ellen Immergut, in a comparative study of the politics of national health insurance in Switzerland, France and Sweden, noted that national health care systems rarely evolve naturally and are always controversial.[148] Immergut identified the source of controversy as a resistance to 'government monopsony': 'the medical profession throughout Western Europe ... preferred programs subsidizing voluntary mutual aid societies to programs of national health insurance; and they preferred programs of national health insurance to programs of national health services'.[149]

In Ireland the medical profession objected most strongly to the creation of a national maternity service. This was motivated by professional protectionism.[150] Nonetheless, many in the medical profession were also deeply influenced by the ideology of Catholic social teaching and, with varying degrees of sincerity, used papal teaching to bolster their arguments against any form of state medicine.[151] Through organisations like the Irish Guild of SS Luke, Cosmos and Damian Society and the Knights of Saint Columbanus[152] they not only drew support but also rubbed shoulders with other professional people, among them government ministers who nurtured a similar Catholic vision.[153] McQuaid had been in regular contact with Stafford Johnson from as early as 1939 in relation to the planned children's hospital for Crumlin and with regard to Catholic medico-ethics.[154] Browne was most probably not fully aware of the power of this parallel world from which he was utterly excluded. However, he fast became convinced that compromise with the IMA was impossible. The fatalistic tinge that this gave to the Minister's subsequent actions was exacerbated by his deteriorating relationship with the head of his own party, Séan MacBride.[155] The atmosphere in government circles had deteriorated to such a degree that Browne's biographer concluded that in the final months, between January and April 1951, the 'issue dominating his strategy' was 'the destruction of the government in order to restore the vision and the idealism of Clann na Poblachta'.[156]

In January 1951 McQuaid confided in a report to the standing committee that the Taoiseach had informed him that the Minister was 'the gravest single embarrassment that the Government endures'.[157] McQuaid was given the impression by the Taoiseach that Browne was the only obstacle to dropping the mother-and-child scheme. McQuaid, aware of the potential public relations disaster, reported to the standing committee in January 1951,

> I do not consider it advisable to give Dr B. and the Clann na Poblachta the chance of going to the country on the basis that the Bishops destroyed the mother and child scheme for *poor* women and children.
>
> But I am convinced that, even at that risk, we may yet be obliged to break this certain introduction into our country of Socialised state Medicine.
>
> I have already broken Dr B.'s scheme to socialize the Cancer Services: and my success so far, I say so far, gives excellent ground for hoping that we can break the free-for-all mother and child scheme.[158]

Nonetheless, McQuaid was willing to endure the bad publicity for the sake of saving the country from 'Socialized state medicine'. In March 1951 McQuaid wrote to Browne, reiterating all of his objections to the scheme and noting, 'if proof be needed of my attitude, I may be permitted to point to many activities of my Episcopate, in particular to the work of the Catholic Social Service Conference founded by me, more especially its Maternity Welfare Centres'.[159] However, McQuaid fought to maintain an established working relationship, one in which the state sought 'to supplement not supplant' voluntary effort in the field of social service.[160] In a report to the standing committee of the Irish Catholic hierarchy in March 1951, McQuaid explained that the free scheme for mothers should be opposed on the basis that 'we shall have saved the country from advancing a long way towards *socialistic* welfare. In particular, we shall have checked the efforts of leftist

Labour elements, which are approaching the point of publicly ordering the Church to stand out of social life and confine herself to what they think is the Church's proper sphere.'[161]

On 5 April 1951 McQuaid wrote to the Taoiseach reiterating the objections put forward in 1947 and 1950 on the grounds that the scheme contravened Catholic social teaching.[162] To McQuaid's dismay, Browne received this objection with joy, noting that the hierarchy had not objected on the grounds of Catholic moral teaching. Exasperated by Browne's tenacity, McQuaid instructed the Taoiseach to explain that 'Catholic Social teaching meant Catholic *moral* teaching in regard to things social.'[163] This was a particularly weak defence, revealing that apart from parroting papal encyclicals and condemning state intervention, the Irish hierarchy had not developed a sophisticated philosophy to support their conviction that the 'subsidiary principle' was the only Christian alternative for Irish society.[164] McQuaid was simply not accustomed to defending his stance; he was used to the days of Ward, when the government approached him and indicated that they would prefer the 'Cath. approach'[sic] to get the 'credit and funding'. Moreover, since the foundation of the Irish state, the Irish hierarchy had stressed the intimate connection between social life and moral behaviour. Catholic social teaching was in effect interchangeable with Catholic moral philosophy. Browne finally resigned on 11 April 1951 when it was clear that the Cabinet would not support his mother-and-child scheme.[165] McQuaid believed that he had secured the balance of power between Church and State. He confided in a letter to the Papal Nuncio, the Most Revd Felici that

> the clash should have come in this particular form and under this Government, with Mr Costello at its head, is a very happy success for the Church. The decision of the Government has thrown back Socialism and Communism for a very long time. No Government, for years to come, unless it is frankly Communist, can afford to disregard the moral teaching of the Bishops.[166]

McKee convincingly argued that the 'Church–State clash' concerning the mother-and-child scheme was 'more apparent than real'. McQuaid was happy to view the controversy as a defining moment in Church–State relations.[167] Evidently, McQuaid believed that a 'clash' between the Catholic Church and the Irish state had been inevitable, as he did not express surprise that the moment had come; he expressed only relief that it had come 'in this particular form and under this Government'. Motherhood provided the perfect *cause célèbre* precisely because the mother was crucial to the moral and physical welfare of the family, and the correct interpretation of motherhood was central to the role of fatherhood. Furthermore, McQuaid felt quite justified in putting himself forward as the champion of motherhood, as he had provided a practical example of social services for mothers, according to Catholic principles, with the CSSC.[168]

The correspondence between the Archbishop of Dublin and the Taoiseach testifies to the fact that Browne did not have the support of the cabinet and that the 'controversy' was as much a product of politics as principle. Horgan's analysis of the months leading up to Browne's resignation also highlights the fact that Browne was less than transparent in his actions, effectively stage-managing his exit from government to maximise damage to Clann na Poblachta. He had become disillusioned with his party and convinced that he could not triumph over the objections of the IMA, with whom he broke off talks on 5 March 1951, three days before the association was due to make its position official.[169] Crucial to Browne's failure, apart from his own strategy, was the fact that his scheme was too ambitious and many in government believed it would prove too costly. Hierarchical objections provided a convenient camouflage for financial imperatives. The real victims of this ideological and political battle were the mothers and infants, a fact virtually obscured by controversy.

While the hierarchy may have thrown back Socialism 'for a very long time', they had not seen the end of the mother-and-child scheme. In fact, it was the publicity given to the 'mother and child controversy' that made resolution a political necessity. The interparty government, weakened by a succession of embarrassing controversies, fell in May 1951. Fianna Fáil resumed the mantle of power and Ryan returned to the portfolio of Health to tackle once again the issue of maternal and child welfare. In September 1952, Ryan sent the Archbishop of Dublin a copy of his *Proposals for Improved and Extended Health Services* which proposed free medical care for women in 'respect of motherhood' and for infants up to six weeks old. Mothers in the lower income group were also entitled to essential nutrients and a cash grant of £4.[170] McQuaid thanked the Minister for his courtesy and expressed the hope that they would be able to settle the spiritual issues at hand: 'An example of such collaboration is to be seen in the adoption act where very grave spiritual issues were involved and, by preliminary discussion, were excellently solved.'[171] Clearly, McQuaid expected a return to the era of 'collaboration', and the fact that his concerns regarding the religion of adopted children had been met in the Adoption Act of 1952 led him to believe that the same would happen with the reorganisation of the health services.

The significance of the 'Browne controversy' was not lost on members of the hierarchy who, although not happy with Ryan's proposals, were anxious to 'avoid a head-on collision'.[172] The proposals only covered children up to six weeks old, the scheme still contained the elements that the hierarchy had objected to, and although they wished to be consulted in the drafting process, Dr Staunton cautioned against directly asking for that privilege 'lest the Government might refuse to acquiesce'.[173] This change in attitude reflected how significant the Browne scandal had been in terms of Church–State relations, and showed that the hierarchy was deeply concerned about public opinion. When Browne had published correspondence between the hierarchy and the Department of Health in April 1951, the hierarchy had been exposed to a considerable degree of attention and criticism. In a particularly frank note to McQuaid, the Archbishop of Cashel, Jeremiah Kinane,[174] explained their predicament: 'although the principle underlying the services in question is wrong, in practice these services will mean very little; so that it would be very difficult to make a case that would appeal to the public'.[175]

The truth was that while objecting to aspects of the scheme, the hierarchy really objected to the principle of a government department introducing a state maternity scheme, regardless of its contents. The hierarchy wished the government to improve housing and other social factors that might impinge on family life, but to leave the existing services with regard to the care of mother and child as they were. Bishop Lucey of Cork, who repeatedly viewed maternity care in terms of male economic citizenship, expressed the hierarchy's opinion:

> The real answer to the problem of the man who cannot afford medical care for his wife and children is not a free mother and child services for all, but a rise in wages – or cut in taxes – sufficient to enable him to pay. In fact, the state whose citizens cannot afford to own their own houses, pay their own doctor and hospital bills, feed and clothe their children etc., is failing in its primary duty to them; the very extent of its 'free' services is proof of its failure as a Government for the common good.[176]

This was basically a plea for the retention of the *status quo* in relation to maternity services. Barrington correctly observed that the hierarchy's suggestions regarding tax cuts 'were hardly within the sphere of the bishops' moral authority', but that was precisely the point: the bishops wished the 'reorganisation' to occur in some other aspect of Irish life that was *not* within their field of concern.[177]

In November 1952 McQuaid wrote to the government enquiring why the hierarchy had not been informed regarding changes to the 1952 White Paper, *Proposals for Improved and Extended Health Services*. He expressed his eagerness to have a 'resolution'.[178] McQuaid was prepared to gamble with a public declaration claiming that he was concerned that 'the apparent lack of hierarchical statement will be misunderstood'.[179] The following day, in a letter to the papal nuncio, he gave private vent to his frustration:

> From Mr de Valera's re-assumption of political leadership, the chief element of note, as far as the Church is concerned, is a policy of distance. The policy is seen in the failure to consult any Bishop on the provision of a Health Scheme. All the present difficulty results from that failure.[180]

Horgan noted that de Valera, while a devout Catholic, had given evidence that 'personal piety was not necessarily a guarantee of subservience', and McQuaid appeared aware and angered by this discretionary capacity.[181] McQuaid went on to reveal a history of difficulty with Fianna Fáil:

> Besides, in assessing the attitude of the Fianna Fáil government, one may never forget the revolutionary past of that Party. On so many occasions, the

Party was on the side opposed to Episcopal directions. While, then, outward courtesies will be accorded, the inner spirit of sympathetic and open collaboration with the hierarchy will be missing from Fianna Fáil Government. Not that anti-Catholic measures may be expected from men who faithfully practise now the Faith, but, as I have said in my present Quinquennial Relatio, a definite Liberalism is always present.[182]

Although a compromise was found, McQuaid viewed it as a defeat: the government, in appearing to concede in principle, had, in fact, given way only in detail.[183] Ryan included an income limit of £600, after which women who wished to avail themselves of the scheme had to pay £1 every year to the health authorities. Bishop Kinane assessed this compromise as 'illusory'; McQuaid believed it to be a 'ridicule of the principle' that the hierarchy defended. Lucey regarded the £1 contribution as 'so much eye-wash' and the entire scheme as tantamount to 'Socialism little by little'.[184] Following a meeting of the hierarchy on 11 April 1953, the committee decided to issue a public statement on the 1952 Health Act which would explain to the public the grounds for their objection to the scheme. Although de Valera managed to stop this statement going to press by arranging an emergency meeting with the Archbishop of Armagh, Dr John D'Alton, the statement is significant as it clearly outlined the hierarchy's justification for intervening in government policy.[185] Moreover, it revealed the vague but fundamental understanding of 'Catholic sociology' that informed the CSSC and many other Catholic social initiatives. The statement explained:

The Church is concerned directly with the spiritual, and the state with the temporal, welfare of men ... Since, however, there are many matters which have both a spiritual and temporal aspect, and since both Church and State have the same subjects, it is the ideal of Catholic sociology that there should be harmonious agreement between the two societies. Such agreement is the most opportune and efficient means of securing, through their joint efforts, the welfare of the human race in all that regards temporal life and the hope of eternal happiness. Should, however, any clash, or, to speak more correctly, apparent clash, arise between spiritual and temporal interests, the spiritual, being the higher, nobler and more important, and the society which deals with them, should prevail.[186]

The hierarchy objected to the state's attempt to separate the temporal from the spiritual in relation to the health and welfare of Irish mothers. The Irish Catholic Church believed that, as the spiritual leaders, their word should 'prevail' in relation to any subject that crossed the line between social and moral welfare. Interestingly, in 1956, when McQuaid was asked by the apostolic nuncio, His Excellency Monsignor Levame, what effect the Health Act had had on the Catholic country, he acknowledged that, as a result of Dr Ryan's concessions, 'the crookedness of the measure was made sufficiently straight to avoid further condemnation'.[187] McQuaid did not consider the Health Act, or any of the proposals suggested at any stage during the 'ten year' battle in the light of their potential impact on maternal welfare; instead he viewed the period in terms of the socialisation of the country and the beginnings of anticlericalism. He complained that the Episcopal committee found, 'both Dr Ryan and Mr Lemass, the acting Taoiseach, mentally incapable of grasping the principles, and the application of the principles, in this Health measure. The latter Minister, as Minister for Industry and Commerce, had been chiefly responsible for the very noteworthy socialisation of our country.'[188]

He concluded,

> Assuming that the position will settle into one of uneasy acquiescence, I fear that the Health Act of 1953 will yet be seen to be one of the unfortunate measures of Mr de Valera's Government that have tended to emphasise the trend towards excessive State intervention, and, I would add, a latent anticlericalism that fears the influence of the Church and will always seek to eliminate that influence from public life.[189]

The historiography of the development of maternity services in Ireland has been almost totally eclipsed by the controversy that developed regarding the 'mother-and-child scheme' first proposed in 1947.[190] Whyte dealt with the mother-and-child scheme as the first 'church-state clash', fitting the narrative of the controversy into the broader tale of Church–State relations and the more immediate context of post-war Ireland in which the previous 'consensus about moral and social questions' was collapsing.[191] Barrington has been correctly credited with providing the most comprehensive treatment of the controversy in the light of the development of public health services in Ireland.[192] Barrington was accurate in interpreting the hierarchy's response as 'defensive action', which is precisely why it appeared so badly organised and unconvincingly argued.[193] McKee stressed the role played by the IMA in galvanising the hierarchy. McQuaid had particularly relied on his medical informants to ensure Catholic control of the new children's hospital in Crumlin and, more generally, to secure the connection between Catholic morality and health care.[194] It would, however, be misleading to view the hierarchy as merely responding to the concerns of the medical profession; they were undoubtedly bolstered and even prompted by the medical profession's response. Nonetheless, in 1952, when the Fianna Fáil government altered the objectionable aspects of the scheme, McQuaid reluctantly withdrew support for the IMA's campaign. During a meeting with the IMA, McQuaid explained that although he still believed that the bill was 'defective', it had 'been amended enough to permit the hierarchy to abstain from either approving or disapproving publicly'.[195] Ironically, McQuaid accepted that the IMA was probably quite confused by the hierarchy's stance: 'It must be conceded that for men of good-will, who are not well trained in philosophy but who have put up a stiff fight and taken a position publicly opposed to the Health Bill, our reasoning must seem rather tenuous.'[196]

The mother-and-child scheme became entangled in a myriad of issues unrelated to health, and perhaps McKee's assessment was most accurate when he concluded that 'the mother-and-child controversy provided a rare though misleading glimpse of the conflicts born of social change'.[197] The state's attempt to deal with maternal health as merely an issue of public health policy provoked fears about the sanctity of the family, the power of professionalism and the role of morality in health care. The controversy contained 'the stuff of legends' with 'its greedy doctors, its scheming bishops, its vacillating politicians, and its Byronic hero'.[198] With such a cast line-up there appeared hardly any room for mothers and children. The controversy with all its colour and star performances managed totally to obscure the tale of what was actually achieved for mothers and their children during this period.

While the mother-and-child scheme was essentially shelved until a compromise was found, the Department of Health, in conjunction with the Dublin maternity hospitals, and Dublin Corporation attempted to introduce parts of the scheme. The situation in the rest of the country remained in virtual abeyance. The neonatal scheme was a partial scheme restricted to infants dealt with by the Dublin maternity hospitals. Nonetheless, the years of preparation and debate contained all the ingredients of the macro controversy. They also revealed the scope for co-operation and contained the only tangible action taken during the years 1947 to 1951.

Notes

1 J. Kavanagh, *Manual of Social Ethics* (Dublin, 1956), p. 54. Kavanagh was one of Archbishop McQuaid's key advisers on ethics. The *Manual of Social Ethics* was written for the students of the Dublin Institute for Catholic Sociology, established in 1954 under the auspices of McQuaid. Cited in P. Conroy, '"From the fifties to the nineties": social policy comes out of the shadows', in Kiely, O'Donnell, Kennedy and Quinn (eds), *Irish Social Policy in Context*, p. 34.

2 Barrington, *Health, Medicine and Politics*, p. 141.

3 MacEntee to the Editor, 16 March 1944, *JMAÉ*, 14:82 (Apr. 1944), 40.

4 Whyte, *Church and State in Modern Ireland*, p. 120.

5 'Memo regarding the incident', 11 June 1945, DDA McQuaid Papers, AB8/B/XVIII/14 (Department of Local Government and Public Health); J. Horgan, *Noël Browne: Passionate Outsider* (Dublin, 2000), p. 94.

6 This was a handwritten letter by McQuaid, to be signed by his secretary Christopher Mangan, to Dr Ward, 7 July 1945, DDA McQuaid Papers, AB8/B/XVIII/14.

7 Whyte, *Church and State in Modern Ireland*, p. 129.

8 T. Farmar (ed.), *The End of An Epidemic: Essays in Irish Public Health 1935–65 by James Deeny* (Dublin, 1998), p. 2. James Andrew Donnelly Deeny (1906–94) served as the Chief Medical Adviser to the Department of Local Government and Public Health between 1942 and 1950.

9 J. Deeny, *To Cure and to Care: Memoirs of a Chief Medical Officer* (Dublin, 1989), p. 25.

10 Deeny, *To Cure and to Care*, pp. 42–3.

11 J. Deeny, 'Infant mortality in the city of Belfast, 1940–41', *JSSISI*, 17 (1943–44),

220–39; J. Deeny, 'Infant feeding in relation to mortality in the city of Belfast', *British Medical Journal*, 1 (Jan. 1944), 146.

12 Barrington pointed out that his very appointment was unusual, as he was not a member of the Department and the normal procedure had been to recruit chief medical officers from within. Barrington, *Health, Medicine and Politics*, p. 155; Farmar, *The End of an Epidemic*, p. 8.

13 Jones claims that the mood of reform infecting Britain and Northern Ireland was also apparent in southern Ireland. See Jones, *'Captain of All these Men of Death'*, p. 192.

14 In 1943 the Irish government established a health embarkation scheme to examine and delouse all emigrants leaving for Britain. Some 55,000 people were examined at the depots in Dublin between 1943 and 1947. See Barrington, *Health Medicine and Politics*, p. 139; Deeny, *To Cure and to Care*, p. 177.

15 Deeny, *To Cure and to Care*, p. 116.

16 Barrington, *Health, Medicine and Politics*, p. 155.

17 The National Health Insurance Society was established by the National Health Insurance Act of 1933 which unified all existing approved societies.

18 'National Health Insurance: Proposals of Most Rev. Dr Dignan', NAI, Dept. Taoiseach, S13570; Barrington, *Health, Medicine and Politics*, pp. 149–52; Whyte, *Church and State*, p. 103–4.

19 Whyte, *Church and State*, p. 114; McKee, 'Church–State relations and the development of Irish health policy', p. 163; S. Riordan, '"A political blackthorn": Séan MacEntee, the Dignan plan and the principle of ministerial responsibility', *IESH*, 27 (2000), 45–51.

20 Riordan, 'A political blackthorn', p. 53.

21 *Ibid.*, pp. 48–9.

22 Barrington, *Health, Medicine and Politics*, p. 154.

23 'A copy of the Irish Medical Association's scheme', p. 7, NAI, Dept. Taoiseach, S13444B.

24 *Departmental Committee on Health Services Report*, September 1945, signed by James Deeny, John Collins, John Garvin, P. J. Keady and Desmond Roche, NAI, Dept. Taoiseach, S 13444B.

25 *Ibid.*

26 *Ibid.*

27 *Ibid.*

28 J. Deeny, 'Epidemiology of enteritis of infancy', *JMAÉ*, 19:112 (Oct. 1946), 155.

29 *Departmental Committee on Health Services Report*.

30 *Ibid.*

31 Barrington, *Health, Medicine and Politics*, p. 165, p. 156.

32 *Departmental Committee on Health Services Report*.

33 *Ibid.*

34 *Ibid.*

35 *Ibid.*

36 *Ibid.*

37 See Chapter 6.

38 Barrington, *Health, Medicine and Politics*, p. 156.

39 See, for example, *Annual Report of the Department of Local Government and Public Health, 1938–9*, p. 39; *Ibid., 1942–3*, p. 54; *Annual Report of the Department of Health, 1949–50*, p. 52.

40 *Health Bill, 1947*, section 21, p. 12.

41 Copy of the Health Bill of 1945 part IV dealt with the control of infectious diseases.

The issues of maternal health and the inspection of schoolchildren were dealt with in the part XI miscellaneous section, NAI, Dept. Taoiseach, S13444B.

42 *Dáil Debates,* vol. 98, col. 1734 (12 December 1945).

43 Sr. Alberta, Dominican Convent, Mother House of the Dominican Order, to McQuaid, 23 January 1946, DDA, McQuaid Papers, AB8/B/XVIII/14. The Dominican Order ran several schools for girls.

44 See note made by McQuaid on letter received from Sr. Alberta.

45 NAI, Dept. Taoiseach, S13444C.

46 Among his advisers were Canon O'Keeffe and Canon Dargan, Memo on new public health bill, DDA, McQuaid Papers, AB8/B/XVIII/14.

47 *Ibid.*

48 Ward to McQuaid, 5 February 1946, DDA, McQuaid Papers, AB8/B/XVIII/14.

49 *Ibid.*

50 Memo O'Súilleabháin to Taoiseach, 27 February 1946 regarding the meeting between Ward and McQuaid on 7 February 1946, NAI, Dept. Taoiseach, S13444C.

51 McQuaid to Ward, 5 March 1946, DDA, McQuaid Papers, AB8/B/XVIII/14.

52 Barrington, *Health, Medicine and Politics,* pp. 174–5, 178; McKee, 'Church–State relations and the development of Irish health policy', p. 167.

53 Memo: Proposals for the Reform of the Health Services, March 1946, NAI, Dept. Taoiseach, S13444C.

54 Memo by J. J. McEligott, 14 February 1946, NAI, Dept. Taoiseach, S13444C. Also cited in Barrington, *Health, Medicine and Politics*, p. 176.

55 *Ibid.*

56 Barrington, *Health, Medicine and Politics*, p. 177.

57 Barrington noted that Irish society was small enough for information to seep out from behind the walls of government buildings. See Barrington, *Health, Medicine and Politics*, p. 179.

58 NAI, Dept. Taoiseach, S14010. Cousins argues that the government could have opted for a Department of Health and Social Welfare. See Cousins, *The Birth of Social Welfare*, pp. 143–7.

59 Dr James Ryan was Minister for Health and Social Welfare from 1947 to 1948 and 1951 to 1954.

60 Part III of the 1947 Public Health Bill dealt with maternity care and the inspection of schoolchildren. Part IV dealt with infectious diseases, NAI, Dept. Taoiseach, S13444D.

61 *Health Bill, 1947* section 21, p. 12.

62 Barrington, *Health, Medicine and Politics*, p. 188.

63 Deeny to Dr Smith, Rockefeller Foundation, New York, 21 May 1947, Royal College of Surgeons of Ireland, Mercer Library, (RCSI, ML) Deeny Papers.

64 *Ibid.*

65 See, for example, M. F. Cox, 'A ministry of public health for Ireland', *JSSISI,* 13 (Oct. 1919), 638–41.

66 'Editorial: The Minister for Health', *JMAÉ,* 19:114 (Dec. 1946), 178. See, for example, 'Editorial: A Ministry of Health?', *JMAÉ,* 14:81 (Mar. 1944), 28–9. Quin, 'A suggested maternity service for Eire', pp. 11–23.

67 As for note 64.

68 James Deeny to Dr Morris Fishbein, editor of the *Journal of the American Medical Association*, Illinois, USA, 31 October, 1947, RCSI, ML, Deeny Papers, Box: Department Correspondence, 1947, 48, 49–50.

69 James Deeny to Dr Reginald Atwater, Managing Editor of the *American Journal of Public Health,* 1790 Broadway (at 58 Street) NY, 19 NY. 31, October 1947, RCSI,

ML, Deeny Papers: Department Correspondence, 1947, 48, 49–50.

70 Deeny to CMA 9/12/47 to Clegg of British Medical Institute, noting that Dillon was challenging the new Health Act, 9 December, 1947, RCSI, ML, Deeny Papers, Department Correspondence.

71 Barrington, *Health, Medicine and Politics*, p. 183.

72 James Staunton (1889–1963), Bishop of Ferns, 1939 to 1963. See B. J. Canning, *Bishops of Ireland 1870–1987* (Ballyshannon, 1987), p. 202.

73 Statement of the Irish hierarchy on the Health Act, 1947, p. 1, DDA, McQuaid Papers, AB8/B/XVIII/14. Also in S13444A

74 *Ibid.*, p. 2.

75 Barrington, *Health, Medicine and Politics*, pp. 186, 187, 190.

76 The 1947 White Paper noted that the school medical service was so inadequate that inspections frequently only took place every three years in a schoolchild's life. Furthermore, this service was not co-ordinated with the maternity and child welfare service. See *White Paper on Health Services, 1947*, p. 15.

77 NAI, Dept. Taoiseach, S2547A.

78 'Minister's note regarding interview with the Archbishop of Cashel', 11 February 1931, NAI, Dept. Taoiseach, S2547A.

79 Barrington, *Health, Medicine and Politics*, p. 188; Farmar, *Patients, Potions and Physicians*, pp. 170–4.

80 Dr Ryan's draft response to the hierarchy's statement, 22 December 1948, NAI, Dept. Taoiseach, S14227.

81 Memorandum for the Taoiseach, sent to the hierarchy, 12 February 1948, DDA, McQuaid Papers, AB8/B/XVIII/14.

82 *Ibid.*, p. 1.

83 *Ibid.*, p. 2.

84 *Ibid.*

85 McKee noted that the Private Practitioners' Group within the IMA was central to organised opposition to the mother-and-child scheme. McKee, 'Church–State relations and the development of Irish health policy', p. 172.

86 *Ibid.*, p. 185.

87 McCann became a member of Browne's National Health Council in 1948.

88 S. McCann, 'The general practitioner in Irish medicine – to-day and to-morrow', *JMAÉ*, 15:87 (Sept. 1944), 33–4.

89 *Ibid.*, p. 34.

90 *Ibid.* p. 35.

91 Horgan noted that Deeny believed McPolin to be guilty of 'dereliction of duty' with regard to his role as medical officer of health for Limerick. Horgan, *Noël Browne*, p. 27.

92 J. McPolin, 'Some aspects of the sociology of the medical profession', *JMAÉ*, 19:110 (Aug. 1946), 118.

93 *Ibid.*, 137.

94 McPolin to Department of Health, 9 July 1947, NAI, Dept. Taoiseach, S13444E.

95 Quin, 'A suggested maternity service for Éire', p. 11.

96 J. A. Ryle, 'The modern concept of social medicine', *IJMSc.*, 271 (July 1948), 289–96.

97 Alex Spain was Master of the National Maternity Hospital between 1941 and 1948.

98 Rotunda Hospital, *Rotunda Bicentenary: Transactions of the International Congress of Obstetricians and Gynaecologists* (7 July 1947–11 July 1947).

99 *Ibid.*, p. 292.

100 *Ibid.*, p. 313.

101 *Ibid.*

102 *Ibid.*

103 *Ibid.*, p. 314.

104 *Ibid.*

105 *Ibid.*

106 *Ibid.*, p. 315.

107 *Ibid.*, pp. 314–15.

108 *Ibid.*, p. 315.

109 See, for example, 'Speech by Dr Ryan', *JMAÉ*, 21:122 (June 1947), 19.

110 Rotunda Hospital, *Rotunda Bicentenary*, p. 317.

111 The Professor of Physic at Trinity College Dublin, T. Gillman Moorhead, described the new Minister as 'approachable' and 'open to any suggestions'. See Rotunda Hospital, *Rotunda Bicentenary*, p. 57.

112 'Editorial: White paper on health services', *JMAÉ*, 21:125 (Nov. 1947), 65.

113 'Editorial: The state and the medical profession', *JMAÉ*, 22:107 (Jan. 1948),17.

114 McPolin, 'Doctors and professional secrecy', *JMAÉ*, 23:107 (Sept. 1948), 40.

115 Farmar, *Patients, Potions and Physicians*, p. 171.

116 Cannon, D. J., 'Dangers in the evolution of the health services', *IER*, 70 (1948), 800.

117 *Ibid.*, p. 804.

118 *Ibid.*, p. 809.

119 Department of Local Government and Public Health, *Report of the Departmental Committee on Health Services* (September 1945).

120 Jackson, *Ireland*, p. 306.

121 The interparty government was made up of Fine Gael, Labour, National Labour, Clann na Poblachta, Clann na Talmhan and six Independents. See Horgan, *Noël Browne*, p. 56; R. Fanning, *Independent Ireland* (Dublin, 1983), p. 163; Jackson, *Ireland*, p. 306.

122 Whyte, *Church and State*, p. 205; Barrington, *Health, Medicine and Politics*, p. 219; Horgan, *Noël Browne*, p. 104, pp. 121–49; N. Browne, *Against the Tide* (Dublin, 1986), pp. 125–88.

123 Barrington, *Health, Medicine and Politics.*, p. 205; Deeny, *To Cure and to Care*, p. 173; Deeny and Browne had fallen out much earlier over the best method of eliminating TB. See Ó hÓgartaigh, *Kathleen Lynn*, pp. 119–20.

124 Horgan, *Noël Browne*, p. 103.

125 McKee, 'Church–state relations and the development of Irish health policy,' p.180.

126 A copy of the letter from P. Ó Cinnéide to Dr J. P. Delaney, 19 August 1948, DDA, McQuaid Papers, AB8/B/XVIII/14.

127 NAI, Dept. Finance, S72/5/49.

128 Fr. James Kavanagh was the professor of social science at University College Dublin between 1966–1973. He became the auxiliary bishop of Dublin in 1973.

129 Department of Health, memorandum for the government Health Bill 1950, NAI, Dept. Taoiseach, S13444G.

130 Kavanagh to McQuaid, 2 June 1950, DDA, McQuaid Papers, AB8/B/XVIII/15, (Dept. of Health).

131 *Ibid.*

132 *Ibid.*

133 *Ibid.*

134 Dr James Staunton, secretary to the hierarchy to Taoiseach, 10 October 1950, DDA, McQuaid Papers, AB8/B/XVIII/15.

135 Dr Staunton, 10 October 1950, DDA, McQuaid Papers, AB8/B/XVIII/15.

136 Present at this meeting was Archbishop McQuaid, and Bishops Browne of Galway and Staunton of Ferns.

137 'Memo of observations of the Minister for Health on various matters relating to the mother-and-child scheme referred to in a letter, dated 10 October, 1950, addressed to the Taoiseach by the Most Rev. J. Staunton, DD, Bishop of Ferns, Secretary to the hierarchy' (undated, c. 12 October 1950), p. 1. Copy in DDA, McQuaid Papers, AB8/B/XVIII/15.

138 *Ibid.*, p. 4.

139 *Casti Connubii*, 1931, Fremantle, *The Papal Encyclicals*, pp. 237–42.

140 McKee, 'Church–state relations and the development of Irish health policy,' p. 171.

141 'Memo of Observations of the Minister for Health', p. 2.

142 *Ibid.*, p. 8.

143 J. A. Costello to Bishop Staunton, 27 March 1951, NAI, Dept. Taoiseach, S14997A. Costello's conversations with McQuaid are detailed extensively in the Archbishop's papers. DDA, McQuaid Papers, AB8/B/XVIII/15.

144 McKee offers a comprehensive examination of all these aspects. See McKee, 'Church–state relations and the development of Irish health policy', pp. 159–94.

145 Note on IMA deputation to Minister of Health (24 Oct. 1950) p. 4, NAI, Dept. Taoiseach, S14997A.

146 *Ibid.*

147 *Ibid.*

148 E. Immergut, *Health Politics: Interests and Institutions in Western Europe* (New York, 1992), pp. 1–2; On how the British Medical Association responded to the introduction of the National Health Service, see H. Leichter, *A Comparative Approach to Policy Analysis: Health Care Policy in Four Nations* (Cambridge, 1979), pp. 178–80.

149 *Ibid.*, p. 39.

150 McKee, 'Church–state relations and the development of Irish health policy', pp. 174–80.

151 Barrington, *Health, Medicine and Politics*, pp. 143–4.

152 A Catholic lay society dedicated to promoting Christianity and consisting primarily of members of the professional classes. See E. Bolster, *The Knights of Saint Columbanus* (Dublin, 1979).

153 McKee traces the links between these organisations, government ministers and members of the hierarchy. See McKee, 'Church–state relations and the development of Irish health policy', pp. 176–8.

154 Stafford Johnson to McQuaid, 30 May 1939, DDA, Byrne Papers (4).

155 Browne, *Against the Tide*, pp. 173–88; Horgan, *Noël Browne*, pp. 111–49.

156 Horgan, *Noël Browne*, p. 132.

157 Report for the standing committee of the hierarchy, 16 January 1951, DDA, McQuaid Papers, AB8/BXVIII.

158 *Ibid.*, p. 3.

159 McQuaid to Browne, 8 March 1951, DDA, McQuaid Papers, AB8/B/XVIII.

160 James Staunton to Taoiseach, J. A. Costello, 10 October 1950, DDA, McQuaid Papers, AB8/B/XVIII.

161 Report to Standing Committee, 3 March 1951: mother-and-child scheme Dr Browne, p. 4, DDA, McQuaid Papers, AB8/B/XVIII.

162 McQuaid to Taoiseach, 5 April 1951, DDA, McQuaid Papers, AB8/B/XVIII.

163 McQuaid's notes on the events of 6 April 1951, DDA, McQuaid Papers, AB8/B/XVIII.

164 The subsidiary principle was essentially the idea that a state could subsidise but not fully fund or control welfare. The 'subsidiary principle' was first expounded by Pope

Pius XI (1922–39) in his encyclical *Quadragesimo Anno*. See O'Leary, *Vocationalism and Social Catholicism in Twentieth-Century Ireland,* p. 18.

165 Horgan, *Noël Browne,* pp. 120–40.

166 McQuaid to the papal nuncio, the Most Revd Ettore Felici, 15 April 1951, DDA, McQuaid Papers, AB8/B/XVIII. See also Cooney, *John Charles McQuaid,* p. 252.

167 Earner-Byrne, 'Managing motherhood', pp. 261–277.

168 T. W. T. Dillon, 'The social services in Éire', *Studies,* 34 (Sept. 1945), 333.

169 Horgan, *Noël Browne,* p. 129.

170 Department of Health, *Proposals for Improved and Extended Health Services* (Dublin, 1952), p. 15.

171 McQuaid to Ryan, 11 September 1952, DDA, McQuaid Papers, AB8/B/XVIII.

172 Dr Staunton to McQuaid, 2 October 1952, DDA, McQuaid Papers, AB8/B/XVIII.

173 *Ibid.*

174 Jeremiah Kinane (1884–1959) Bishop of Waterford and Lismore 1933–42 and Co-adjutor Archbishop 1942–46, succeeded to the See of Cashel in September 1946. Canning, *Bishops of Ireland,* p. 241.

175 Bishop Kinane to McQuaid, 14 October 1952, DDA, McQuaid Papers, AB8/B/XVIII.

176 *Irish Independent,* 6 Nov. 1952.

177 Barrington, *Health, Medicine and Politics,* p. 217.

178 McQuaid to Lemass, 6 November 1952, DDA, McQuaid Papers, AB8/B/XVIII.

179 *Ibid.*

180 McQuaid to papal nuncio, Most Revd Gerald O'Hara, 7 November 1952, DDA, McQuaid Papers, AB8/B/XVIII.

181 Horgan, *Noel Browne,* p. 127,

182 McQuaid to Papal Nuncio, 7 November 1952.

183 Barrington, *Health, Medicine and Politics,* p. 229.

184 Kinane to McQuaid, 28 January 1953; McQuaid note on top of Kinane's letter, 29 January 1953; Lucey to McQuaid, 29 January 1953 and 9 February 1953, DDA, McQuaid Papers, AB8/B/XVIII.

185 Memo stating that the Taoiseach and Minister for Health had convinced D'Alton to withdraw hierarchical statement from the press, NAI, Dept. Taoiseach, S13444J.

186 Statement on the Health Bill, 1953, p. 2, DDA, McQuaid Papers, AB8/B/XVIII.

187 McQuaid to Levame, 14 April 1956, DDA, McQuaid Papers, Nuncio Box.

188 *Ibid.*

189 *Ibid.*

190 While the 1945 public health bill dealt with maternity services, it was not until the 1947 bill that the title mother-and-child was given to services.

191 Whyte, *Church and State,* p. vii, p. 195.

192 Barrington, *Health, Medicine and Politics,* pp. 137–250.

193 *Ibid.,* p. 191.

194 This box contains a series of correspondence from 1936 to 1939 between Archbishop Byrne, Stafford Johnson and McQuaid regarding a new children's hospital. Stafford Johnson first mooted in 1936 the idea of lobbying the Hospitals' Commission to prevent the 'amalgamation by Protestants' of two children's hospitals by suggesting a Catholic alternative. McQuaid invested much time and energy in ensuring that the new hospital was under Catholic control. Our Lady's Hospital for Sick Children in Crumlin opened in 1957 under the care of the Sisters of Charity, with the Archbishop of Dublin as manager. See DDA, Byrne Papers, (4) Hospitals General; See also, Ó hÓgartaigh, *Kathleen Lynn,* pp. 104, 105, 127.

195 McQuaid's handwritten note regarding a meeting between the IMA, himself and the Archbishop of Cashel, DDA, McQuaid Papers, MCS AB8/B/XVIII.

196 *Ibid.*
197 McKee, 'Church–state relations and the development of Irish health policy', p. 194.
198 Horgan, *Noël Browne*, p. 91.

6

Maternity on the ground:
the Dublin experiment, 1945–56

The compelling voice of the thousands of children who have died over the last few years should find a quick answer.[1]

In 1944, TWT Dillon understandably complained that although health planning had become 'front-page news in Éire', previously the only 'references to the subject were the criticisms of outspoken doctors and the soothing statements of the Minister in his annual reports to the Dáil'.[2] However, while the mother-and-child scheme was being 'messed about with', Deeny began the groundwork with a Dublin experiment.[3] The development of a 'free neonatal' scheme was based on co-operation between the Department of Health, Dublin Corporation and three Dublin voluntary maternity hospitals, and it revealed the complexities inherent in negotiating new health initiatives. Although the free neonatal scheme encountered many of the same obstacles as the national mother-and-child scheme, its success was testament to the fact that a free scheme did not mean the end of charity and morality. Ironically, the Dublin free scheme was terminated because a national mother-and-child service finally became operational in 1954. However, its temporary success offered an insight into both the level of resistance and the potential for compromise.

The Dublin experiment: conflict and co-operation

Neonatal mortality is defined as death within the first month of life,[4] and post-neonatal as those deaths occurring after the first month and before the end of the first year.[5] In 1932 the Department of Local Government and Public Health reported that 'a very large proportion of infants do not survive the first month of life, thus indicating the operation of antenatal or congenital causes or complications occurring at or immediately subsequent to confinement'.[6] The department interpreted the high rate of neonatal mortality as an indication of the need for antenatal supervision and ready access to medical assistance (see Table 6.1).[7] This conclusion was drawn principally because neonatal mortality was more common in rural areas,

'which points to the lack of institutional facilities in connection with con-
finements in such districts and to the difficulty often experienced of sum-
moning skilled medical assistance on time'.[8] The disadvantage of an urban
environment was thought to take hold after the first month, where the ravages of city life outweighed the benefits of medical facilities.[9] Infant mortality was offered as the primary reason for the proposed improvements of
the health services in the 1947 White Paper:

> Progress towards the achievement of a population of healthy children is an
> indispensable foundation for the attainment of a higher level of health in the
> people as a whole and for this reason the introduction of improved measures
> for safeguarding the lives and health of mothers and children is the first item
> in the programme of proposed reforms.[10]

Table 6.1 National neonatal mortality rates for males and females, 1938–54

Year	Male	Female
1938	30	26
1939	32	26
1940	30	26
1941	34	26
1942	31	24
1943	37	29
1944	37	29
1945	35	28
1946	32	26
1947	32	26
1948	25	21
1949	28	22
1950	26	20
1951	29	21
1952	25	21
1953	25	19
1954	26	19

Source: Compiled from the Department of Health, *Annual Report of the Registrar General
Report, 1950* and Central Statistics Office, *Report of Vital Statistics, 1953–54*

   The White Paper drew heavily on the departmental report of 1945, pointing to the exceptional nature of the maternity and child welfare services
available in Dublin and the dominance of the three maternity hospitals.[11]
The Department of Health noted that the infant mortality rate in Dublin
city had 'assumed such dimensions that a drastic change of provision relating to infant welfare is called for'.[12] The main problem in Dublin was identified as gastro-enteritis, which killed an average of 520 infants per annum
between 1942 and 1947.[13] The high death rate resulting from gastro-enteritis
had led to a focus both on pregnancy as the preliminary phase of infant care

and on an intensive campaign of protection during the first year of life. In this respect, the White Paper heralded a new era of co-operation between Dublin Corporation and the maternity hospitals in a bid to ensure that the city could provide a domiciliary service, an infant clinic service, an emergency night-and-day infant service and approximately thirty cots in each hospital to service the domiciliary clinics.[14] It was envisaged that ultimately this infant protection scheme would be integrated with the antenatal and postnatal care of the mother and thus a 'continuous and complete service' would be afforded.[15]

The acting medical officer in charge of child welfare for Dublin Corporation, Morgan Crowe, described 'infant loss of life' as the biggest problem facing the public health worker. He noted that the death rate among infants in Dublin during the war was 113 per 1,000, which was a considerable increase on the 1938 figure of 77 per 1,000 live births.[16] However, Crowe was determined to absolve the local authorities of all the blame:

> In this country, however, legislation to further child health, introduced in the last years of alien government, has not been properly implemented. For this the local authority is sometimes blamed, but before doing this it is well to be familiar with the limitations of our system of local administration. In this country, the Local Government Department maintains, by virtue of its 50 per cent recoupment on approved expenditure, a controlling influence on local activity, a control often used to damp local initiative.[17]

Although Crowe was optimistic that the state was 'about to tackle' the issue in a 'comprehensive way', his article revealed the degree of tension between central and local government.

Crowe was representative of the Corporation's mindset: he had repeatedly drawn attention to the plight of the poor expectant mother, deprived of nutrition, rest, privacy and government attention.[18] A strong advocate of Catholic charitable involvement, he had pledged his support to McQuaid's maternity scheme and had encouraged other local initiatives.[19] Crowe refused to regard maternal and child welfare as purely a medical problem and, like TWT Dillon, he resented the government's sudden interest and apparent attempts to consider only the immediate aspects of maternal health:

> The relationship between poverty and subnormal health has been established in other countries, and these surveys do furnish data suggesting that poverty may play a similar role here. However, this is a matter which is obscured by statements from responsible authorities to the effect that no significant degree of want exists in this country.[20]

The new Department of Health had to combat more than professional protectionism; it had to defend its apparently new interest in maternal and child welfare, previously the domain of local authorities and voluntary initiative. All three of the Dublin maternity hospitals had established antenatal clinics by 1935, saving the Department of Local Government and Public Health a great deal of money and organisational resources. The Rotunda was paid £150 a year for its clinic and the Coombe and National Maternity Hospital were paid £75 each until 1947 when the grants were increased to £300 and £150 respectively.[21] This was a relatively minor increase considering that between 1940 and 1948 the overall cost of Dublin Corporation's maternity and child welfare scheme rose from £17,800 per annum to £94,800.[22] In June 1940 the Department of Local Government and Public Health was paying the Infant Aid Society £90,000 to distribute free milk to necessitous mothers and to children under five years of age; under pressure this grant was increased in June 1941 to £125,000.[23] In the context of an appalling world war this was significant, as in many other respects severe cutbacks were introduced and real wage levels 'plummeted'.[24] The corporation had negotiated and co-ordinated all the voluntary and statutory services and, together with the three hospitals, had contributed enormously not only to a greater understanding of the social dimensions of maternal and child health, but also to highlighting the dire reality for many poor mothers. It was extremely difficult for both the hospitals and the corporation to accept the department's intensified interest and repeated attempts to focus purely on the medical aspects of care.

In 1945, following the departmental committee's report on the health services, Ward, the Parliamentary Secretary, contacted the three maternity hospitals in Dublin to request their assistance in introducing a neonatal scheme.[25] The idea was to co-ordinate the resources and services provided by the corporation, the maternity hospitals and the department in an attempt to protect the health of infants during the first year of life, free of charge.[26] Deeny, who became the driving force behind the experiment, wished to integrate infant health care into the system already available to mothers. He wanted the hospitals to take responsibility for supervising all infants under one year of age, which had previously been the function of the corporation. This, he envisaged, could be done through a clinic service, an emergency night-and-day service, domiciliary visiting and, if necessary, hospital confinement – all of which was outlined subsequently in the 1947 White Paper. All children over one year of age would be referred, as before, to the corporation's child welfare clinics for future supervision. The death rate of Dublin infants from gastro-enteritis was the impetus and the justification for providing such a neonatal scheme free to all mothers.[27] While all three hospitals responded favourably, the National Maternity Hospital warned that the scheme would not be a 'panacea', and that social conditions had to be rectified if a long-term improvement was to be secured.[28] Archbishop McQuaid was the chairman of the National Maternity Hospital, and the response was very much in keeping with the arguments presented by various members of the hierarchy and medical profession in the years ahead. In fact, the hospital's response was a subtle indication of where the battle lines would lie: the hospitals wanted more finance, not more interference.

Negotiating the particulars of the infant protection scheme proved a slow and tortuous process. In May 1946, six months after Ward had approved the scheme, no substantial progress had been made, and Deeny complained to the Assistant Secretary of the department that, in view of the fact that there were twenty preventable infant deaths a week, he found the corporation's delay 'hard to understand'.[29] The issue was one of control. The corporation found it hard to accept the level of autonomy that the maternity hospitals demanded, considering that it was the corporation which was expected to sanction funding for the venture out of its annual budget.[30] Furthermore, the scheme allowed the voluntary maternity hospitals to take over responsibility for the supervision and care of infants in the first year of life – a function normally carried out by the corporation. The corporation was used to co-ordinating Dublin maternity facilities, but it was unaccustomed to such a level of co-operation. The neonatal scheme sought, in effect, to integrate the services provided by the voluntary hospitals and the corporation. Despite the corporation's reservations concerning the degree of interdependence being introduced under the scheme, they were apparently unable to understand how this would also make the maternity hospitals anxious with regard to their autonomy, which was already appreciably undermined by financial dependency on sweepstake funds and grant aid.[31]

In July 1946, Dr Russell, the medical officer of health for Dublin Corporation, met with the Masters of the three hospitals. During this meeting the Masters expressed their objection to the proposals to allocate each hospital a health zone. The zoning was an attempt to divide the city into health regions for administrative purposes, and it was suggested that mothers would be referred to the maternity hospital in charge of their region. The Masters objected on the grounds that the mothers should have 'freedom of choice in attending hospitals'.[32] The Department of Health intended to divide Dublin County Borough into ten administrative zones for the purposes of the neonatal scheme and eventually to extend the boundaries of the scheme to include maternity services. Accordingly, a public health clinic would be established in each district for the purposes of child welfare and the ante- and postnatal supervision of Dublin mothers.[33] The department envisaged that the maternity hospitals would staff the clinics that fell within their traditional areas. Falkiner of the Rotunda hospital summed up the hospitals' demands: all medical appointments should be made by the board of each hospital, and a booking system should be initiated whereby only the infants delivered in hospitals would be treated free by the hospital.[34] These demands mirrored in many respects the central concerns of the medical profession with regard to the planned state medical service for mothers. In essence, the hospitals wished to maintain control over professional appointments, and they were concerned that in agreeing to participate in the scheme they would be swamped by the corporation and the state. Furthermore, they wished to safeguard the mother's choice with respect to the care of her child, which of course had the added advantage of protecting each hospital's traditional clientele. Finally, the hospitals were not willing to take the ultimate responsibility for the welfare of all of Dublin's children and therefore stressed the element of follow-up care. By restricting their services to children born in their hospitals, the Masters were ensuring that they controlled the element of medical care, and the corporation and government were left with the ultimate responsibility for the social welfare of mothers and children.[35] Essentially, the hospitals sought to strike a balance between autonomy and co-operation.

In September 1946 the Minister for Local Government and Public Health, Séan MacEntee, received a deputation from Dublin Corporation in an attempt to settle the deadlock between the corporation and the hospitals. MacEntee explained that he wished to see a reorganisation of the maternity and child welfare scheme and argued that this was not 'a simple problem of finding more houses, better living conditions, more food'.[36] It was of course totally disingenuous to imply that housing, social conditions and food were 'simple problems', but it was obvious that the government was establishing its justification for interfering in the arena of medical welfare. Focusing purely on health care was part of MacEntee's grand plan to 'unscramble the proverbial egg' that was the dual Department of Local Government and Public Health.[37] The government was attempting to separate health care from social welfare needs. The decision to employ Deeny was testament to this new approach. Deeny criticised the corporation for using social conditions as an excuse for inaction, and the hospitals for citing lack of beds as an excuse for delaying the creation of a comprehensive system to save babies' lives:

> To talk about housing, or about extra hospital beds, is actually to avoid the main issue. It is if you like the counsel of defeatism. We can actually go after the disease. We can try to find how it spreads from child to child. We can educate parents in the various ways and means of prevention and so on.[38]

In response to arguments that the existing system needed not alteration but investment, Deeny claimed that an 'extension of your present service is merely extension of an advice service'.[39] Under the existing system, mothers received free antenatal care and advice. However, if they or their baby needed further medical treatment, they were expected to pay, unless they qualified under public assistance legislation. Deeny suggested that the neonatal scheme would offer a free 'specialised service' to back up the antenatal system.[40]

Dublin Corporation was reluctant to accept such a medically based service, repeating the need for nutritional care for the mother and urging the government to subsidise food products for poor mothers.[41] Lillie O'Shea-Leamy, a Dublin City councillor, believed that malnourished mothers bearing children were the 'root' of the problem. She pointed out that 'a new poor' were unwilling to attend the Catholic Social Service Conference and St John kitchens.[42] Although the corporation was in favour of the subsidisation of voluntary effort, it recognised a need for greater state involvement in the provision of welfare.[43] The focus of the meeting was on infant mortality. Nevertheless, it was evident that preventive medicine raised more questions regarding the appropriate response to maternal and child welfare than it answered. Apart from the controversial issue of control, there was the essential dilemma as to where health care ended and welfare provision began. The corporation was ideally placed to co-ordinate both aspects of maternity care. However, it tended to assume an authoritarian approach, and the hospitals were anxious that their independence would be sacrificed if they became too heavily involved in any scheme directed by the corporation.

In March 1947 the Minister for Health, Dr Ryan, wrote to inform the corporation that a scheme had been submitted to the corporation for consideration a year previously, and that the department was still awaiting a response. The Minister stressed that the corporation's failure to implement the scheme would constitute a breach of their promise to co-operate. Furthermore, it would 'entail a very grave responsibility for the continuance of this excessive mortality'.[44] The corporation, apparently impervious to such emotional blackmail, continued to stress that the department's exclusively medical approach to maternal and child welfare was partial and did not address the fundamental issues. Crowe, the acting medical officer of health, explained,

> It must be stressed that the causes of these high rates [of infant mortality] go further than the consulting-room or dispensary, and are not so much a question of medicine. The causes are created and maintained by the number of insanitary structures allowed to function as dwellings, by the type of food expectant mothers and children must consume, and by the lack of training in the hygiene of motherhood in our schools. The alleviation of poverty and the introduction of health education are matters beyond the scope of the Corporation.[45]

Although the corporation's response amounted to a disclaimer of responsibility, it did reflect a general belief that the problem of infant mortality in particular and maternal policy in general was far more complicated than medical intervention. Nonetheless, the Department of Health had to resist this argument as defeatist in order to justify the reorganisation of the medical mother-and-child services. In 1951 an internal memo regarding the report of the joint committee of the Royal College of Obstetricians and Gynaecologists and the British Paediatric Association noted,

> It furnishes us with abundant evidence that nursing and medical care are most important factors in reducing neo-natal mortality but it also furnishes evidence to show that social and economic factors are also most important. Any attempt to use the figures furnished to show that the poor are not getting adequate medical care is very vulnerable to attack. It is probably true to a large extent but it is not proved by the fact that the infant mortality rates are higher among the poorer classes. I think our safest line is to admit that nutrition, housing etc. are important factors but to maintain that proper medical care is the most important single factor.[46]

This memorandum revealed the defensive attitude that the department had assumed by 1951. It also highlighted the incongruous position in which the department found itself: in order to justify intervening to provide a better health service for mothers and children, it had to play down other social factors that potentially impaired maternal health.

In January 1949 a conference was held at the Department of Health regarding the expansion of the mother-and-child service in Dublin County Borough between the Department of Health, the corporation and the three maternity hospitals. Deeny defended his mother-and-child scheme as the best compromise between what they wished to achieve and what they could realistically expect to accomplish. The new Master of the Rotunda, Dr O'Donel Browne, expressed concern that the services provided at hospital clinics might encroach on private practice. Deeny explained that under his scheme mothers who attended private doctors and who were in need of specialist treatment or maternity accommodation would obtain it free of charge.[47] In general, the hospitals expressed themselves willing to provide comprehensive care free of charge for mothers and infants up to the age of six weeks. However, the hospitals were obviously anxious regarding the national controversy. In August, Dr O'Donel Browne explained,

> There are but few who would oppose a better mother and child health service … I feel certain that this maternal and child health scheme would be a move in the right direction, but painful delays, obscure Departmental obstacles, and any suggestion of division of control, cannot but hinder progress and foster antagonism. I know we would do our utmost to help the Minister and the Corporation, but we would require a free hand and our wants would have to be supplied promptly and in good faith.[48]

Later that month Deeny meet with O'Donel Browne to resolve the outstanding issues. O'Donel Browne explained to Deeny the reasons for delay on the hospitals' part: the central concern was autonomy, particularly when it came to deciding which hospital controlled which section of Dublin in the new zoning plan. Both the Rotunda and Coombe appeared content to serve their traditional areas, but the National Maternity Hospital apparently desired to 'move in on Crumlin', a new suburban housing area.[49] Finally, in September 1949, it was agreed to maintain the traditional service areas of the three hospitals until the new Coombe hospital was built.[50] Under the plan devised by the Department of Health, the Rotunda would continue to administer care to infants born in the Dublin north-west, north and north central areas, and the hospital would staff a clinic at Larkhill. The Coombe would continue to service the Dublin south-west and south areas, including a clinic in the Crumlin/Kimmage area, which witnessed a population explosion in the 1940s and 1950s. Finally, the National Maternity Hospital would be responsible for neonatal care in the Dublin south central, south-east and north-east areas, and also hold a clinic in Dun Laoghaire.[51] The department reiterated that this plan did not affect a patient's choice to apply to any hospital for care, but it did mean that the clinic in her area would be staffed by a designated hospital.[52] Deeny was anxious that the Dublin working-class population should be fairly evenly distributed between the three hospitals. However, the hospitals were anxious to remain in control of staffing policy, lest the voluntary character of each institution be compromised by the new scheme.

A series of meetings between the Department of Health, the corporation and the three maternity hospitals took place between January 1949 and February 1950.[53] By April 1950 the neonatal scheme was up and running. The Department of Health reported that after preliminary discussions between the hospitals and the corporation, the hospitals had agreed to provide a health care service for children up to the age of six weeks. The idea that the neonatal scheme should be scaled down to six weeks had originated from the *Report of the Consultative Child Health Council and the Neonatal Infants Scheme* submitted in October 1948.[54] Noël Browne had established the Consultative Council on Child Health in May 1948 under the chairmanship of M. W. Doran who was also chairman of the Hospitals' Commission. The council was charged with reviewing the child welfare provisions in Dublin and making recommendations to pave the way for forthcoming legislation. Deeny was vehemently against the idea of limiting the neonatal scheme to the care of infants under the age of six weeks. He pointed out that he had already secured the co-operation of the corporation and had been working on the implementation of the scheme for two years.[55] The scheme entailed the examination of each child born in hospital, and follow-up visits if necessary. Deeny did not believe that it would take much more accommodation to cater for infants up to the age of one year. Nonetheless, the limitation of the hospitals' role to the neonatal period formed only part of the process of compromise, and the corporation continued to care for children between the age of six weeks and five years.[56] In 1948 the Department of Health drew explicit attention to the issue of neonatal mortality with the stark observation that in the previous twenty-five years the death rate for infants under the age of one month had shown 'practically no improvement'.[57] In this context the department explained its new neonatal scheme:

> Under the agreed arrangements, infants born in the hospitals are medically examined before their discharge. After their discharge those living in Dublin are visited regularly by nurses and, if necessary, by doctors. Clinics are conducted by the hospitals, to which mothers are encouraged to bring their infants for care and advice. It is the aim to have each child medically examined at least once between the date of discharge from hospital and the time it reaches the age of six weeks.[58]

However, the department, conscious at that stage of the climate of distrust with regard to state intervention in the arena of family medicine, stressed that participation in the scheme was voluntary and free of charge and that no infant would be examined 'without the consent of the parents or guardians'.[59] The department went on to advertise the merits of the scheme, explaining what each hospital had to offer and how facilities had been improved in order to protect infants during this fragile period of their lives. The Rotunda, in addition to the existing twenty cots for infants born in the hospital and not yet discharged, had been equipped with a new unit of thirty cots specifically for the neonatal scheme, and the service was supervised by two paediatricians. The Rotunda's unit was officially opened on 27 January 1951. The National Maternity Hospital was provided with eight extra cots in addition to the thirty existing ones. The unit, supervised by two paediatricians, opened its doors on 1 February 1951.[60] Finally, the Coombe Lying-In Hospital had been equipped with sixteen cots and one paediatrician. Dr Ryan officially opened this unit on 18 September 1951.[61] Nevertheless, an internal departmental report later that year indicated that the beginning of the scheme did not mean the end of tension. The corporation claimed that the hospitals were failing to supply records, that they ran their clinics at unsuitable times for mothers, and that at the clinics the hospital staff continuously changed, which meant that mothers were not familiar with the people caring for their children. Finally, the hospitals were failing to hand out nutrients at the clinics when necessary, but instead sent the mothers to the corporation's clinics, thereby necessitating further travelling for the mother and child.[62] The department concluded that the problem was a general one of attitude:

> Most of the existing difficulties could be smoothed out if co-operation and goodwill on the part of the hospitals were forthcoming. Unfortunately our experience so far has been that the hospitals are proving very difficult. They resent being queried or asked to justify anything they do. Their attitude is: give us freedom and we'll do the job. Their idea of freedom seems to be liberty to spend the Corporation's money without having to justify their expenditure in any way.[63]

The report pointed out that the National Maternity Hospital had threatened to shut down the scheme if all their demands were not met. There was undoubtedly another side to the story of integration, however: the observations of the Department of Health and the corporation reveal the inherent difficulty in altering a system of co-operation to one of integration. The voluntary hospitals were accustomed to receiving relatively uncomplicated and generous funding from the sweepstakes, which resulted in little intrusion. The grants from the corporation which they had received under the old mother-and-child welfare scheme was for continuing to run pre-existing antenatal clinics. The hospitals had earned the grants under the original scheme because they qualified on the basis of their existing operation. However, the neonatal scheme was a project started from scratch and instigated by the Department of Health. The lines of control and power were considerably more complicated, and the voluntary hospitals evidently felt compromised by the new process of assimilating resources.[64]

The path to co-operation in the neonatal scheme had not been smooth. However, it was achieved in half the time it took to reach a compromise on a similar scheme for mothers. In support of private practitioners, the maternity hospitals initially refused to extend the same scheme to mothers.[65] However, by July 1954 the Rotunda agreed to operate the scheme 'without prejudice to negotiations by the IMA with the Minister on behalf of their members'.[66] In 1955 the intensive neonatal scheme was terminated. The department explained that it had been started under the Health Act of 1947 and had been free to all. However, under the Health Act of 1953 only infants whose mothers were eligible under section 16 would be eligible for free treatment under section 17.[67] An internal memo explained:

> It must be remembered that the Scheme started as the first instalment of the free Mother and Child Scheme which was then visualised. We were anxious to get the Scheme working and we were liberal with requests for payments. We agreed to a system under which hospitals were more or less to spend as they liked and to have the expenses made good by the Corporation. We did all these things with our eyes open as the Scheme was only a first step. The whole arrangement was to be reviewed at the end of a year, in any case, it was visualised that it would be merged in the wider Scheme for a Mother and Child Service. The wider Scheme never materialised and we have been left with the original rather unsatisfactory arrangements.[68]

The weary tone of this memorandum reflected the department's disillusionment after years of wrangling over 'a simple matter of introducing a simple scheme'.[69] However, the neonatal scheme could be abandoned precisely because a national maternity scheme had been introduced, notwithstanding the fact that it fell short of the comprehensive service envisaged in 1945. The separate scheme for neonatal care was rendered obsolete, as intensive and free supervision of the infant for the first six weeks of life formed part of the modified mother-and-child scheme introduced under the Health Act 1953. In terms of post-neonatal mortality, the infectious disease, gastroenteritis, had been drastically reduced, and with a nationwide programme for pre- and postnatal care there was every reason to hope that post-neonatal mortality would remain under control.

In fact, the new focus on the neonatal period was an indication of the confidence felt in the light of improved maternal and child welfare services. Neonatal and post-neonatal mortality have different causes, which Loudon breaks down into endogenous and exogenous factors. Neonatal mortality is caused primarily by environmental factors and inadequate antenatal supervision, whereas neonatal mortality is caused by prematurity, congenital malformations and birth injury.[70] Post-neonatal mortality was therefore much more the preserve of the hospitals, requiring medical intervention. In the same year that the neonatal scheme was terminated, the Department of Health reported that the infant mortality rate of 39 per 1,000 live births was the 'lowest figure ever recorded in the country'.[71] However, neonatal mortality remained a concern throughout the 1960s, and the Department of Health noted in 1956 that while Ireland's national mortality rate compared well with other European countries, the neonatal rate was 'proportionately worse': Sweden had a rate of 13, Ireland 23 and Spain 28 per 1,000 live births.[72] This concern was more an indication of a shifting emphasis in medical infant care indicated by the new phrase 'neonatology', meaning the study and science of the new-born and first coined in the 1950s, than any new mortality trend.[73] In 1957 the department noted the new interest in prenatal life, as for the first time vital statistics had taken account of foetal deaths occurring after twenty-eight weeks of pregnancy.[74] Evidently, the medical focus was once again shifting: in the same year Ireland, along with Sweden and the Netherlands, had been invited to participate in a World Health Organisation study of prenatal mortality.[75]

In 1966 the Department of Health attributed the successful and sustained decline in infant mortality in Ireland to the improved services.[76] However, it pointed to the need for further improvement and a change in focus to mortality in the first week and stillbirth, both of which had remained consistent features in maternal and infant health figures. The department continued to recognise maternal and child welfare as an essential health platform and, cognisant of Ireland's demographic profile, actually considered that Ireland should place an even higher premium on developing a proper service to cater for its relatively high birth rate.[77] It noted that the maternity grant payable to women in the lower income bracket per confinement was to be doubled to £8, and women who had multiple births would receive a grant per live-born child.[78]

The meaning of the mother-and-child scheme to Dubliners

When the Health Act of 1953 was finally passed, the department explained that there was to be

> a full maternity care service (medical, surgical, midwifery, hospital and specialist services) free to persons in the lower and middle income groups and to certain hardship cases, and at a small contribution (initially £1 a year and in any case not exceeding £2 a year) for others. Provision is made for choice of doctor and choice of patient and for supplying obstetrical requisites, free of charge, for domiciliary confinements.[79]

Mothers in the lower income group were entitled to free care for their infants up to six weeks after the birth, and a £4 cash grant for each confinement. These mothers were also entitled to free milk for themselves while expecting or nursing, and for their children up to the age of five years. In order to avail herself of the grant, a woman in the lower income bracket had to apply three months prior to confinement, furnishing the department with a doctor's or midwife's certificate. By 1957, 28,622 maternity grants were paid, which represented 47 per cent of all births.[80] Following ongoing negotiations with members of the medical association[81] the department announced in 1955 that, while previously maternity services for the lower income group had been given by dispensary doctors only, under new regulations any medical practitioner who had an agreement with the health authority could provide the service.[82] As a result of the objections by the medical profession and the hierarchy, mothers were entitled to a choice of doctor – an option denied to them in the original proposals. From 31 March 1956, free medical care to mothers and infants was extended to the middle-income group (which was defined as adult persons with less than £600 per annum).[83] By the end of 1954 the corporation noted that the numbers of mothers and children attending the welfare clinics had 'diminished as mothers were being cared for by Medical Practitioners'.[84] In 1956 the mother and child welfare service was renamed, omitting the word mother as it now catered only for children.[85]

In theory, the scheme entitled all mothers, even those in the top income bracket, who could participate on the basis of a nominal contribution of £1 per annum, to a free maternity service. In reality, the scheme was never actually extended to the mothers in the upper income bracket. In May 1954 the wheels of politics intervened again when the second interparty government came to power. McQuaid was immediately relieved to have Costello back at the helm and reported to the papal nuncio that the new Minister for Health, Dr Thomas F. O'Higgins[86] had 'made a public declaration in consonance with principles of Catholic sociology'.[87] O'Higgins introduced a bill that allowed him to phase in the mother-and-child scheme, which, in effect, meant that the upper income group of mothers never benefited from the scheme. O'Higgins also introduced the Voluntary Health Insurance Act, 1957, which covered all those not protected by public schemes. Barrington noted that the establishment of the Voluntary Health Insurance Board 'indicated a new kind of partnership between government, the medical profession and the idealised "voluntary" spirit of Irish Catholic moralists'.[88]

Dublin was, in real terms, least affected by the introduction of a mother-and-child scheme because it had the best maternal and child welfare service in operation prior to the Health Act of 1953. As was repeatedly noted, the Dublin maternity service operated primarily through the maternity hospitals and the corporation. Nonetheless, as a result of the introduction of a national service which encompassed all but the wealthiest of mothers, many more Dublin mothers were entitled to free medical care as a right. Despite arguments put forward by the Catholic hierarchy and the IMA stating that the existing service, which covered necessitous cases, was sufficient, there were several mothers who had been unable to afford the medical attention they required. In May 1949, Dr Ita Brady, the acting chief medical officer for Dublin, wrote to the department on behalf of a Mrs C. The latter was pregnant for the seventeenth time and, owing to debility and general ill health, had been attending the antenatal clinic at the Rotunda. The hospital was concerned about the overcrowding in Mrs C.'s home and the possibility of complications during the birth.[89] The hospital wished to admit Mrs C. but, as a 'public assistance case', she was supposed to be admitted to St Kevin's hospital, and would not be covered if admitted to any other hospital.[90] However, as Mrs C. was a high-risk case, it was believed that she needed the specialist treatment available in the Rotunda.[91] The Minister 'raised no objections to abnormal maternity cases going to the Rotunda under the mother and child welfare scheme'.[92]

The Minister, at that time was Noel Browne, and, after a series of such cases were submitted to the department for special consideration, he suggested a 'general sanction' and consulted Mr Lyons of Dublin County Council regarding a solution.[93] Lyons explained that these cases were 'half-an-inch above the Public Assistance level' and therefore the maternity and child welfare scheme was purely a consultation service for them. If these women were advised to seek hospital treatment they were expected to pay out of private funds, which was 'often a grave hardship'.[94] Browne believed that the mother-and-child service would 'adjust the position', but in the meantime recommended that the health authority be afforded a 'reasonably free hand'.[95]

Although the Health Act of 1953 was never extended to cover women in the higher income group, it catered for those maternity cases 'half-an-inch above public assistance level'.[96] Moreover, and in spite of the controversy, the mother-and-child scheme survived free of moral prerequisites: the underlying assumption was that Irish mothers were entitled to care as citizens, not necessarily as wives. The universal nature of the scheme broadened the rights of citizenship, rendering (in theory) assistance independent of need and morality. Symbolically, this scheme altered the landscape, not just of welfare assistance in Ireland, but also of female citizenship. Women became entitled, as a right, to free care during pregnancy, regardless of their marital status, thereby separating their welfare from the role of fatherhood and the presumptions of family power. This was exactly what many, in and out of the Catholic Church, had feared when they criticised the act for falling short of Catholic moral and social teaching by encroaching on the sanctity of paternity. Fr. Coyne, when reviewing the 1952 version of the scheme, considered it not in the light of motherhood, but in terms of its potential threat to fatherhood:

> There is something sacred and primary and personally intimate and holy and inviolate in the privileges and duties of paternity: a married man is more a man, when he shoulders, alone, the proud burden of responsibility for wife, mother and child ... By all means, let the State give generous, lavish indirect help and refrain from burdening: but let it keep its necessarily clumsy, almost sacrilegious methods out of this sphere of life at least.[97]

This view was echoed time and again in relation to any state benefit or assistance that addressed the needs of the mother directly. The same fears were manipulated in a more blatant fashion by a Franciscan Friar, the Revd

Fr. Paul, OFM in *The People*, a Wexford local newspaper, who appealed to the most basic sense of ownership inherent in the patriarchal family:

> The physical health of our Irish mothers and children would have become primarily the concern of the State ... We assert, quite flatly, that this is primarily *our* concern: they are *our* mothers, *our* children, not the State's ... Do you know what that could mean in practice? Any Tom, Dick or Harry of a State Official, could instruct *your* children, *your* wife, *your* mother, *and instruct them all wrong*? But he might be a Catholic? Sure. Or he might be a Protestant. Or a Jew. Or an agnostic. Or an atheist. The Scheme made no provision for that. He might be anything. Look. You who are reading this have probably some idea of the strange and twisted approach to sexual problems which characterises certain schools of modern medicine, especially certain schools of psychological medicine ... How would you like *your* wife to be 'instructed' in the killing of your child in her womb? How would you like her to be counseled on the practice of artificial conception-control? Or, if you were childless, how would you like her to be told that the remedy for her childlessness lies in artificial insemination? And do you think that our Bishops could see this situation about to arise and still sit back calmly and say nothing?[98]

While the style of journalism may have varied from *Studies* to *The People*, the message did not: Irish mothers belonged to the family, the society, the medical profession and the Church, but *not* to the state. A state maternity service was regarded as 'an Open Sesame' for the state to intervene between man and wife. The battle fought in their name was not about mothers; it was about jurisdiction and possession.

The Irish Housewives' Association (IHA) unanimously approved of the mother-and-child scheme on the grounds of equal citizenship. The association protested outside the Department of Health when Browne resigned in April 1951, holding placards that read, for example, 'Equal Rights to Happy Motherhood' and 'Healthy Mothers, Healthy Children, Healthy Nation'.[99] The IHA statement was clearly cognisant of maternal health as a right protected in the Constitution:

> We, the committee of the IHA, affirm our belief that the principle of equal opportunities, enshrined in our Constitution, should be applied to the sphere of health to those least able to fend for themselves: the mothers and children of Ireland. We consequently re-affirm our support of the Mother and Child Scheme as proposed by the Minister for Health.[100]

While the tone of the protest was maternalistic in the mode of first-wave feminists, it was also framed in the syntax of rights, and clearly sought to reclaim the debate on maternal and child welfare for women. Its annual report of 1950–51, while asserting the organisation's 'non-party, non-sectarian' credentials, reiterated this theme: 'We affirm our belief in the equal rights of all Irish women to happy motherhood, and deplore the resignation of a Minister for Health who had done so much in his term of office for the health of the community.'[101]

The new health act was not the answer to all prayers. Social workers found much of their time was spent informing mothers of their new rights, of which they seemed oblivious, and helping them fill out the necessary forms. In 1957, Miss Eleanor Holmes, the social worker for the Rotunda hospital expressed her frustration:

> It has been noted that patients of all categories were singularly ignorant of the benefits to which they were entitled. Few had heard of the Health Act under which a large majority qualified for treatment at a free or reduced rate. Much time was spent in advising them to what clerical offices and Departments to make applications for both Health Act and statutory benefits.[102]

Nevertheless, the implications of the new policy with regard to health care entitlement stretched far beyond the technicalities of pregnancy, impacting on the social rights of all mothers. The 1953 act, however flawed and ultimately partial, represented the beginning of an era that would support mothers, regardless of their family ties. In 1954 the Assistant Secretary to the Department of Health wrote to the Rotunda hospital requesting that they stop demanding marriage certificates prior to antenatal care. He explained that, under the 1953 Health Act, all women were entitled to care, and therefore a woman could argue that her rights were infringed by the hospital's policy. In a tone cognisant of changing times and lingering social strictures, he explained: 'The request for the certificate is an embarrassment to the single woman or the woman who married only a short time before the expected birth of the baby, if she wishes to conceal the fact, as she should be at liberty to do.'[103]

As citizens, women had the right to care and did not have to submit to religious, voluntary or official zeal. Mothers themselves appeared to be indicating that they were uncomfortable with the charitable nature of certain ventures and wished to accept assistance to which they were entitled, rather than help of which they were deemed deserving. As the Master of the Coombe, J. Kevin Feeney, observed in 1951, 'It has been found in the case of our poor mothers, that there is a marked reluctance to attend the excellent Catholic Social Services Conference Dining Centres, and they seem to prefer milk which is offered by the Maternity and Child Welfare Centres as a substitute.'[104] In 1957, Sean MacEntee hinted at the ways in which Irish society, and in particular the venerable pillars of that community, had to adapt to changing times:

> And yet, though principles remain immutable, times change and existing institutions, however long-established or even, by origin, imperishable they may be, must adapt themselves and their practices to the new circumstances. This is the very condition of progress, and indeed of survival. In its wisdom the Church at all times has been alive to this truth, and in recent years, in the regulation of its liturgy and its observances, has given many instances of its readiness to meet the exigencies of the times, so that it may continue to be effective in its mission. In that fact there is a lesson which I trust will not go unheeded by the traditionalists among us, whether we be doctors or laymen.[105]

Hinting, of course, at the battles fought and the bitter pills swallowed by clergy and medical profession alike, MacEntee took considerable credit for the improvement in public health over the decade, claiming 'that without the legislation, and without the driving force of the officers of my Department which made it effective, it is very doubtful indeed if the improvement would have been so marked and so encouraging'.[106]

The health act did not mean the end to all hardship: the 'simple problem' of housing and poverty lingered, and the unmarried mother in particular needed more than free care *during* pregnancy. However, Mrs D., who wrote to Archbishop Byrne in 1938 wondering why neither the Catholic Church nor the state was interested in her welfare, may have looked at the debacle that became known as the 'mother-and-child controversy' with a wry smile. In 1956 she would have been entitled to a free maternity scheme, a cash grant of £4 per confinement and a hot meal at the maternity centres of the CSSC, which were not phased out until the mid-1970s.[107]

Notes

1 Deeny, 'The lost town', p. 146.
2 Dillon, 'Public health planning', p. 433.
3 Deeny, *To Cure and to Care*, p. 174.
4 *Annual Report of the Department of Health, 1950–1951*, p. 14.
5 Loudon, *Death in Childbirth*, p. 485.
6 *Annual Report of the Department of Local Government and Public Health, 1932–3*, p. 54.
7 *Ibid.*
8 *Ibid.*
9 *Ibid.*
10 Department of Health, *White Paper on Health Services*, p. 18.
11 *Ibid.*, p. 33.
12 *Ibid.*, p. 32.
13 Section C: Gastro-Enteritis Control Section Memo to Sub Committee, *Report of the Consultative Child Health Council 1949*, p. 1, NAI, Dept. Health, A116/167.
14 *Ibid.*, p. 33.
15 *Ibid.*
16 M. Crowe, 'Conditions affecting child health in Éire', *IJMSc.*, 255 (Mar. 1947), 92; *Annual Report of the Department of Local Government and Public Health, 1938–9*, p. 37.
17 Crowe, 'Conditions affecting child health in Éire', p. 100.
18 *Ibid.*, p. 92.
19 Crowe to McQuaid, 29 October 1943, DDA, CSSC (2).
20 Crowe, 'Conditions affecting child health in Éire', p. 93.
21 Preliminary Estimates Mother and Child Welfare, 1927–48, NAI, Dept. Health, M34/0.
22 J. E. Cummins, city manager and town clerk, estimated costs of the Dublin Co Borough maternity scheme, NAI, Dept. Health, M34/0.
23 'Free Milk Scheme: General', NAI, Dept. Health, M34/1, vol. III.
24 C. O'Grada, *A Rocky Road: The Irish Economy since the 1920s* (Manchester, 1997),

p. 18. See also M. E. Daly, *Social and Economic History of Ireland since 1800* (Dublin, 1981), pp. 156–7.

25 'Memo: Progress of the present scheme to reduce infant mortality', NAI, Dept. Health, M34/17.

26 'Memo: Explaining the origins of the mother and child scheme', NAI, Dept. Health, M34/17.

27 'Gastro-enteritis and "sick baby" clinic arrangements, Dublin Corporation', NAI, Dept. Health, M34/5.

28 Holles St to Department of Local Government and Public Health, 5 November 1945, NAI, Dept. Health, M34/17.

29 Deeny to Assistant Secretary of the Department of Local Government and Public Health, 21 May 1946, NAI, Dept. Health, M34/17.

30 J. Keane of the corporation to Dr Deeny, 27 May 1946, NAI, Dept. Health, M34/17.

31 M. Coleman, 'The origins of the Irish Hospitals' Sweepstake', *Irish Economic and Social History,* 29 (Nov. 2002), 40–55. See also Farmar, *Patients, Potions and Physicians,* p. 166.

32 Hernon, the city manager, sent the Department a memo drawn up by Dr Russell regarding his meeting with the Masters of the maternity hospitals, 27 July 1946, NAI, Dept. Health, M34/17.

33 Department of Health to the Coombe regarding the neonatal scheme under the maternity and child health service, NAI, Dept. Health, M34/49, Vol. II.

34 *Ibid.*

35 It is important to stress that the hospitals already provided a considerable amount of social assistance to mothers via their almoner departments.

36 Report on meeting between Health Department and Dublin Corporation, 25 September 1946, NAI, Dept. Health, M34/17.

37 *The Irish Times* (25 Feb. 1944).

38 NAI, Dept. Health, M34/17.

39 *Ibid.*

40 *Ibid.*

41 *Ibid.*

42 *Ibid.*

43 'Maternity hospitals clinical reports', *IJMSc.,* 312 (Aug. 1951), 825. The almoner of the Coombe Hospital noted a 'marked reluctance' among the poorer mothers to attend the Catholic Social Service Conference.

44 Minister to Corporation, 25 March 1947, NAI, Dept. Health, M34/17.

45 Hernon sent this memo by Crowe to the Department on 12 May 1947, NAI, Dept. Health, M34/17.

46 'Infant mortality statistics', unsigned memo, 19 January 1951, NAI, Dept. Health, M134/65.

47 Memo on conference in connection with expansion of the mother-and-child service in Dublin County Borough, 17 January 1949, NAI, Dept. Health, M34/17.

48 T. D. O'Donel Browne, 'The coming years', *IJMSc.,* 284 (Aug. 1949), 683.

49 Memo by Deeny regarding a conversation with the Master of the Rotunda, O'Donel Browne, 24 August 1949, NAI, Dept. Health, M34/49, vol. II.

50 This was not complete until 1967. Feeney, *The Coombe Lying-in Hospital,* p. 167.

51 Department of Health to the city manager, 20 September 1949, NAI, Dept. Health, M34/49, Vol. II.

52 *Ibid.*

53 Minutes of the following meetings: 17 January 1949, 30 September 1949, 14 and 23 February 1950, and 14 March 1950, NAI, Dept. Health, M34/55.

54 Notes regarding a preliminary departmental conference held in Department of Health, 12 November 1948. NAI, Dept. Health, M34/55.

55 *Ibid.*

56 *Annual Report of the Department of Health, 1950–1*, p. 51.

57 *Ibid.*, p. 14.

58 *Ibid.*, p. 51

59 *Ibid.*

60 *Ibid.*, p. 52.

61 Feeney, *The Coombe Lying-in Hospital*, p. 331.

62 'Coombe neonatal scheme: internal report', 3 July 1950, NAI, Dept. Health, M134/57.

63 *Ibid.*

64 Feeney noted, with regard to the original plans for the 'infants' scheme', that 'administration would have been difficult'. With regard to the mother-and-child scheme, he believed that the hospitals accepted it because they had 'no alternative'. See Feeney, *The Coombe Lying-in Hospital*, p. 152. Browne opened the paediatric unit in the Rotunda on 27 January 1951. See T. A. Clarke and T. G. Matthews, 'The development of neonatal paediatrics at the Rotunda', in Browne (ed.), *Masters, Midwives and Ladies-in-Waiting*, p.132; Farmar makes a brief reference to the scheme, noting that the bishops considered it 'creeping socialism'. See Farmar, *Holles Street 1894– 1994*, p. 127.

65 Darby to Taoiseach, 21 April 1951, NAI, Dept. Health, M100/119.

66 'Dublin Co. Borough medical care at the three maternity hospitals: memo regarding Rotunda authority, 17 July 1954, NAI, Dept Health, M103/53.

67 Mother and child welfare scheme – neonatal scheme undated memo concerning the neonatal scheme under the Health Act 1953, NAI, Dept. Health, M111/12.

68 Internal memo, unsigned *c.* 1955, NAI Dept. Health, M111/12.

69 Deeny, *To Cure and to Care*, p. 174.

70 Loudon, *Death in Childbirth*, p. 485.

71 *Annual Report of the Department of Health, 1953–4*, p. 10.

72 *Ibid.*, *1955–6*, p. 15.

73 Browne, *Masters, Midwives and Ladies-in-Waiting*, p. 118.

74 *Annual Report of the Department of Health, 1957–8*, p. 14.

75 *Ibid.*, p. 30.

76 See Department of Health, *Health Services and their Future Development* (January, 1966), p. 20.

77 *Ibid.*, p. 21.

78 *Ibid.*, p. 48.

79 *Annual Report of the Department of Health, 1953–4*, p. 21.

80 *Ibid.*, *1956–7*, p. 29.

81 'General practitioner medical care for mothers and infants', NAI, Dept. Health, M100/ 135.

82 *Annual Report of the Department of Health, 1954–55*, p. 21.

83 *Ibid.*, *1956–7*, p. 2.

84 J. A. Harrison, *Report of the Medical Officer of Health in the City of Dublin for the Year 1954* (Dublin, 1955), p. 21.

85 J. B. O' Regan, *Report of the Medical Officer Health City of Dublin for the Year 1957* (Dublin, 1957), p.26.

86 Minister for Health from 1954 to 1957.

87 Copy of a letter from McQuaid to the Nuncio, Levame, DDA, McQuaid papers, Nuncio Box.

88 Barrington, *Health, Medicine and Politics*, p. 247.

89 Ita D. Brady to County Secretary, 12 May 1949, NAI, Dept. Health, M8/2.
90 This is now St James's Hospital.
91 Internal departmental memo, 4 June 1949, NAI, Dept. Health, M8/2.
92 Unsigned memo, 28 June 1949, NAI, Dept. Health, M8/2.
93 Unsigned memo, 7 March 1950, NAI, Dept. Health, M8/2.
94 *Ibid.*
95 *Ibid.*
96 *Ibid.*
97 E. J. Coyne, 'Health Bill, 1952', *Studies*, 42 (1953), 6.
98 *The People* (2 June 1951). Emphases in the original text.
99 There is a wonderful photograph of this protest in *The Irish Times* (18 Apr. 1951).
100 Tweedy, *A Link in the Chain*, p. 73.
101 *Ibid.*
102 *Irish Journal of Medical Science*, Annual Report of the Rotunda Hospital, 1957, p. 30.
103 O Muireadaigh to Bayne, 5 May 1954, NAI, Dept. Health, M100/255.
104 J. K. Feeney, 'Report of the Coombe', *IJMSc.*, 312 (Aug. 1951), 825.
105 Minister for Health, S. MacEntee, 'Speech to the IMA', *JIMA*, 41:242 (Aug. 1957), 61.
106 *Ibid.*
107 Purcell, *Catholic Social Service Conference*, p. 30.

7

Illegitimate motherhood, 1922–60

May I place before you my sorrow and plead of you to do something to help my Eldest Daughter she is Eldest of 14 children … She is 20 years old … in the year of 1933 she had a Baby Girl. She is four year old I then placed the case in Hands of Rev Fr D. cc. failing to get the Boy to marry her she was only 16 years old. I acted on the advice of Fr D. I took the Baby a Brough (*sic*) it up as one of my own … I let her mother go out to work. She picket (*sic*) up with another Boy and he would not marry her because she had a child. She is after having a Baby Boy for this young man … Her father casted her out of her Home and only late has brough her Home … No where will give her help … I am not able to do anything for her as my youngest is only 12 months old. Their seems to Be no one who will give her a kind word your Grace. She is not Bad only Foolish she was a good Catholic. And now she has not any friend in the world to give her a cup of Tea only myself and if I turn her out with her children (God) knows what would be her end.[1]

The whole question of unmarried mothers is one of the most difficult problems we have got to deal with. We have not thought out any settled policy … we haven't made our minds up as to the best course to pursue and the only opinion we have is that it is not desirable to associate them in very large numbers.[2]

In 1939, on completion of an international study (including Ireland) on illegitimacy, the League of Nations concluded, 'The conception of legitimacy is a function of the conception of the family peculiar to each social order, and this in turn is generally the outcome of religious ideas.'[3] In the Irish 'social order', the concept of illegitimacy extended in practice, if not in name, to the unmarried mother: she was an illegitimate mother. The status of the mother was legitimated by marriage, reflecting a cultural understanding of the family as patriarchal and only *bona fide* when headed by a male obligated to the role of fatherhood by marriage. This underlying assumption informed much of the care and support that Irish mothers received during this period and was essentially based on 'religious ideas' of morality. While unmarried mothers were isolated in Irish society, the same assumptions governed their treatment as influenced the policy in relation to all mothers, and the issue of responsibility dogged this aspect of social service as it did maternity services in general. In fact, in relation to unmarried mothers the ambiguity between health and morality lent itself even more successfully to paralysis and manipulation, allowing the central government to renege on its responsibility on the grounds that the issue was too morally sensitive for the ostensibly secular hands of government.

The social context for moral angst

The trend of a slightly declining birth rate and increased illegitimacy persisted (to the dismay of many) after Irish independence: the annual average for the decade 1920 to 1930 was 58,700 legitimate and 1,706 illegitimate live births; for the decade 1930 to 1940 it was 55,212 and 1,893 respectively (see Tables 7.1 and 7.2).[4] What was remarkable, in fact, was the relative stability of the relationship between legitimate and illegitimate births rates until the 1970s. Illegitimate births still accounted for only 2.7 per cent of births in 1971 by 1979 that percentage had increased to 4.5.[5]

In the 1920s, as society began to assess the meaning of independence in terms of social and moral order, attention was paid to these statistics. Independence not only led to a greater level of moral and cultural introspection, it also highlighted the trail of unmarried mothers to Britain, a social pattern that caused great embarrassment to the fledgeling Irish state. If infant mortality, in general, was a barometer of poverty and effective public health administration, illegitimacy was an indicator of slacking social control and moral decline.

In the turbulent early years of the Irish Free State, pregnancy outside wedlock became a symbol of the perceived moral degeneration of the nation.[6] In 1927, the *Report of the Commission on the Relief of the Sick and Destitute Poor* acknowledged the increase in illegitimate births but declared, 'Our belief is that with returning stability of government and the gradual tightening of the reins of discipline, both governmental and parental, that we may look forward to a decrease in the number of these births.'[7] However, three years later a committee established to review criminal law found little improvement in the social situation, and attributed the climate of immorality 'primarily to the loss of parental control and responsibility during a period of general upheaval'.[8] Illegitimacy was offered as concrete proof, and it was pointed out that statistical evidence revealed that births outside the confines of the family had increased since 1925 at 'an unprecedented rate'.[9] Even more alarming was the claim that 'extraneous sources' indicated that a number of such births were not registered and therefore not represented in the final statistical tally.[10] Ascertaining the real figure of illegitimate births was problematic, given the tendency of mothers to conceal these births, if possible, or flee to Britain. However, the committee noted an increase in illegitimate births from 1.98 per cent of the total number of

Table 7.1 Number and percentage of illegitimate births for Ireland, 1922–73

Year	Rate	Illegitimate	Year	Rate	Illegitimate
1922	2.6	1,520	1948	3.3	2,165
1923	2.6	1,624	1949	3.1	2,006
1924	2.6	1,677	1950	2.6	1,627
1925	2.7	1,662	1951	2.5	1,588
1926	2.8	1,716	1952	2.5	1,619
1927	2.9	1,758	1953	2.1	1,340
1928	3.0	1,788	1954	2.1	1,310
1929	3.2	1,853	1955	2.0	1,234
1930	3.2	1,863	1956	1.9	1,173
1931	3.4	1,925	1957	1.7	1,032
1932	3.2	1,819	1958	1.6	976
1933	3.4	2,004	1959	1.6	959
1934	3.5	2,030	1960	1.6	968
1935	3.3	1,946	1961	1.6	975
1936	3.3	1,908	1962	1.8	1,111
1937	3.2	1,813	1963	1.8	1,157
1938	3.3	1,878	1964	2.0	1,292
1939	3.2	1,781	1965	2.2	1,403
1940	3.2	1,824	1966	2.3	1,436
1941	3.5	1,975	1967	2.5	1,540
1942	3.7	2,419	1968	2.5	1,558
1943	3.8	2,448	1969	2.6	1,642
1944	3.9	2,567	1970	2.6	1,708
1945	3.9	2,626	1971	2.7	1,842
1946	3.9	2,642	1972	2.9	2,005
1947	3.4	2,348	1973	3.1	2,167

Source: For the numbers of illegitimate births, see Department of Local Government and Public Health, Department of Health, *Annual Reports of the Registrar-General*, 1922–52 and Central Statistics Office, *Reports on Vital Statistics, 1953–73*

births registered in 1913 to 3.20 per cent in 1929.[11] There appears to be little doubt that the figures recorded for illegitimate births were distorted by an under-registration as a result of social pressure. The registrar-general, when drawing attention to the much higher infant mortality rate for illegitimate infants, argued

> The accuracy of these figures, however, is open to some doubt. When the deaths of illegitimate infants are co-related to the corresponding births the proportion of the former is so high as to suggest that a considerable deficiency exists in births registered as illegitimate. A test search in the records for the births of illegitimate infants whose deaths were registered within one year failed to reveal more than 54 per cent of the births. It is inferred that many births that are really illegitimate are registered as legitimate.[12]

Table 7.2 Illegitimate births per 1,000 registered births for Dublin County and
Dublin County Borough (from 1930 Dublin City), 1923–49

Year	Dublin County	Dublin County Borough/City
1923	3.08	2.49
1924	2.64	2.68
1925	3.18	3.26
1926	2.59	2.79
1927	2.65	3.00
1928	2.54	2.62
1929	3.28	2.85
1930*	4.46	3.09
1931	3.68	3.25
1932	3.48	3.04
1933	3.45	3.16
1934	3.25	2.79
1935	4.47	2.50
1936	3.04	2.46
1937	3.39	2.52
1938	4.10	2.56
1939	3.39	2.28
1940	3.17	1.98
1941	3.09	2.53
1942	3.11	2.39
1943	3.52	2.90
1944	3.40	3.00
1945	3.20	3.00
1946	3.20	2.70
1947	3.10	2.80
1948	2.90	2.50
1949	2.50	2.40

Note:* From 1930 Dublin County Borough was relabelled in tables Dublin City

Source: Figures compiled from Department of Local Government and Public Health,
Department of Health, *Annual Reports of the Registrar-General*, 1923–49

However, when the illegitimate mortality figures are considered over several decades it is safe to conclude, as was the case in Northern Ireland,
England and Wales, although not to the same extent, that the mortality rate
was considerably higher among these more vulnerable infants.[13]

In 1932 *The Lancet* noted that the 'problem of the care of the illegitimate
child appears to be becoming more serious than formerly in the Irish Free
State'.[14] This gloomy prediction was made following a speech given by the
Garda Commissioner, General Eoin O'Duffy, to the Society for the Prevention of Cruelty to Children.[15] Substantiating his pessimism, O'Duffy bom-
barded the society with some Dublin crime statistics for 1929, 1930 and

1931. During those three years 32 infants had been murdered and there were 154 convicted cases of concealment of birth and 29 cases of abandonment.[16] O'Duffy, a devout Roman Catholic, was hugely concerned with the rate of sexual crime and, as Finnane convincingly argues, he represented 'an obsession with the visibility of sex' in Ireland, which resulted in an avoidance of the 'context and harm of serious sexual offending'.[17]

The lens of morality limited social vision and inhibited any serious consideration of the economic and social costs of pregnancy outside wedlock. The initial discussions regarding the topic focused on the reasons for this moral deterioration, parental responsibility, legal measures for the curtailment of sexual activity and the need for the separate moral rehabilitation of unmarried mothers.[18] Even the most earnest attempts to improve conditions for the unmarried mother were paralysed by arguments of moral complicity, despite the counter-concern of proselytism. Revd M. H. MacInerny of the Irish Vigilance Association, who eloquently expressed the common fear that these 'girls' were the 'principal harvest' of soul-snatchers, still felt the need to justify his concern for these women.[19] Locating the evil in Dublin, where the 'huge octopus' of proselytism was centred, he explained that these mothers were so desperate 'to rid themselves of the unwelcome fruit of their folly' that they were not in a fit state to protect the faith of their children.[20] As a safeguard for the children, not the mothers, he urged 'purely Catholic institutions to shelter' them. Nonetheless, he also had to defend himself from the charge that to provide for unmarried mothers was tantamount to condoning their moral sin.[21]

There is little doubt that the moral aspect of pre- or extra-marital sex hampered the development of social services for the mothers of illegitimate infants and seriously affected the shape and tenor of any services available. Consequently, it was only when an even stronger religious argument, that of proselytism, was proffered that the issue of services for the unmarried mother and her child could be confronted and the social response questioned: 'Its seems quite clear that the policy of hounding unfortunate girls from their native districts, in the absence of proper Catholic institutions to receive them, is fraught with disaster ... This policy, if policy it should be styled, simply places a premium on proselytism and prostitution.'[22]

Not surprisingly, Revd MacInerny's solution for the care of Catholic unmarried mothers was institutional care supervised by nuns, as this approach facilitated religious protection, physical shelter and moral regeneration, as well as a strong element of restraint which contained an implicit degree of punishment.[23] In approaching the issue of unmarried motherhood from the perspective of crime and punishment, the social conscience was appeased and satiated: the problem was neither ignored nor condoned. Nor was its real complexity accommodated. This approach to the issue of illegitimate motherhood was not new and had its origins in nineteenth-century rescue work, which was bolstered by the prevalent fear of proselytism.[24]

The *Report of the Commission on the Relief of the Sick and Destitute Poor* of 1927 was one of the first inquiries after political independence that dealt with the issue of the unmarried mother and her child. Both the witness testimonies (those that survive) and the final report are revealing as they isolated key themes that plagued the issue of the unmarried mother for the succeeding decades: the need for appropriate institutional services for mother and child, the issue of moral rehabilitation and the fear of proselytism, the role of religious and/or voluntary organisations, the emigration of unmarried mothers to Britain, and the difficulty of defining an official policy for the care of unmarried mothers and their children. The second report of significance that raised similar issues, the *Report of the Committee on the Criminal Law Amendment Acts (1880–85) and Juvenile Prostitution*, otherwise known as the Carrigan Report, was completed in 1931. The Carrigan Report, guided by the conviction that the 'moral condition' in Ireland was challenged by modernity and only legislation could rectify the situation, sought to raise the age of sexual consent from sixteen to eighteen years of age and reform the laws relating to prostitution.[25]

The Carrigan Report painted a picture of an Ireland in moral decline with rising illegitimacy, the widespread use of birth control and increased prostitution. Significantly, this report was never published, revealing, as both Kennedy and Finnane argue, the tendency to suppress controversial information regarding sexual morality in Ireland.[26] Perhaps, as Finnane speculates, independent Ireland did not wish publicly to acknowledge that it was following a trend in morality not dissimilar to that across the border and the Irish Sea. Thus the report languished in the Department of Justice files.[27] As the Department of Justice reasoned, 'Unless these statements are exaggerated … the obvious conclusion to be drawn is that the ordinary feelings of decency and the influence of religion have failed in this country … It is clearly undesirable that such a view of conditions in the Saorstat should be given wide circulation.'[28]

The social response to the unmarried mother and child

> Neither should children be punished for the sins of their parents … An Irish Legislation will, I hope, remove such civil disabilities, and deal with the repentant and erring woman in a way that she also will obey the tender order of Divine Mercy: "Go, thou, and sin no more."[29]

The central argument in favour of providing services for the unmarried mother was the 'innocence' of her offspring. The campaigner for widows' rights, J. P. Dunne, claimed to be in favour of keeping mother and child together, as he explained in his paper: 'The care of illegitimate children would demand delicate circumspection, and unless the mother was an actual degenerate I would not deprive her of the companionship and affection of her child.'[30] However, he was a member of the Committee of Inquiry into Widows' and Orphans' Pensions in 1933 and signed the majority report which recommended that the illegitimate child of a widowed mother would not be deemed a dependent child – a necessity for the mother's qualification for a pension.[31] Evidently, like many others who claimed that they were not against the unmarried mother retaining guardianship of her child, Dunne did not believe that she should be offered any financial assistance to do so. Irish society was distinctly reluctant to allow social policy to bend to the dictates of what was culturally considered moral transgression. In reality, this meant that, despite the rhetoric, Irish society was not willing to facilitate illegitimate motherhood by offering such mothers the assistance it offered institutions and foster parents. This reluctance was in keeping with Catholic moral teaching.

Contemporaries were capable of making the connection between the high infant mortality rate and children born outside wedlock. However, there were few practical solutions proffered and rarely any public statement questioning the validity of the societal rejection of this form of motherhood. In 1937, Mrs Maud Walsh of Dublin Corporation, when reviewing social services for Irish mothers, described the death rate of illegitimate infants as 'a cause for discontent' and attributed the high rate to methods of dealing with unmarried mothers which had yielded 'insufficient results'.[32] The disproportionately high illegitimate death rate was the strongest incentive to improve services for the unmarried mother, and in this respect the motivation for action was not dissimilar to that which prompted welfare provision for all mothers, though progress was slower for the unmarried mother and her child.[33] Dublin Corporation was remarkable for its inclusive attitude to the unmarried mother, a policy driven by the dedicated Kerry Reddin, who ran the mother and child welfare services until his sudden death in 1953. Reddin insisted that unmarried mothers be 'visited in the ordinary way on the district and obtain all the services that are provided for other mothers. Their records are kept as in the case of married women, and they are addressed as married women in the Clinics.'[34] In accordance with contemporary notions of social respectability, treating unmarried mothers as married women in public was a way of protecting them from social censor.

The Hospitals' Commission believed that the growing contemporary concern about the high death rate of illegitimate babies was the main reason for creating new services for unmarried mothers:

> The death-rate of approximately 295 per 1,000 births in 1929 of illegitimate children, compared with 140 and 105 in Northern Ireland and England respectively rendered it essential that active measures be taken to reduce the mortality of infants born out wedlock.[35]

Acknowledging that the 'whole problem bristles with difficulties' and in keeping with the general social consensus, the Hospitals' Commission viewed the 'innocent' child as the main victim.[36] Evidently aware of the possible accusation of moral complicity, the report carefully expressed the view that the problem of the unmarried mother was one that begged a 'solution'. It was clear that the commission recommended social services, which would accommodate the social reality for the benefit of the children in question.

There existed a general belief, substantiated by Catholic doctrine, that the name of Irish motherhood was besmirched by the few who became pregnant outside the legal and religious boundaries of the family. The papal encyclical *Casti Connubii*, issued in 1931, noted with dismay the social tendency to support illegitimate motherhood:

> We are sorry to note that not infrequently nowadays it happens that through a certain inversion of the true order of things, ready and bountiful assistance is provided for the unmarried mother and her illegitimate offspring (who, of course, must be helped in order to avoid a greater evil) which is denied to legitimate mothers or given sparingly or almost grudgingly.[37]

The view that assistance to the unmarried mother in some way slighted the married mother had resonances in Irish society. Furthermore, papal teaching was taken very seriously by many who worked in social welfare. Anneenee Fitzgerald-Kenney[38] acknowledged that contact with the unmarried mothers of boarded-out children revealed the hopelessness of their position. She noted that these unmarried mothers often had 'insufficient food and clothing in their own case; lack of money for the necessary care of health for themselves, no knowledge of how to obtain it free … Added to which there is often the embittering influence of the contempt in which she may be held.' She admitted that it was 'increasingly evident that all unmarried mothers need advice and assistance and this should be extended to those also who do not come to private or public charities; but who are struggling along in misery and loneliness without asking assistance from any one.' Nonetheless, she concluded, 'At the same time we cannot afford to ignore the warnings of His Holiness Pope Pius XI', referring to *Casti Connubii*.[39]

E. W. McCabe, the vice-chairman of the Irish Adoption Society, noted some eighteen years after *Casti Connubii* that the only legislation introduced to help the unmarried mother with the economic consequences of her 'sin' was the Affiliation Order Act of 1930. This act, McCabe argued, involved 'great trouble and expense with little or no outcome – in only two out of a hundred cases before the court was paternity successfully established and the man solvent'.[40] As long as the role of women in Irish society was defined as subsidiary to the institution of the family, maternity could only be discussed and understood in terms of its impact on the distribution of family power. Although this understanding of maternity had a fundamental effect on legislation for all mothers, it was devastating for the unmarried mother, whose lone motherhood set her adrift from society, a society with a limited, purely political understanding of female citizenship. The married mother had a husband to articulate her citizenship; a widowed mother drew her entitlement through her bereaved status; an unmarried mother was rendered voiceless.

McCabe expounded on the impossible situation faced by illegitimate mothers who attempted to care for their children:

> If she keeps the child personally under her own roof, she has the great
> annoyance and provocation of her pharisaical and uncharitable neighbours,
> who can make life a most unpleasant and upsetting experience for the wretched
> girl, who has been forced, in most cases, to leave her home ... Since she has
> no husband to maintain her she must seek work to provide for herself and her
> child, and this raises the difficulty as to the care of the child during her
> absence.[41]

It was hardly surprising that post-conception matrimony, colloquially
known as 'shotgun weddings', was a strategy of survival for many women
facing single motherhood in Ireland.[42] In 1936 the Department of Local
Government and Public Health reported on the Mountjoy home for unmarried mothers, run by the Saint Patrick's Guild, noting that the 'spiritual outlook in that Home is splendid and many of the mothers have been married
before leaving the Home'.[43] This approach to the problem of the unmarried
mother was also very cost-effective: upon marriage the illegitimate child
became the responsibility of the father rather than the state. Furthermore,
society was more forgiving of mothers who sought to legitimise their mistake by marriage, even if that marriage took place shortly before or after
the birth. It was a friendlier world if a woman attempted moral restitution
and much easier for her child, who would no longer be marked out as illegitimate by that 'stigmatising document' – the birth certificate.[44]

In view of the social anxiety regarding Ireland's perceived slide into immorality and the governmental predisposition to suppress the circulation of
unsavoury evidence, the lack of policy relating to unmarried mothers and
their children was hardly surprising. The fact that the moral connotations
of the 'problem of the unmarried mother' had real and deadly consequences
did little to spur action. Dereliction of duty in this regard characterised all
administrations until the 1970s.

The unmarried mother and government policy

Defensive action characterised government policy in relation to unmarried
mothers and their children throughout the period: only as problems arose
were measures devised and even then belatedly. There was no vision or
long-term strategy. The issue of cost, though rarely explicitly mentioned,
was also a major factor behind inaction. It was cheaper, in monetary terms,
to allow the problem of the unmarried mother float in a moral never-never
land. Hovering below moral concerns were financial practicalities. On many
levels, therefore, the intervention of religious and voluntary organisations
was seen as both appropriate and cost-effective. Irish governments in this
area, as in others, relied heavily on the infrastructure and personnel of the
various religious groups of all creeds. In fact, this became a default policy.

Table 7.3 Rates of infant mortality compared to illegitimate infant mortality, 1923–50

Year	Infant mortality (per 1,000 births)	Illegitimate mortality (per 1,000 births)
1923	66	344
1924	72	315
1925	68	287
1926	74	322
1927	71	288
1928	68	307
1929	70	295
1930	68	251
1931	69	267
1932	67	240
1933	60	209
1934	56	265
1935	62	260
1936	66	305
1937	67	258
1938	61	227
1939	62	193
1940	60	246
1941	68	239
1942	62	262
1943	76	250
1944	72	273
1945	66	194
1946	59	200
1947	63	220
1948	47	149
1949	51	131
1950	45	78

Note: The rates given for infant mortality from 1923 to 1931 are inclusive of illegitimate death rates, whereas the rates provide from 1932 to 1950 are exclusive of illegitimate deaths and thus provided a more accurate picture of the discrepancy between the rates of legitimate and illegitimate infant mortality

Source: Compiled from the Department of Local Government and Public Health, Department of Health, *Annual Reports of the Registrar-General, 1923–50*

The lack of any concrete policy afforded a degree of discretion and often evasion, leaving complicated social issues like the unmarried mother in practical limbo for years. This process was supported in no small way by societal reluctance to confront an uncomfortable moral and social quandary.

The extraordinarily high mortality rate among illegitimate infants was one of the main motivations for action, but even this emotive call on officialdom did not exact radical action (see Table 7.3). From the outset the Department of Local Government and Public Health acknowledged that the illegitimate death rate (particularly in Dublin) did much to swell overall infant mortality rates.[45] For 1925 and 1926 the reports of the registrar-general indicated that the illegitimate death rate was five times that of legitimate infants and that one out of every three infants born out of wedlock did not survive the first year of life.[46] The department argued that while 'illegitimate infants [were] handicapped by constitutional and environmental disadvantages that tend[ed] to a heavy incidence of infant mortality', these adverse factors did not account for the 'disproportionately high' death rate compared to other countries.[47] The international factor, or rather the national embarrassment factor, was strong in terms of both these mortality statistics and the noted presence of Irish unmarried mothers in Britain. The department made the connection between this mortality index and the 'difficult problem of dealing with the case of the unmarried mother', but concluded evasively that this problem 'lies in the main outside the sphere of Child Welfare services'.[48]

The central problem was that there was no service that dealt specifically with the unmarried mother *and* her child. The inspectors of boarded-out children, in theory in charge of illegitimate or orphaned children, were, in reality, the only ones who consistently highlighted the connection between the treatment of the unmarried mother and the welfare of illegitimate children. The case of the unmarried mother lay outside the domain of child welfare services; in fact, there was no specific service for the unmarried mother. As the Department of Local Government and Public Health's witness informed the Commission on the Relief of the Sick and Destitute Poor, there was no 'settled policy' in relation to the unmarried mother. The department believed implicitly in institutionalisation and a hierarchy of transgression: the first time 'offender' should be separated from the repeat 'offender'. Segregation and institutionalisation were seen as the most appropriate response to the unmarried mother, as this isolated her from the general community and carried with it the implications of detention: the loss of freedom as a result of sin. The department was 'strongly opposed' to the policy of allowing the mother to board out her child and return to the work market, as this 'relieve[d] the mother of responsibility', the acceptance of which was viewed as a crucial aspect of her rehabilitation.[49]

McArdle, while giving evidence before the Commission on the Relief of the Sick and Destitute Poor on behalf of the Department of Local Government and Public Health, was evidently uncomfortable. He repeatedly stated that there was no policy and that the department had not made up its mind. When questioned by Senator Jennie Wyse-Power regarding the role of the religious orders in the institutional care of unmarried mothers, he was unable to provide any detailed information regarding the running of these homes.[50] When pressed on the issue of the county home as the main resource available to unmarried mothers and their children, he acknowledged that this was not ideal but was the best that could be done at present. Prior to Irish independence, many unmarried mothers were accommodated in workhouses, which were converted into county homes in the early days of the Irish Free State. Nevertheless, many commentators believed that the change was only symbolic and that the old, inadequate and degrading system continued under the Irish administration.[51] In 1930 there were 868 unmarried mothers maintained in Poor Law institutions and a further 160 by Poor Law authorities in extern institutions.[52] Maria Luddy pointed out that the county home offered the 'chief refuge' for the unmarried mother.[53] In 1939 there were 772 unmarried mothers in Poor Law institutions and 338 extern institutions, those run by private bodies.[54] County homes continued to play the largest role in the institutionalisation of unmarried mothers throughout the 1930s, 1940s and 1950s despite repeated calls for more 'suitable' accommodation.

As a result of its investigations, the *Report of the Commission on the Relief of the Sick and Destitute poor, including the Insane Poor* called for alternative accommodation to the county home for the unmarried mother. The Department of Local Government and Public Health responded to this pressure by turning to religious orders to provide so-called 'special homes' and to open magdalen asylums.[55] The department categorised unmarried mothers according to moral degradation, wishing the 'intractable problem' of the 're-peat offender' to be dealt with in magdalen asylums.[56] The 'better class' of girl was, ideally, catered for in religious special homes. While praising the work of the religious special home at Bessboro,[57] the department explained that 'it is now generally accepted that the number of unmarried mothers in the County Homes should be diminished and that encouraging results can be anticipated if special provision is made to help them' (see Tables 7.4 and 7.5).[58] The Department acknowledged that the

> policy of the special institution recommends itself on the ground of economy, for unless active measures designed to enable them [unmarried mothers] to return eventually to the work-a-day world are taken at the critical time, they are in danger of becoming a permanent burden on the ratepayers or of drifting into a life of degradation.[59]

The inspectors of boarded-out children also called for the provision of special mother and baby homes, noting 'with alarm the consequences of bringing up children' in county homes.[60] The consequence was a chain of institutionalisation in which children reared in the county home often returned with illegitimate pregnancies in early adulthood. This was a concern expressed throughout the period, and even as late as 1972 at the Kilkenny conference on social services for the unmarried mother.[61] In 1971, Dr Meagher had conducted a study of 400 unmarried mothers attending the National Maternity Hospital. He noted that there was an 'over representation of girls who have themselves been illegitimate and who have grown up in the emotionally sterile, unisexual atmosphere of an institution'.[62]

Table 7.4 Numbers of unmarried mothers maintained in county homes, 1928–42

Year*	Mothers in county homes
1928	970
1929	—
1930	903
1931	868
1932	936
1933	914
1934	889
1935	964
1936	859
1937	832
1938	841
1939	772
1940	1018
1941	879
1942	783

Note: *The figures for each year were taken on 31 March of the following year

Source: Compiled from the Department of Local Government and Public Health, *Annual Reports of the Department of Local Government and Public Health*, 1928–1942

Table 7.5 Numbers of unmarried mothers in special homes, 1928–42

Year*	Bessboro	Sean Ross Abbey	Manor House	Total
1928	65	—	—	65
1929	—	—	—	—
1930	—	—	—	—
1931	—	—	—	160
1932	93	173	—	266
1933	108	193	—	301
1934	131	168	—	299
1935	109	176	60	345
1936	110	146	76	332
1937	150	105	56	311
1938	120	129	64	313
1939	98	153	69	320
1940	98	170	81	349
1941	—	—	—	342
1942	—	—	—	352

Note: Sean Ross Abbey, Roscrea opened in 1930 and Manor House, Castlepollard opened in 1935. From 1941 onwards only total figures were given for the three homes rather than separate figures for each

Source: Compiled from the Department of Local Government and Public Health, *Annual Reports of the Department of Local Government and Public Health*, 1928–42

In 1943 the Joint Committee of Women's Societies and Social Workers[63] (JCWSSW) lamented that many unmarried mothers still had no option but the county home.[64] Lighting on the issue of class, the JCWSSW opined that most of these girls were 'drawn from the poorest classes' and often had more than one illegitimate pregnancy.[65] The issue of class permeated most debates on unmarried mothers and their children, and informed policy decisions. The official preference for a system of special homes run by religious orders satisfied both the angle of moral rehabilitation and class anxieties. The basic idea was that the county home would be the resort only of the 'poorest class', whereas the special homes would be reserved for the 'better type of girl'. There were also places allocated in most county homes for the admittance of unmarried mothers and their children. Furthermore, there were three mother and baby homes administered by the Poor Law authorities generally for working-class unmarried mothers: Pelletstown on the Navan Road in County Dublin under the control of the Dublin Board of Assistance, the Auxiliary Home, Kilrush, County Clare and a home at Tuam under the Galway Board of Health and Public Assistance. These homes were also operated by religious bodies: Pelletstown by the Sisters of Charity of St Vincent de Paul, the Auxiliary Home, Kilrush by the Sisters of Mercy, and the Tuam home by the Bon Secours Sisters.[66]

Magdalen asylums throughout the country co-operated with the local authorities in catering for women with more than one illegitimate child.[67] Lay magdalen asylums dated from the eighteenth century and were, in effect, reformatories which placed a heavy emphasis on the spiritual rehabilitation of prostitutes or women considered moral degenerates.[68] In the early nineteenth century the various Catholic congregations began to take over the asylums, and by the twentieth century they were considered Catholic institutions.[69] However, this was clearly not always the case as, for example, the magdalen asylum in Leeson St. in Dublin city centre was for unmarried mothers from the Church of Ireland.[70] In Dublin the main asylums were St Mary's Asylum and Reformatory, High Park Refuge Convent, Drumcondra (1833) and St Mary's Asylum in Donnybrook (1798) under the Sisters of Our Lady of Charity and Refuge, St Patrick's Asylum, Crofton Rd., Dunlaoghaire, and St Mary's Asylum, 104 Gloucester St. (1822) under the Sisters of Mercy.[71] Between 1922 and 1933 three new homes run by Catholic nuns came on stream: Bessboro home in Cork,[72] Shan Ross Abbey in Roscrea,[73] and the Manor House, Castlepollard in County Westmeath were all administered by the Sisters of the Sacred Heart of Jesus and Mary.[74] There was also St Gerard's, 39 Mountjoy Square, Dublin,[75] which admitted 'paying cases and selected destitute ones'[76] and only operated for six years.[77] These homes were for the reception of the 'better type of girl' which was social code for women from middle-class backgrounds who, it was deemed, were less likely to fall more than once. The special religious homes admitted women from all over the country. For example, in 1928 Bessboro received women from Cork, Kilkenny, Waterford, Tipperary and Kerry.[78] In

1930 it was noted that mothers came from as far away as Monaghan and Leitrim.[79] These homes were funded through a capitation system, whereby the state paid a grant per mother and per child.[80] Furthermore, despite the reservations of the Minister for Justice, James Fitzgerald-Kenney regarding the 'extension of the principle' of dependence, [81] the homes were also allocated sweepstake funds.[82] This money was used to help fund maternity wings attached to special homes.[83]

Dublin was the destination for many unmarried mothers, and the Department of Local Government and Public Health described the tendency as 'somewhat remarkable'.[84] Of the 551 illegitimate births registered in the city in 1931, only 335 were found to be 'chargeable to the city'.[85] Each local authority was responsible for the welfare of the illegitimate children born of women from its area. However, the social shame led many countrywomen to flee to Dublin for anonymity.[86] Such was the fear of social discovery that many countrywomen opted for the precarious fate of the unknown, escaping to Dublin rather than seeking refuge in the relevant county home. Societies such as the Saint Patrick's Guild and the Catholic Protection and Rescue Society frequently dealt with requests for assistance from all over the country. The Catholic Protection Society, for example, dealt with 1,003 requests for assistance in 1927.[87] In the same year, the guild received 5,988 letters regarding the protection of Catholic children.[88] In 1932 the Legion of Mary, which ran the Regina Coeli hostel for Catholic unmarried mothers and their children, noted that the welfare of these women had been almost entirely neglected, with disastrous consequences for the spiritual welfare of both mother and child:

> Outside the Union or the Protestant Homes those without means have been entirely unprovided for in Dublin. There is a reluctance to face the Union. Moreover the latter only admits Dublin girls, so for the large number of those flying from the country there was only the Protestant home. The result has been disaster in a great number of cases.[89]

In general, Catholic unmarried mothers from Dublin who remained within the Irish system were either sent to St Patrick's Home, Pelletstown, to one of the various magdalen asylums in the city or to the Legion of Mary hostel established in 1930. Protestant mothers were received at the Bethany home in Orwell Road, Rathgar;[90] these women were also accepted in Pelletstown, but the preferred option was to send mothers to homes that catered specifically for their religious needs. The strong association between illegitimacy and morality meant that all the homes, Protestant and Catholic, stressed the aspect of rehabilitation and the spiritual future of the child. Protection societies such as the Catholic Rescue and Protection Society and the Saint Patrick's Guild functioned primarily for the spiritual protection of Catholic children. However, this inevitably meant that they came in contact with the unmarried mother.

The various mother and baby homes throughout the country were largely

autonomous with respect to in-house rules, as there were no policy guidelines laid down by any government during the period. Therefore, no clear
conclusions can be drawn regarding the policies of these homes or the actual periods of detention for most inmates. However, the position outlined
in the 1927 report into the relief of the sick and destitute poor revealed the
general approach to the detention of unmarried mothers, which remained
largely intact until the 1960s. Conforming to the general view that these
unmarried mothers were fundamentally 'ill' and in need of 'reform' and
'treatment', the report separated the unmarried mothers into two categories: those 'amenable to reform' and the 'less hopeful cases'.[91] The 'less
hopeful' were those who had fallen more than once or those considered
feeble-minded or inherently evil. At a loss *vis-à-vis* the particulars of care or
how to confront this social and moral problem, the report shied away from
specifics by offering a free hand to local health authorities:

> Experience would indicate that the treatment of these cases should not be too
> tied up with regulations or be too hide-bound and that the results are more
> often attained by individual care. We, therefore, recommend that Boards of
> Health should be allowed an almost complete discretion in the matter of dealing
> with and paying for this class through the agency of the Rescue Societies and
> other voluntary organisations.[92]

When referring to the institutional care of unmarried mothers, the report
stressed that the detention of mothers for a period of one year was in no
sense 'penal'. However, the validity of this argument was somewhat vitiated
by a subsequent recommendation that 'repeat offenders' be detained for
two years.[93] The report explained that 'the object of our recommendations
is to regulate control according to individual requirements, or in the more
degraded cases, to segregate those who have become sources of evil, danger and expense to the community'.[94] The 'expense' could of course be interpreted as a moral or financial one, but the emphasis was on the latter.
The commission urged that no woman should be discharged until she had
given a guarantee that she could provide for her child 'either by paying
wholly or partially for maintenance in the home or boarding it out with
respectable people approved by the Board of Health'.[95] These recommendations were predicated on the assumption that legal powers would be introduced, to allow for the detention for at least one year of unmarried mothers who sought assistance. No such legal powers were ever introduced. Tables
7.6 and 7.7 reveal the level of movement in special homes for unmarried
mothers and babies for two sample years, 1935 and 1940.

In the Bessboro home in Cork, according to the Department of Local
Government and Public Health, women were, as a matter of policy, 'detained for a period of one year, and [were] trained to useful occupations,
housework, cooking, needlework, laundry work, diary management, poul-
try rearing, gardening and farming'.[96] However, by 1930 the matron of the
home explained that 'a number of the girls are weak willed and have to be

Table 7.6 Movement in and out of special homes, 1935

Inmates:	Bessboro	Sean Ross Abbey	Manor House
Expectant mothers	109	176	60
Mothers with children	6	12	12
Births	96	157	38
Discharges:			
Mothers with children	29	80	10
Mothers alone	81	102	5
Children boarded-out	7	31	0
Children adopted	15	12	3
Children to nurse by mothers	1	80	1
Children to rescue homes	0	3	1
Maternal deaths	0	0	0
Infant deaths	25	54	4
Mothers in institutions	127	139	51
Children in institutions	79	129	33

Source: Department of Local Government and Public Health, *Annual Report of the Department of Local Government and Public Health, 1935–36* (Dublin, 1936), p. 162

Table 7.7 Movement in and out of special homes, 1940

	Bessboro	Sean Ross Abbey	Manor House
Mothers:			
In institution on 31 March	98	170	81
Admitted			
Discharged			
To employment			
To parents			
Married			
Other			
Maternal deaths	0	0	2
Children:			
In institution on 31 March	98	164	62
Admitted	87	164	117
Discharged	45	109	63
Remaining	102	159	82
Children boarded-out	11	36	7
Children adopted/sent to schools or institutions	20	9	27
Infant deaths	38	58	34

Source: Department of Local Government and Public Health, *Annual Report of the Department of Local Government and Public Health*, 1940–1 (Dublin, 1941), p. 81

maintained in the Home for a long period to safeguard them against a second lapse'.[97] In 1932 the matron allegedly reported that some 'girls first received into the Home [1922?] are still there and have no desire to leave it. These girls have a great influence for good over the newcomers.'[98] The questionable virtue of long periods of detention was repeatedly stressed from a moral perspective. In 1934 it was noted that few women released from the special religious homes relapsed, and those who did 'spent only a short period in the special homes either because of the death of the first child or through the interference of relatives'.[99] Frequently, the mothers were kept until their child was old enough to be admitted into an orphanage or industrial school.[100] The fact that during her stay the mother paid for the maintenance of her child and herself by manual labour is also likely to have influenced the development of a long-stay policy.[101] Hearn pointed out that the 'commercial spirit' in many magdalen laundries concerned the factory inspector, Martindale, who worried that it would 'swamp the spirit of reform'.[102]

Alice Litster, as an inspector for boarded-out children, argued for the early release of unmarried mothers from county homes on the grounds of child welfare. She noted that the practice of allowing unmarried mothers to leave county homes to take up employment while boarding out their children had 'on the whole been justified'.[103] She cited Offaly and Leitrim, where this policy was enforced routinely, and the results were promising, with only two women in Leitrim returning to the county home on the grounds of a second pregnancy. The reason proffered by certain county homes for not following this policy was the character of the mothers: the authorities argued that they 'would inevitably return to the county home with a second illegitimate child'.[104] A policy of detaining women on the grounds that they may be 'prone to relapse' afforded an extraordinary degree of discretionary power at the hands of county home officials and the religious orders that ran the special homes.

Although, as noted, there was no legal basis for the policy, mothers were detained indefinitely in most of the institutional homes, with the average stay amounting to two years. In 1949 the *Report of the Consultative Child Health Council* noted that the tendency to detain unmarried mothers in institutions for between eighteen and twenty-four months for the purposes of house and laundry work continued.[105] The policy of long-term detention remained the norm until the late 1950s, even though evidence suggested throughout the 1930s and 1940s that it was one of the reasons expectant Irish unmarried mothers fled to Britain.[106] Until legal adoption was introduced in 1952, mothers usually stayed in an institution until their children were old enough to be transferred to an orphanage or industrial school. Legal adoption meant that illegitimate infants could be adopted within six to eight weeks of birth, which allowed the mother to leave the mother and baby home shortly after birth.[107] The period of detention also afforded a sense of punishment, and it was noted in the 1960s that unmarried mothers with their first child were provided with 'speedy adoptions' whereas 'repeat offenders' were required to wait longer for adoption to be finalised.[108]

Those unmarried mothers who attempted to brave life outside the institution, if denied parental or familial protection, were fated to a precarious existence with no legal protection. The two Department of Local Government and Public Health inspectors of boarded-out children, Anneenee Fitzgerald-Kenney and Alice Litster repeatedly stressed the harsh existence that these women and their children endured at the hands of society. The majority of these women were engaged in domestic service, their wages were small and 'their history militates against them and they are obliged to accept what is offered'.[109] It was hardly surprising that, in the majority of cases, contribution to the upkeep of their child was 'found impracticable'. While Fitzgerald-Kenney was a strong advocate of special religious homes, crediting them with preventing infanticide by providing the desperate mother with a haven, she did criticise the training that the women received.[110] She noted that the women were principally trained in agricultural work but she believed that domestic training was a more practical option, as on their return to 'independent life, they can earn higher wages … and agricultural work with its many opportunities seems to lead more easily to further lapses'.[111] However, in the absence of policy guidelines and legal safeguards, unmarried mothers were literally at the mercy of society, the county home or the religious mother and baby homes.

In terms of legislation, there were two acts passed during the 1930s that dealt directly with illegitimacy: the Illegitimate Children (Affiliation Orders) Act, 1930 and the Legitimacy Act, 1931.[112] The affiliation act allowed an unmarried mother to sue a putative father in her own right for maintenance of his child. Prior to this act, the only recourse for an unmarried mother was via a case of seduction taken by her parent, guardian or employer, based on loss of service.[113] The legitimacy act allowed for the legitimatisation of a child born outside wedlock if the parents married after the birth. Neither of these acts dealt specifically with the welfare of the unmarried mother. [114] However, in 1934 and 1939, two acts were passed that had a greater impact on the welfare of the unmarried mother and her child than any other legislation passed prior to World War II. The 1934 Maternity Registration Act ensured that all institutions providing care for mothers had to be registered, undergo inspections, and keep records.[115] In return for compliance, these institutions could apply for grant assistance under the maternity and child welfare system. This act was consciously crafted with a view to reducing the high death rate of illegitimate infants by monitoring the standards in all maternity homes. The Parliamentary Secretary, Dr Ward, made no secret of the act's intentions, noting that the abnormally high death rate of illegitimate infants meant that 'one must come to the conclusion that they are not looked after with the same care and attention as that given to ordinary children'.[116] In 1939 the Public Assistance Act allowed for the free medical care of all people unable to pay. Obviously this covered most unmarried mothers. However, the same legislation made the unmarried mother legally responsible for the financial upkeep of her illegitimate child, even while that child was maintained in an institution.[117]

The paucity, content and debate surrounding the legislation introduced reflected some deeply held convictions regarding the unmarried mother which facilitated inertia and neglect. For example, throughout the Dáil debates on affiliations orders, deputies repeatedly stressed that the legislation was a 'charter of these children of illicit love', rather than support (in a financial or moral sense) for the unmarried mother.[118] Senator O'Farrell reminded the Senate that these mothers were not 'saints or martyrs' and urged that the bill be for child protection rather than maternal benefit.[119] The Minister for Justice, Fitzgerald-Kenney was no less ambiguous in his arguments against *in camera* hearings for affiliation orders:

> It has to be recognised that there are a considerable number of immoral women in the world. It is quite possible that a woman, through her own fault, may apply for a fourth, fifth, or even sixth affiliation order against different men … Is she not to be known? Is her name never to be published? Such a woman is a danger to the community really. Is it not really better that her name should be known? It seems to me that it is. Let us take an example of one of the commonest forms of blackmail that you can come across. Suppose a girl is a servant and is in the employment of a respectable, well-to-do business man. She meets someone outside and is seduced. He is probably a penniless person. Public opinion would condemn her less if they thought that she had been seduced by the man in whose employment she was, than if she had been seduced by somebody outside. There is a big temptation to her to bring the charge against her employer.[120]

The Minister outlined the scenario of a female, class-based conspiracy against respectable men whereby the mother, since 'all mothers are not completely virtuous women', would encourage her daughter to sue her employer rather than her pauper lover for the upkeep of her child. He did not envisage this tactic in the case of a 'respectable woman whose daughter fell by accident' but a 'certain class of people' to whom 'illegitimacy seems to be almost hereditary'.[121] The Minister evidently touched a middle-class chord, as Deputy Jameson declared, 'I would not like to be alone in my house with any clever and designing servant girl if my wife was away for a night or two' if the *in camera* provision was maintained. After all, he cautioned, the Bill was not dealing with a 'highly moral class of people'.[122]

This 'class of people' was largely left to languish in county homes or fend for themselves amid a society that actively discriminated against their existence as a family unit. The *in camera* clause was eventually accepted, although Luddy argues that, rather than affording the women anonymity, it protected the men who were therefore not publicly named.[123] However, many contemporaries considered that *in camera* also protected the women involved from public humiliation or unnecessary exposure in a society that was largely disapproving of sex outside wedlock. Even the incredible death toll among illegitimate infants did not result in any dynamic response to the situation of single mothers and their children. The response to unmarried motherhood revealed many conflicting and contradictory attitudes in Irish society: sympathy was mixed with punishment, morality with finance, condemnation masked fear and facilitated emotional cowardice, and reality was banished to institutions or Britain.

A problem for 'the clergy': Irish unmarried mothers in Britain

The emigration of Irish unmarried mothers to Britain became a recurring theme throughout the period, merging eventually in the 1970s with the abortion debate. This propensity of Irish unmarried mothers to emigrate to Britain rather than avail themselves of services or family support at home not only reflected badly on Irish social services but also caused national embarrassment. The idea that Ireland's moral linen was washed in Britain was anathema to the aspirations of the new state. There was also a real fear for the souls of these children in 'Protestant Britain'. These two points did most to motivate the Irish Catholic charities, and eventually the state, to take steps to end this prenatal emigration.

It was voluntary workers in Britain who first brought the issue of Irish unmarried mothers in Britain to the attention of the Irish authorities. In 1929, Margaret Kerr of the Edinburgh Catholic Enquiry Office wrote to the Catholic Archbishop of Dublin, Dr Byrne, that many Irish women, most of them 'useless, feckless and in grave danger', were blackening the name of all Irish women in Scotland. Despite the fact that she attributed their downfall to the influence of 'the gay life through pictures and dance halls', she noted that many were so ashamed of their pregnancy that they signed themselves into the poorhouses as Protestants.[124] Evidently Mrs Kerr wondered why the fate of these women was not causing the same degree of concern in their native country.[125]

In 1931 the Saint Patrick's Guild, under the chairmanship of Mary Josephine Cruice, conducted the investigation into the situation in Britain.[126] Cruice gathered information from organisations in London, Liverpool, Manchester, Leeds and Scotland. This was to be the first of many impressionistic investigations into the subject carried out during the first half of the twentieth century. As a result of the work of Irish voluntary organisations and of complaints from British charitable organisations, negotiations began in 1930 to establish a repatriation scheme to bring these mothers and their infants back to Ireland.[127] In November 1931, the rudiments of the repatriation scheme were agreed upon in the offices of Mr John Dulanty, the Irish High Commissioner in London, by officials from the Irish Department of Local Government and Public Health and representatives of Catholic social welfare societies in Britain.[128] The repatriation scheme only covered first-time unmarried mothers who had conceived in Ireland, and the Irish government only covered 50 per cent of the costs.[129] The Irish committee for the supervision of the repatriation promised by the department during the 1931 meeting in the High Commissioner's office never materialised. As a result, the Irish Catholic Protection and Rescue society operated the repatriation scheme in lieu of any official action, a role they were officially designated by Archbishop McQuaid on his succession to the Catholic See of Dublin in 1941. George Craven, of the Crusade and Rescue Society, when writing to Miss Cruice in 1937, perhaps put his finger on the reasons why the repatriation scheme was not wholeheartedly embraced by the Irish government: 'I think your problems would be intensified if you had to deal with all the cases of pregnant Irish girls who find their way to this country.'[130]

The Department of Local Government was aware of the continuance of the prenatal emigration of Irish unmarried mothers to Britain. In 1935 the general inspector for the Department of Local Government and Public Health, Mrs Crofts, visited London and Liverpool to inquire into the problem of the Irish unmarried mother. As a result of her investigations she noted two major problems: the lack of facilities in Ireland, which encouraged Irish women to flee, and the tendency of young girls to abandon their religion and become pregnant within a year of emigration.[131] The association of the problem with religious defection facilitated the department's inclination to seek the aid and manpower of the various religions. Crofts recommended two preventive measures: training schools attached to convents for girls wishing to emigrate and special homes to take care of Irish single mothers *in* Ireland.[132] However, the department continued to rely on many religious and voluntary organisations to cater for the immediate needs of unmarried mothers and their children.

The Irish government's response to the publicity generated by Irish unmarried mothers in Britain was to put moral pressure on the Irish Catholic hierarchy 'to imitate the zeal' of its English counterparts.[133] When the government decided in 1938 to approach the Catholic hierarchy officially regarding the issue the Secretary of the Department of External Affairs, Joseph Walshe,[134] argued that the layman was 'particularly helpless' when faced with the issue of unmarried mothers. He explained 'I could go further and say that even a State Department can effect very little. Its moral and religious aspects and the extreme care and delicacy required for handling it point inevitably to a Church organisation of some kind.'[135] Walshe seemed genuinely convinced that this was not a state responsibility and that it was appropriate 'to put the responsibility for this matter where it really belongs, namely, on the shoulders of the clergy'.[136] The status of the unmarried mother was much more ambiguous than that of her married counterpart, and her health and welfare fell more readily into the category of moral duty than state responsibility.

The 'Emergency': the Irish unmarried and emigrant welfare, 1940–56

The Emergency was a period of introspection in Irish social life and thus brought many social issues to the fore, among them illegitimacy and infanticide, both of which appeared to increase.[137] Under wartime pressure, cracks began to show in the repatriation scheme. In 1940 the Irish Catholic Protection and Rescue Society (ICPRS) expressed concern that English agencies were sending Irish women back to Ireland under false pretences, promising them certain care and conditions that were not, in fact, available in Ireland.[138] It transpired that the Westminster Committee, frustrated with the pace of the scheme under the directorship of the ICPRS, had turned to the Saint Patrick's Guild.[139]

The ICPRS was possessive of its status as the 'chosen organisation' in relation to the repatriation scheme. However, it was also concerned about the very real dangers of an *ad hoc* approach to the repatriation of such vulnerable people. As Litster discovered, many of these women returned home to Ireland equipped only with a letter addressed to the inspector of the Department of Local Government and Public Health. Litster outlined the case of one unmarried mother who had been resident in London. After treatment for haemorrhage, a month prior to confinement, she was sent home to Ireland. Coupled with the physical risks to this patient, she was also emotionally distraught when she discovered that she had been misinformed in Britain and that, according to the Irish system would not be dealt with in Dublin, but would have to enter her local county home.[140]

Litster, accustomed to relying on and co-operating with voluntary organisations, and mindful of the sensibilities of the Dublin charity network, contacted Cruice of the Saint Patrick's Guild, requesting that she deal directly with the Westminster Committee before matters worsened.[141] By May 1940 the issue had been raised with the chief medical officer of Health in England, Dr Arthur Newsholme, by a concerned Catholic social worker, Mrs Helen Murtagh. Murtagh secured an agreement from Newsholme that each repatriation case would be thoroughly investigated and the relevant people in Éire contacted before any woman was sent home.[142] However, as Murtagh indicated in a letter in early May 1940 to the Saint Patrick's Guild, there appeared to be some confusion in Britain as to whether the Irish state was willing to take these women back into the country.[143] Murtagh drew a clear distinction between Irish women who became pregnant in Britain and those who arrived pregnant. She believed that those impregnated in Britain were the responsibility of the British state, but seemed dismayed by the lack of concern displayed by the Irish authorities for the souls of babies conceived in Éire. In her letter to Cruice she explained the situation in the context of the devastation of war:

> The Irish women in this country who are pregnant are attending the Public
> Health departments in the usual way. We have taken eight into Woodville, but

as Woodville is the only Catholic Home, with a capacity for 14, it is difficult. The Bishop is building but the war has stopped the operation and altogether the position is worrying as the Irish girls are being taken into Salvation Army and other homes. I have before me a list of 22 planted all over the city. Some of these are definitely Birmingham cases as they have lived here a year and got into their trouble over here. There are an isolated few who have run over here already pregnant; is the Irish Free State willing to have these women returned to their country?[144]

Cruice forwarded the letter to Litster, who wrote personally to Murtagh to explain the Irish system, which amounted to no more than a policy whereby first-time pregnancies were catered for in special homes and 'repeat offenders' were sent to the county homes.[145] On paper the deficiency of Irish provisions for unmarried mothers was highlighted. Murtagh was not privy to the much more enlightening report that Litster had compiled in November 1939 on the Irish services. In this report Litster outlined the deficiencies in the Irish system in terms of infant mortality:

> The chance of survival of an illegitimate infant born in the slums and placed with a foster-mother in the slums a few days after birth is greater than that of an infant born in one of our special homes for unmarried mothers. I except the Manor House, Castlepollard, in which the infantile death rate is comparatively low. In theory, the advantage should lie on the side of the child institutionally born. Pre-natal care, proper diet, fresh air, sufficient exercise, no arduous work, proper and comfortable clothing, freedom from worry, the services of a skilled doctor, the supervision and attention of a qualified nurse, all should be available and should make for the health of the expectant mother and the birth and survival of a healthy infant … Cleanliness, medical attention, dietetic knowledge, all the human skill may continue to preserve child life should be at hand. Yet any infant born in any other circumstances appears to have a better chance of life.
>
> I have grave doubts of the wisdom of continuing to urge Boards of Health and Public Assistance to send patients to the special homes so long as no attempt is made to explore the causes of the abnormally high death rate.
>
> The illegitimacy birth rate shows an upward trend. In 1916 it was 1530; in 1925 it was 1662. We cannot prevent the birth of these infants. We should be able to prevent their death.[146]

The illegitimate infant

The focus of concern was on the illegitimate baby rather than the mother, an approach facilitated by the fact that the Department of Local Government and Public Health had not delegated one member of staff to look after the care and welfare of these women. The issue of infant mortality, which provided the impetus for a reorganisation of maternity services in general, proved to be the only factor that interested the state in terms of the welfare of unmarried mothers. Litster, as the general inspector for the Department of Local Government and Public Health, concerned herself more than any other member of the department with the fate of these neglected families, but even her attempts were restricted, censored and ignored. Litster became a skilled mediator between the voluntary sector and the state, by paying the necessary deference to religious etiquette and co-ordinating the limited resources available.

Subsequent to her communication with Litster, Murtagh travelled to Ireland in search of a solution to the problem of Irish unmarried mothers in Britain. On 22 August 1942 she was received in the Archbishop's Palace in Drumcondra.[147] Apart from treating Mrs Murtagh to a tour of his Catholic Social Welfare Bureau, McQuaid arranged meetings for her with the Ministers of Justice, Public Health, External Affairs and the Taoiseach, an honour Mrs Murtagh had not expected: 'I did not imagine I should have the privilege of meeting Mr de Valera or his Ministers.'[148] With McQuaid as an ally, Murtagh had managed to work for several days with 'Mr MacEntee's Department' and with Litster in particular.[149]

As a result of this visit, Murtagh wrote to inform McQuaid that she would approach Bishop Griffin and Cardinal Hinsley with a view to securing a policy that all Irish babies would be baptised before leaving Britain.[150] She also promised to try to stop 'exaggerated reports getting to the press' and to try to find employment for Irish unmarried mothers post childbirth.[151] The concern regarding the employment prospects of unmarried mothers was new and most definitely prompted by the Archbishop of Dublin. McQuaid took a particular interest in the moral and physical welfare of female emigrants, and he believed that if the women were punished by social exclusion they would fall prey to greater sin and exploitation.[152] Murtagh described herself as 'very impressed' with the CSWB and indicated that she had urged the Minister for Local Government and Public Health, MacEntee, to co-operate with the welfare initiative by notifying the bureau of any women who emigrated to Britain.[153]

However, Murtagh was shocked at the standard of care provided for unmarried mothers and their babies: 'I could not help comparing them with our night nurseries', she wrote, 'where every mother can stay with her baby; all because the Ministry of Health pays again and again to build future citizens.'[154] Murtagh explained to Miss Myerscough of the CSWB that the English had moved away from the policy of institutionalising unmarried mothers and their babies in large homes, as this system 'produced a community of depressed and despairing women absolutely unemployable'.[155] She stressed that 'physically the case concern[ed] the Public Health authorities' and although she might be in a maternity hospital or a home the unmarried mother received the same medical attention. The voluntary organisations were denominational, and the public health authority co-operated with these initiatives *provided* they complied with 'regulations laid down by the Ministry of Health'.[156] Whether the mothers were in an institution or a special home they were usually transferred after three months to a hostel where they were gradually reintegrated into the working world.[157] The English approach to the welfare of unmarried mothers also relied heavily on the religious aspects of care. However, the British state was adamant that the medical responsibility had to be fulfilled.

Disquiet was evident in Ireland also. In 1942 an examination of the Dublin board of assistance discovered that 'maladministration was rampant' throughout the system of care relief.[158] In relation to unmarried mothers and their children, it noted that the mothers were 'either deliberately or carelessly forgotten by those responsible'.[159] As a result of this investigation three wardmasters were 'punished', one nun-nurse resigned and the director of the community at Pelletstown considered disciplinary measures as a result of irregularities by the matron's assistant. The following year a 'prolonged examination' of St Kevin's Hospital, which accommodated unmarried mothers, was completed.[160] Yet again, neglect was discovered and the conclusion was that the principal problem was that no one seemed to know who was responsible for such cases. The report recommended that a new department of registration and records should be founded. In relation to St Patrick's home in Pelletstown, it stated,

> It will be necessary to make a detailed report of the girls and children in St Patrick's Home – where the girls come from, their mental condition, how they should be treated, when they should be discharged and many other questions, about which divergent opinions are expressed and on which a definite policy has never been decided.[161]

In 1943 the JCWSSW reported on services for unmarried mothers in Ireland. Their report focused primarily on the child, noting the lack of progress that many of these children made in institutions:

> These illegitimate children start with a handicap. Owing to the circumstances of their birth, their hereditary [sic], the state of mind of the mother before birth, their liability to hereditary disease and mental weakness, we do not get, and could not expect to get, the large percentage of healthy vigorous babies that we get in normal circumstances. This is noticeable in the institutions we visited.[162]

While the joint committee articulated the general assumption that illegitimate babies died so frequently because of the hereditary roots in sin, the committee also voiced a growing conviction that circumstances played a large part in the death toll. Although the committee believed that the mother had 'committed an offence', they still argued that she deserved more than an institution.[163] However, they believed that 'economic difficulties and public opinion' made it impossible for illegitimate mothers to keep their children and therefore they recommended that she be paid instead of the institution to look after her child:

> We do not think this plan would encourage a woman in wrong-doing – wrong doing in which – though there were two guilty partners, she and the innocent children are frequently the only sufferers – the man getting off scot-free. The

very fact of having the responsibility of a child to look after and her affection for the child would tend to prevent a second offence. We could emphasise the benefit to the child of the care of even one parent.[164]

Although the committee couched their suggestion of financial assistance in terms of its moral and child-care benefits, it was still a radical proposal and one not realised until the introduction of an unmarried mothers' allowance scheme in 1973. Sensitive to public opinion and the reality of social hostility, the committee expressed surprise that there was no legal adoption 'in view of the hardships occasioned by its lack'.[165]

Litster was perhaps the most vocal advocate of legal adoption within government circles. Aware of the social condemnation of unmarried mothers and the reality of institutional care, she argued for legal adoption as early as 1937, when she noted that the 'passing of such an act in the Saorstát would do much in my opinion to give security and the chance of a happy life to many unfortunate children'.[166] She was unable to understand the religious objections to a legal adoption act, as the informal method of adoption that existed in the country was 'open to many possibilities of abuse', and there were frequently no safeguards to ensure that the religion of a child was respected after adoption.[167] In December 1939 Litster met with the Principal Officer of the Department of Justice, Mr J. E. Duff,[168] in an attempt to convince him of the need for legal adoption in Ireland. During this meeting, Mr Duff explained that the principal objections were religious: 'an unmarried mother might consent to the adoption of her child by persons or societies of different religion'.[169]

In 1945 the Department of Justice approached McQuaid concerning the issue of legal adoption, and the Archbishop indicated that he did not consider it possible to legalise adoption and protect the religious faith of illegitimate children. The department 'deduced from the general tone of his reply that he was not in favour of any legislation on the subject', and the Minister 'decided to drop the full adoption proposals'.[170] This reluctance on the part of the Archbishop to have informal arrangements legalised was in keeping with his general policy in relation to issues of health, welfare and morality. McQuaid was wary of secular legislation that would not bend if necessary to ensure that Catholic welfare was paramount. Moreover, as the state had repeatedly expressed the desire for the clergy to 'shoulder' the responsibility of unmarried mothers, it was hardly surprising that the department agreed to let the matter of adoption drop.

There is evidence that many of the Catholic voluntary agencies working on behalf of illegitimate children were in favour of legal adoption. In the early years of the Emergency, the Saint Patrick's Guild undertook an examination of foster care in Ireland and discovered that there was a shortage of foster homes as a result of wartime conditions.[171] The guild declared itself in favour of some form of legal adoption.[172] As the war progressed, the various rescue agencies in Dublin became more vocal regarding their support for legal adoption. In November 1943, Archbishop McQuaid attended

the opening of a conference of all the Catholic societies[173] involved in rescue work, during which 'special attention' was given 'to fosterage and the
reasons ascertained for suggestions that there was no longer an adequate
number of Foster Mothers' [sic].[174] At the end of the conference, Fr. Francis
J. Kenny of the Rotunda Girls Aid Society and Sister M. Collette of the Saint
Patrick's Guild expressed themselves in favour of 'a Law permitting legal
adoption'.[175] The Chairman, Mr C. P. Glennon of the Catholic Protection
and Rescue Society, reminded all present that 'he thought there would be
objections from Ecclesiastics to proposals for an Adoption Act'.[176] The objection to legal adoption was not based on a fundamental objection to adoption *per se*, but to a law that did not protect the religion of illegitimate
children.

Deterred temporarily from pursuing legal adoption, the state could not
ignore the increasing death rate of illegitimate children in institutional care.
The Registrar-General repeatedly highlighted the peril of institutional care
for illegitimate infants. In 1934 in Dublin of the 54 deaths in Dublin County
and 74 of the 104 deaths in Dublin City, 44 were in institutions and in the
city 74 of the 104 deaths were in institutions.[177] The Department of Local
Government and Public Health pointed out that these institutional deaths
were usually caused by an epidemic 'which spreads quickly among children
and wipes out the weaklings'. However, the crucial factor was not the possible weakness of these infants, but the fact that 'nurseries are laid out to
accommodate too many children and the provision for isolation is not adequate'.[178] Clustered cots in institutional wards provided the infectious disease with a deadly feeding-ground.

Table 7.8 Illegitimate infant deaths in institutions, 1933

Institution	Admission	Deaths
Pelletstown	155	53
Tuam home	120	42
Bessboro	64	25
Sean Ross Abbey	160	60

Source: Department of Local Government and Public Health, *Annual Report of the Department of Local Government and Public Health, 1933–34*, (Dublin, 1934), p. 148.

In 1939 the annual inspector's report noted that the death rates in the
various unmarried mother's homes around the country were undesirably
high: Bessboro home, Cork had an infantile death rate of 47 per cent, Shan
Ross Abbey, Roscrea had a death rate of 18 per cent, the Manor House,
Castlepollard a rate of 7 per cent, and St Patrick's Home, Pelletstown and
the home in Tuam, County Galway had rates of 23 per cent and 15 per cent

respectively.[179] By 1943, Litster noted that the rate in Bessboro was a staggering 61 per cent, and Shan Ross Abbey and the Tuam home had rates of 35 per cent, whereas Castlepollard and Pelletstown had shown 'a satisfactory decrease'.[180] In response to the declining death rate in the last two homes, Litster declared that the 'conclusion that overcrowding was responsible for a previous higher death rate cannot be avoided'.[181] According to Deeny, Litster's reports led him to shut Bessboro down and dismiss the sister in charge, despite the fact that the Bishop of Cork, Dr Lucey, complained to the nuncio, Archbishop Robinson. Deeny claimed that his actions were vindicated.[182]

In 1946, as chief medical adviser, Deeny requested an examination of the Regina Coeli hostel in Dublin as he considered it to be a 'very serious source of enteritis cases'.[183] Dr Daly visited the hostel on 12 and 19 of August and reported to Deeny that there were only seven permanent members of staff, no qualified nurse and doctor to provide care for the babies and unmarried mothers resident in the hostel.[184] In 1946 there were 220 inmates, many of whom were unmarried mothers and illegitimate children.[185] The mothers were afforded lodgings in the hostel and were sent to one of the maternity hospitals to give birth.[186] The legion's policy was to encourage mothers to go out to work and leave their babies in the hostel.[187] It was hoped that this would enable the mothers to remain the guardians of their children. Daly believed that 'a considerable amount of money would need to be spent in repair, decoration, furnishing and suitable equipment before it could be considered suitable. The voluntary effort, beyond doubt laudable, in my opinion is unable to cope with the situation in a satisfactory manner.'[188] He reported that hygiene was 'fairly satisfactory', that each baby had its own bottle and that the departmental policy of encouraging natural feeding was not possible when the mothers had to go out to work.[189] However, the departmental policy was to encourage voluntary effort in this regard, and while Deeny was in favour of this approach, he was determined that the state should inspect these premises and ensure that the proper money was available to render such effort viable and safe.

In 1945, 156 babies had been admitted to the hostel and 48 had died.[190] In 1946, 85 infants were admitted and 33 died of gastro-enteritis, seven of these having been admitted before January 1946.[191] In September 1946, Dr Murphy recommended that, in order to reduce infant mortality in the institution, visiting medical officers should be appointed, a day and night nurse provided, and an isolation ward established with a separate kitchen and sterilisation unit for infant feeding.[192] Despite regular meetings between Deeny and the staff of the hostel, it took another year before Frank Duff, the chairman of the Legion of Mary, agreed to the employment of a doctor.[193] In May 1948, in response to the level of infant mortality, Deeny removed the hostel's exemption from inspection. Under the 1934 Registration Act, the hostel should have been obliged to keep records and undergo annual inspections. However, due to the Legion's resistance to outside interference and the department's dependence on voluntary initiatives with regard to the care of unmarried mothers, the hostel had been granted an exemption in November 1934.[194]

Deeny was aware of the sensitive nature of interfering in the running of Catholic voluntary effort, considering the lack of official initiative in this area, and so he secured the agreement of the Archbishop that improvements were necessary.[195] By denying the legion an exemption to the requirements of the 1934 Registration Act, Deeny had ensured that the hostel would have to submit to improvements or it would not qualify as a maternity home under the existing legislation. He noted that the hostel had confessed it was unable to comply with the regulations, and Deeny considered this 'an excellent opportunity' to enable the department to 'achieve some necessary improvements'.[196] Deeny was considerably more supportive of the legion's attempts to maintain mother and baby together than his predecessor, the medical inspector Charles E. Lysaght, who reported in 1942:

> My own personal view is that the retention of unmarried mothers and children in this Hostel is altogether wrong. St Patrick's Home, Pelletstown appears to me the proper place for all such cases where they are under the care of nurses; better facilities are available. In this connection it is only right to point out that St Patrick's Home is overcrowded.[197]

Lysaght recommended Pelletstown, despite overcrowding, for medical reasons, but he paid no heed to the psychological and emotional benefits of the policy operated in the Regina Coeli hostel. Deeny, however, commended the tenacity of the legionaries, and believed that were it not for

> the hostel these children would be for the most part in Industrial Schools. Separation of mother and child would in most cases be complete. The hostel has kept mother and child together and has saved the State the cost of maintenance for children in Industrial Schools. Many of the mothers have been married possibly to men not the fathers of their children and 14 children have been happily settled with them. For many employment has been secured in which they may keep their children with them. This represents an effort to meet a growing problem constructively.[198]

Deeny not only appreciated a constructive approach to the care of the unmarried mother and her baby, he was also capable of seeing the saving in emotional and monetary terms. However, Deeny at no point questioned whether the care of unmarried mother and illegitimate children should rest in the hands of the appropriate religious body:[199]

> The sort of self-sacrifice and devotion which animate the Legionaries who work in the Hostel is to my mind the fine flowering of a self less humanity. It is certainly not something which may readily be replaced by paid labour. It should not be beyond our powers to find a means of co-operating with the Legion in fighting infant mortality without running counter to the ideals of its constitution.[200]

In this respect, Deeny was consistent with government policy and the Department of Health's response to maternal welfare in general. The state had the responsibility to ensure the medical well-being of all mothers and children. However, this did not militate against co-operation with voluntary organisations which were best placed to cater for the moral elements of care. Deeny, along with most of his contemporaries, did not question that the unmarried mother was a moral problem with social consequences. Duff was extremely appreciative of the department's understanding of illegitimacy as a moral problem and he informed McQuaid that his meeting with the departmental officials was 'not like a conference of officials but of very earnest Catholics'.[201] Nonetheless, Duff thanked the Archbishop for giving him permission to use his name 'in the event of the going being bad', adding that despite the fact that this measure had not proved necessary, he was sure it would 'have been decisive in the case of things being in the balance'.[202] This remark reflected Duff's confidence in the power of his Archbishop's name, and the fact that, despite the legitimate concerns regarding the infant mortality rate in his hostel, he found nothing in the Department of Health's attitude to make him feel the need for clerical support. He was among like-minded men.

Deeny agreed with the departmental policy of encouraging religious effort in the care of the unmarried mother and her child, but he believed that this relationship should be formalised and pursued in conjunction with legal adoption. In response to the *First Interim Report of the Child Health Consultative Council*, Deeny clearly outlined what he believed was necessary in order to solve the 'high illegitimate death rate':[203]

> Two things are necessary – one is the active intervention of the Church in this matter, and the other is a proper Adoption Act. As regards the first, the Medical Section has approached the various Ministers at different times during the past 7 or 8 years and Ministers in turn have made tentative approaches to the Bishops, but no concrete result has been achieved. This has largely been due to the tentative nature of the approach which has always been on a purely personal basis and has never reached a formal submission to the bishops on the matter. [204]

Deeny believed that the state had an obligation to provide a legal basis for the adoption of illegitimate children, as this was a matter of public health: children were dying because they could not legally secure a life outside an institution.[205] In keeping with his general approach to health care, Deeny believed that there was no room for the 'purely personal basis': the role of the Church should be official and adoption legalised. Deeny saw no problem in dividing the care of the unmarried mother and her child between the moral need for rehabilitation and the medical right to care. Similarly, he did not believe that his free mother-and-child scheme, available for *all* mothers, was incompatible with the system of voluntary and religious support clinics such as the CSSC. Deeny simply wished the system of maternity and child welfare to be official and to have a strong legal foundation that would enable the state to provide an adequate system of public health care.

Litster, after years of negotiating the haphazard system of care provided by the Church and the state, had some sobering observations to make, and many of her reports on maternal and child welfare, the impact of poverty and the consequence of no legal adoption were shocking. In 1948, Litster prepared a report for the IRCPS regarding the repatriation scheme, which she submitted for departmental approval before sending it to Archbishop McQuaid. In this report, years of frustration manifested themselves in a tone of unapologetic condemnation of Irish negligence with regard to the welfare of so many citizens. She began by stating that until the Irish confronted the problem at home there was little point in attempting to stem or correct the flow of pregnant single mothers to Britain. The version that made it into the Catholic Protection and Rescue Society booklet read as follows:

> It is useless deploring the flight of these unmarried mothers to England unless better facilities are offered to them at home. Secrecy is the unmarried mother's first and greatest need and so many refuse to remain at home because they see little hope of preserving their secret. Apart from the services of a few voluntary societies in Dublin, such as ours, all of which are constantly in financial difficulties, the only facilities available for the unmarried mother are the County Homes and three Special Mother and Baby Homes. The local authorities maintain the girls in these institutions, and a girl has little chance of going free until she has remained almost two years with her child in the institution. The result is the abnormal flight to England with consequent danger to both mother and infant.[206]

The original draft prepared by Litster was a much more hard-hitting document. Not surprisingly, it did not even make it to McQuaid before it was severely edited. Unlike other social commentators of the time, Litster considered the illegitimate children beyond the bounds of their souls, noting that they were entitled to citizenship:

> I do feel however that the Irish unmarried mother should be encouraged to return home, not only for her own sake, but much more for the Child's sake. Apart altogether from the question of religious upbringing, these babies are our own; they are entitled to Irish citizenship; above all the country needs them. From the point of view of Church and State, there are no unwanted babies.[207]

However, her sentiments did not survive internal censorship as the implicit criticism targeted both Church and State, and coming from a departmental inspector would have been incredibly damaging if afforded public circulation. In fact, the exodus of Irish single mothers had led people like Litster to ask a few fundamental questions about the services provided at home, and in explaining the reasons why she believed Irish women opted for Britain she was no less circumspect. Miss Litster explained:

The Irish unmarried mother in Great Britain who has gone there to avoid local knowledge of her condition is reluctant to return to Ireland. (*What have we to offer her here in comparison with the concealment, comfort and facility for adoption offered in Great Britain?*) In this country she can obtain shelter during her waiting time, good food and care, skilled attention during confinement, care, attention and kindness to her baby.[208]

The censor removed Litster's central question, thereby changing completely the tone and veracity of the report.[209] Litster was clear that, in her view, Irish society as a whole colluded in, facilitated or merely turned a blind eye to a policy of exclusion, institutionalisation and public shunning of these women and their children. Litster did not hesitate to inform the department of the consequences of communal negligence and the price of a stalemate between Church and State, which she believed contributed to a lack of public initiative in this field. In another report in May 1948, decrying the absence of legal adoption, she described the discovery of three abandoned infants (two dead) in Dublin in the previous fortnight. She noted, 'These three hapless babies are not the only infant martyrs of convenience, respectability and fear. The Church is perhaps waiting for the State to do something. The State is perhaps hoping the Church will do something.' [210] This was a particularly perceptive observation, the verity of which would become apparent only a few years later, when the issue of Church or State responsibility would manifest itself in the 'mother-and-child controversy'. Litster identified the social attitude as central to the death of innocent illegitimate infants, and the lack of any co-ordinated policy between Church and State as playing a crucial role in keeping the issue at the fringes of social policy. The uncertainty caused by the lack of any policy on the part of the department *vis-à-vis* the issue of morality and health negatively affected the development of various forms of social service, leading to much vacillation and, she believed, loss of life.

In 1952, Monsignor Cecil Barrett, chairman of the Catholic Protection and Rescue Society, published a pamphlet on adoption in order to outline Roman Catholic anxieties regarding the practice.[211] Barrett was evidently preoccupied with the safety of souls and the cause of rehabilitation, condemning those who 'dabble in private adoption work' for making it 'too easy for the unmarried mother'.[212] However, he did defend the many mothers who 'simply cannot care for their child' because of a hostile community: 'Many such mothers love their infants, but in order to safeguard their reputation and that of their families they must offer them for adoption.'[213] Nonetheless, he feared that legal adoption might remove the aspect of spiritual care and establish in Ireland the 'purely humanitarian' trend of other countries whereby illegitimate pregnancy was regarded as a mistake rather than a sin.[214] Under this system not only would the 'rents in the mother's spiritual fabric' fail to be repaired, but her baby's soul might be lost to bureaucracy.[215]

Unmarried mothers' welfare: the legalisation of health and adoption

In November 1949, Barrett contacted the Minister for Health, Noël Browne, requesting an extension of the maternity and child welfare grant. He wanted the grant to be paid in respect of children up to sixteen years of age instead of the existing age limit of five. He argued that this would help to cover the high cost of foster care and prevent some children from going to industrial schools, which he regarded as the 'easy way out'.[216] Barrett also requested that the regulations should cover not only children of widows, deserted and unmarried women but also illegitimate children of married mothers.[217] Browne's response was not only clear with regard to where the Department of Health believed the divide between health and moral welfare lay, but also showed that they believed the new mother-and-child scheme would legislate for this divide:

> The Minister fully appreciates the valuable work being done by these voluntary bodies but it is difficult to maintain they should be regarded as administering to the health of their charges rather than to the social and moral welfare. The introduction of a scheme to be administered by local authorities and to provide a comprehensive health service for all mothers and for all children up to 16 years, which it is hoped to put into effect in a short time, will leave only the maintenance and education of children to be provided by voluntary effort where the public assistance services do not meet their needs.[218]

While the mother-and-child scheme took four more years of debating before it was enacted in a modified form, it was clear that the Department of Health from the mid-1940s regarded this scheme as part of their policy to cater for the health of unmarried mothers and their offspring. In terms of policy, the state was also clear: state departments would cater for the medical care of these mothers and the formalisation of adoption practices, but other aspects of care fell into the sphere of morality, and that was the Church's field of responsibility. Indeed, the way in which compromise was finally reached between the Catholic Church and the Irish state with regard to legal adoption, was considered by McQuaid as a model for future co-operation concerning the delicate matter of legislation for a national maternity service.

The Adoption Society, a pressure group in favour of legal adoption, began to lobby local authorities for their support in 1948, by pointing out the benefits of legal adoption in terms of costs and lives.[219] The vice-chairman of the society, E. W. McCabe, argued in terms of infant mortality: 'All of these children carry the stigma of their birth, and suffer the social punishment of their state, though they are as innocent of any sin against morality or society as the highest born in the land.'[220] Despite the fact that the majority of local authorities petitioned by the Adoption Society had pledged their support by the end of 1950, the Minister for Justice, Séan MacEoin decided in November 1950 that he would not introduce any such legislation.[221] The

Minister believed that adoptive parents did not need protection, and he was concerned that the legalisation of adoption would jeopardise the rights of the family. He did not consider adoption in terms of infant mortality or the welfare of the unmarried mother.[222]

The Attorney General, Charles Casey, was even more explicit in his explanation for not favouring a legalisation of adoption when he asked, 'how can a Catholic logically demand or permit any legislation which would endanger the soul of a single child?'[223] Although he did consider the position of the unmarried mother, he did so in terms of the 'inalienable' rights of the family:

> If the word 'inalienable' is to be given any meaning at all, it may mean that no mother of an illegitimate child can alienate her right and duty to provide according to her means for the religious and moral, intellectual, physical and social education of her child. In other words, if she cannot allow her child to be irrevocably adopted, can the State pass legislation enabling her to do so?[224]

Casey considered the issue purely from the perspective of principle, and, despite referring to the 'mental anguish of the unmarried mother', in truth that mattered less to him than the rights of legitimate families. Legal adoption faced the same ethical and moral hurdles as the comprehensive maternity service: the Catholic understanding of the family was more important to many than social reality. There was no consideration of other religious groups and their needs. Casey appeared to relish the idea of the 'counter-attack' which his speech would engender, telling McQuaid that he was sure it would 'come hot and heavy. I shall enjoy that in my bed.'[225] For the Attorney General, legal adoption was an opportunity to defend the Catholic principles.

McQuaid was not opposed to legal adoption in principle.[226] He was aware of private adoptions arranged in his diocese by societies such as the Catholic Protection and Rescue Society, and he played a significant role in supervising the adoption of Irish children by American couples.[227] However, the Archbishop's concern was always the spiritual welfare of Catholic children. While he acknowledged that the state had a responsibility in terms of the physical welfare of children, he was nervous that legal adoption would no longer be under his control or flexible in terms of spiritual welfare. The controversy over the mother-and-child scheme in 1950–51 distracted McQuaid and the interparty government from any persistent consideration of legal adoption.

Nevertheless, the Adoption Society continued to pursue the aim of legal adoption, principally on behalf of adoptive parents and illegitimate children. In November 1951 the Society introduced a private members bill and officially approached the Catholic hierarchy through Cardinal D'Alton of Armagh.[228] In January 1952 the Catholic hierarchy agreed in principle to legal adoption, that provided there were sufficient spiritual safeguards to ensure that the religious faith of the child was protected. The episcopal committee drew up certain safeguards allowing for the creation of an adoption board, with a member of each religious denomination represented who had the right to refuse any application for adoption.[229] All these stipulations were honoured in the Adoption Act of 1952. Ironically, Irish adoptions within Ireland only had a limited period of popularity between 1960 and 1980; by the mid-1980s the majority of single mothers kept their children (see Table 7.9).[230]

Table 7.9 Number of adoption orders received for the years 1957 to 1969

Year	Illegitimate births	Adoption orders
1957	1,032	752
1958	976	592
1959	959	501
1960	968	505
1961	975	547
1962	1,111	699
1963	1,157	840
1964	1,292	1,003
1965	1,403	1,049
1966	1,507	1,178
1967	1,540	1,493
1968	1,547	1,343
1969	1,638	1,224

Source: NAI, Clandillon papers, Box (1) Facilities available by or with the aid of the Department of Health for unmarried mothers, c.1971

Rethinking the unmarried mother 'problem', 1950s–1960s

The Emergency brought the unmarried mother to the attention of the maternity hospitals, who began to notice an increased number of such women coming through their doors as a result of travel restrictions.[231] The hospitals reflected the subtle changes in Irish society and the ghosts of previous concerns that lingered during the 1950s.[232] They began to issue reports each year of the numbers of unmarried mothers dealt with and the actions taken by the hospital on their behalf, from referral to other organisations to advice or mediation with parents. It was obvious that the vast majority of Irish unmarried mothers availed themselves of legal adoption, approximately 90 per cent between 1953 and 1972.[233] It was evident that the 'problem of the unmarried mother' was a growing one. In 1956 the almoner of the Rotunda, Eleanor Holmes, observed, 'The purely social and moral problems of the unmarried mother and her child have continued to absorb a relatively large proportion of time in comparison to that devoted to other patients.'[234]

While the almoner reflected the class bias of the 1920s, calling for a small home for the 'better type of Roman Catholic girl', she also expressed new thinking with regard to the social definition of a positive outcome. Instead of regarding marriage as the best solution to the situation of the unmarried mother, she cautioned against such hasty action, noting that it often led to 'marital discord' later. She regarded it as better that the women should '"weather the storm" than spend her life in an unhappy marriage'.[235] The same year the Coombe expressed a similar philosophy, urging co-operation between various agencies that worked with the unmarried mother in order to 'prevent premature decisions which may be afterward regretted'.[236]

The unmarried mother's problems were no longer regarded in a purely moralistic framework although undertones lingered, they were increasingly regarded as 'emotional, personal, family and material'.[237] The social shame of an illegitimate pregnancy continued to be relevant in the decision-making process, but the official mind had come around to the idea that the extended family should, if possible, be the first resort and the institution only the second option and a short-term respite:

> The attitude of these girls' parents has been found to be of the utmost importance. Recrimination and/or punitive action or urgings to get rid of the baby as soon as possible, or to get married had to be understood. The impact of the disaster on the young girl's family has had to be considered and in most instances it was felt that if no other adult relative could give shelter during the pregnancy, a home for mothers and babies was the wisest answer, and gave the girl time to work out the best plan for the future from conflicting family advice and pressure.[238]

In 1954, Margaret Horne, the almoner at the Rotunda, cited the story of Rita as an example of how the unmarried mother could be assisted successfully. Rita was nineteen years of age and alone in Dublin. She did not have the support of her boyfriend and vacillated between keeping her child or putting it up for adoption. Her main reasons for opting for adoption were financial and social. The social worker approached Rita's employer to ensure that her job was held for her and secured her accommodation. Rita kept her child. The social worker did not encourage Rita to opt for adoption; instead she facilitated Rita's decision, which was by far the harder social option.[239]

Eileen Conroy noted that by the 1940s a shift had occurred in American literature regarding the unmarried mother: her situation was increasingly depicted as 'a manifestation of psychopathology rather than immorality'.[240] The notion of 'dysfunction' crept into social work theory with regard to the family in general, and the unmarried mother became the personification of this concern. Conroy argues that these 'psychoanalytic concepts about the single mother never really held sway in the UK or Ireland'.[241] However, these assumptions did inform reports like those emitted from the social work department of the Rotunda hospital throughout the 1950s and 1960s. This attitude to the unmarried mother was also reflected in the 1972 report of Kilkenny Social Services, *The Unmarried Mother in Irish Community*, which stated, 'Of course, among unmarried mothers there is inevitably a higher proportion of girls who are psychiatrically disturbed in the first place, than among a control group of others and so at one time or another we may expect that this group of unmarried women would show a high psychological vulnerability.'[242]

By the late 1950s in Ireland the 'case-work' approach to the unmarried mother predominated, rather than that of moral rehabilitation.[243] The themes were 'patience and understanding', infiltrated with a continued class bias and a partiality for a psychological profiling of the unmarried mother as disturbed and maladjusted. She remained 'deviant' and her behaviour continued to be a 'problem'. However, sociological research began to point increasingly to social reasons for unmarried motherhood. In her thesis on the Irish unmarried mother submitted in 1967, Sister Mary Creegan concluded that there appeared 'to be no such person as the typical unmarried mother'. [244] She noted the criticism of contemporary social research which warned against perpetuating the 'image of the unmarried mother as poor, uneducated and mentally disturbed when in fact professionals working with these women feel many are middle-class, educated and "normal" women'.[245] For Creegan, difficulties for the unmarried mother arose from her social and cultural context:

> In a family-structured society unmarried motherhood almost inevitably constitutes a problem for the individual mother and her child, and for society as a whole. From the point of view of the individual mother, in our culture at least, an illegitimate pregnancy is likely to be a source of great tension and emotional stress. Difficulties inherent in the situation may be increased by the social hostility directed towards her.[246]

The unmarried mother exerted her own pressure: the rate of Irish abortions in Britain caused considerable alarm in Ireland.[247] In 1959 the almoner of the Rotunda hospital noted that many unmarried mothers continued to go to England 'and are frequently referred back here as being Irish pregnancies and therefore not England's responsibility'.[248] In spite of the introduction of legal adoption and greater social awareness of the difficulties and anxieties facing these women, prenatal emigration persisted. In 1967, Creegan also observed the 'number of Irish girls who go to Britain when they discover they are pregnant', concluding that this was due to the weight of social censor in Ireland, ignorance and/or fear of Irish social services, and a desire for secrecy. She claimed that many professionals were not comfortable with the repatriation scheme, as it was often 'carried to extremes': she cited one case of a girl who had not lived in Ireland since she was eight years of age who was repatriated.[249] By 1969 the introduction of the British Abortion Act of 1967,[250] the ICPRS were alleging that the reasons for this voyage had altered from adoption to abortion.[251] The proximity of the two islands, the cultural precedence of emigration, and the social condemnation of these women meant that, for many, Britain was far too tempting an escape route. The ICPRS lamented that, in spite of the help offered and the legalisation of adoption, 'the old prevalent belief that one must go to England to preserve secrecy seems to die hard'.[252]

It was acknowledged repeatedly that the 'drift to England' would continue until Irish society accommodated the unmarried mother and her child into its social and legal framework.[253] This social pattern threw cold water on moralistic hypotheses about 'condoning promiscuity'; it also raised questions about the realities of raising a child as a lone parent in Ireland. By the early 1970s the unmarried mother's rights became the new theme and foremost among them was the right to retain the guardianship of her child.[254] A far cry from the sentiments of *Casti Connubii*, it was now considered 'grossly hypocritical … to preserve the dignity of family life at the expense of the incomplete family'.[255] These social changes were reflected by the closure of the special mother and baby homes established in the early 1920s and 1930s: the Sean Ross Abbey home in Roscrea ceased operations in 1969, Manor House in Castlepollard followed suit in 1971 and Bessboro home became the centre of adoption services for the Sacred Heart order known as the Sacred Heart Adoption Society, which only ceased adoption placements in 1998.[256]

It was gradually accepted by social commentators that the services provided for the unmarried mother reflected social attitudes. The Kilkenny conference held in 1971 typified this growing awareness:

> In any consideration of community services for the unmarried mother it is important to understand society's attitude towards both the unmarried mother and her child, because it is ultimately society's attitude which will determine the level of care that both will receive and accordingly will determine how valuable a member of the community the unmarried mother's child will be when he becomes an adult.[257]

Dr Peter Birch, the Roman Catholic Bishop of Ossory, speaking at the conference, noted that as long as society tolerated the 'conditions of rejection' then the community was 'tacitly helping to contribute to the problem of the unmarried mother'. He noted that 'social attitudes, social philosophy and legislation clearly' reflected what he dubbed a 'moralistic' approach inappropriate to the late twentieth century.[258] The conference report articulated the growing culture of rights, expressing the contention that it was a mother's 'fundamental right' to be able to keep her child.[259] Legislation in the 1970s gave teeth to this right by facilitating financially and legally the unmarried mother as guardian of her child.

The Social Welfare Act of 1973 entitled unmarried mothers to maintenance allowances and children's allowance, which was, as Kennedy argues, ideologically tantamount to 'stepping on to a new planet'.[260] The allowance was introduced following a recommendation by the Commission on the Status of Women (1972), which was established to report on the status of women in Irish society.[261] This recommendation 'created the economic possibility for solo-motherhood' and knitted the single mother into the social welfare fabric of Irish society that sought to protect and support the Irish family.[262] The introduction of the Unfair Dismissals Act in 1977 ensured that women would not lose their jobs as a result of a pregnancy.[263] This offered women the most basic economic protection from social prejudice with regard to illegitimacy. These legislative changes were not a panacea for all the social or economic difficulties encountered by the lone mother in Ireland. However, they reflected a new era of rights-based welfare that protected these women from the rawest forms of discrimination.

Notes

1 Mrs B. to Byrne, 21 July 1937, DDA, Byrne papers, AB 7, Charity Cases, Box 6, July 1935–May 1937. The girl was dispatched to High Park Convent (magdalen asylum in Drumcondra).

2 Mr Thomas McArdle, witness on behalf of the Department of Local Government and Public Health. See Commission on the Relief of the Sick and Destitute Poor, *Report* (Dublin, 1927), pp. 14–15.

3 League of Nations, *The Study on the Legal Position of the Illegitimate Child* (Geneva, 1939), p. 5.

4 E. W. McCabe (Vice-Chairman, Adoption Society), 'The need for a law of adoption', *JSSSI*, 102 (8 Apr. 1949), 188.

5 In 1989, illegitimate births were 11.9 per cent and by 2000 they accounted for 31.8 per cent of births. See Kennedy, *Maternity in Ireland*, pp. 82–3.

6 Kunzel noted that in American history unmarried motherhood has engaged fears regarding class, race, ethnicity, sexuality and family. See R. G. Kunzel, *Fallen Women, Problem Girls: Unmarried Mothers and the Professionalization of Social Work, 1890–1945* (Yale, 1993), pp. 5 and 51.

7 Commission on the Relief of the Sick and Destitute Poor, *Report*, p. 73.

8 *Report of the Committee on the Criminal Law Amendments Acts (1880–85)*, p. 12.

9 *Report of the Committee on the Criminal Law Amendments Acts*, p. 8.

10 *Ibid.*, p. 9.

11 *Ibid.*, p. 8.

12 Department of Local Government and Public Health, *Annual Report of the Registrar-General, 1932* (Dublin, 1933), p. xiii.

13 See the reports of the Registrar-General for the years 1923 to 1930 when comparative figures are recorded.

14 Ireland correspondent, 'The care of illegitimate children,' *The Lancet*, 2 (11 Nov. 1932), 1073.

15 O'Duffy was also a member of the Carrigan Committee. McGarry noted that O'Duffy's *in camera* submissions to the Carrigan Committee detailed 'the relatively widespread existence of serious sexual offences such as rape, incest, and child abuse'. See F. McGarry, *Eoin O'Duffy: A Self-Made Hero* (Oxford, 2005), p. 157.

16 The State Book at Central Criminal Court, Dublin City between 1924 and 1950 bears witness to 219 cases of infanticide and/or concealment of birth.

17 Finnane, 'The Carrigan Committee', 520–1, 530.
18 Revd R. S. Devane, S.J, 'The unmarried mother: some legal aspects of the problem', *IER*, 23 (1924), 55; 'The unmarried mother and the Poor Law commission', *IER*, 31 (1928), 561–82; 'The legal protection of girls', *IER*, 37 (1931), 20–40; 'The dance hall,' *IER*, 37 (1931), 170–94.
19 M. H. MacInerny, 'The souper problem in Ireland', *IER*, 18 (1922), 140.
20 *Ibid.*, p. 141.
21 See also, Devane, 'The unmarried mother: some legal aspects of the problem', pp. 55–67.
22 MacInerny, 'The souper problem in Ireland,' p. 143.
23 *Ibid.*, p. 144.
24 M. Luddy, 'Prostitution and rescue work in nineteenth-century Ireland', in M. Luddy, and C. Murphy (eds), *Women Surviving: Studies in Irish Women's History in the 19th and 20th Centuries* (Dublin, 1990).
25 Finnane, 'The Carrigan Committee', p. 523. The committee was established as a result of legal changes in England and Scotland in 1922 and Northern Ireland in 1923, which meant that Ireland's legislation was considerably more lenient with regard to sexual offences against young persons. F. Kennedy, 'The suppression of the Carrigan report,' *Studies*, 89:356 (2000), 354.
26 Finnane, 'The Carrigan Committee', p. 536; Kennedy, 'The suppression of the Carrigan report', pp. 354–62.
27 Finnane, 'The Carrigan Committee', p. 522.
28 Confidential Department of Justice Report on the Committee on the Criminal Law (Amendment) Acts, p. 13, NAI, Attorney General 2000/10/1235; also cited in Finnane, 'The Carrigan Committee', p. 527.
29 J. P. Dunne, 'Poverty problems for a patriot parliament', *JSSSI*, 74–5 (1922–23), 197.
30 *Ibid.*
31 *Report of the Committee of Inquiry into Widows' and Orphans' Pensions*, 1933, p. 27
32 The report of a meeting of municipal authorities in *The Lancet*, 2 (25 Sept. 1937), 763.
33 The National Council of the Unmarried Mother and her Child was established in Britain in 1917 as a result of concern regarding the mortality rate of illegitimate infants. See K. Kiernan, H. Land, J. Lewis (eds), *Lone Motherhood in Twentieth Century Britain* (Oxford, 1998), p. 98.
34 M. J. Russell, *Report on the State of Public Health in the City of Dublin for the Year 1938* (Dublin, 1939), p. 78.
35 Hospitals' Commission, *First General Report 1933–34*, p. 54.
36 *Ibid.*
37 *Casti Connubii* (On Christian Marriage), 31 December, 1931, quoted in Fremantle, *The Papal Encyclicals,* p. 242.
38 A. Fitzgerald-Kenney was an inspector for boarded-out children between 1903 and 1935.
39 Annual Report of the Department of Local Government and Public Health, 1933–4, p. 325.
40 E. W. McCabe, 'The need for a law on adoption', *JSSSI*, 102 (8 Apr. 1949), 181.
41 McCabe, 'The need for a law on adoption', p. 181.
42 As Kennedy argues, the 'shotgun' wedding was a strategy employed by all social classes in Ireland for dealing with a pregnancy outside wedlock and was still practised in the 1960s. See Kennedy, *Cottage to Crèche*, p. 27.
43 'Report on "Lowville" Ballsbridge', 22 April 1936, NAI, Dept. Health, M34/16.

44 McCabe, 'The need for a law of adoption', p. 179.
45 See *Annual Report of the Department of Local Government and Public Health, 1922–5,* pp. 57, 110; *Ibid., 1927–8,* p. 42; *Ibid., 1928–9,* p. 47.
46 *Ibid., 1922–5,* p. 110.
47 *Ibid.*
48 *Ibid.,1927–8,* p. 42; for a discussion of Wyse Power's significance, see M. O'Neill, *From Parnell to De Valera: A Biography of Jennie Wyse Power, 1858–1941* (Dublin, 1991).
49 Commission on the Relief of the Sick and Destitute Poor, *Report,* p. 15.
50 *Ibid.*
51 *Ibid..*
52 *Annual Report of the Department of Local Government and Public Health, 1931–2* (Dublin, n.d.), p. 138.
53 M. Luddy, 'Moral rescue and unmarried mothers in Ireland in the 1920s', *Women's Studies,* 30 (2001), 799.
54 Garrett pointed out that 70 per cent of unmarried mothers were accommodated in poor law institutions and this remained the case until the late 1950s. See P. M. Garrett, 'The abnormal flight: the migration and repatriation of Irish unmarried mothers', *Social History,* 25 (2000), 332.
55 See, for example, *Annual Report of the Department of Local Government and Public Health,1927–8,* p. 86; *Ibid., 1928–9,* p. 114; *Ibid., 1930–1,* p. 129.
56 *Annual Report of the Department of Local Government and Public Health, 1931–2,* p. 129.
57 There are several spellings given for this home (Bessborough, Bessboro, Besboro). Bessboro is used throughout this study.
58 *Annual Report of the Department of Local Government and Public Health, 1928–9,* p. 113.
59 *Ibid., 1930–1,* p. 129.
60 *Ibid., 1928–9,* p. 217.
61 Kilkenny Social Services, *The Unmarried Mother in the Community: A Report on the National Conference on Community Services for the Unmarried Parent 1972* (Kilkenny, 1972)
62 *Ibid.,* p. 16.
63 The JCWSSW represented the following organisations: Society of Girl Guides, Irish Countrywomen's Association, Irish Matron's Association, Saor an Leanbh, Irish Schoolmistresses Association, Irish Women's Workers' Union, Mothers' Union, National Council of Women, Women Graduates' Association of Nation University and Trinity College Dublin, Women's Citizens' Association, Women's National Health Association, Holy Child Association, and the Society for the Prevention of Cruelty to Children. NAI, Dept. Taoiseach, S9278; See also C. Clear, '"The women can not be blamed": the commission on vocational organisation, feminism and 'home makers' in independent Ireland in the 1930s and '40s', in O'Dowd, and Wichert (eds), *Chattel, Servant or Citizen,* pp. 179–86.
64 JCWSSW, Memo on Children in Institutions Boarded-out and Nursed Children (June, 1943), p. 2, NAI, Clandillon Papers, Box 3.
65 *Ibid.*
66 *Annual Report of Department of Local Government and Public Health, 1928–9,* p. 47.
67 *Ibid., 1932–33,* p. 130.
68 In 1766, Lady Arabella Denny founded the earliest recorded magdalen asylum in Ireland as a shelter for teenage Protestant unmarried mothers. In the nineteenth century, the Good Shepherd nuns ran asylums in Cork, Belfast, Limerick, Waterford

and New Ross. The Mercy Sisters ran asylums in Galway, Tralee and Dun Laoghaire. The largest asylum in England and Ireland was run by the Sisters of Our Lady of Charity in Drumcondra in Dublin, known as High Park (see note 1). See P. Burke Brogan, 'The Magdalene experience', in P. Kennedy (ed.), *Motherhood in Ireland*, pp. 164–5; M. Luddy 'Prostitution and rescue work in nineteenth-century Ireland', in Luddy and Murphy (eds), *Women Surviving*, p. 61.

69 *Ibid.*, p. 66.

70 M. J. Russell, *Report on the State of Public Health in the City of Dublin for the Year 1936* (Dublin, 1937), p. 76.

71 Williams, *Dublin Charities*, pp. 156–62.

72 *Catholic Directory and Almanac, 1931*, p. 263. Conway noted that in 1921 the bishop of Cork purchased land from the Quaker family Pike and gave it to the Sisters of Sacred Heart of Jesus and Mary to establish a mother and baby home. This home became Bessboro home and later became the Sacred Heart Adoption Society, which ceased adoption placements in 1998. See E. Conway, 'Motherhood interrupted: adoption in Ireland', in Kennedy (ed.), *Motherhood in Ireland*, pp. 182–3.

73 Sean Ross Abbey opened its doors in 1930. See *Annual Report of the Department of Local Government and Public Health, 1930–1*, p. 129.

74 *Ibid., 1931–2*, p. 128; Department of Local Government and Public Health, *Report of the Conference on Public Health and Social Services, 1930*, p. 88.

75 St Gerard's was established in 1933 under the lay control of the Catholic organisation, Saint Patrick's Guild. See *Annual Report of the Department of Local Government and Public Health, 1933–4*, p. 148.

76 *Ibid., 1934–5*, p. 179.

77 The home closed in 1939. See *Annual Report of the Department of Local Government and Public Health, 1939–40*, p. 42.

78 *Annual Report of the Department of Local Government and Public Health, 1928–9*, p. 47.

79 *Annual Report of the Department of Local Government and Public Health, 1930–1*, p. 129.

80 The rate was three shillings a day for mother and child in 1928. See *Annual Report of the Department of Local Government and Public Health, 1928–9*, p. 47.

81 Dáil Éireann, *Official Reports of the Debates*, vol. 34, col. 383, 20 February 1931.

82 Coleman, 'The origins of the Irish Hospital Sweepstake', pp. 40–55; *First General Report of the Hospitals' Commission, 1933–34*, pp. 54–5; *Third General Report of the Hospitals' Commission, 1937*, pp. 7 and 145.

83 Bessboro home in Cork, for example, had a new maternity wing opened in 1930.

84 *Annual Report of the Department of Local Government of Public Health, 1931–32*, p. 59.

85 *Ibid.*

86 Kunzel noted that in American culture during the same period, unmarried mothers frequently felt compelled to seek anonymity in urban areas. See R. G. Kunzel, *Fallen Women, Problem Girls: Unmarried Mothers and the Professionalization of Social Work, 1890–1945* (Yale, 1993), p. 67.

87 Catholic Protection and Rescue Society, *14th Annual Report of the Catholic Protection and Rescue Society*, (Dublin, 1928), p. 3.

88 Saint Patrick's Guild, *Annual Report of the Saint Patrick's Guild, 1927–8*, p. 9.

89 The Regina Coeli Hostel, 5 October 1930–11 May 1932, p. 7, DDA, Byrne papers, Lay organisations (1)

90 NAI, Department of Health, A121/57 and A24/6.

91 Commission on the Relief of the Sick and Destitute Poor, *Report*, p. 68.

92 *Ibid.*
93 Powell noted that this report revealed a 'patriarchal dimension', conferring a criminal status of unmarried mothers. See Powell, *The Politics of Irish Social Policy*, p. 179.
94 Commission on the Relief of the Sick and Destitute Poor, *Report*, p. 69.
95 *Ibid.*
96 *Annual Report of the Department of Local Government and Public Health, 1922–25*, p. 56.
97 *Ibid., 1930–1*, p. 130.
98 *Ibid., 1932–3*, p. 55.
99 *Ibid., 1933–4*, p. 179.
100 Children were generally not accepted into industrial schools before the age of two.
101 See F. Finnegan, *Do Penance or Perish: Magdalen Asylums in Ireland* (Oxford, 2004), pp. 35, 228–9.
102 M. Hearn, *Thomas Edmondson and the Dublin Laundry: A Quaker Businessman, 1837–1908* (Dublin, 2004), p. 134.
103 *Annual Report of Department of Local Government and Public Health, 1928–9*, p. 217.
104 *Ibid.*
105 *Report of the Consultative Child Health Council, 1949* part 'F' *Infant (illegitimate) Death Rate in the city of Dublin*, p. 3, NAI, Dept. of Health A116/167; During the same period the average stay in the evangelical homes of America decreased from six months to two months. See Kunzel, *Fallen Women*, p. 89.
106 'Memorandum for the Government: Report of the Commission on Emigration and Other Population Problems', p. 2, NAI, Dept. Taoiseach, S12424B.
107 Sr. M. F. Creegan, 'Unmarried mothers: an analysis and discussion of interviews conducted in an Irish mother and baby home', MA, University College Dublin, 1967, p. 7.
108 *Ibid.*, p. 7.
109 *Annual Report of the Department of Local Government and Public Health, 1927–8*, p. 93.
110 Guilbride argued that almost all cases of mothers who committed infanticide before the Irish courts between 1920 and 1950 were classified as 'poor and destitute' and unmarried. See A. Guilbride, 'Infanticide: the crime of motherhood', p. 173.
111 *Annual Report of the Department of Local Government and Public Health, 1934–5*, p. 411.
112 Both these pieces of legislation seemed more concerned with establishing paternity and relieving the local authority of the financial burden of illegitimacy. See L. Earner-Byrne, 'The boat to England: an analysis of the official reactions to the emigration of single expectant Irishwomen to Britain, 1922–1972', *IESH*, 30, (Nov. 2003), 57.
113 For an explanation of this act, see *Annual Report of the Department of Local Government and Public Health, 1930–1*, p. 122.
114 Luddy, 'Moral rescue and unmarried mother in Ireland in the 1920s', p. 811; Powell noted that the Legitimacy Act reflected Catholic social teaching. See Powell, *The Politics of Irish Social Policy*, p. 162.
115 Robins noted that the registration act was introduced largely to control private nursing homes that became refuges for unmarried mothers. See J. Robins, 'Public policy and the maternity services in Ireland during the twentieth century', in Browne (ed.), *Masters, Midwives and Ladies-in-Waiting*, pp. 289–91.
116 *Dáil Debates*, col. 1218, vol. 50, (7 February, 1934).
117 Cherish pointed out that the 1939 act only obliged fathers to maintain their legitimate

children. See Cherish, *Proceedings of the Conference on the Unmarried Parent and Child in Irish Society* (Dublin, 1974), p. 6.

118 Senator Comyn, Seanad Éireann, *Seanad Debates,* col. 827, vol. 13 (26 March 1930).

119 Seanad Éireann, *Seanad Debates,* cols 704–5, vol. 13 (19 March 1930).

120 *Ibid.*, cols 708–9, vol. 13 (19 March 1930).

121 *Ibid.*

122 *Ibid.*, col. 836, vol. 13 (26 March, 1930).

123 Luddy, 'Moral rescue and unmarried mothers in Ireland in the 1920s', p. 812.

124 Margaret Kerr to Miss Monaghan, 14 December 1929, sent to Archbishop Byrne. DDA, Byrne Papers, Lay organisations (2).

125 Kerr of Catholic Enquiry Office, Scotland to Archbishop, 20 July 1932.

126 The Saint Patrick's Guild was taken over by the Sisters of Charity in May 1944.

127 See also L. Earner-Byrne, '"Moral repatriation": the response of Irish unmarried mothers in Britain', in P. Duffy (ed.), *To and from Ireland: Planned Migration Schemes c. 1600–2000* (Dublin, 2004), pp. 155–74.

128 *Annual Report of the Department of Local Government and Public Health, 1931–2,* p. 129–30; Litster, A., 'Report on the unmarried mother, in Great Britain and at home', 8 May 1948. NAI, Clandillon, Box (3).

129 Memo on repatriation of Irish girls by the Catholic Rescue Society, *c.* 1941, NAI, Clandillon, Box (3).

130 Craven to Cruice, 17 April 1939, NAI, Dept. Health, M34/16.

131 Crofts's report, 28 February 1935, NAI, Dept. Health, A124/23.

132 *Ibid.*

133 Department of External Affairs, J. Walshe to the Secretary of the Department of Local Government and Public Health, Hurson, 27 May 1939, NAI, Clandillon, Box (3,) Letters/Reports setting up of repatriation scheme UK/Ireland, 1939–50.

134 Keogh described Joseph Walshe as 'unquestionably one of the most influential of the senior civil servants in the area of church-state relations'. See Keogh, *The Vatican, the Bishop*, p. 126; Jackson describes him as a devout Catholic. See Jackson, *Ireland*, p. 297.

135 Department of External Affairs, J. Walshe to the Secretary of the Department of Local Government and Public Health, Hurson, 15 December 1938, NAI, Clandillon, Box (3), Letters/Reports setting up of repatriation scheme UK/Ireland, 1939–50.

136 Walshe to Hurson, 25 October 1938.

137 Guilbride noted that between 1940 and 1946 there were forty-six cases of infanticide before the Central Criminal Court, whereas there had been fewer than twenty such cases during the previous fifteen years. See Guilbride, 'Infanticide: the crime of motherhood', p. 178. While the number of illegitimate births increased, so did the number of legitimate births. The actual rate fluctuations were minimal during this period, according to figures given by the Registrar-General.

138 'Memo from Litster to Secretary of Department of Local Government and Public Health', 20 May 1941, Letters/Reports setting up of repatriation scheme UK/Ireland, 1939–50.

139 *Ibid.*

140 Memo by Litster, 13 June 1940, Letters/Reports setting up of repatriation scheme UK/Ireland, 1939–50.

141 *Ibid.*

142 Murtagh, 22 Augustus Rd., Edgbaston Birmingham, to Litster, 15 May 1940. Letters/Reports setting up of repatriation scheme UK/Ireland, 1939–50.

143 Murtagh to Cruice, 1 May 1940.

144 *Ibid.*

145 Litster to Murtagh, 11 May 1940.
146 Miss Litster, 'Report on unmarried mothers in Ireland', 29 November 1939. This section was deleted by internal censors from the final report. Letters/Reports setting up of repatriation scheme UK/Ireland, 1939–50.
147 McQuaid's memo regarding the meeting with Mrs Murtagh, 22 August 1942, DDA, McQuaid Papers, AB8/B/XIX, (CSWB).
148 Mrs Murtagh to McQuaid, c. July 1942, DDA, McQuaid Papers, AB8/B/XIX.
149 Ibid.
150 Ibid.
151 Ibid.
152 Opening speech of the CSWB, 16 June 1942, DDA, McQuaid Papers, AB8/B/XIX.
153 Murtagh to McQuaid, c. August 1942, DDA, McQuaid Papers, AB8/B/XIX.
154 Ibid.
155 Murtagh to Myerscough, 20 October 1942, DDA, McQuaid Papers, AB8/B/XIX.
156 Ibid.
157 Ibid.
158 MacEntee to Taoiseach, 10 June 1942, NAI, Dept. Taoiseach, S12956.
159 Ibid.
160 St Kevin's Hospital, 1 James St, Co. Dublin was the former workhouse for the South Dublin Union and continued throughout the twentieth century to cater for many public assistance patients. It also had a small maternity unit and catered for some unmarried mothers. See Barrington, Health Medicine and Politics, pp. 122, 142 and 201.
161 'General review and report on progress of the commissioners for the Dublin board of assistance', NAI, Dept. Taoiseach, S12956
162 Report of the Joint Committee of Women's Societies and Social Workers, June 1943, p. 3, NAI, Clandillon Papers, Box (2).
163 Ibid.
164 Ibid., p. 4.
165 Ibid., p. 6.
166 Litster internal memo, 15 July 1937, NAI, Dept. Health, A124/12.
167 Litster to McArdle, 13 December 1939, NAI, Dept. Health. A124/12.
168 The Minister for Justice at the time was Padráig Ruithléis
169 'Memo on adoption of children' in NAI, Clandillon papers, Box (3). This fear was repeatedly raised. See, for example, Dáil Debates, vol. 132, col. 1108 (11 June 1952). Another crucial concern was the transfer of rights from 'natural parents' to adoptive parents. See, for example, Dáil Debates, vol. 101, col. 2584 (27 June 1946).
170 D. Roche to the Attorney General, 11 June 1945, NAI, Attorney General 2000/10/3058.
171 Report of the Saint Patrick's Guild (c. 1941). DDA, McQuaid Papers, Lay organisations: Catholic Protection and Rescue Society.
172 Ibid.
173 The following societies attended: Catholic Protection and Rescue Society, the Sacred Heart Home in Drumcondra, Sisters of Charity of St Vincent de Paul, Regina Coeli Hostel, Legion of Mary, Rotunda Girls Aid Society, Society for the Protection of Destitute Catholic Children, Holles Street Hospital, Saint Patrick's Guild and St Bridget's Orphanage, Eccles Street.
174 Report of the meeting of Catholic societies and organisations interested in rescue work, 28 November, 1943, Stephen's Green, Dublin. DDA, McQuaid Papers, Lay organisations: Catholic Protection and Rescue Society
175 Ibid., p. 5.

176 *Ibid.*
177 Department of Local Government and Public Health, *Annual Report of the Registrar-General, 1934,* (Dublin, 1935), p. xxxvi.
178 *Annual Report of the Department of Local Government and Public Health, 1933–4,* p. 147.
179 *Inspector's Report on the Number of Unmarried Women Maintained by the Poor Law* (16 August 1939), p. 3, NAI Clandillon papers, Box (2).
180 *Annual Report, Year Ended 31 March, 1943* (Litster, 17 December 1943), p. 3. NAI, Clandillon papers, Box (2)
181 *Ibid.*
182 Deeny, *To Cure and to Care,* p. 85.
183 Deeny to Dr Daly, 7 August 1946, NAI, Dept. Health, M134/60.
184 Daly to Deeny, 6 September 1949, NAI, Dept. Health, M134/60.
185 List of institutions (having 100 or more inmates) in Dublin Co. Borough with preliminary population figures (marked confidential not for publication), Census of population, 1946, NAI, Dept. Health, M34/44.
186 *Ibid.*
187 'Report on Regina Coeli', Dr James Deeny, 12 November 1848, NAI, Dept. Health, M134/60.
188 *Ibid.*
189 *Ibid.*
190 Ten of these infants had been admitted prior to 1945.
191 NAI, Dept. Health, M134/60.
192 Dr Murphy to Deeny, 10 September 1946, NAI, Dept. Health, M134/60.
193 Memorandum by Deeny, 19 December 1947, NAI, Dept. Health, M134/60.
194 Regina Coeli exemption under section 6 of Registration Act, 1934, NAI, Dept. Health, M134/58.
195 Chief Medical Adviser Memorandum, 20 May 1948, NAI, Dept. Health, M134/60.
196 Chief Medical Adviser Memorandum, 7 October 1948, NAI, Dept. Health, M134/60.
197 'Report of the Regina Coeli', C. E. Lysaght, 6 June 1942, NAI, Dept. Health, M134/60.
198 'Report on Regina Coeli', Dr James Deeny, 12 November 1948, NAI, Dept. Health, M134/60.
199 Jones's assessment of Deeny is the most perceptive. He was, as she describes him, a 'Catholic populist', whose traditional views moderated his sometimes aggressive 'reformist zeal'. See Jones, *Captain of All these Men of Death*, p. 194.
200 *Ibid.*
201 Frank Duff, Legion of Mary, to Archbishop McQuaid, 21 December 1948, DDA, McQuaid Papers, Lay organisations: Legion of Mary.
202 *Ibid.*
203 The tone of Deeny's response to the Child Health Council's report might have been influenced by the growing tension between him and certain members of the medical profession. In particular, Deeny and Dr Bob Collis, a highly regarded paediatrician and member of the council, had several disagreements regarding the way in which gastro-enteritis should be tackled. Deeny was quick to tell Duff of the Legion during their meeting on 18 December 1948 that 'Collis was not a representative' of the Department of Health. See Duff to McQuaid, 21 December 1948, DDA, McQuaid Papers, Lay organisations: Legion of Mary; *Consultative Child Council*, NAI, Dept. Health, M34/55; Deeny, *To Cure and to Care*, pp. 94–7
204 Memorandum by chief medical adviser in response to *First Interim Report of the*

Child Health Consultative Council, 4 November 1948, p. 4, NAI, Dept. Health, M100/91 vol. II, p. 5.

205 *Ibid.*, p. 6.

206 Extract from 1952 report of the Catholic Protection and Rescue Society of Ireland, NAI, Dept. Taoiseach, S11582E.

207 Litster, 'Unmarried mother, in Great Britain and at home', 8 May 1948, *Implementation of the Children's Acts 1945–51*, NAI, Clandillon papers, Box (3). This section was deleted by internal censors from the final report.

208 *Ibid.*

209 *Ibid.*

210 Litster. 'Unmarried mother, in Great Britain and at home, 8 May 1948.

211 C. Barrett, *Adoption: The Parent, the Child, the Home* (London, 1952).

212 *Ibid.*, p. 13.

213 *Ibid.*, p. 18.

214 *Ibid.*, p. 23.

215 *Ibid.*, p. 24.

216 Cecil Barrett to Noël Browne, 29 November 1951, NAI, Dept. Health, A128/29.

217 Internal memorandum, 2 May 1950, NAI, Dept. Health, A128/29.

218 Department of Health to Barrett, 31 July 50.

219 Whyte, *Church and State,* p. 185.

220 McCabe, 'The need for a law of adoption', pp. 179–80.

221 Whyte, *Church and State,* p. 187.

222 MacEoin continued to object to legalised adoption during the readings of the adoption bill in 1952 on these grounds and on the basis that the religious welfare of an illegitimate child could not be guaranteed. See, for example, *Dáil Debates*, vol. 132, cols. 1107–16 (11 June 1952).

223 Charles Casey in a speech given to the law students' debating society, 13 February 1951, NAI, Attorney General, 2000/10/3058.

224 *Ibid.*

225 *Ibid.*

226 Whyte, *Church and State,* p. 192.

227 See M. Milotte, *Banished Babies*. Goulding confirms that these American adoptions took place through Bessboro home in Cork. See J. Goulding, *The Light in the Window* (London, 2005), p. 65.

228 John D'Alton (1882–1963) became Archbishop of Armagh in June 1946 and was appointed Cardinal by Pope Pius XII on 12 January 1953. See Canning, *Bishops of Ireland*, pp. 48–9.

229 'Notes on legal adoption', 3 January 1952, NAI, Attorney General, 2000/10/3058.

230 Conroy noted that the mid–1980s witnessed this shift from adoption to single-parenthood. She pointed out that in 2000 there were only eighty non-relative adoption orders granted in respect of children placed by their Irish birth mothers. See Conroy, 'Motherhood interrupted', p. 184.

231 'Annual report of the Rotunda', *IJMSc.*, 258 (Aug. 1947), 237.

232 Between 1922 and 1970 on average 1,900 illegitimate births were registered per annum. This figure increased temporarily during the Emergency (1939–45), reaching 2,626 in 1945 and declining again in the early 1950s. The steady and persistent increase began from 1971 onwards. See Central Statistics Office, *Report on Vital Statistics*, 1955–73. See also Kennedy, *Cottage to Crèche*, fig. 2.3, p. 31.

233 Kilkenny Social Services, *The Unmarried Mother in the Community*, p. 14.

234 'Annual report of the Rotunda', *IJMSc.*, 335 (Nov. 1956), 5.

235 *Ibid.*

236 'Annual report of the Coombe', *IJMSc.*, 335 (Nov. 1959), 108.
237 'Annual report of the Rotunda', *IJMSc.*, 336 (Nov. 1960), 4.
238 *Ibid.*
239 Horne, 'An almoner's work in a maternity hospital', 106.
240 Conroy, 'Motherhood interrupted', p. 185.
241 *Ibid.,* p. 185.
242 Kilkenny Social Services, *The Unmarried Mother in Irish Community*, p. 20.
243 *IJMS,* 'Annual Report of the Rotunda', 1957, p. 30.
244 Creegan, 'Unmarried mothers', p. 3.
245 *Ibid.,* p. 5
246 *Ibid.,* pp. 9–10.
247 McAvoy, 'Before Cadden: abortion in mid-twentieth-century Ireland', pp. 147–63. The number of women citing Irish addresses in British abortion clinics rose from 64 in 1968 to 577 in 1971. See *Dáil Debates,* vol. 263, col. 516 (2 November 1972).
248 'Annual Report of the Rotunda Hospital', *IJMSc.,* 406 (October, 1944), 5.
249 Creegan, 'Unmarried mothers', p. 6.
250 Jackson argued that the Irish 'abortion trail' to Britain began long before 1967. See P. Jackson, 'Outside the jurisdiction: Irish women seeking abortion', C. Curtain, P. Jackson and B. O'Connor (eds), *Gender in Irish Society* (Galway, 1987), pp. 203–23.
251 *Report of Meeting with the Maternity Medical Social Workers in London,* 29 April 1969, pp. 6–7, DDA, McQuaid Papers, Lay Organisations: Catholic Protection and Rescue Society
252 Catholic Protection and Rescue Society, *56th Annual Report of the Catholic Protection and Rescue Society, 1969,* (Dublin, 1970), p. 1.
253 Kilkenny Social Services, *The Unmarried Mother in the Community*, p. 28.
254 *Ibid.,* p. 10.
255 *Ibid.,* p. 11.
256 Conroy, 'Motherhood interrupted', pp. 182–3.
257 Kilkenny Social Services, *The Unmarried Mother in the Community*, p. 9.
258 *Ibid.,* pp. 9–10.
259 *Ibid.,* p. 10.
260 Kennedy, *Cottage to Crèche*, p. 219. See also J. Beale, *Women in Ireland: Voices of Change* (Dublin, 1986), p. 60.
261 Cited in Kennedy, *Cottage to Crèche*, p. 110.
262 *Ibid.,* p. 112.
263 Conroy, 'Motherhood interrupted', p. 184.

Conclusion

In 1954 Revd Cornelius Lucey, the Catholic Bishop of Cork, complained that motherhood had gone out of fashion particularly among urban mothers:

> There is no doubt that many housewives, in particular, feel the urge for greater freedom from domestic ties and that this is a factor that predisposes them towards having small rather than large families. This too is in accordance with the spirit of the age. They see no sufficient reason why they should give up going out to pictures, dances, races, clubs or perhaps jobs, for the sake of children ... Another factor militating against motherhood is the impression abroad that frequent childbearing leads to physical and mental breakdown. No evidence, however, has ever been adduced to support this view.[1]

Apart from associating 'materialism' with urban living, and urban living with anti-family values, the Bishop was also expressing a very real fear that mothers themselves were shying away from motherhood. While modern living may have provided a more comprehensive welfare medical system, it was also part of the process that changed people's perceptions about the quality and standard of life. Dr Robert W. Collis, a leading paediatrician with a very different outlook to that of Revd Lucey also concluded that women were becoming active agents of change within the family structure:

> The good, large, happy, healthy family is an ideal, but the large, unhappy, unhealthy family where the mother is a drudge is that which we would be more likely to arrive at by such a policy. This is no proper solution to our population problem. The women themselves have made their views plain by their actions. We should only degrade and demoralise ourselves and relapse into callousness towards our neighbours' sufferings if we reverted to the over-large family as the general rule.[2]

In the 1960 annual report, the Coombe hospital declared that the 'old type of "Coombe Grande-Multipara" who regarded it as a matter of pride and social obligation to have her baby at home at all costs, is now almost extinct'.[3] The hospital was receiving fewer and fewer mothers with more than seven children, and more and more mothers were opting for hospital births. Evidence that Irish society was reconsidering the definition of motherhood came not just in the extinction of the 'dangerous multipara', but also in the fact that contemporaries were increasingly frustrated at their inability to help those mothers still producing more children than they wished. In 1957 the social worker at the Rotunda hospital expressed her dismay at not being able to help a mother facing her twelfth pregnancy who asked 'would she ever stop having babies'. The social worker's quandary was how to assist such mothers who felt trapped by their numerous pregnancies 'in a constructive, yet ethical way'.[4] By 1964 the Catholic National Maternity Hospital had introduced a family planning clinic, which 'was the outcome of an increasing awareness of the real potential problems which uncontrolled fertility presented in many patients'.[5] At this clinic, women were provided with information regarding the 'safe period', as artificial contraception was still illegal and morally unacceptable to the Catholic ethos of the hospital. However, the hospital reported that women who attended the clinic did so for 'social' rather than medical reasons.[6]

There was no social revolution in Ireland between 1922 and 1960, but it was a period of vital evolution which helped to redefine and redirect the future of Irish motherhood. While Irish society persisted in maintaining the ambiguities inherent in all cultures – where ideals and reality compete for space in legislation and social policy – there was a perceptible shift during this period from moral control to secular entitlement. Pregnancy is biologically determined and motherhood is culturally defined, and during the first forty years of independence increased biological knowledge and the changing cultural definition of maternity altered the landscape of social welfare and social awareness.

The degree to which national values shape the policy-making process is virtually impossible to quantify and can only be surmised through crude measurements such as the probable impact of religion, social perceptions of gender, and the cultural ideology of the family. However, it is easier to research the significance of the agents of change, the men and women of the civil service, the medical profession and the voluntary sector, who sought to change the basis and standard of care offered to Irish mothers and their children. The civil servants, like Dr James Deeny and Alice Litster, who worked within the system to expand and improve the conditions of mothering and the chances of child survival, played an invisible but important role in the history of maternity policy and provision in Ireland. Much of this history depended on the efforts, errors, co-operation and resistance of individuals who propelled change or defended the *status quo*.

In examining the role of the voluntary organisations on the ground and the complications inherent in co-operation between different religious groups, this book has revealed the progressive impact of charitable assistance, and also the inhibiting effect of sectarian hostility. The issue of religion and welfare motivated many voluntary workers to became involved in maternity welfare in order to 'protect' the souls of mother and child. The fear of proselytism gave the poor mother some small amount of leverage in a world in which she had very little real power. Nonetheless, the divisive aspect inherent in the denominational approach to welfare also restricted the opportunities for co-operation amongst voluntary groups and allowed agencies to exercise a form of moral control over necessitous mothers. The fact that many of the voluntary initiatives were subsidised by the state maternity and child welfare grant also meant that official monies could be used to impose subjective religious or moral codes in return for assistance.

Archbishop McQuaid's involvement in maternal and child welfare in Dublin exposed the potential and limitations of voluntary welfare. The Archbishop was adamant that 'the physical health and social welfare of the people were not divorced from their spiritual welfare. What life was, when it began and when it ended, was defined within the Church's teachings.'[7] Consequently, he set about ensuring that Roman Catholic welfare provision was sufficient to ward off any Protestant or multidenominational competition. While the involvement of the CSSC in maternity welfare increased the aid available to Dublin mothers, it had the negative effect of curtailing the work of other non-sectarian organisations, most notably the St John Ambulance Brigade. Furthermore, McQuaid was sensitive to the potential of state power and determined that the only source that would intervene on the preserve of the family and compromise the role of the father would be a benevolent and discretionary source under his auspices. McQuaid viewed motherhood as a potential source for either moral power or social disruption. Consequently, he was determined that the Catholic church should control maternal welfare. To this end he pursued a policy of co-operation with the state, a strategy that served him well initially, both with respect to the threat of non-sectarian competition and in terms of his involvement in state decisions.

However, as a result of an arrogant policy of rigid protocol and Catholic supremacy, McQuaid allowed himself, and the Catholic hierarchy, to become embroiled in a political controversy over the introduction of a free maternity scheme in 1951. A thorough analysis of the controversy reveals that the dynamics were much more complicated than McQuaid using Dr Noël Browne as his 'pawn' against communism.[8] In fact, it is apparent that for both the Archbishop and the Minister for Health, motherhood was a means to an end. Dr Browne used the maternity scheme to render 'the destruction of government'[9] and McQuaid wished to maintain the Church's position in the administration of welfare and to control state intervention in the private lives of citizens. The Catholic hierarchy won the battle but eventually lost the war. The introduction of the modified mother-and-child scheme in 1953 altered what mothers were entitled to on the grounds of their citizenship rights. Unlike the widows' and orphans' pension of 1935 and the family allowances of 1944, the free maternity service was available to women irrespective of their marital status. While the mother-and-child scheme was by no means the panacea for all social ills, it symbolised a significant blow to the connection between morality and health.

An indication of the tenuous concept of female citizenship is revealed in the treatment of the unmarried mother who, according to the moral ethos of the state, was an 'illegitimate mother'. Despite the rhetoric in favour of maintaining the mother-and-child bond there was virtually no official attempt to support that aim in the case of the single mother and her infant. The principle of intervention into the welfare of the unmarried mother was similar to the principle behind maternity welfare in general: the protection of the infant. In the case of the single mother, however, the impact was much more decisive. Bereft of whatever security the conventional family offered, the single mother faced a term in institutional care until her child was old enough to be either adopted or sent to an industrial school. With the notable exception of the Legion of Mary, no organisation sought to empower the single mother to retain guardianship of her child.

The only official state action taken which vaguely impacted on the welfare of unmarried mothers was the repatriation scheme and legal adoption. Both these measures were billed as child protection measures and were prompted by religious concerns regarding the soul of the unborn child. The repatriation scheme established in the 1930s was motivated by shame and a desire to ensure that Protestant families in Britain did not adopt Irish infants. Furthermore, the mother was not entitled to repatriation on the basis of her citizenship but on the condition that her child had been conceived within the Irish state. In other words, she was assisted to return to her home country on the basis of the probable citizenship of the father of her infant and the citizenship rights of the unborn child. Nevertheless, the unmarried mother was afforded access to free maternity care under the Health Act of 1953 and, in view of the fact that the babies of unmarried mothers died more frequently than any others in the Irish state, this was most definitely a preventive health measure. While access to free maternity care and legal adoption offered the unmarried mother some protection, therefore, her fate revealed the conditional nature of female citizenship. Single motherhood was virtually untenable in a society hostile to unorthodox families, and in reality the Irish unmarried mother had to surrender her right to motherhood.

This book also highlights one other frequently overlooked aspect regarding the history of twentieth-century Ireland: a virtual public health revolution. This is revealed in the crudest form as statistically the maternal and infant mortality rates were drastically reduced. As a result of the level of controversy surrounding health policy initiatives during this period, there has been a tendency to overlook this remarkable improvement in the life expectancy of infants and mothers.[10] This success story stands in stark contrast to the intransigence of other social issues such as high emigration and complicates perspectives that have characterised this period as wholly stagnant and bleak.

Maternal and child welfare, more than any other public health issue, crossed the line between social and medical welfare, material and spiritual well-being, duty and responsibility. It was the quintessential 'boundary issue'[11] that facilitated the exorcising of profound cultural anxieties regarding morality and health, and the evolving relationship between the family, the state and the Catholic Church. Central to the debates and controversies regarding maternity policy were attempts to ascertain an appropriate balance between assistance and intervention. When did assistance become intervention? Who was best placed to give assistance, and on what basis should a mother qualify? The dilemma between assistance and intervention was not particular to Ireland: international anxiety in relation to quality and quantity of population had led to policies regarding maternal welfare all over Europe and in parts of the USA. In each country the cultural and social realities resulted in very different policies, but there was one common feature: the issue of motherhood indirectly became an issue of public debate and concern. In Ireland maternity debates provided the arena for more disturbing debates on the role of the state, the citizen and the Catholic Church, the nature of health care provision and entitlement, and the line between family privacy and family protection. Ultimately, the compromises arrived at reflected the deeper compromises made in the evolution of the Irish state and the shifting of crucial power relationships.

Notes

1   *Minority report for the Commission on Emigration and Other Population Problems* by Revd C. Lucey, 1 July 1954, NAI, Dept. Taoiseach, S14249A/1, p. 7. It should be noted that there were no statistics to support Revd Lucey's claims.

2   Reservation no. 1 by W. R. F. Collis and Arnold Marsh, to the Majority report of the Commission on Emigration and Other Population Problems, 1948–54, NAI, Dept. Taoiseach, S14249 Annex, p. 217.

3   *Annual report of the Coombe Hospital, 1960,* p. 7.

4   *Annual report of the Rotunda Hospital, 1957,* p. 32.

5   *Annual report of the National Maternity Hospital, 1964,* p. 94.

6   *Ibid.*

7   Inglis, *The Moral Monopoly,* pp. 56–60.

8   Cooney, *John Charles McQuaid,* p. 252.

9   Horgan, *Noël Browne,* p. 130.

10 A point made more recently by both Ó hÓgartaigh and Clear. See M. Ó hÓgartaigh, 'Health and Souls: The Foundation of Crumlin's Children's Hospital', unpublished; Clear, 'Women in de Valera's Ireland, 1932–48', pp. 104–14.

11 Martha Dertick cited in Immergut, *Health Politics,* p. 1.

Bibliography

State Papers (Ireland)

Attorney General Files.
Department of Health Files.
Department of Taoiseach Files.
State Book at Central Criminal Court, Dublin City 1924–50.

Official publications

Cameron, C. A., *How the Poor Live* (Dublin, 1904).
Cameron, C. A., *Report upon the State of Public Health in the City of Dublin for the Year 1915* (Dublin, 1916).
Cameron, C. A., *Report upon the State of Public Health in the City of Dublin for the Year 1916* (Dublin, 1917).
Central Statistics Office, *Report on Vital Statistics*, 1955–73.
Commission on Emigration, *Report of the Commission on Emigration and Other Population Problems 1948–54* (Dublin, 1956).
Commission on the Relief of the Sick and Destitute Poor, *Report of the Commission on the Relief of the Sick and Destitute Poor, including the Insane Poor* (Dublin, 1927).
Committee of Inquiry into Health Insurance and Medical Services, *Committee of Inquiry into Health Insurance and Medical Services, Interim Report* (Dublin,1925).
Committee of Inquiry into Health Insurance and Medical Services, *Committee of Inquiry into Health Insurance and Medical Services, Final Report* (Dublin, 1927).
Committee of Inquiry into Widows' and Orphans' Pensions, *Committee of Inquiry into Widows' and Orphans' Pensions, Reports*, 1933.
Consultative Child Health Council, *Report of the Consultative Child Health Council, 1949*, NAI, Department of Health, A116/167.
Dáil Éireann, *Official Reports of the Debates of Dáil Éireann*, 1922–73.
Department of Health, *Annual Reports of the Department of Health*, 1945–58.
Department of Health, *Annual Reports of the Registrar-General*, 1946–54.
Department of Health, *White Paper on Health Services: Outline of the Improvement of the Health Services 1947*.
Department of Health, *Proposals for Improved and Extended Health Services* (Dublin,

1952).

Department of Health, *Health Services and their Future Development* (Dublin, 1966).

Department of Local Government and Public Health, *Annual Reports of the Registrar-General*, 1921–1945.

Department of Local Government and Public Health, *Annual Reports of the Department of Local Government and Public Health*, 1922–44.

Department of Local Government and Public Health, *Report of the Conference between the Department of Local Government and Public Health and Representatives of Local Public Health and Public Assistance Authorities, 1930* (known also as *Conference on Social Services, 1930*) (Dublin, 1930).

Department of Local Government and Public Health, *Report of the Conference on Public Health and Social Services, 1930* (Dublin, 1930).

Department of Social Welfare, *First Report of the Department of Social Welfare, 1947–49* (Dublin, 1949).

Department of Social Welfare, *A Guide to Social Services* (Dublin, 1950).

Dublin Corporation, *Dublin Corporation Reports*, 1930–70.

Government Publication, *Bunreacht na hEireann (Constitution of Ireland) 1937* (Dublin, 1997).

Harrison, J. A., *Report of the Medical Officer of Health in the City of Dublin for the Year 1954* (Dublin, 1955).

Hospitals' Commission, *First General Report, 1933–34*.

Hospitals' Commission, *Third General Report, 1937*.

Hospitals' Commission, *Fifth General Report, 1939–41*.

League of Nations, *The Study on the Legal Position of the Illegitimate Child* (Geneva, 1939).

Medical Council of Ireland, *Report of the Gastro-Enteritis Survey of Dublin City, 1964–66*.

Municipal Corporation of the City of Dublin, *Minutes of the Municipal Corporation of the City of Dublin*, 1930–70.

O'Regan, J. B., *Report of the Medical Officer of Health in the City of Dublin for the Year 1957* (Dublin, 1957).

Political and Economic Planning, *Report on the British Social Services: A Survey of the Existing Public Social Services in Great Britain with Proposals for Future Development* (London, 1937).

Russell, M. J., *Report on the State of Public Health in the City of Dublin for the Year 1936* (Dublin, 1937).

——*Report on the State of Public Health in the City of Dublin for the Year 1938* (Dublin, 1939).

——*Report on the State of Public Health in the City of Dublin for the Two Years Ending December 31ˢᵗ 1940* (Dublin, 1941).

Seanad Éireann, *Seanad Debates*.

Reports of Non-Governmental Organisations

Catholic Action, *Catholic Action: Principles and Practice* (Dublin, 1934).

Catholic Protection and Rescue Society, *16ᵗʰ Annual Report of Catholic Protection and Rescue Society, 1929* (Dublin, n.d.).

Catholic Protection and Rescue Society, *56th Annual Report of the Catholic Protection and Rescue Society, 1969* (Dublin, 1970).

Civics Institute of Ireland, *Annual Reports of the Civics Institute of Ireland Ltd.*, 1939–46.

Cherish, *Proceedings of the Conference on the Unmarried Parent and Child in Irish Society* (Dublin, 1974).

Coey Bigger, E., *Welfare of Mothers and Children, Ireland*, Vol. 4 (Carnegie UK Trust, 1917).

Irish Catholic Directory and Almanac for 1920 (Dublin, 1920).

Irish Catholic Directory and Almanac for 1931 (Dublin, 1931).

Irish Journal of Medical Science, 'Annual reports of the Dublin maternity hospitals', 1930–58.

Kilkenny Social Services, *The Unmarried Mother in the Community: A Report on the National Conference on Community Services for the Unmarried Parent 1972* (Kilkenny, 1972).

Lynn, K. and R. Hayes, *Sinn Fein Public Health Department: Public Health Circular No. 1* (Dublin, 1918).

Lyon, S., *Report on Survey Covering the Employment, Social and Living Conditions of Irish Emigrants (First Generation) in Great Britain* (1948).

Nicholson, J., *Mother and Baby Homes: A Survey of Homes for Unmarried Mothers* (London, 1968).

Rotunda Hospital, *Rotunda Hospital Bicentenary: Transactions of the International Congress of Obstetricians and Gynaecologists* (7 July 1947–11 July 1947).

Saint Patrick's Guild, *Annual Report of the Saint Patrick's Guild, 1927–8.*

Samaritan Fund, *Marrowbone Lane: Samaritan Fund* (Dublin, c.1943).

Society of St Vincent de Paul, *Annual Report of the Society of St Vincent de Paul* (Dublin, 1928).

Society of St Vincent de Paul, *Reports of the Council of Ireland, 1939–45.*

St John Ambulance Brigade, *Annual Report, 1935.*

——*St John Ambulance Brigade in Ireland: Welfare Department 15 Years of Work 1920–1935* (Dublin, 1935).

Williams, G. D., *Dublin Charities: Being a Handbook of Dublin Philanthropic Organisations and Charities* (Dublin, 1902).

WNHA of Ireland, *Infant Mortality and Infant Milk Depots* (Dublin, 1908).

Contemporary newspapers, journals and magazines

The Catholic Bulletin
Irish Catholic Directory
The Catholic Directory and Almanac
Church of Ireland Gazette
Irish Citizen
The Irish Ecclesiastical Record
The Irish Independent
The Irish Journal of Medical Science
The Irish Press
Irish Rosary

The Irish Times
The Journal of the Irish Free State Medical Union (1937–41)
The Journal of the Irish Medical Association (1951–60)
The Journal of the Medical Association of Eire (1941–51)
The Journal of the Statistical and Social Inquiry Society of Ireland
The Lancet
Model Housekeeping
The Standard
Studies
Woman's Life
Woman's Mirror

Pamphlets

Barrett, C., *Adoption: The Parent, the Child, the Home* (London, 1952).
Brown, S. J., *Catholics and the League of Nations* (Dublin, 1929).
Cahill, E., *The Catholic Social Movement* (Dublin, 1931).
Catholic Social Service Conference, *Food Supplies: Food and Dietetics* (Oct. 1944).
Catholic Social Service Conference, *Handbook of the Catholic Social Service Conference, 1945.*
Catholic Truth Society, *The Problem of Undesirable Printed Matter Suggested Remedies: Evidence of the Catholic Truth Society of Ireland Presented to the Departmental Committee of Inquiry 1926* (Dublin, 1926).
Cherish, *An association of Unmarried Parents: Conference on 'the Unmarried Parent and Child in Irish Society'* (Dublin, 1974).
CSSC, *The Handbook of the Catholic Social Service Conference* (Dublin, 1945).
Davidson, E. G., *The Mother's Union: Its Vision Our Failure* (Dublin, 1936).
Duffy, L., *Pensions for Widows in Saorstát Éireann: A Popular Guide to the Widows' and Orphans' Pensions Act, 1935* (Dublin, 1936).
Dunne, P. 'Waiting The Verdict': Pensions or Pauperism: Necessitous Widows and Orphans in the Free State* (Dublin, c. 1930).
Inghram, E., *The Care and Management of Baby,* I (Dublin, 1914).
——*The Care and Management of Baby,* II (Dublin, 1914).
Reilly J., *Our Food Problem: A National Survey* (Cork, 1942).
Sir John Lumsden, *St John's Ambulance: A Brief Account of the History and Work of the Order and Brigade* (Dublin, n.d.).
St John Ambulance Brigade, *Official Handbook of the St John Ambulance Brigade, 1950* (Dublin, 1950).
St John Ambulance Brigade, *St John's Ambulance Brigade Golden Jubilee 1904–1954: Souvenir Handbook* (Dublin, 1955).
Watson, A. M., *The Future Development of the Councils of Social Welfare Movement* (National Council of Social Service, London 1944).
WNHA, *Infantile Mortality and Infant Milk Depots,* (Dublin, 1908).
WNHA of Ireland, *The Golden Jubilee 1907–1957: The Women's National Health Association of Ireland* (Dublin, c. 1957).

Papers

Archbishop Byrne Papers (Dublin Diocesan Archives).
Archbishop McQuaid Papers (Dublin Diocesan Archives).
Clandillon Papers (National Archives). Please note the Clandillon Papers are currently with the Department of Health, where they are being microfilmed and recollated.
De Valera Papers, (University College Dublin, Archives).
Deeny Papers (Royal College of Surgeons of Ireland, Mercer Library).
MacEntee Papers (University College Dublin, Archives).
McGilligan Papers (University College Dublin, Archives).
Marsh Papers (Trinity College Dublin).

Articles and Chapters

Anon., 'Comments on the foregoing article', *Studies*, 27:105 (Mar. 1938), 24.
Anon., 'The education of the public', *JIFSMU*, 3:14 (Aug. 1938), 33.
Beaumont, C., 'Women and the politics of equality: the Irish women's movement 1930–1943,' in Valiulis and Dowd (eds), *Women and Irish History*, pp. 173–88.
Bock, G., 'Antinatalism, maternity and paternity in National Socialist Racism', in Bogdan, J. C., 'Childbirth in America, 1650–1900', in Apple (ed.), *Women, Health and Medicine in America*, p. 114.
Burke, H., 'Foundation stones of Irish social policy, 1831–1951, in Kiely, O'Donnell, Kennedy and Quinn (eds), *Irish Social Policy*, p. 11.
Burke Brogan, P., 'The Magdalene experience', in Kennedy (ed.), *Motherhood in Ireland*.
Cahill, E., 'The social bond: a study in Christian sociology', *IER*, 26 (1925), 58.
——'The Catholic social movement', *IER*, 36 (1930), 572–87.
Clarke, T. A., and T. G. Matthews, 'The development of neonatal paediatrics at the Rotunda', in A. Browne (ed.), *Masters, Midwives and Ladies-in-Waiting*, pp. 118–59.
Clear, C., 'The decline of breast-feeding in twentieth-century Ireland', in A. Hayes and D. Urquhart (eds), *Irish Women's History* (Dublin, 2004), pp. 187–98.
——'Women in de Valera's Ireland, 1932–48: a reappraisal', in G. Doherty and D. Keogh (eds), *De Valera's Irelands* (Cork, 2003), pp. 104–14.
——'"A living saint if ever there was one": work, austerity and authority in the lives of Irish women of the house, 1921–1961', in J. Hill and C. Lennon (eds), *Luxury and Austerity* (Dublin, 1999), pp. 212–29.
——'No feminine mystique: popular advice to women of the house in Ireland 1922–1954', in Valiulis and O'Dowd (eds), *Women and Irish History*, pp. 189–205.
—— '"The women can not be blamed": the commission on vocational organisation, feminism and "home makers" in independent Ireland in the 1930s and '40s', in M. O'Dowd and S. Wichert (eds), *Chattel, Servant or Citizen: Women's Status in Church, State and Society* (Belfast, 1995), pp. 179–86.
Cleary, Revd M. P., 'The Church of Ireland and birth control', *IER*, 38 (1931), 624.
Coakley, A., 'Mothers and poverty', in Kennedy, *Motherhood in Ireland*, pp. 207–17.
Coleman, M., 'The origins of the Irish Hospitals' Sweepstake', *Irish Economic and Social History*, 29 (Nov. 2002), 40–55.

Collis, W. and D. M. Minabbawy, 'Investigation into the condition of malnutrition in children and wives of unemployed men in Dublin', *JMAÉ*, 11:64 (Oct. 1942), 43–5.

—— and N. Sheehan, 'Investigation into the condition of malnutrition in the children and wives of unemployed men in Dublin', *JMAÉ*, 11:63 (Sept. 1942), 31–4

Conroy, P., 'Maternity confined – the struggle for fertility control', in Kennedy (ed.), *Motherhood in Ireland*, pp. 127–38.

——'"From the fifties to the nineties": social policy comes out of the shadows', in Kiely, O'Donnell, Kennedy and Quinn (eds), *Irish Social Policy*, pp. 33–50.

Conway, E., 'Motherhood interrupted: adoption in Ireland', in Kennedy (ed.), *Motherhood in Ireland*, pp. 181–93.

Cousins, M., 'The introduction of children's allowances in Ireland, 1939–1944', *Irish Economic and Social History,* 27 (November, 1999), 35–55.

Cox, M. F., 'A ministry of public health for Ireland', *JSSISI*, 13 (Oct. 1919), 638–41.

Coyne, E. J., 'Health Bill 1952', *Studies*, 42 (1953), 6.

Craft, M., 'The development of Dublin: the southern suburbs', *Studies* (Spring 1971), 79.

Crew, D. F. (ed.), *Nazism and German Socialism, 1933–1945* (London, 1994), pp. 110–40.

Crowe, M., 'Conditions affecting child health in Éire', *IJMSc.*, 255 (Mar. 1947), 96.

Cunningham, J. F., 'Mother and child service: the medical problem', *Studies*, 40 (June 1951), 150.

Curtain, M., 'Failure to breastfeed: a review of the feeding history of 1,007 infants', *IJMSc.*, 346 (Oct. 1954), 447.

Daly, M. E., 'Wives, mothers, and citizens: the treatment of women in the 1935 Nationality and Citizenship Act', *Éire-Ireland* (Winter, 2003), 244–64.

——'"Turn on the tap": the state, Irish women and running water', in Valiulis and O'Dowd (eds), *Women and Irish History,* pp. 206–19.

——'Social structure of the Dublin working class, 1871–1911', *Irish Historical Studies*, 23:100 (Nov. 1982), 159–94.

——'The Irish family since the Famine', *Irish Journal of Feminist Studies,* 3:2 (Autumn, 1999), 1–21.

D'Cruze, S., 'Women and the family', in Purvis (ed.), *Women's History in Britain, 1850–1945*, pp. 51–76.

Deeny, J., 'Infant mortality in the city of Belfast, 1940–41', *JSSISI*, 17 (1943–44), 220–39.

——'Infant feeding in relation to mortality in the city of Belfast', *British Medical Journal*, (Jan. 1944), 146.

——'Epidemiology of enteritis of infancy', *JMAÉ*, 19:112 (Oct. 1946), 155.

Devane, Revd R. S., SJ, 'The unmarried mother: some legal aspects of the problem', *IER*, 23 (1924), 55.

——'The unmarried mother and the Poor Law Commission', *IER*, 31 (1928), 561–82.

——'The dance hall', *IER*, 37(1931), 170–94.

——'The legal protection of girls', *IER*, 37 (1931), 20–40.

Digby, A., 'Poverty, health and the politics of gender in Britain, 1870–1948', in A. Digby and J. Stewart (eds), *Gender, Health and Welfare* (London, 1996), pp. 67–90.

—— and J. Stewart, 'Welfare in context', in Digby and Stewart (eds), *Gender, Health and Welfare*, pp. 1–31.

Dillon, T. W. T., 'The social services in Eire', *Studies*, 34 (Sept. 1945), 331.

Dockerlay, G. C., 'Diet in pregnancy', *JMAE*, 12:70 (Apr. 1943), 39.

—— and W. R. Fearon, 'Ante-natal nutrition in Dublin: a preliminary survey', *IJMSc.*, 128 (Aug. 1939), 80.

Dunne, E., 'Action and reaction: Catholic lay organisations in Dublin in the 1920s and 1930s', *Archivium Hibernicum*, 48 (1994), 107–18

Dunne, J. P., 'Poverty problems for a patriot parliament', *JSSSI*, 74–5 (1922–23), 197.

Dunwoody, J., 'Child welfare', in Fitzpatrick (ed.), *Ireland, the First World War*, pp. 69–75.

Earner-Byrne, L., 'The boat to England: an analysis of the official reactions to the emigration of single expectant Irishwomen to Britain, 1922–72', *IESH*, 30 (Nov. 2003), 57.

——'"Managing motherhood": negotiating a maternity service for Catholic mothers in Dublin,1930–54', in *Social History of Medicine*, 20:2 (Aug. 2006), pp. 261–77.

Falkiner, N., 'Maternity hospital clinical reports: Rotunda', *JMAÉ*, 11:64 (Oct. 1942), 43–5.

Fearon, W. R., 'The national problem of nutrition', *Studies*, 27:105 (Mar. 1938), 17.

——'Deficiency diseases: nutritional problems of to-day', *JMAÉ*, 9:49 (July 1941).

Feeney, J. K., 'Report of the Combe', *IJMSc.*, 312 (Aug.1951), 825.

Finn, 'Women in the medical profession in Ireland, 1876–1919', in B. Whelan (ed.), *Women and Paid Work in Ireland, 1500–1930* (Dublin, 2000), pp. 102–19.

Finnane, M., 'The Carrigan committee of 1930–1 and the "moral condition of the Saorstát"', *IHS*, 33:128 (Nov. 2001), 519–36.

Fuchs, R., 'Morality and poverty: public welfare for mothers in Paris, 1870–1900', *French History*, 1:3 (Sept. 1988), 288–311.

Garret, P. M., 'The abnormal flight: migration and repatriation of Irish unmarried mothers', *Social History*, 25 (2000), 330–43.

Gallagher, J. G., 'Causes of maternal mortality', *IJMSc.*, 188 (Aug. 1941), 499.

Geary, R. C., 'The future population of Saorstát Éireann and some observations on population statistics', *JSSISI*, 89 (1935–36), 20.

Grier, J., 'Eugenics and birth control: contraceptive provision in North Wales, 1918–1939', *Social History of Medicine,* 11:3 (December, 1998), 443–58.

Guilbride, A., 'Infanticide: the crime of motherhood', in Kennedy (ed.), *Motherhood in Ireland*, pp. 170–80.

Hall, L. A., 'Marie Stopes and her correspondents: personalizing population decline in an era of demographic change', in R. Peel (ed.), *Marie Stopes: Eugenics and the English Birth Control Movement,* (London, 1997), pp. 27–48.

Hamill, J. 'Childcare arrangements within the Belfast linen industry', in B. Whelan (ed.), *Women and Paid Work in Ireland 1500–1930* (Dublin, 2000), pp. 120–32.

Harrison, B., 'Women and health', in Purvis (ed.), *Women's History in Britain 1850–1945*, p. 58.

Hartigan, M., 'The religious life of the Catholic laity of Dublin, 1920–1940', in Kelly and Keogh (eds.), *History of the Catholic Diocese of Dublin*, pp. 331–48.

Hensey, B., 'The health services and their administration', in Litton (ed.), *Unequal Achievement*, pp. 147–64.

Hilliard, B., 'Motherhood, sexuality and the Catholic Church', in Kennedy (ed.), *Motherhood in Ireland*, pp. 139–59.

Hoggart, L., 'The campaign for birth control in Britain in the 1920s', in A. Digby and

J. Stewart (eds), *Gender, Health and Welfare* (London, 1996), pp. 143–66.

Holmes, E. A., and I. Keogh, 'Medical social work at the Rotunda', in Browne (ed.), *Masters, Midwives and Ladies-in-Waiting*, pp. 199–239.

Horne, M., 'An almoner's work in a maternity hospital', *Journal of the Irish Medical Association*, 34:202 (Apr. 1954), 105.

Jackson, P., 'Outside the jurisdiction: Irish women seeking abortion', in C. Curtain, P. Jackson and B. O'Connor (eds), *Gender in Irish Society* (Galway, 1987), pp. 203–23.

Jones, G., 'Eugenics in Ireland: the Belfast Eugenics Society, 1911–15', *IHS*, 28:109 (May 1992), 80–95.

Kavanagh, J., 'Social activist,' *Studies*, 87:348 (Winter 1998), 372–7.

Kelly, A., 'Catholic Action and the development of the Irish welfare state in the 1930s and 1940s', *Archivium Hibernicum*, 53 (1999), 109.

Kelly, J., 'Infanticide in eighteenth-century Ireland', *IESH*, 19 (1992), 5–26.

Kennedy, F., 'Two priests, the family and the Irish constitution,' *Studies*, 87:348 (Winter 1998), 353–64.

——'The suppression of the Carrigan report', *Studies*, 89:356 (2000), 54–362.

Kennedy, P., 'Childbirth in Ireland', in Kennedy (ed.), *Motherhood in Ireland*, pp. 77–88.

Kiely, G., 'From colonial paternalism to national partnership: an overview of Irish social policy', in Kiely, O'Donnell, Kennedy and Quinn (eds), *Irish Social Policy*, p. 3.

Keogh, D., 'Towards a biography of an archbishop,' *Studies*, 87:348 (Winter 1998), 37–343.

Koven, S., and S. Michel, 'Womanly duties: maternalist politics and the origins of welfare states in France, Germany, Great Britain, and the United States, 1880–1920', *American History Review*, 95:4–5 (1990), 1076–108.

Lambert, S., 'Irish women's emigration to England, 1922–60: the lengthening of family ties', in A. Hayes and D. Urquhart (eds), *Irish Women's History* (Dublin, 2004), pp. 153–67.

Lawson, W., 'Infant mortality and the Notification of Births Act, 1907, 1915', *JSSISI*, 13 (October 1919), 479–97.

Lee, J. J., 'Aspects of corporatist thought in Ireland: the Commission on Vocational Organisation 1939–43', in A. Cosgrave and D. McCartney (eds), *Studies in Irish History Presented to R. Dudley Edwards* (Dublin, 1974), pp. 324–46.

——'Women and the church since the famine,' in MacCurtain and Ó Corrain (eds), *Women in Irish Society*, pp. 37–46.

——'Society and culture', in Litton (ed.), *Unequal Achievement*, pp. 1–20.

Lewis, J., 'Gender and welfare in the late nineteenth and early twentieth centuries', in A. Digby and J. Stewart (eds), *Gender, Health and Welfare* (London, 1996), pp. 208–28.

Lucey, Revd, 'On a recent study in social science', *IER*, 41 (1933), 375.

Luddy, M., 'Moral rescue and unmarried mothers in Ireland in the 1920s', *Women's Studies*, 30 (2001), 797–817.

——'Prostitution and rescue work in nineteenth-century Ireland', in Luddy and Murphy (eds), *Women Surviving*.

McAvoy, S., 'Before Cadden: abortion in mid-twentieth-century Ireland', in D. Keogh, F. O'Shea and C. Quinlan (eds), *The Lost Decade: Ireland in the 1950s* (Cork, 2004), pp. 147–63.

——'Regulation of sexuality in the Irish Free State', in Malcolm and Jones (eds), *Medicine, Disease and the State in Ireland*, p. 257.

McCabe, E. W., 'The need for a law on adoption', *JSSSI*, 102 (8 Apr. 1949), 181.

McCann, S., 'The general practitioner in Irish medicine – to-day and to-morrow', *JMAÉ*, 15:87 (Sept. 1944), 33–4.

McCarthy, E., 'Public health problems created by louse infestation', *IJMSc.*, 266 (Feb. 1948), 67.

McDougall, M. L., 'Protecting infants: The French campaign for maternity leaves, 1890s–1913,' *French Historical Studies,* 13 (Spring, 1983), 79–105.

MacEntee, S., 'Speech to the IMA', *JIMA*, 41:242 (Aug. 1957), 61.

MacInery, M. H., 'The souper problem in Ireland', *IER*, 18 (1922), 140.

Mcintosh, T., 'Profession, skill, or domestic duty? Midwifery in Sheffield, 1881–1936, *Social History of Medicine,* 11:3 (Dec. 1998), 381–402.

McKee, E., 'Church–state relations and the development of Irish health policy: the mother-and-child scheme, 1944–53', *Irish Historical Studies*, 25:98 (Nov. 1986), 159–94.

McKevitt, Revd P., 'The Beveridge plan reviewed', *IER*, 61 (1943), 150.

Maclashin, A., 'Social policy: 1957–82', in F. Litton (ed.), *Unequal Achievement*, pp. 203–24.

McMahon, D., 'The politician – a reassessment', *Studies*, 87:348 (Winter 1998), 344–52.

——'John Charles McQuaid, Archbishop of Dublin, 1940–72', in Kelly and Keogh (eds), *History of the Catholic Diocese of Dublin*, pp. 349–80.

Macnicol, J., 'Welfare, wages and the family: child endowment in comparative perspective, 1900–1950' in Cooter (ed.), *In the Name of the Child*, pp. 244–75.

McPolin, J., 'Some aspects of the sociology of the medical profession', *JMAÉ* 19:110 (Aug. 1946), 118.

MacSweeney, C. J., 'A public health programme for Éire', *IJMSc.*, 170 (Feb. 1940), 54.

Manning, M., 'Women in Irish national and local politics 1922–1977', in MacCurtain and Ó Corain (eds.), *Women in Irish Society: The Historical Dimension*, pp. 92–102.

Mellanby, E., 'Nutrition and childbearing', *The Lancet*, 2 (1933), 1131–7.

Michael, S., and S. Koven, 'Womanly duties: maternalist politics and the origins of the welfare states in France, Germany, Great Britain and the United States, 1880–1920', *American History Review*, 4:95 (Oct. 1990), 1076–108.

O'Callaghan, M., 'Language, nationality and cultural identity in the Irish Free State, 1922-7: the *Irish Statesman* and the *Catholic Bulletin* reappraised', *IHS*, 24:49 (Nov. 1984), 226–45.

Ó Cinneide, S., 'The development of the home assistance service', *Administration*, 17 (1969), 284–308.

O'Connor, A., 'Women in Irish folklore: the testimony regarding illegitimacy, abortion and infanticide', in MacCurtain and O'Dowd (eds), *Women in Early Modern Ireland*, pp. 304–17.

O'Dwyer, I., and A. L. Mulhall, 'Midwifery', in Robins (ed.), *Nursing and Midwifery in Ireland in the Twentieth Century.*

Ó'Grada, C., '"The greatest blessing of all": the old age pension', *Past and Present* 175 (May, 2002), 124–61.

O hOgartaigh, M., 'Dr Dorothy Price and the elimination of childhood tuberculosis,' in J. Augusteijn (ed.), *Ireland in the 1930s: New Perspectives* (Dublin, 1999), pp. 67–82.

——'Flower power and "mental grooviness": nurses and midwives in Ireland in the early twentieth century', B. Whelan (ed.), *Women and Paid Work in Ireland, 1500–1930* (Dublin, 2000), pp. 133–47.

——'Women, politics, and public health: the Babies' Clubs in Ireland and the Children's Bureau in the US', in C. Burns, Y. V. O'Neill, P. Albou, J. G. Rigáu-Pérez (eds), *Proceedings of the 37ᵗʰ International Congress on the History of Medicine* (Texas, 2001), pp. 99–103.

——'St Ultan's: a women's hospital for infants', *History Ireland* (July/August, 2005), pp. 36–9.

——'Health and souls: the foundation of Crumlin Children's Hospital', unpublished.

Pateman, C., 'The patriarchal welfare state', in Gutman (ed.), *Democracy and the Welfare State*, pp. 231–60.

Quin, J., 'A suggested maternity service for Eire', *IJMSc.*, 229 (Jan. 1945), 11–23.

Reddin, K., 'The maternity and child welfare clinic – its origin, scope and trend', *IJMSc.*, 77 (May 1932), 222.

Reddin, N., 'Lost to Rathmines', *The Irish Times* (30 Dec. 1943).

Reid, J. S., and J. Mackintosh, 'The influence of anaemia and poor social circumstances during pregnancy', *The Lancet*, 2 (1937), 1389–92.

Riley, D., 'Some peculiarities of social policy concerning women in wartime and postwar Britain', in Higonnet, Jenson, Michel and Collins Weitz (eds), *Behind the Lines*, pp. 260–71.

Riordan, S., '"A political blackthorn": Séan MacEntee, the Dignan plan and the principle of ministerial responsibility', *IESH*, 27 (2000), 44–62.

Robins, J., 'Public policy and the maternity services in Ireland during the twentieth century', in Browne (ed.), *Masters, Midwives and Ladies-in-Waiting*, p. 289.

Russell, M. J., 'The health of Dublin', *JIFSMU*, 3:17 (Nov. 1938), 56–8.

——'The health of Dublin', *JIFSMU*, 5.29 (Nov. 1939), 54–6

Ryle, J. A., 'The modern concept of social medicine', *IJMSc.*, 271 (July 1948), 289–96.

Saraceno, C., 'Redefining maternity and paternity: gender, pronatalism and social policies in Fascist Italy', in Bock and Thane (eds), *Maternity and Gender Policies*, pp. 204–5.

Sheehy, D., 'Archbishop McQuaid: legend and history', *Doctrine and Life*, 53:2 (February 2003), 102–10.

——'Archbishop McQuaid: the diocesan administrator', *Doctrine and Life*, 53:3 (Mar. 2003), 166–9.

——'Archbishop McQuaid: pastoral programme', *Doctrine and Life*, 53:4 (April 2003), 215–20.

Solomons, B., 'The prevention of maternal morbidity and mortality', *IJMSc.*, 88 (Apr. 1933), 175.

——'The dangerous multiplara', *The Lancet*, 2 (7 July 1934), 8–11.

Spain, A., 'Maternity services in Éire', *IJMSc.*, 229 (Jan. 1945), 1–11.

Stephenson, J., 'Women, motherhood and the family in the Third Reich', in Burleigh (ed.), *Confronting the Nazi Past: New Debates on Modern German History* (London, 1996).

Tierney, G. J., 'Maternal mortality', *IJMSc.*, 82 (Oct. 1930), 603.

Travers, P., 'Emigration and gender: the case of Ireland, 1922–1960', in O'Dowd and Wichert (eds), *Chattel, Servant or Citizen*, pp. 187–99.

——'Irish female emigration, 1922–1971', in P. O'Sullivan (ed.), *The Irish World*

Wide Vol. 4: Irish Women and Irish Migration (London, 1995), pp. 146–67.

Valiulis, M., 'Neither feminist nor flapper: the ecclesiastical construction of the ideal Irish woman', in O'Dowd and Wichert (eds), *Chattel, Servant or Citizen*, pp. 168–78.

Wanrooji, B. P. F., 'Italy: sexuality, morality and public authority,' in Eder, Hall and Hekma (eds), *Sexual Cultures in Europe*, pp. 114–37.

Ward, M., 'The League of Women Delegates and Sinn Féin', *History Ireland*, 4:3 (Autumn, 1996), 37–41.

Weiss, J. H., 'Origins of the French welfare state: poor relief in the Third Republic, 1871–1914', *French Historical Studies,* 13 (Spring, 1983), 47–78.

Books

Anderson, Bonnie S. and Judith P. Zinsser, *A History of their Own: Women in Europe from Prehistory to the Present,* Vol. 2 (New York, 1988).

Anderson, M., *Approaches to the History of the Western Family 1500–1914* (London, 1980).

Apple, R. D., *Women, Health, and Medicine in America: A Historical Handbook* (New York, 1990).

Arensberg, C. M., and S. T. Kimball, *Family and Community in Ireland* (Clare, 1968).

Augusteijn, J. (ed.), *Ireland in the 1930s: New Perspectives* (Dublin, 1999).

Barrington, R., *Health, Medicine and Politics in Ireland 1900–1970* (Dublin, 1987).

Beale, J., *Women in Ireland: Voices of Change* (Dublin, 1986).

Behan, B., *Mother of all Behans* (London, 1984).

Bock, G. and P. Thane (eds), *Maternity and Gender Policies: Women and the Rise of European Welfare States, 1880–1950* (London, 1991).

Bolster, E., *The Knights of Columbanus* (Dublin, 1979).

Bourke, J., *Husbandry to Housewifery: Women, Economic Change, and Housework in Ireland 1890–1914* (Oxford, 1993).

Bowen, D., *Souperism: Myth or Reality?* (Cork, 1970).

Brasnett, M., *Voluntary Action: A History of the National Council of Social Service 1919–1969* (London, 1969).

Brown, T., *Ireland: A Social and Cultural History, 1922–1985* (London, 1985).

Browne, A., *The Story of the Rotunda Hospital* (Dublin, 1976).

——(ed.), *Masters, Midwives and Ladies-in-waiting, the Rotunda Hospital 1745–1995* (Dublin, 1995).

Browne, N., *Against the Tide* (Dublin, 1986).

Browne, P., *Thanks for the Tea, Mrs Browne: My Life with Noël* (Dublin, 1998).

Cahill, E., *The Framework of a Christian State: An Introduction To Social Science* (Dublin, 1932).

Calder, A., *The People's War: Britain 1939–1945* (London, 1992).

Canning, B. J., *Bishops of Ireland 1870–1987* (Ballyshannon, 1987).

Carr-Saunders, A. M., *World Population: Past Growth and Present Trends* (Oxford, 1936).

Cassell, R. D., *Medical Charities, Medical Politics: The Irish Dispensary System and the Poor Law, 1836–1872* (Woodbridge, 1997).

Clear, Caitríona, *Nuns in Nineteenth-Century Ireland* (Dublin, 1987).

——*Women of the House: Women's Household Work in Ireland 1922–1961: Discourses, Experiences, Memories* (Dublin, 2000).

Collis, W. R. F., *Marrowbone Lane, A Play in Three Acts* (Dublin, 1943).

——*The State of Medicine in Ireland* (Dublin, 1943).

——*To be a Pilgrim* (London, 1975).

Connolly, L., *The Women's Movement: From Revolution to Devolution* (New York, 2002).

Cooney, J., *John Charles McQuaid: Ruler of Catholic Ireland* (Dublin, 1999).

Cooter, R. (eds.), *In the Name of the Child: Health and Welfare 1880–1940* (London, 1992).

Corish, P., *The Irish Catholic Experience: A Historical Survey* (Dublin, 1985).

Cousins, M., *The Birth of Social Welfare in Ireland, 1922–1952* (Dublin, 2003).

Cowell, J., *A Noontide Blazing: B. Lyons Thorton, Rebel, Soldier, Doctor* (Dublin, 2005).

Cronin, M., *Primer of the Principles of Social Science* (Dublin, 1934).

Cullen Owens, R., *Louie Bennett*, (Cork, 2001).

Daly, M. E., *Social and Economic History of Ireland Since 1800* (Dublin, 1981).

——*Dublin: The Deposed Capital. A Social and Economic History, 1860–1914* (Cork, 1984).

——*The Buffer State: The Historical Roots of the Department of the Environment* (Dublin, 1997).

——*The Spirit of Earnest Inquiry: The Statistical and Social Inquiry Society of Ireland* (Dublin, 1997).

——Deeny, J., *To Cure and to Care: Memoirs of a Chief Medical Officer* (Dublin, 1989).

Desmond, B., *Finally and in Conclusion: A Political Memoir* (Dublin, 2000).

Dowling, J., *An Irish Doctor Remembers* (Dublin, 1955).

Dwork, D., *War is Good for Babies and Other Young Children: A History of the Infant and Child Welfare Movement in England, 1898–1918* (London, 1987).

Eder, X., L. Hall and G. Hekma (eds), *Sexual Cultures in Europe: National Histories,* (Manchester, 1999).

Fallon, B., *An Age of Innocence: Irish Culture 1930–1960* (Dublin, 1998).

Fanning, R., *Independent Ireland* (Dublin, 1983).

Farmar, T., *Holles Street 1894–1994: The National Maternity Hospital – A Centenary History* (Dublin, 1994).

——(ed.), *The End of an Epidemic: Essays in Irish Public Health 1935–65 by James Deeny* (Dublin, 1998).

——*Patients, Potions and Physicians: A Social History of Medicine in Ireland* (Dublin, 2004).

Farrell, B. (ed.), *De Valera's Constitution and Ours* (Dublin, 1988).

Farren, G. *From Condemnation to Celebration: The Story of Cherish, 1972–1997* (Dublin, 1998).

Feeney, J., *John Charles McQuaid: The Man and the Mask* (Dublin, 1974).

Feeney, J. K., *The Coombe Lying-in Hospital* (Dublin, c. 1980).

Fennell, D., (ed.), *The Changing Face of Catholic Ireland* (Washington DC, 1968).

Ferriter, D., *'Lovers of Liberty?': Local Government in Twentieth-Century Ireland* (Dublin, 2001).

——*The Transformation of Ireland, 1900–2000* (London, 2004).

——*Mothers, Maidens and Myths: A History of the ICA* (Dublin, n.d.).

Finnegan, F., *Do Penance or Perish: Magdalen Asylums in Ireland* (Oxford, 2004).

Fitzpatrick, D. (ed.), *Ireland, the First World War* (Dublin, 1986).

Fleetwood, J. F., *The History of Medicine in Ireland* (Dublin, 1983).

Foster, R. F., *Modern Ireland, 1600–1972* (London, 1988).

Fox, R. M., *Louie Bennett: Her Life and Times* (Dublin, 1957).

Fremantle, A., *The Papal Encyclicals in their Historical Context* (New York, 1956).

Fuller, L., *Irish Catholicism Since 1950: The Undoing of a Culture* (Dublin, 2004).

Geary, L. M., *Medicine and Charity in Ireland, 1718–1851* (Dublin, 2004).

Gélis, J., *History of Childbirth: Fertility, Pregnancy and Birth in Early Modern Europe* (Cambridge, 1991).

Gillis, J. R., L. A. Tilly and D. Levine, *The European Experience of Declining Fertility, 1850–1970: A Quiet Revolution 1850–1970* (Cambridge, 1992).

Glass, D. V., *Population: Policies and Movements in Europe,* (New York, 1968).

Gutman, A., (ed.), *Democracy and the Welfare State* (Oxford, 1988).

Hall, L., *Sex, Gender and Social Change in Britain since 1880* (London, 2000).

Hearn, M., *Thomas Edmondson and the Dublin Laundry: A Quaker Businessman, 1837–1908* (Dublin, 2004).

Heclo, H., *Modern Social Politics in Britain and Sweden: From Relief to Income Maintenance* (London, 1974).

Hensey, B., *The Health Services of Ireland* (Dublin, 1988).

Higonnet, M. R., J. M. Jenson, S. Michel and M. Collins Weitz (eds), *Behind the Lines: Gender and the Two World Wars* (London, 1987).

Horgan, J., *Noël Browne: Passionate Outsider* (Dublin, 2000).

Hufton, O., *The Prospect Before Her: A History of Women in Western Europe, Volume One 1500–1800* (London, 1997).

Hug, C., *The Politics of Sexual Morality in Ireland* (New York, 1999).

Humphrey, J. A., *New Dubliners: Urbanization and the Irish Family* (London, 1966).

Immergut, E., *Health Politics: Interests and Institutions in Western Europe* (New York, 1992).

Inglis, T., *Moral Monopoly: The Catholic Church in Modern Irish Society* (Dublin, 1987).

Jackson, A., *Ireland, 1798–1998* (Oxford, 1999).

Jalland, P., *Women and Marriage and Politics, 1860–1914* (Oxford, 1986).

Jones, G., *'Captain of All These Men of Death': The History of Tuberculosis in Nineteenth and Twentieth Century Ireland* (New York, 2001).

Kavanagh, J., *Manual of Social Ethics* (Dublin, 1956).

Keane, M., *Ishbel, Lady Aberdeen in Ireland* (Newtownards, 1999).

Kearns, K. C., *Dublin Tenement Life: An Oral History* (Dublin, 1994).

——*Dublin's Lost Heroines: Mammies and Grannies in a Vanished City* (Dublin, 2004).

Kelly, G., *Medico-Moral Problems* (Dublin, 1960).

Kelly, J., and D. Keogh (eds), *History of the Catholic Diocese of Dublin* (Dublin, 2000).

Kennedy, E. R., *The Irish, Emigration, Marriage, and Fertility* (California, 1973).

Kennedy, F., *Cottage to Crèche: Family Change in Ireland* (Dublin, 2001).

Kennedy, P., *Maternity in Ireland: A woman-centred perspective* (Dublin, 2002).

——*Motherhood in Ireland: Creation and Context* (Cork, 2004).

Kenny, J., *Principles of Medical Ethics* (Cork, 1953).

Kenny, M., *Goodbye to Catholic Ireland* (London, 1997).

Keogh, D., *Twentieth-Century Ireland: Nation and State* (Dublin, 1994).

——*The Vatican, the Bishops and Irish Politics 1919–1939* (Cambridge, 1986).

Keogh, D., F. O'Shea and C. Quinlan (eds), *The Lost Decade: Ireland in the 1950s* (Cork, 2004).

Kerrigan, G., *Another Country: Growing up in '50s Ireland* (Dublin, 1998).

Kiely, G., A. O'Donnell, P. Kennedy and S. Quinn, (eds), *Irish Social Policy in Context* (Dublin, 1999).

Kiernan, K., H. Land and J. Lewis, *Lone Motherhood in Twentieth Century Britain* (Oxford, 1998).

King, T., *Mothercraft* (London, 1939).

Kunzel, R. G., *Fallen Women, Problem Girls: Unmarried Mothers and the Professionalization of Social Work, 1890–1945* (Yale, 1993).

Larkin, E., *The Roman Catholic Church in Ireland and the Fall of Parnell 1888–1891* (North Carolina, 1979).

Leavitt, J. W., *Brought to Bed: Childbearing in America, 1750–1950* (Oxford, 1986).

Lee, J. J., *The Modernisation of Irish Society 1848–1918* (Dublin 1981).

——*1912–1985: Politics and Society* (Cambridge, 1989).

Leichter, H., *A Comparative Approach to Policy Analysis: Health Care Policy in Four Nations* (Cambridge, 1979).

Lewis, J., *The Politics of Motherhood: Child and Maternal Welfare in England, 1900–1939* (London, 1980).

——(ed.), *Women's Welfare, Women's Rights* (London, 1983).

Litton, F. (ed.), *Unequal Achievement: The Irish Experience, 1957–1982* (Dublin, 1982).

Llewelyn Davies, M., *Maternity: Letters from Working-Women* (London, 1984, 1st editon, 1915).

Loudon, I., *Death in Childbirth: An International Study of Maternal Care and Maternal Mortality 1800–1950* (Oxford, 1992).

Luddy, M., *Hanna Sheehy Skeffington* (Dundalk, 1995).

—— and C. Murphy (eds), *Women Surviving: Studies in Irish Women's History in the 19th and 20th Centuries* (Dublin, 1990).

McCullagh, D., *A Makeshift Majority: The First Inter-Party Government, 1948–51* (Dublin, 1998).

MacCurtain, M. and D. Ó Corrain (eds), *Women in Irish Society: The Historical Dimension* (Dublin, 1978).

McGarry, F., *Eoin O'Duffy: A Self-Made Hero* (Oxford, 2005).

McKenna, Revd L., *The Church and Social Work* (Dublin, 1928), p. 117.

Macnicol, J., *The Movement for Family Allowances, 1918–1945: A Study in Social Policy Development* (London, 1980).

Mahon, E., C. Conlon and L. Dillon (eds), *Women in Crisis Pregnancy* (Dublin, 1998).

Malcom, E, and G. Jones, *Medicine, Disease and the State in Ireland, 1650–1940* (Cork, 1999).

Meenan, F. O. C., *St Vincent's Hospital 1834–1994: An Historical Portrait* (Dublin, 1995).

Meenan, J., *George O'Brien* (Dublin, 1980).

Miller, D. W., *Church, State and Nation in Ireland 1898–1921* (Dublin 1973).

Milotte, M., *Banished Babies: The Secret History of Ireland's Baby Export Business* (Dublin, 1997).

Mitchell, D., *A 'Peculiar' Place: The Adelaide Hospital, Dublin 1839–1989* (Dublin, 1989).

Morrissey, T. J., *William J. Walsh, Archbishop of Dublin: No Uncertain Voice* (Dublin, 2000).

Moynihan, M. (ed.), *Speeches and Statements by Eamonn de Valera*.

Mulvihill, M., *Charlotte Despard: A Biography* (London, 1989).

Murphy-Lawless, J., *Reading Birth and Death: A History of Obstetric Thinking* (Cork, 1998).

Newsholme, A., *Evolution of Preventive Medicine* (London, 1927).

——*Fifty Years in Public Health: A Personal Narrative with Comments* (London, 1935).

Noonan, J. T., *Contraception: A History of its Treatment by the Catholic Theologians and Canonists* (Cambridge, 1965).

Nowlan, K. B., and T. D. Williams, *Ireland in the War Years and After, 1939–51* (Dublin, 1969).

Oakley, A., *Becoming a Mother* (Oxford, 1979).

——*Women Confined: Towards a Sociology of Childbirth* (Oxford, 1980).

——*The Captured Womb* (Oxford, 1984).

O'Brien, J. V., *'Dear Dirty Dublin': A City in Distress, 1899–1916* (Berkeley and Los Angeles, CA, 1982).

Ó Broin, L., *Frank Duff: A Biography* (Dublin, 1982).

O'Carroll, J. P., and J. A. Murphy, (eds), *De Valera and his Time* (Cork, 1986).

O'Connell, Cardinal, *The Reasonable Limits of State Activity* (Dublin, 1920).

O'Connell, J., *Doctor John: A Crusading Doctor and Politician* (Dublin, 1989).

O'Connor, V. A., and M. S. Parkes, *Gladly Learn and Gladly Teach: Alexandra College and School 1866–1966* (Dublin, 1983).

O'Dowd, M., and S. Wichert (eds), *Chattel, Servant or Citizen: Women's Status in Church, State and Society* (Belfast, 1995).

O'Grada, C., *Ireland Before and After the Famine: Exploration in Economic History 1800–1930* (Manchester, 1988).

——*Ireland: A New Economic History 1780–1939* (Oxford, 1994).

——*A Rocky Road: The Irish Economy since the 1920s* (Manchester, 1997).

Ó hÓgartaigh, M., *Kathleen Lynn, Irishwoman, Patriot, Doctor* (Dublin, 2006).

O'Leary, D., *Vocationalism and Social Catholicism in Twentieth-Century Ireland* (Dublin, 2000).

O'Mahony, C., *In the Shadows: Life in Cork 1750–1930* (Cork, 1997).

O'Neill, M., *From Parnell to De Valera: A Biography of Jennie Wyse Power, 1858–1941* (Dublin, 1991).

Pedersen, S., *Family, Dependence, and the Origins of the Welfare State: Britain and France, 1914–1945* (New York, 1993).

Peillon, M., *Contemporary Irish Society: An Introduction* (Dublin, 1982).

Pember Reeves, M., *Round About a Pound a Week* (London, 1979, 1st edition, 1939).

Porter, D., *Health, Civilization and the State: A History of Public Health from Ancient to Modern Times* (London, 1999).

Powell, F. W., *The Politics of Irish Social Policy, 1600–1990* (New York, 1992).

Preston, M., *Charitable Words: Women, Philanthropy, and the Language of Charity in Nineteenth-Century Dublin* (Westport, CT, 2004).

Prunty, J., *Dublin Slums, 1800–1925: A Study in Urban Geography* (Dublin, 1998).

Purcell, M., *Catholic Social Service Conference, Golden Jubilee 1941–1991* (Dublin, 1991).

Purvis, J. (ed.), *Women's History in Britain, 1850–1945: An Introduction* (London, 1995).

Quine, M. S., *Population Politics in Twentieth-Century Europe: Fascist Dictatorships and Liberal Democracies* (London, 1996).

Rafferty, M., and E. O'Sullivan, *Suffer Little Children: The Inside Story of Ireland's Industrial Schools* (Dublin, 1999).

Rathbone, E., *The Disinherited Family* (London, 1927).

Reynolds, S., *France Between the Wars: Gender Politics,* (London, 1996).

Robins, J., *The Lost Children: A Study of Charity Children in Ireland 1700–1900* (Dublin, 1980).

——*Nursing and Midwifery in Ireland in the Twentieth Century: Fifty Years of an Board Altranais (the Nursing Board) 1950–2000* (Dublin, 2000).

Roche, D., *Local Government in Ireland* (Dublin, 1982).

Saunders, K., and P. Stanford, *Catholics and Sex: From Purity to Perdition* (London, 1992).

Scanlan, P., *The Irish Nurse. A Study of Nursing in Ireland: History and Education 1718–1981* (Drumlín, 1991).

Shorter, E., *A History of Women's Bodies* (London, 1983).

Skocpol, T., *Protecting Soldiers and Mothers: The Political Origins of Social Policy in the United States* (Boston, MA, 1992).

Sleeman, J. F., *The Welfare State: Its Aims, Benefits and Costs* (London, 1973).

Solomons, B., *One Doctor in his Time,* (London, 1956).

Solomons, M., *Pro Life? The Irish Question* (Dublin, 1992).

Soloway, R. A., *Demography and Degeneration: Eugenics and the Declining Birthrate in Twentieth-Century Britain* (Durham, NC, 1995).

Spring Rice, M., *Working-Class Wives: Their Health and Conditions* (London, 1981, 1st edition, 1939).

Tweedy, H., *A Link in the Chain: The Story of the Irish Housewives Association 1942–1992* (Dublin, 1992).

Ussher, A., *The Face and Mind of Ireland* (London, 1949).

Valiulis, M. G., and M. O'Dowd (eds), *Women and Irish History: Essays in Honour of Margaret McCurtain* (Dublin, 1997).

Ward, M., *The Missing Sex: Putting Women into Irish History,* (Dublin, 1991).

——*Unmanageable Revolutionaries: Women and Irish Nationalism* (London, 1995).

——*Hanna Sheehy Skeffington: A life* (Cork, 1997).

Whelan, B., (ed.), *Women and Paid Work in Ireland 1500–1930* (Dublin, 2000).

Whyte, J. H., *Church and State in Modern Ireland 1923–1979* (Dublin, 1980).

Young, L., *Out of Wedlock* (New York, 1954).

Unpublished sources

Creegan, M. F., 'Unmarried mothers: an analysis and discussion of interviews conducted in an Irish mother and baby home', (MA, University College Dublin, 1967).

Fee, G., 'The effects of World War II on Dublin's low-income families 1939–1945' (Ph.D., University College Dublin, 1996).

Ferriter, D., 'A peculiar people in their own land' catholic social theory and the plight of rural Ireland 1930–1955' (Ph.D., University College Dublin, 1996).

Harkin, P., '*La Famille, fruit du passé, germe de l'avenir*: family policy in Ireland and Vichy France' (M.A., University College Dublin, 1991).

Hartigan, M., 'The Catholic laity of Dublin, 1914–1939' (Ph.D., National University of Ireland, Maynooth, 1992).

McCarthy, G., 'Moral and political attitudes of the catholic hierarchy: an analysis of Lenten pastoral 1932–1945' (MA, University College Dublin, 1989).

Riordan, S., 'The unpopular front: the catholic revival and Irish cultural identity 1932–48' (MA, University College Dublin, 1990).

Index